Platoni

As prose dramatic te
audience as an alter
dialogue form is expl
dominant public mode of communication of his time. The oral performance of his works is suggested both by the pragmatics of the publication of literary texts in the classical period and by his original role as a Socratic dialogue-writer and the creator of a fourth dramatic genre. Support comes from a number of pieces of evidence, from a statue of Sokrates in the Academy (fourth century BC) to a mosaic of Sokrates in Mytilene (fourth century AD), which point to a centuries-old tradition of treating the dialogues in the context of performance literature and testify to the significance of the image of 'Plato the prose dramatist' for his original and subsequent audiences.

NIKOS G. CHARALABOPOULOS is Lecturer in the Department of Philology at the University of Patras.

CAMBRIDGE CLASSICAL STUDIES

PLATONIC DRAMA AND ITS ANCIENT RECEPTION

NIKOS G. CHARALABOPOULOS
University of Patras, Greece

CAMBRIDGE
UNIVERSITY PRESS

CAMBRIDGE
UNIVERSITY PRESS

University Printing House, Cambridge CB2 8BS, United Kingdom

One Liberty Plaza, 20th Floor, New York, NY 10006, USA

477 Williamstown Road, Port Melbourne, VIC 3207, Australia

4843/24, 2nd Floor, Ansari Road, Daryaganj, Delhi - 110002, India

79 Anson Road, #06-04/06, Singapore 079906

Cambridge University Press is part of the University of Cambridge.

It furthers the University's mission by disseminating knowledge in the pursuit of education, learning and research at the highest international levels of excellence.

www.cambridge.org
Information on this title: www.cambridge.org/9781108439411

First published 2012
First paperback edition 2017

A catalogue record for this publication is available from the British Library

Library of Congress Cataloging in Publication data
Charalabopoulos, Nikos G., 1969–
Platonic drama and its ancient reception / Nikos G. Charalabopoulos, University of Patras, Greece.
pages cm. – (Cambridge classical studies)
Includes indexes.
ISBN 978-0-521-87174-7 (hardback)
1. Plato – Criticism and interpretation. 2. Plato. Dialogues.
3. Greek literature – History and criticism. I. Title.
PA4291.C47 2012
184 – dc23 2012002189

ISBN 978-0-521-87174-7 Hardback
ISBN 978-1-108-43941-1 Paperback

CONTENTS

FIGURES

PREFACE

As a writer of prose dramatic texts, Plato found himself in a constant dialogue with the dramatists of the stage. This book examines the nature of this engagement as well as the ways in which Plato's dialogues would have been presented by the author and read by their original audience as an alternative type of theatrical composition.

The introductory chapter ('Setting the stage') comments on the 'paradox' of the dialogue form and suggests whether Plato's writing of dialogues was the appropriation by a young and ambitious author of the dominant public mode of communication of his time. A discussion on the terminology applied concludes this opening section.

Chapter 2 ('The metatheatre of dialogue') relocates Plato in his original context in view of the prehistory of the dialogue form and the evidence for the literary production of the other Socratics. Basic features of the dialogues tell the story of the emergence of a fourth dramatic genre in fourth-century Athens that transcends its theatrical counterparts. Passages from the *Symposium*, the *Republic*, the *Laws* provide the evidence for this metatheatrical reading.

Chapter 3 ('Performing Plato') deals with the performance aspect of Plato's works. A number of ancient authorities, beginning with Aristotle, read the Platonic dialogue as a prose genre in the context of dramatic production. The pragmatics of the publication of literary texts in the classical period strongly suggests an oral performance of the dialogues. The evidence from *Tht.* 143b–c corroborates this view.

Chapter 4 ('Plato's "theatre": the fragments') discusses a number of pieces of evidence, from the statue of Sokrates in the Academy (fourth century BC) to the mosaic of Sokrates in Mytilene (fourth century AD) that point to a centuries-old tradition of treating the dialogues in the context of performance literature. Their reception, no less than the dialogues themselves, testifies to the significance of the image of 'Plato the prose dramatist' for his original and subsequent audiences.

The concluding section ('Finale') summarises the argument of the book while pointing to the importance of reading Plato as the first prose playwright.

An appendix on the alleged Platonic connections of an inscribed marble fragment excavated in the Academy serves as a coda.

ACKNOWLEDGEMENTS

As a thoroughly revised version of my Cambridge Ph.D. thesis this book has been in the making for quite some time. A number of people have provided their help and comments throughout this period whom I would like here to mention – despite running the risk of omitting some of them.

To begin with, a scholarship from the Greek State Scholarships Foundation (I.K.Y.) made my studying abroad possible. The Faculty of Classics has also supported me financially all these years and I express my deep gratitude.

Prof. J.-Th. Papademetriou was the one who opened for me the prospect of graduate studies abroad back in the early 1990s. Prof. M. Thomadaki introduced me to the world of academic conferences and theatre semiotics. Both have helped me in the development of my own identity as a scholar. I thank them with nostalgia and pleasure.

Dr E. Lyngouri-Tolia, former Director of the Third Ephorate of Prehistoric and Classical Antiquities, has given her permission for photographing the Academy inscription M 3120 – published here for the first time. Credits for the photo go to Giorgos Ioannou and his colleagues. Special thanks to Joyce Reynolds, Stephen Tracy and Yiannis Tzifopoulos whose expertise in epigraphy was instrumental in my reading the inscription.

For their helpful remarks on parts or the whole of my thesis I am grateful to Andrea Capra, Tim Duff, Jason König, Spyridon Rangos. I also thank Pierre Destrée for allowing me to read the manuscript of the book he has co-edited with F.-G. Hermann, *Plato and the Poets* (Mnemosyne Supplement 328, Brill).

The Faculty of Classics of Cambridge University has been a friendly and welcoming environment all these years thanks to the hospitality of its members. James Warren, Sara Owen, Johannes

Haumbold, Barbara Graziosi, Polly Low, Liz Irwin, Emily Greenwood, Noriko Yasumura, Thalia Papadopoulou and Iannis Konstantakos have seen to this. Judith Waring, Lina Undicino, Steve Kimberley and the rest of the staff of the Classics Faculty Library have facilitated immensely my work with their warmth and understanding.

The publication of this book owes a lot to the patience of Michael Sharp and Liz Hanlon, editors for the Cambridge University Press, who both tolerated and encouraged me throughout this long period of revision. Especially Liz had to put up with my occasional failures to abide by the deadlines.

Special thanks to my examiners, Malcolm Schofield and Chris Gill, whose helpful suggestions saved me from a number of errors. David Sedley has perceptively commented on an earlier draft. His steadfast support and guidance all these years has been a source of inspiration for me.

The greatest debt is owed to my supervisor Pat Easterling. I do not think I will ever thank her properly for all her patience, affection and infinite support all these years. This book would never have been written had she not encouraged me in the first place. Needless to say, not only has she followed through its different phases but she has stood by me in every possible way since I left Cambridge. I will always be in your debt, Pat.

I would rather end on a personal note – the reader is asked to forgive the emotional tone. Never will I be able to express in words how much I owe to my mother and the memory of my father. My father inspired in me the love for the Ancients and, especially, Plato. My mother has been for me the inexhaustible source of love and comfort throughout the difficult years. Σᾶς εὐχαριστῶ καὶ τοὺς δυό.

NOTE ON SPELLING

In the spelling of the Greek names I have tried to avoid latinised forms as much as possible. Except for familiar names (e.g. Plato, Achilles) I have mostly used a transliteration more faithful to the original (for instance, 'Thoukydides' instead of 'Thucydides'). I do not replace k with c but χ is everywhere transliterated as ch. Finally, the isolated page numbers in parentheses in the main text or the footnotes are cross-references to pages and notes of this book.

ABBREVIATIONS

Ancient authors and their works are abbreviated according to *LSJ*^{9} and *OCD*^{3}, in each case opting for the less ambiguous suggestion. Texts are cited from the most recent Oxford Classical Text or, where none exists, from the most recent Teubner edition. In all other cases the editions used are given by the name of the editor and those not included in the References are cited in full in the following list. Periodicals are cited according to the abbreviations used in *L'année philologique*. For journals not included there and all other works I use the following abbreviations.

Adler	A. Adler (ed.) *Suidae Lexicon*, 5 vols. Leipzig, 1924–38
AMB	*Acta Musica Byzantina*
ANRW	*Aufstieg und Niedergang der Römischen Welt*. Berlin, 1972–
APSR	*The American Political Science Review*
Aujoulat	N. Aujoulat (ed.) *Synesius: Opuscules*. 3 vols. Paris, 2004–8
BACAP	*Proceedings of the Boston Area Colloquium in Ancient Philosophy*. Lanham, 1986–
Bartelink	G. J. M. Bartelink (ed.) *Palladio: la storia Lausiaca*. Verona, 1974
BAW	*Bayerische Akademie der Wissenschaft*
Bethe	E. Bethe (ed.) *Onomasticon*. Leipzig, 1900
BT	*Bibliotheca Teubneriana*
C&H	*Culture and History*
CAD	E. Csapo and W. J. Slater (eds.) *The Context of Ancient Drama*. Ann Arbor, 1995

CAH	*Cambridge Ancient History*
CamQ	*The Cambridge Quarterly*
CHHP	K. Algra, J. Barnes, J. Mansfeld, and M. Schofield (eds.) *The Cambridge History of Hellenistic Philosophy*. Cambridge, 1999
Cousin	V. Cousin (ed.) *Procli Commentarium in Platonis Parmenidem*. Paris, 1864
CPF	*Corpus dei Papiri Filosofici Greci e Latini*. Florence, 1989–
DAGM	E. Pöhlman and M. L. West (eds.) *Documents of Ancient Greek Music*. Oxford, 2001
*DFA*²	A. W. Pickard-Cambridge, *The Dramatic Festivals of Athens*, 2nd edn with supplement and corrections revised by J. Gould and D. M. Lewis. Oxford, 1988
DK	H. Diels and W. Kranz (eds) *Die Fragmente der Vorsokratiker*, 3 vols, 6th edn. Berlin, 1952
Diels	H. Diels (ed.) *Simplicii in Aristotelis physicorum libros quattuor priores commentaria*. Berlin, 1882
Dilts	M. R. Dilts (ed.) *Scholia in Aeschinem*. Stuttgart and Leipzig, 1992
Dodge	B. Dodge (ed.) *The Fihrist of al-Nadīm*. New York, 1970
DPhA	R. Goulet (ed.) *Dictionnaire des Philosophes Antiques Vol. I*. Paris, 1989
DPhA Suppl.	R. Goulet (ed.) *Dictionnaire des Philosophes Antiques, Supplément*. Paris, 2003
*DTC*²	A. W. Pickard-Cambridge, *Dithyramb, Tragedy and Comedy*, 2nd edn revised by T. B. L. Webster. Oxford, 1962
Dübner	Fr. Dübner (ed.) *Scholia Graeca in Aristophanem*. Paris, 1842
EL	*The European Legacy*

Entretiens	*Entretiens Fondation Hardt pour l'étude de l'antiquité classique*
FGrHist	F. Jacoby (ed.) *Die Fragmente der Griechischen Historiker*. Berlin, 1923–
GOTR	*Greek Orthodox Theological Review*
Gow–Page	A. S. F. Gow and D. L. Page (eds.) *The Greek Anthology: Hellenistic Epigrams*. 2 vols. Cambridge, 1965
Hansen	G. C. Hansen (ed.) *Sokrates Kirchengeschichte, Die griechischen christlichen Schriftsteller des ersten Jahrhunderts, new series 1*. Berlin, 1995
HCT	A. W. Gomme, A. Andrews and K. J. Dover (eds.) *A Historical Commentary on Thucydides*. Oxford, 1945–81
HGP	W. K. C. Guthrie *A History of Greek Philosophy*. Cambridge, 1962–81
Hilgard	A. Hilgrand (ed.) *Grammatici Graeci I. 3: Scholia in Dionysii Thracis Artem Grammaticam*. Leipzig, 1901
Holwerda	D. Holwerda (ed.) *Scholia in Aristophanem II. 3: in Aves*. Groningen, 1991
IEG^2	M. L. West (ed.) *Iambi et Elegi Graeci Vol. II*, 2nd edn. Oxford, 1992
IG	*Inscriptiones Graecae*. Berlin, 1873–
IGD	A. D. Trendall and T. B. L. Webster (eds.) *Illustrations of Greek Drama*. London, 1971
IJMES	*International Journal of Middle Eastern Studies*
IJPT	*International Journal of the Platonic Tradition*
JAAC	*Journal of Aesthetics and Art Criticism*
JACh	*Journal of Agrarian Change*
Jan	K. Jan (ed.) *Musici Scriptores Graeci*. Leipzig, 1895

JECS	*Journal of Early Christian Studies*
JLA	*Journal of Late Antiquity*
JPhil	*The Journal of Philology*
JR	*The Journal of Religion*
JRAS	*The Journal of the Royal Asiatic Society*
Kroll	G. Kroll (ed.) *Procli Diadochi in Platonis Rem Publicam Commentarii*, 3 vols. Leipzig, 1899–1901
KRS	G. S. Kirk, J. E. Raven and M. Schofield (eds.) *The Presocratic Philosophers*, 2nd edn. Cambridge, 1983
LIMC	*Lexicon Iconographicum Mythologiae Classicae*. Zurich, Munich and Düsseldorf 1981–97
L–P	E. Lobel and D. L. Page (eds.) *Poetarum Lesbiorum Fragmenta*. Oxford, 1955
LPGN	P. M. Fraser and E. Matthews (eds.) *Lexicon of Personal Greek Names*. Oxford 1987–2005
LSJ^9	H. G. Liddell, R. Scott and H. S. Jones, *A Greek–English Lexicon*, 9th edn with a revised supplement. Oxford, 1996
MIMC^3	T. B. L. Webster and J. R. Green (eds.) *Monuments Illustrating Old and Middle Comedy*, 3rd edn. *BICS* Suppl. 39. London, 1978
MINC^3	T. B. L. Webster, J. R. Green and A. Seeberg (eds.) *Monuments Illustrating New Comedy*, 3rd edn. *BICS* Suppl. 50. London, 1995
MITS^2	T. B. L. Webster (ed.) *Monuments Illustrating Tragedy and Satyr Drama*, 2nd edn. *BICS* Suppl. 20. London, 1967
NGDM	S. Sadie and J. Tyrell (eds.) *The New Grove Dictionary of Music and Musicians*. London, 2001
NM	National Museum of Greece

OCD^3	S. Hornblower and A. Spawforth (eds.) *The Oxford Classical Dictionary*, 3rd edn revised. Oxford, 2002
OCT	Oxford Classical Texts
Patillon–Bolognesi	M. Patillon and G. Bolognesi (eds.) *Aelius Théon Progymnasmata*. Paris, 1997
PCG	R. Kassel and C. F. Austin (eds.) *Poetae Comici Graeci*. Berlin, 1983–
Pfeiffer	R. Pfeiffer (ed.) *Callimachus Volumen II: Hymni et Epigrammata*. Oxford, 1953
PG	J.-P. Migne (ed.) *Patrlogia Graeca*. Paris, 1857–66
PLPLS	*Proceedings of the Leeds Philosophical and Literary Society*
PMG	D. L. Page (ed.) *Poetae Melici Graeci*. Oxford, 1962
PMM	*Plainsong and Medieval Music*
PPS	*Perspectives on Political Science*
PS	*Philosophical Studies*
PT	*Poetics Today*
QJS	*Quarterly Journal of Speech*
RE	A. Pauly, G. Wissowa and W. Kroll (eds.) *Real-Encyklopädie der classischen Altertumswissenschaft*. Stuttgart, 1893–1978
RPhLang	*Recherches sur la philosophie et le langage*
da Rios	E. da Rios (ed.) *Aristoxenus Elementa Harmonica*. Rome, 1954
Russell	D. A. Russell (ed.) *'Longinos' On the Sublime*. Oxford, 1964
SEC	*Studies in Eastern Chant*
SEG	*Supplementum Epigraphicum Graecum*. Amsterdam, 1924–
Spengel	L. Spengel (ed.) *Rhetores Graeci Vol. I*. Leipzig, 1853

SSR	G. Giannantoni (ed.) *Socratis et Socraticorum Reliquiae*. Naples, 1990
TrGF	B. Snell, R. Kannicht and S. Radt (eds.) *Tragicorum Graecorum Fragmenta*. Göttingen, 1971–2004
TS	*Theatre Survey*
TSP	*Tulane Studies in Philosophy*
Uhlig	G. Uhlig (ed.) *Grammatici Graeci I.1: Dionysii Thracis Ars Grammatica*. Leipzig 1883
VQR	*Virginia Quarterly Review*
Wehrli	Fr. Wehrli (ed.) *Die Schule des Aristoteles: Dikaiarchos*, 2nd edn. Basel and Stuttgart, 1967
Worthington	I. Worthington (ed.) *Dinarchus and Hypereides*. Warminster, 1999
ZMW	*Zeitschrift für Musikwissenschaft*

I

SETTING THE STAGE

The 'paradox' of the dialogue form

The literary form of Plato's works has always been felt by scholars to be an extraordinary feature, and has generated a number of responses as a result. According to the historical/biographical explanation this form was natural because the dialogues were records of actual Socratic conversations. A political answer is also possible, namely that it was Plato's device to avoid persecution for the publication of his unorthodox views. The majority of approaches, however, are those adducing philosophical considerations. One type of answer, related to the so-called 'proto-essay' view of the dialogues, resolves the paradox by cancelling it. Since Plato's works are *philosophical* writings, their form has hardly any bearing on their content; hence it makes no real difference whether a philosopher expresses himself in treatises or resorts to more literary forms. The dialogue is simply one format for the presentation of the author's arguments. The dialogues are philosophical texts in which theories are expounded, positions are argued for or against, and, significantly, theoretical systems are carefully constructed. Argumentation forms the sole means of producing legitimate propositions. Unwarranted premises, deficient syllogisms or other fallacies are painstakingly discovered by the modern reader, who may then pronounce judgement on the quality of the writer as a thinker. Given that Plato, whether he would like it or not, has been placed at the head of the Western philosophical tradition, he is evidently to be viewed as conforming with the image of the archetypal *philosopher*. What is uttered counts for much more than the way this utterance is made, or, to put it differently, the content takes precedence at the expense of the form. On such a reading, the dialogue form seems, understandably, something of an oddity that may be ignored, explained, or explained away.[1]

Another solution to the 'paradox' derives from an alternative method of interpretation, developed partly as a reaction to the predominance of the content-oriented reading. Here the focus of attention has shifted from the *what* to the *how* of the text. Characterisation and the pragmatics of conversation are more thoroughly examined as less irrelevant to a proper understanding of a dialogue. Ambiguity and irony become prime interpretative tools. Most important, the recorded and implied action, the things done, gets carefully analysed as a necessary complement to the arguments expressed, the things said. The variations in setting and the detailed descriptions of, say, cancelled departures or late arrivals do not represent dispensable embellishments but contribute to the overall philosophical character of the work. While endorsing the image of Plato *the philosopher*, this approach attempts, at the same time, to 'save the appearances', that is, to show that form equals and corroborates content as a means for the expression of philosophical truths. Therefore the dialogue form is welcomed as a successful device for pedagogical and (meta)philosophical purposes. It is this realisation of the philosophical significance of the dialogue that resolves the 'paradox'. Accordingly, Plato's dialogues are considered the archetypal *philosophical dramas*.[2]

[1] For a survey of suggested answers to the question of the dialogue form see Sayre (1995) 1–10; Moes (2000) 1–24; Gill (2006); Byrd (2007) 365–74; Lavery (2007) 191–5; Rowe (2007a) 1–7; Griswold (2008). A neat example of this content-oriented line of interpretation is Beversluis' (2000) statement that for Plato the dialogue form is 'a *carte blanche* stylistic format . . . the ideal vehicle for celebrating his mentor and concluding his own philosophical investigations' (20). An alternative, admittedly original, philosophical expanation of the 'paradox' has been suggested by Sedley (2003a): Plato remained faithful to composing dialogues because 'conversation, in the form of question and answer, is the structure of thought itself . . . these same question-and-answer sequences can legitimately be read by us as *Plato thinking aloud*' (1). See Rowe (2007a) 33–7 for a critique.

[2] Press (2007) remarks that in Plato's dialogues 'drama is a form of argument and argument a form of drama' (5). For this dialogical interpretative mode see the articles in Press (1997). The pedagogical/protreptic function of the dialogue has been argued for, among others, by the members of the 'Tübingen School'. See Szlezák (1999) and, for a critical reappraisal Mann (2006). For more answers to the 'paradox' of the dialogue form based on this 'dramatic' approach see Desjardins (1988); Griswold (1988); Klagge and Smith (1992); Press (1993) and (2000); Gonzalez (1995); Nails (1995); Gill and McCabe (1996); Hart and Tejera (1997); Michelini (2003a); Yamagata (2005) 122–4.

Now there can be no doubt that the recognition of the dramatic nature of the dialogues restores a longed-for balance and moves scholarship towards the right direction of a holistic interpretation of Plato. All the same, despite their opposition as regards the philosophical significance of the dialogue form, both the 'proto-essay' and the 'dialogical' view have been developed out of a common matrix: the conceptual framework of modern insitutionalised philosophical discourse. It is very likely then that the question of why Plato wrote dialogues reveals more about modern readers' expectations than about authorial dilemmas.[3] For the problem arises only if one would expect Plato to have followed the normative genre of philosophical writing, that of the treatise. As long as one's perception draws on elements pertinent to later, ultimately modern, experiences, there will always be present a split between Plato the formidable dialectician and Plato the literary artist.[4] The division has a rather prescriptive character, favouring a model of the irrelevance or, at best, the subordination, of the artist to the thinker. Consequently, even when the drama of the dialogues comes to the fore and is duly acknowledged, there is still in many cases a tendency to show that these formal aspects are no less liable to philosophical use and interpretation.[5] Content then still

For the interrelation between the drama and the philosophy in the dialogues see Krentz (1983); Stokes (1986); Frede (1992); Rossetti (1993); Rutherford (1995); Tejera (1999); Giuliano (2000a); Corlett (2005); MacCabe (2006); Kahn (2010). Cossutta (2003) offers arguments in favour of the inherent dialogism of Plato's dialogues using current philosophical terminology. For a critique of the dialogical model see recently Beversluis (2006).

[3] Intriguingly, although one can find articles with exactly that title, namely why Plato wrote dialogues (Hyland 1968), there is, so far as I am aware, no scholarly text bearing on 'Why Aischylos wrote tragedy' or 'Why Sappho composed monodies'.

[4] Vlastos (1991) characteristically asserts that 'the artist in Plato could not have displaced the philosopher. We must assume that philosophical inquiry was the *primum mobile* in the composition of those earlier dialogues no less than of any he was to write thereafter' (52–3).

[5] A number of scholarly contributions that reveal the intrinsic value of the dramatic aspect in Plato are worth mentioning. In her insightful book Gordon (1999) emphasises the extralogical elements of the Socratic/Platonic dialectic (e.g. emotional engagement 19–42, images 135–72) and treats Plato as a dramatist (63–92). In his lengthy article Gifford (2001), in an exemplary way, examines Plato's use of tragic irony in *Republic* I. In the first two chapters of an ambitious study Blondell (2002) offers the most comprehensive discussion of the subject by giving her own version of a dramatic reading of Plato (4–37) and examinig the reasons that led Plato to the use of the dialogue form (37–52). Finally, Puchner (2010) offers the most promising interpretation of Plato as a prose dramatist so far by arguing persuasively that he was a radical theatre reformer (3–35).

legitimises form and the original unity of the Platonic dialogue is cancelled for the sake of a selective reading, though one more comprehensible to a modern taste.[6]

Chronology

A similar tendency to appeal to the expectations of the audience each time has been at work in the vexed problem of the Platonic chronology. The standard view throughout the twentieth century has been that, as regards their period of composition, Plato's works may be divided into early, middle and late dialogues. This tripartition, backed up by the results of stylometry, goes, as a rule, hand in hand with a developmentalist theory about Plato's philosophical route. In the early dialogues Plato's main objective is to draw the portrait of his master by presenting and elaborating on the basic tenets of the historical Sokrates while still writing under his spell (*Ion*, *Laches*). In his middle works he has left the Socratic legacy behind and produces his own fully formulated doctrines, such as the Theory of Forms, expounded and defended by a Platonic Sokrates, now more of an authorial creation and mouthpiece (*Republic*, *Symposium*). In his last phase Plato, disillusioned and more critical than ever, scrutinises basic principles of his doctrines while indulging in the technicalities of dialectic and dogmatic exposition and gradually dispensing with Sokrates as a mouthpiece (*Sophist*, *Laws*). The scheme provides also for transitional dialogues that cover the borderline between two periods such as the *Gorgias* (early–middle) and the *Theaetetus* (middle–late).

A reaction to this consensus has recently been articulated. Those who argue against the traditional division point out the arbitrary

[6] Ancient commentators seem to have followed a rather different way. The author of the *Prolegomena*, a Neoplatonic introduction to Plato of the late sixth century AD, provides seven answers to the 'paradox' of the dialogue form (15. 1–67 Westerink), only one or two of which are likely to be found in modern scholarship. On the other hand, Rowe's (2006a) attractive position that Plato resorted to dialogue as a means to overcome the 'radical difference of perspective' between himself and his audience 'combined with the urgent requirement to communicate (to change others' perspectives)' (10) restores Plato as a flesh-and-blood thinker who was writing for *his* contemporaries. Long (2008) articulates a provocative but salutary warning, namely that it is almost impossible to discover a meaningful answer for Plato's use of dialogue form that is applicable to his entire corpus.

grounds on which it is founded. Evidence from stylometry should be treated with caution, not least because of the pitfalls inherent in the use of literary techniques, such as the avoidance of hiatus, for establishing chronological order. That the philosophy of the historical Sokrates may be traced in and retrieved from the early/Socratic dialogues is a premise not fully supported by the evidence. Sokrates' theses may sometimes differ greatly among the early dialogues (cf., for example, his hedonistic views in the *Protagoras*), while to extract a philosophical edifice out of arguments addressed to particular interlocutors in specific moments requires a certain leap in reasoning. In any case one is not entitled to take Sokrates, or any other main speaker, as Plato's mouthpiece because this violates the principle of authorial anonymity imposed on us by Plato's choice of not speaking *in propria persona*. Finally, there is no compelling reason why criticism of distinctive doctrines should necessarily mean Plato's wholesale rejection of them – as the arguments against the Theory of Forms in the *Parmenides* might imply.[7]

Admittedly it is not very easy to decide whether the 'traditionalists' or the 'revisionists' present a more persuasive case. It is true that the developmental model has served Platonic scholarship very well for the last hundred years or so, offering a plausible hermeneutic paradigm that accounts for stylistic and philosophical affinities or discrepancies among the dialogues. At the same time, that model remains essentially little more than a very influential interpretation that often does not do justice to the wealth of textual evidence and suffers from the circular character of some of its premises – such as the relationship between the early dialogues and the philosophy of the historical Sokrates. On the other hand, this urge to 'dethrone' the developmental thesis may in fact be due to no other reason than a predictable fatigue on the part of the scholarly community.[8] Or, it may be that the success of the

7 A recent instantiation of this debate with solid argumentation from both factions is to be found in Annas and Rowe (2002). For a critique of developmentalism as well as a survey of various chronological taxonomies see Nails (1995) 53–135. Cf. Rowe (2003a) 104–6, 119–22 and (2007b) 90–2; Bonazzi et al. (2009).

8 So Sedley (2003a), for whom the attacks on the model 'represent, so far at least, little more than the understandable fact that people are getting bored of it' (7).

tripartite division has turned a working hypothesis into a self-fulfilling prophecy. Equally important to the question of chronology is the context in which this 'battle of arguments' is aired. The developmentalist edifice will stand or fall primarily on philosophical grounds.[9]

I wish to draw attention to the importance of this feature in order to put the debate into perspective. As has been the case for more than two millennia now, it is the self-image of the communities of Plato's readers, laymen, teachers and exegetes alike, that sets the agenda for Platonic interpretation.[10] In modern times this community is a scholarly one, consisting of teachers of and researchers on Plato in universities and other academic institutions. Any new reading of his dialogues is legitimate to the degree that it deepens the community's understanding of the author's content or method of philosophising. Developmentalism has proved so hugely influential precisely because it familiarises Plato's compositions for a modern professional philosopher by (a) signposting turning points in Plato's intellectual explorations, so that the theories he held in different periods of his life may be safely mapped out, and (b) building an implicit belief in the superiority of a later over an earlier dialogue on philosophical grounds. As a result, the interpreter gains a more or less direct access to Plato's arguments, bypassing the admittedly awkward dialogue form and placing him safely in the company of later thinkers. He can also flatter himself that Plato's later, hence more authoritative, word on issues of argumentation and dialectics comes closer to modern preoccupations – as shown, for example, by a comparison between what is said about knowledge in the *Theaetetus* and Wittgenstein's theories. But this

9 It should be noted, however, that there are developmentalists whose criterion is the evolution of Plato not as a philosopher but as a literary author: Li Volsi (2001) postulates three chronological groups on the basis of Plato's use of the dramatic, narrative or the mixed form. Similarly, the acceptance of Plato's philosophical development does not necessarily commit one to the early–middle–late scheme, as the neo-unitarian approaches adopted by Kahn (1996) and Rowe (2007a) aptly prove (cf. Kahn 2000; Griswold 1999 and 2000).

10 Tigerstedt (1974); Gerson (2005). Interestingly, Platonism as a comprehensive, trans-historical philosophical system extracted from Plato's texts but not confined to them seems to have been an invention of the Roman period, between the first century BC and the second century AD. For a brief survey of the development of the Platonist tradition see Brittain (2008).

chronological taxonomy does more than recreate an updated Plato: it gives Sokrates a philosophy of his own. And this is a prize that is unlikely to be abandoned today. If Sokrates and Plato do not have a recognisable system or a successful method, or both, as philosophers, then they, along with Aristotle, will cease to act as the founding figures for the Western philosophical tradition and need to be replaced by, say, St Augustine or Thomas Aquinas – not an option for a post-Renaissance frame of mind.

This is the reason why I believe that, unless another model offers a more appealing portrait of Sokrates and Plato *qua* philosophers, the tripartite division will continue to enjoy its privileged status, regardless of its arbitrariness as a latter-day construct. For it is clearly a product of the evolutionism and scientific optimism of the late nineteenth and early twentieth centuries, with a firm belief in linear progress and the model of the natural sciences as the ultimate road to knowledge. Similarly, the reaction to that pattern may be rooted in post-war experiences and currents of thought. That Plato did not hold doctrines and use Sokrates as his mouthpiece, thereby committing himself to an intentional anonymity, echoes postmodernist theories on the 'death of the author'. The construction of the Platonic dialogue as an open-ended, ambiguous, ironic text and of philosophising as a limitless question-and-answer process may run parallel to the modern rhetoric of the liberal, democratic, anti-authoritarian societies of Western culture.[11] In other words, it is almost inevitable that Platonic scholars will be influenced by the cultural milieu and scholarly traditions they live in – witness the geographical distribution of, say, the analytical philosophers, the esotericists, the Straussians, the dialogists. Of course there is nothing improper in using the interpretation of the dialogues as

[11] On the origins of the current hermeneutical models in Platonic studies see Taylor (2002). The reluctance to accept a 'doctrinal' Plato may stem in part from his appropriation by Nazi Germany and the discovery of totalitarian tendencies in his political thought as the cases of Crossman and Popper demonstrate (cf. recently Forti 2006). One way Platonists could defend their author was to deny that he is committed to the arguments Sokrates puts forward in the *Republic* or the *Laws*, for example, and that one should not read Kallipolis as a blueprint for social reform (Strauss). For the demonisation of Plato as a proto-anti-Jew see Goldhill (2004) who holds that Plato's views have been 'instrumental in shaping Hitler's fascist state and the communism of the Soviet Union. *Plato has a lot to answer for*' (195, emphasis added).

a means of fostering group or school identities provided that the reading will bring us closer to Plato and not vice versa.[12]

It is in this light that the question over the standard tripartite taxonomy could be fruitfully engaged with. Despite the extremely slim evidence available, it would be worth trying to investigate the relative or even absolute dates of composition for particular dialogues whenever possible. The evidence from stylometry may prove useful but cannot be trusted unreservedly. There is always the possibility that revised and inauthentic dialogues could affect the results, or that a non-chronological explanation could be developed for clusters of stylistically close dialogues – the intended audience, for instance. Most importantly, whatever knowledge is acquired cannot be used as a pretext for hypothesising about the evolution of Plato's thought. A professional reader of Plato today would have a lot to gain if he were willing to free himself of the notion that the value of a dialogue *as a work of philosophy* depends heavily on how old its author was when he composed it. There is no such criterion for judging Euripides' tragedies *as poetry* or Isokrates' speeches *as oratory*. I see no compelling reason why Plato should be treated differently.

The premise of a Socratic philosophy retrievable from the early dialogues is also problematic. There is nothing in the texts themselves that invites the reader to harmonise the arguments of Sokrates in the dialogues and produce a defensible theoretical system. For instance, the difference between the incomposite soul of the *Phaedo* and the tripartite soul of the *Republic* is not *necessarily* explicable in terms of Plato's abandoning an earlier, Socratic doctrine of a single, rational soul in favour of his own belief in a composite soul with an irrational, lower part that accommodates our desires and passions. It may not even be clear why this 'inconsistency' should matter. The issue is whether Sokrates convinces his friends about the immortality of his soul and theirs, a few hours before leaving them for ever, or whether he teaches Plato's ambitious brothers the necessity for a just society in which citizens

[12] As Penner (2007) rightly says, 'the point of studying Socrates and Plato is not simply to identify their errors from modern philosophical points of view, but to learn from them enough to see how much modern philosophical work could be improved with some deep study of Plato, and of Socrates in Plato' (5).

consider themselves brothers and for the deterrence of civil strife at any cost. Arguments are always contextualised. They are apparently the most important element in the Platonic textual edifice but not the only one; the means not the end.[13]

That is why Plato can portray Sokrates arguing for positions that are not always compatible with each other. The condemned prisoner of the *Crito*, the satirist of the *Ion*, and the stubborn debater of the *Protagoras* share the same name, love for discussion, and authoritative stance, but to think of them as the same *individual* misses the point. They are three characters inhabiting a different fictional world in each dialogue. Evidently they need to comply with a minimal set of features evoked by the name of Sokrates, but this is a process carried on in the context of the Socratic literature and the Platonic dialogues in particular. It is often overlooked that Sokrates the philosopher is Plato's literary creation, the indisputable hero of his philosophical dramas who confronts opponents, fights for his rights, constructs utopias. As a leading speaker in most of the dialogues he dominates the discussion, but one should resist confusing the hero with the mouthpiece. In ancient classical drama even privileged views or paradigms are always challenged and make the latter notion redundant. Mouthpieces are expendable and often flat and dry. Heroes are not.[14]

The fictional nature of the genre of the Socratic dialogue makes the search for the historical Sokrates in Plato a misguided enterprise. Not that any doubts about whether he ever existed may be seriously raised. It is rather that we can never access his thoughts in an unmediated manner because he wrote nothing. In the present state of evidence all we are left with are three literary portraits by

[13] For an attractive presentation of the standard identification of the Sokrates of the early dialogues with the historical Sokrates, referred to by the author as the Early Dialogue Thesis, see Graham (1992). Cf. Penner (2002); Rowe (2006a). On the composite nature of the soul see Miller (2006); Ferrari (2007a); Rowe (2007a) 164–85; Lorenz (2008); Barney et al. (forthcoming).

[14] Therefore I endorse Wolfsdorf's (2004: 38) alternative to the mouthpiece theory, namely the conception of Sokrates 'as Plato's favoured character' who 'expresses or develops views Plato intended to advance' although 'Plato did not intend to endorse all the views Socrates asserts'. See also Trabattoni (2003); Gill (2007, 62–3). In the case of the *Theaetetus* Sedley (2002) argues for 'a radical separation of the speaker Socrates . . . from a master dramatist Plato' (312). On the other hand, Rowe (2007a: 15–20) insists on the complete identification of Plato with Sokrates.

Aristophanes, Plato and Xenophon. It was all too predictable that the reconstruction of Sokrates and his philosophy should result from dismembering the Platonic corpus. In this way, one body of texts could suffice to provide on its own direct access to the theories of two of the greatest thinkers ever. This economical solution offered by developmentalism contributed immensely to its success among Plato's modern professional readers.[15]

For the modern historian of philosophy does not get much help from a thinker who lacks a body of extant writings in which his basic doctrines are stored. Admittedly there have been a couple of other ancient philosophers who wrote nothing and their views, like Sokrates', are known from the texts of their followers, namely Pythagoras and Epiktetos. But in the latter's case the surviving document called *Discourses*, written by his student Arrianos, is a faithful record of the master's teachings, from which his doctrines may be directly engaged with – in sharp contrast with the style of the Platonic dialogues. As for Pythagoras, his silence was not so much of a problem because his image as a pioneer in mathematics, harmonics and the philosophy of numbers is in all probability a construction of later Pythagoreanism, whereas in reality he was probably a sage who taught about metempsychosis and the salvation of the soul (*KRS* 238). But neither the image of the sage nor metaphysical claims verging on the religious were fitted for a non-conformist, rational iconoclast as Sokrates must have been. The founder of dialectic and the champion of reasoned argument could not but reflect the post-Enlightenment thought-world of his modern readers.[16]

[15] The impossibility of recovering the historical Sokrates – or the historical Plato for that matter – is argued for by Michelini (2003b). Osborne (2006) provides a persuasive philosophical explanation for the incompatibility of Sokrates' theses in different dialogues. For the most recent expression of the *status quaestionis* on the Socratic problem see Dorion (2011). Cf. Morrison (2006); Prior (2006); Cooper (2007); Trapp (2007a).

[16] The quest for the historical Sokrates appears to have some similarities with that for the historical Jesus. In both cases the scholarly reconstruction of the 'man behind the myth', as it were, exhibits an unmistakable zealot's commitment to the liberation of these historical figures from their traditional textual/cultural context, with the ultimate goal of deplatonising and dechristianising them respectively (a: Sokrates *vs* Plato; open-ended elenchus *vs* doctrinal exposition; b: Jesus *vs* Christ; synoptic gospels *vs* John; scholarly community *vs* Church).

All in all, it may be argued that the privileged status of the prevailing division of the Platonic corpus into three chronological groups derives mainly from a barely admitted anxiety on the part of the humanities to get prestige by appropriating the methods of the sciences. The argument that it tells a persuasive story about Plato's evolution from a Socratic to an independent thinker is for the most part a circular one. The recovery of the philosophy of the historical Sokrates answers rather to the psychological need to avoid a crucial gap in the history of Western philosophy – an example of collective *horror vacui*. Having said as much, there is absolutely no intention on my part to belittle the important contribution that developmentalism has brought to Platonic studies. The pitfall lies in its being accepted as the only philosophically legitimate taxonomy. If the notion of philosophy could one day be redefined so that it came closer to what Plato and his original audiences must have understood by the word, namely more of a way of living than merely an academic discipline, perhaps then a more flexible context may be envisaged for the accommodation of alternative readings.

In conclusion, it may be noticed that *every* taxonomy of the Platonic corpus is to a certain degree an act of superimposition. Each dialogue should be read *primarily* as an independent, integral piece of dramatic literature, appreciated on its own terms, since this is how the original public first came to know it. Naturally, access to the full corpus makes group-division an inevitability. It would be preferable then to distinguish between those patterns that follow the few clues incorporated in the texts (setting, participants, dramatic date) and those based on similarities or differences in the doctrines expounded. Without my implying any value-judgement, it may be noticed that the second class invites greater involvement on the part of the interpreter. I would personally be more favourable to viewing the early–middle–late division as only one useful classification *among others*. Ancient readers worked with a number of taxonomies, based on philosophical and literary criteria alike, often observing cross-references between them (pp. 178–92). It would be wise for the moderns to follow their lead and explore the possibilities offered by alternative classifications such as the arrangement according to the dramatic date of the dialogues, sometimes suggestive of a biography of Sokrates (from the *Parmenides* to the *Phaedo*).[17] The full exploitation of the interpretative potential of acknowledged Platonic trilogies or tetralogies may prove equally rewarding. Since taxonomies create interpretative worlds for the readers, much could be gained from the exploration of these long-ignored *kosmoi*.

Authenticity

The question of the authenticity of the dialogues has been aligned with that of their chronology in both ancient and modern times. The anonymous author of the *Prolegomena to Plato's Philosophy*, a Byzantine introduction to Plato (6th cent. AD), considers the two issues interdependent (*Prol.* 26.1–2 Westerink). Nor should it be forgotten that Campbell resorted to stylometry in order to prove that the *Sophist* and the *Statesman* were authored by Plato. The reason for this combined treatment is pretty clear. Any classification presupposes a body of texts as its basis. It is a prerequisite that this body is free from any forgeries, imitations or wrongly attributed works. Otherwise, any conclusions drawn may run the risk of projecting distorted pictures.

To find out whether an author has in fact composed a particular text is not simply a matter of historical accuracy. Authenticity is a heavily charged notion that engenders expectations and boundaries. Genuine works receive the haloes of imprimatur, and are considered of superior quality to any of their unlucky competitors ('the worst of the genuine works is better than the best of the spurious ones'). The concomitant value-judgement implies that the group of the texts recognised as authentic defines the author and controls its reception. Since forgery is by definition a disease affecting the corpus of great writers the challenge (and temptation) for interpreters is a huge one.

[17] Zuckert (2009) maps out the philosophical significance of precisely such an arrangement. In her view, if read as a sequence of texts in terms of their dramatic dates, the Platonic corpus embodies a narrative of the rise, development and limitations of Socratic philosophy.

In the case of an ancient author with a substantial literary output like Plato it was predictable that his corpus would be augmented with additional material from early on. Demosthenes and Plutarch, to name but two, have suffered a similar fate. But the need to 'cleanse' Plato from his 'pseudo'-self is much more urgently felt because for his readers, unlike theirs, doctrinal coherence has been an imperative goal that could be easily jeopardised if any conclusions were to rely on the wrong kind of texts. As any fight against spuriousness rests on a clear vision of genuineness, there needs be postulated a body of texts above suspicion with which the rest may be compared and tested. It has been possible for twentieth-century scholars to agree on a relatively fixed number of dialogues, including the most famous ones, the authenticity of which is taken for granted. Any doctrinal, linguistic, stylistic or thematic divergences from the main features of this core could form the basis for the athetisation of any suspicious piece. For instance, the apparently opposite views argued in relation to the choice between a citizen's rights and his obedience to his city favoured in the *Apology* and the *Crito* respectively could problematise the status of the latter, while the passionate and unanswered tirade against Sokrates could raise doubts for the *Clitophon*, as the unprecedented interest in Sokrates' *daimonion* and his mysterious powers could do for the *Theages*.

This method of reaching a more reliable Platonic corpus has evidently the mark of mathematical reasoning by postulating axioms and proceeding from premises to conclusions on the basis of a set of rules that guarantee the soundness of the results reached. In practical terms, a suspected text is examined from as many aspects as possible (content, style, setting, language) so that the degree of its conformity with the normative dialogues may be determined. The criterion of authenticity therefore relates to how well the identity of a suspect work agrees with what one may expect of Plato the author of philosophical dialogues. This portrait in turn is a product of deduction on the evidence of a set of texts generally accepted as Plato's own compositions. It is this canon that validates the whole enterprise, playing a role equivalent to that of 'the first principle beyond hypothesis' of the *Republic*.

A canon, however, is by definition a construction reflecting the expectations of, and the norms imposed by, those groups undertaking the formation of such an authoritative list, in the present case Plato's professional readers. Any pretensions to crystallisation notwithstanding, *a canon of authorised Platonic dialogues is constantly in the making*. Take for example the famous debate on the genuineness of the *Seventh Letter*.[18] There are indeed factual and psychological reasons for this, whether it be the general distrust felt towards the extant pieces of ancient epistolography when they are attributed to well-known authors, the eagerness or reluctance of critics to listen to Plato's 'own' words without the mediation of his literary characters, or the strong claims made in the letter about the inadequacy of writing to convey any truth. One additional source of anxiety has been the claim that knowledge of the Good is not accessible to man through rational means only, but following a long philosophical training and companionship it springs suddenly in the soul and thereafter nurtures itself (341c–d). Depending on the interpreter's feelings for transcendent reality and the dominance of reason in Plato's philosophy, he will be more liable to argue for or against the authenticity of the letter.[19]

The 'fluidity' of the Platonic canon is also proved by the number of dialogues that have come under suspicion during the last two centuries or so of scholarly research. Today it may seem difficult to realise that among the athetised texts there once featured works like the *Phaedrus*, the *Ion*, the *Lysis*, and the *Menexenus*, or that there are still voices raised in favour of the spuriousness of the *Crito* (Thesleff 1982, 208–10 [355–7]) or, even, the *Laws* themselves (Tejera 1999, 291–308). Furthermore, in recent years there has been a tendency to put back into the picture dialogues that recent consensus had proclaimed dubious, if not inauthentic, as is the case with the *Hippias Major* (Woodruff 1982), the *Clitophon* (Slings 1999; Bowe 2007), the *Alcibiades* (Denyer 2001), the *Minos* and the *Hipparchus* (Mulroy 2007). Even those works considered spurious already in antiquity, namely the

[18] For the most recent discussion on the subject in favour of Platonic authorship see Liatsi (2008). Cf. also Knab (2006) 1–17; Tuozzo (2011) 31–44. Schofield (2006), on the other hand, considers the letter spurious (14–19).

[19] Nevertheless a non-transcendental, anti-'mystical' reading of the passage always remains a possibility. This is, for instance, what Baltes (1997) in another context is doing when arguing that the Form of Good in the *Republic* cannot really be beyond Being (ἐπέκεινα τῆς οὐσίας 6.509b9). Cf. also Ferber (2003).

Sisyphus or the *Demodocus*, have their defenders (Li Volsi 2001, 221–3). The shift in scholarly appreciation of these particular texts may serve as a reminder that the question of authenticity is as open nowadays as it has always been.

My first point, then, is that the canon of genuine Platonic works may be thought of as *conditionally* fixed. Instead of a rigid division between 'authentic' and 'spurious' dialogues, one would rather not overlook a third body of 'dubious' or 'ambivalent' ones that, in a sense, act as go-betweens and may be occasionally classified under either group depending on scholarly consensus from time to time. The proper evaluation of this 'grey zone' among the inherited corpus serves as a healthy reminder that the canon is flexible and that the criteria for authenticity are themselves liable to change. The possibility that Plato authored revised versions of his dialogues while at the same time encouraging dialogue-writing in the Academy has led at least one interpreter to introduce the idea of 'semi-authenticity' (Thesleff 1982, 94–6 [241–3]). Evidently revision and shared authorship could in principle compromise the textual data forming the very basis of authenticating techniques such as stylometry. In other words, it is rather difficult to avoid the impression that canonisation and its opposite carry with them an inherent element of 'charitable arbitrariness' lying beyond the reach of the most severe argumentation.

Realising that the transition from 'Plato' to 'pseudo-Plato' and vice versa is mediated by 'quasi-Plato' benefits the scholarly reception of the inherited corpus – and this is my second point. Whereas a condemned dialogue is virtually destined to fall into interpretative obscurity, as the lack of commentaries in the case of the *Eryxias*, the *Hipparchus*, or the *Minos* suggests, a dialogue that enjoys at least the benefit of the doubt such as the *Theages* has a chance to fare better. Whatever merits as pieces of literature and/or philosophy dialogues of ambiguous authenticity may display, their treatment as texts worthy of serious attention greatly benefits Platonic studies for at least three reasons: (a) some of these works may well have been fourth-century compositions by writers familiar with, if not participants in, the Academic tradition of the first two generations after Plato's death; (b) the writing of short dialogues in the Platonic style by authors unrelated to the Academy may be indicative of

Plato's popularity among the general public and the features they chose to duplicate could point to some tendencies in his reception outside his school; (c) there always remains the possibility that a genuine work may lie 'hidden' in this group so that any collective devaluation of the not-agreed-to-be-certainly-genuine dialogues is not such a wise course to follow.

That is why the growing tendency to put back into the picture dialogues formerly ignored because of their suspected authorship signals a very promising turn in the full appreciation of the whole Platonic corpus. It might be better for the interpreter not to let any suspicions of spuriousness prejudice him against a serious consideration of any dialogue, especially if there is a lot to be gained from a thorough reading – as the recent commentators of the *Clitophon*, the *Alcibiades* and the *Theages* amply prove.[20] Perhaps the quest for the 'purgation' of the transmitted corpus needs be put into a more generous perspective. Over-criticism usually leads to the extreme of over-athetisation attested in nineteenth-century scholarship, an ultimately self-defeating practice. If, for instance, the only dialogues to be considered genuine beyond any doubt are the ones mentioned by Aristotle or the first generation of Academics, then there is not very much left outside, say, the *Republic*, the *Laws*, the *Menexenus*, the *Hippias Minor* or the *Phaedo*. On the other hand, it is all too natural that in the course of the decades and centuries following Plato's death the body of his work should have been augmented through accretion and agglomeration – mostly for the same reasons that lie behind the formation of, say, the Hippocratic corpus. The line distinguishing genuine dialogues from later additions is indeed a very fine one. It may be wiser therefore to adopt a more charitable attitude towards those texts traditionally ascribed to Plato and leave every possibility open.

[20] Whereas Slings (1999, 234) and Denyer (2001, 24–5) accept Platonic authorship for the *Clitophon* and the *Alcibiades* respectively, Joyal (2000, 131) concludes that the author of the *Theages* is a member of the early Academy. All three, however, seem to give the authenticity issue no more than its proper due (Slings 1999, 227–34; Joyal 2000, 121–34; Denyer 2001, 14–26). The question is by no means settled: the authenticity of the *Clitophon* is rejected by Rowe (2003b) but defended in Kremer (2004), while Smith (2004) argues against that of the *Alcibiades* only to be rejected by Jirsa (2009). Mulroy's (2007) posits a Platonic milieu for both the *Minos* and the *Hipparchus*.

My suggestion, in other words, is to treat Thrasyllos' canon as the ultimate starting point. According to a record of the current consensus on the authenticity of the Platonic dialogues (Cooper 1997, v–vi), nine out of the thirty-five works included in his tetralogies, i.e. approximately one fourth of the whole, have been deemed either doubtful (*Alcibiades*, *Clitophon*, *Hippias Major*) or outright spurious (*Alcibiades Second*, *Hipparchus*, *Lovers*, *Theages*, *Minos*, *Epinomis*). Although there are reasons to suspect that the taxonomist's numerological fancies have their say in the pattern of the classification ($4 \times 9 = 36$), this does not prove *ipso facto* that he would intentionally insert in his collection so many works known to him to be inauthentic nor that his ploy would remain for so long undetected had he chosen to do so. The group of dialogues Thrasyllos appended to his tetralogies and clearly specified as spurious is a strong argument against any such large-scale tampering with the inherited material on his part. If, then, the presence of any spurious dialogues in his taxonomy is not due to a deliberate act of his, it follows that he had reasons to regard all thirty-five texts as genuine. Given the degree of arbitrariness inherent in every canonisation and in the agendas all taxonomists wish to promote, modern scholars no less than ancient readers, it seems to me a defensible 'verdict' to treat all nine disputed dialogues as Plato's or, at least, Platonic, while, at the same time, leaving the burden of proof with the athetisers.

At the end of this discussion one concluding remark on the subject may not be out of place. Without wishing to challenge the validity of or the necessity for distinguishing true Platonic dialogues from those falsely bearing this label, I think this quest for the authentic Plato has some resonances of a founding myth. Since there is no evidence that he wrote a dialogue that has been lost to us (the missing part of the unfinished *Critias* and the supposed *Philosopher* and *Hermocrates* come closer to that), the search for genuine works meant the purging of Thrasyllos' canon. Much as early modern archaeologists ignored or, occasionally, destroyed the later strata in an excavation until they reached the classical finds, early modern professional readers of Plato wanted to discover his real body of writings amidst the debris that had unavoidably been attached to it by the first century AD. This line of reasoning assumes that (a) it is *absolutely certain* that Thrasyllan tetralogies incorporate un-Platonic material and (b) modern scholarship is better equipped than its ancient equivalent to solve the problem. Now there seems to be no compelling reason to support (a), unless one resorts to the circular argument of some texts' discrepancy with Plato's philosophical persona, a construction based on other 'more canonical' texts.[21] As for (b), it may be rather construed as a gesture of self-assertion by a newly formed community against its (perceived) predecessors, in line with the scientific optimism of the times. The situation today looks rather more promising as Platonic scholars are willing to abandon the arrogant rejection of most ancient and Byzantine commentators and learn from them, acknowledging their own debt to these professional readers of old. Perhaps then the fact that the Byzantine teacher whose lectures have been recorded in the *Prolegomena*, accepted all the dialogues of the Thrasyllan canon as genuine, except for the *Epinomis*, may serve as a cautionary reminder for any unwarranted tendency towards athetisation.[22]

Plato in his original context

A first step towards the recovery of the integrity of the Platonic dialogue and its author would be its rehabilitation into its historical context. Instead of reading back into Plato a fixed model of doing and/or writing philosophy, a subsequent development meaningful in terms of a given tradition, it would be preferable to go back to the fifth and fourth centuries BC and seek to establish the meaning of his writings against the background of contemporary production

[21] Interestingly, none of the currently suspected dialogues seems to contain a lot that would add to the edifice of Platonic philosophy, at least in terms of rational argumentation or analytic thought. But the reader comes across some topics that may not easily comply with the standard image of Plato: one is reminded of the discussion on Sokrates' divine sign or *daimonion* (*Theages*) or the admonition to study and worship the celestial objects verging on astrology (*Epinomis*). On the spurious dialogues of the Platonic corpus see Döring et al. (2003).

[22] In the relevant discussion (26.1–13) the author of the *Prolegomena* records the general consensus on the spuriousness of the *Sisyphus*, the *Demodocus*, the *Halcyon*, the *Eryxias* and the *Definitions* (attributed to Speusippos), all works excluded from Thrasyllos' tetralogies, and rejects the authenticity of the *Epinomis* on the authority of the 'divine Proklos' (26.7). On the Platonic corpus in general see Irwin (2008).

of texts. As prose dramatic compositions, i.e. works that consist of the words and deeds of their characters without the intervention of an authorial voice, the dialogues were immediately comparable to the other dramatic texts of the period, to wit plays. Theatre was a dominant mode of discourse throughout the fourth century and tended to infiltrate any sort of public or publicised communication. It seems reasonable to assume that Plato's writings would be defined and received in relation to their poetical predecessors and contemporaries. The author himself does not seem to have been unaware of this. Indeed, features of his dialogues point to an underlying dialectics with dramatic poetry, exemplified by comment on and appropriation of dramatic techniques and conventions. A reading that takes as its starting point this dialectical relationship not only contextualises Plato's works but may also reveal an additional dimension: the possibility that the dialogues were liable to be read as the Platonic equivalent to the dramatists' plays.

Although in the last decade a number of voices pointing to this alternative have been raised, the scholarly community still seems rather reluctant to speak of Plato as a producer of pieces of dramatic literature. Even supporters of dialogical or dramatic interpretations feel the need to use terms from the theatrical vocabulary with qualification lest they wrongly imply too close an association with theatre proper. The argument that makes it so difficult for Plato to be read as a composer of dramas is based mostly on (a) his disparagement of anything related to the public performance of poetry – epic, dramatic, or otherwise; (b) the conception that theatre and philosophy are two rival and mutually exclusive types of discourse;[23] (c) the assumption that a Platonic dialogue was neither intended for nor depended on theatrical performance for its completion as a work of literature;[24] (d) the lack of evidence for the staging of the dialogues or Plato's association with theatre in any way.

[23] See, for example, Murray (2003).

[24] This is precisely Blondell's (2002) main argument for her claim that Plato's dialogues were not dramas (22). She prefers to think instead that the reader is invited to envisage the action of a dialogue in his mind (48). See her insightful discussion on the extent to which Plato may be justifiably considered a dramatist (14–37).

It is only fair to say that both (a) and (b) are firmly rooted in what is amply documented in the dialogues themselves. The attacks on poetry in the *Ion*, the *Republic* and the *Laws* hardly need any rehearsing. Similarly, on more than one occasion poetry, in general, and tragedy, in particular, are condemned as promoters of false wisdom and pleasure that damage the soul and lead men astray from the truly wise and happy life of the philosopher. Yet these attacks, and the famous ancient quarrel, seem to be part of Plato's strategy to demarcate a territory for philosophy and construct her as the only legitimate authoritative mode of discourse in the polis (pp. 71–7). Even if Plato really thought that the notion of the philosopher-poet would be a contradiction in terms, an unlikely assumption in itself, this does not change the fact that he appropriated the poets' methods to fight back against them. No matter what the characters in a dialogue say, their fictional status points to the continuum of the dialogue with the rest of the dramatic genres. For the Platonic dialogue displays two defining features of all drama, namely authorial effacement and role-playing. There is absolutely no reason why a full production in the manner of plays was not an option for its presentation. Therefore (c) simply begs the question and cannot stand as an objection to calling Plato a dramatist. It is important to bear in mind that in fourth-century Athens there were alternative modes of staging to the theatrical production in public festivals. As for (d), I would wish, for the present, to remark that the sources may not prove so silent after all.

The present study is precisely an attempt to reconstruct the way Plato presented himself to his original audience as the creator of an alternative drama as his own response to the existing theatrical genres. My basic assumption is that Plato's contemporaries would have responded to his writings, and to the rest of the products of Socratic literature for that matter, as pieces of dramatic fiction featuring the heroised Sokrates as the leading character practising philosophy. Fourth-century audiences would not fail to notice the special character of Platonic drama in comparison with a play: minimal physical action and movement, overwhelming presence of argumentation, absence of a singing chorus, lack of institutionalised presentation, to name but a few. These differences would have earned for Plato the title of an experimental, even eccentric, prose dramatist with a particular agenda, namely persuading people to turn to the life of philosophy – but a dramatist nonetheless. The fact that, only a generation after his death, Plato's successors did not go on composing philosophical plays should not be read back to his own lifetime and lead one to question the intrinsic unity and interdependence between Plato's philosophy and Plato's theatre.

The development of the Platonic dialogue as the new type of drama is the subject of Chapter 2. In the wake of some ancient views that define dialogue as a piece of dramatic literature (pp. 24–32), a survey of the prehistory of the prose dialogue (pp. 32–49) and of the other Socratic writers (pp. 49–56) puts Plato in his historical context. On the basis of evidence from the dialogues themselves, Plato re-emerges as both a writer who proposed his own prose drama as an alternative to the poets' plays, a rival and successor of Aristophanes or Euripides, and a thinker who employs the then dominant mode of public discourse to promote his ideas, in the tradition of the philosopher-poets Parmenides and Empedokles (pp. 56–103). Chapter 3 deals with the dialogues as pieces of performance literature. A number of remarks by ancient authorities indicate that the dialogues were treated as performable texts from early on (pp. 104–29). The nature of the publication of literary texts in classical Athens (pp. 129–40), the doxographical tradition and the evidence from *Tht.* 142a–143c (pp. 140–54) suggest that an oral presentation of the dialogues, dramatisation not excluded, should be considered a serious possibility. It is significant that the interpretation of the dialogues as pieces of theatre is a standard feature of the reception of Plato throughout antiquity. The fragments of this tradition are collected and thoroughly examined in Chapter 4. These consist of (a) a classical bronze statue-group depicting Papposilenos and Dionysos (pp. 159–78); (b) the arrangement of the Platonic corpus in trilogies and tetralogies in antiquity (pp. 178–92); (c) the evidence from a second-century AD papyrus fragment for the performance of the *Cratylus* and the rest of the dialogues of the second Thrasyllan tetralogy (pp. 192–6);

(d) the testimonies of Plutarch and Athenaios on the production of Plato's dialogues as dinner theatre in Rome (pp. 197–206); (e) a couple of editorial signs in a second-century AD Plato papyrus that might be construed as evidence for the 'ekphonetic' performance of Platonic texts (pp. 226–38); (f) a fourth-century AD mosaic in Mytilene depicting a scene from the *Phaedo* with Sokrates, Simmias and Kebes (pp. 238–55). A final section summarises the main argument of the present study and points to the significance of the image of 'Plato the prose playwright' in antiquity (pp. 256–7).

A short essay has been appended to the main body of the book. It is a discussion on an inscribed marble fragment excavated in the Academy which has been thought to bear the names of characters from the Platonic dialogues. The conclusion reached is that on the present state of evidence the Platonic connection of the inscription must be ruled out (Appendix).

Terminology

A short note on the terminology applied may be apposite here. When applied to Plato's dialogues the term *metatheatre* is throughout the book used with a meaning quite different from the usual one. In semiotics metatheatricality refers to the self-reflexive function of the language when the very fact of the theatrical transaction is alluded to during the performance (e.g. asides addressed to the audience, play within the play). Here I mean the evocation of theatrical discourse in the framework of dialogic text and its impact on and significance for the generic identity of the dialogue. In my version, the prefix 'meta-' loses much of its self-reflexive force of 'speaking about x by means of x' (the proper term in such a case would rather be 'metadialogical') and takes a referential meaning of 'in relation / response to x', 'in the context of x'. Plato's works are metatheatrical texts in the sense that they are prose dramas that define themselves in constant dialogue with their counterparts in verse through emulation and transcendence.

Similarly, the differentiation between *theatre/theatrical* and *drama/dramatic* is not so rigidly observed. In semiotics the first pair is associated with the pragmatics of the performance, whereas the latter refers to the mode of fiction meant for stage production.[25] I follow this distinction when the written document ('dramatic text') and the performance ('theatrical text') need to be distinguished. In general, however, 'theatre' and 'theatrical' are given a broader meaning and refer to the cultural phenomenon and its associations as experienced by the Greeks of the classical period. 'Drama' and 'dramatic', in turn, are mostly used in the context of discussions on literary genres.

Finally, *performance* is used for those activities which comprise (a) an oral/aural and/or visual dimension, (b) an audience of listeners and/or spectators and (c) a set of conventions recognised by a certain community. 'Performance literature' denotes those texts intended for oral delivery in a given context by one or more voices. In classical Greece almost the whole of literary production in verse and prose alike would fall under the category of 'performance texts' (Blondell 2002, 23).

[25] Dobrov (2001) offers a succinct discussion of metatheatricality in ancient Greek drama (1–53). On the semotics of theatre see Elam (1980); Pavis (1982); Alter (1990); Fischer-Lichte (1992); de Marinis (1993); Ubersfeld (1999); Postlewait and Davis (2003). For definitions of theatrical performance see Osipovich (2006). On performance studies see Davies (2008).

2

THE METATHEATRE OF DIALOGUE

Ancient views

Definitions

A reasonable starting point for any attempt at approaching the original context for the production and reception of Plato's works would be a brief overview of how that genre of dialogue was defined in ancient literature. Admittedly, there seem to be only three cases in extant writings in which definitions of dialogue are given. Although all three passages come from late sources, their standardised formulation attests to a uniform tradition prevalent throughout the late Roman and early Byzantine times. This in turn has in all probability reflected theoretical considerations on the nature of prose dialogue during the preceding periods.[1]

The earliest testimony is a passage from Albinos' *Prologos*, a short introduction to Plato from the second century AD. The same definition is repeated word for word by Diogenes Laertios about a century later. Whether this is a case of direct copy or not, both authors evidently draw from a broader theoretical background, recording what must have by then been consolidated into common knowledge. According to these authors dialogue is

λόγος ἐξ ἐρωτήσεως καὶ ἀποκρίσεως συγκείμενος περί τινος τῶν πολιτικῶν καὶ φιλοσόφων πραγμάτων, μετὰ τῆς πρεπούσης ἠθοποιΐας τῶν παραλαμβανομένων προσώπων καὶ τῆς κατὰ τὴν λέξιν κατασκευῆς. (Alb. *Intr.* 147.18–21 = Diog. Laert. 3. 48)[2]

[1] The fullest discussion of the ancient definitions of dialogue is found in Nüsser (1991) 87–100. The most comprehensive study of the history of this literary genre still remains Hirzel (1895).

[2] The latest edition of Albinos' work is Reis (1999). I use his text and follow him in keeping the pagination of Hermann's *BT* edition (cf. also the review by D'Ancona 2002). He argues that the *Prologos* is Albinos' own introduction to his edition of Gaios' lectures. Göransson (1995) has argued that *Prologos* is the written version of a lecture delivered

speech composed of question and answer on some political or philosophical topic, having the proper delineation of characters employed and the artistic treatment in terms of diction.

This is a concise statement of the basic constituents of a dialogic text. It is a prose work (λόγος) composed of the verbal exchanges in a question-and-answer format uttered by *dramatis personae* (προσώπων). As in any piece of literature these figures must speak and act in character (ἠθοποιΐας). The dialogue is also defined by a particular type of diction (λέξις) while its subject matter relates to political and philosophical issues. These points are further elaborated in the next chapter of the *Prologos*, in essence a commentary on this definition. There Albinos seems to think of the dialogue in terms of an orally performed text (λόγος . . . προφορικός 147.23–4) as well as producing a taxonomy of dialogic characters, distinguishing the philosopher, the sophist and the layman while attributing to each of them their respective patterns of behaviour (148.3–8). In addition, he considers this definition as a 'certificate' of generic identity: any prose text not displaying the features outlined there should be denied the name of dialogue (148.13–15).

Two more points in this explanatory chapter need to be particularly mentioned because they reveal the context out of which such definitions were developed:

(a) The division of the uttered speech (λόγος προφορικός) into two types in relation to the form of delivery, namely the continuous exposition (κατὰ διέξοδον λεγόμενος 147.25) and the exchange of questions and answers (ὁ δὲ κατ᾽ ἐρώτησιν καὶ ἀπόκρισιν *ibid.*). This typology may be related to Stoic theories of the distinction between rhetoric and dialectic, but a reader with basic knowledge of Plato will not fail to notice some correspondence to the division of his dialogues into narrated and dramatic ones.[3] That the dialectical conversation is considered the 'trademark' of the literary dialogue (147.25–6) suggests the significance of the dramatic element in the dialogic texts.

by Gaios and merely recorded by Albinos, possibly the only surviving portion from Gaios' *Hypotyposeis of Platonic doctrines* (52). For a slightly earlier commented edition see Nüsser (1991). Albinos' definition has been recently discussed by Ford (2008) 34–5.

[3] Cf. Nüsser (1991) 46–7. For διέξοδος in the sense of narrative see *LSJ*[9] s.v. II.

(b) The explicit association of dialogue with mimetic literature, especially theatre. This is clear not only from the employment of terminology derived from literary theory (ἠθοποιΐα, λέξις), but from Albinos' twice drawing a parallel between tragedy and dialogue. As regards the content, the appropriate types of subject matter for these genres are mythology and philosophy respectively (147.30–148.1). In the case of diction the metrical character of tragedy and comedy are juxtaposed to the Attic prose of the dialogue (148.9–13).[4] As well as establishing its generic affinity with theatre these passages underline what differentiates dialogue from dramatic poetry. It may be reasonably concluded that *Albinos defines dialogue as a philosophical drama in prose.*

This conclusion raises the question of the status of this definition in relation to Plato's writings. It seems reasonable to assume that the first two chapters of the *Prologos* deal with issues pertaining to the dialogue as a literary genre with no reference to specific works; the more so since Albinos signals the transition from the genre to Plato's texts in the opening of the third chapter (148.19–20). This impression, however, is rather illusory. The elements of the definition (dialectical exchange, characterisation, philosophical content, refined Attic prose), though applicable to a certain degree to later works, point to the products of Socratic literature as the paradigmatic texts of the genre. Plato's importance in the post-classical tradition makes it highly unlikely that theorists would not assign him a special status among his fellow-writers. The recognition of the philosopher and the sophist as stock-figures in dialogic writing is quite telling. The explicit reference to the Platonic dialogue in the third chapter does not mean that the opening chapters were not supposed to bear directly on Plato. The absence of a second definition proves in fact the contrary. It is possible then that such definitions were modelled on the dialogues of Plato, even though they were invariably intended for all relevant texts.

It is now time to turn to the other extant definition. It is found in the *Prolegomena to Platonic Philosophy*, the written version of the lectures delivered by a Christian student of Olympiodoros in

[4] The addition here of the enigmatic πλάσμα as the proper medium of composition for history is to be associated with the reference to Thoukydides a couple of sentences later (148.15).

Alexandria or Constantinople in the second half of the sixth century AD. A comparison with Albinos and Diogenes demonstrates the continuity in the theory of dialogue from Roman to Byzantine times as the author of the *Prolegomena* records practically a version of the formula in use four centuries earlier. At the same time, some variations indicate a new emphasis on certain aspects. A Byzantine student of Plato would have to learn the following definition:

Διάλογος τοίνυν ἐστὶν λόγος ἄνευ μέτρου ἐξ ἐρωτήσεως καὶ ἀποκρίσεως ποικίλων προσώπων συγκείμενος μετὰ τῆς προσηκούσης αὐτοῖς ἠθοποιΐας. (14.4–6 Westerink)[5]

Dialogue then is an unmetrical speech composed of questions and answers exchanged by various characters that have been appropriately delineated.

Anonymous for the most part reproduces the traditional formula but differs in three points: (a) he substitutes προσηκούσης for πρεπούσης and, more significantly, ποικίλων for παραλαμβανομένων; (b) he omits the phrases on the political and philosophical subject matter and the proper diction of the dialogue; (c) he inserts the qualification that the dialogue is not a verse composition (ἄνευ μέτρου). These changes result in the suppression of the element of content, already not the dominant factor in the earlier formulation. Consequently, the *Prolegomena* version is based exclusively on formal criteria. The disqualification of the subject matter as a distinguishing mark of the genre might have been generated by the appearance of works like Loukianos' satirical dialogues which proved that the genre was not a monopoly of the philosophers.[6] I think it more plausible, however, that the answer lies rather in a tendency to express the dramatic identity of the dialogue in stronger terms. The notion of ποικιλία was frequently employed in Neoplatonic hermeneutics to signify the

[5] The most recent edition of the *Prolegomena* is Westerink et al. (1990). The date and authorship of the text are discussed in the introduction (lxxxviii–lxxxix). For discussion and comparison with the earlier definition see Nüsser (1991) 95–100. Cf. Hoffmann (2006) 613–14.

[6] On the other hand, Diogenes Laertios, although writing almost a century after Loukianos, does not feel obliged to change the received definition.

style of variety typical of all the works of art of which the Neoplatonists disapproved.[7] The selection from a gallery of characters was evidently a technique utilised by the dramatic poet. To speak of the dialogic characters in terms of their theatrical counterparts is simply a statement that both dialogues and plays derive from the same dramatic matrix. This is also implied by the qualification that the dialogue is a prose genre, or literally 'a speech/text without metre'. This addition would have been unnecessary if it were not the only reason for justifying a separate classification: the use of prose is the only feature that distinguishes dialogue from comedy and tragedy. Anonymous' words immediately after the definition leave no room for doubt whatsoever:

Τὸ δ' 'ἄνευ μέτρου' πρόσκειται διὰ τὸν κωμικὸν καὶ τραγικὸν λόγον ἔμμετρον ὄντα· σύγκειται γὰρ καὶ αὐτὸς ἐξ ἐρωτήσεως καὶ ἀποκρίσεως ποικίλων προσώπων μετὰ τῆς δεούσης ἠθοποιΐας. (14.6–10 Westerink)

The designation 'unmetrical' has been added because comic and tragic speech is metrical; for this is also composed of questions and answers exchanged by diverse characters that have been suitably delineated.

The near identity between these two types of dramatic literature is so intensely felt here that a transposition takes place: a standard definition of dialogue is applied lock, stock and barrel to tragedy and comedy. Not only is dialogue defined as prose drama but drama itself may in turn be described as 'versified dialogue'. Once again it is the Platonic text that has been implied all along, as the author goes on to explain what differentiates Plato from the playwrights, given that both use almost the same literary form (14.11–29 Westerink). The author of the *Prolegomena* preserves what may be safely described as the strongest ancient statement that the Platonic dialogue is a metatheatrical prose drama. But this association was not invented in the sixth century AD. Given that the dominant theatrical genre in his time was not tragedy and comedy but mime he could hardly have drawn on contemporary practice either.[8] Therefore, he must have echoed earlier interpretations.

7 See Westerink et al. (1990) lxiv, 64 n. 137.

8 For performances of mime in early Byzantine theatre see Webb (2008a) 95–138. Cf. Solomos (1964) 17–67; Puchner (2002) 312–7; Mullet (2010) 227–9.

Albinos' definition is also conceivable in the context of a close relationship between Plato's and the poets' dramas.[9] In the pages to come it will be shown that the origin of this viewpoint, attested in literary and archaeological evidence from different periods, may plausibly be traced back to Plato's lifetime. The Byzantine lecturer was simply more outspoken than others.

Fragments of a monograph

Generic definitions are not the only extant testimonia that speak in favour of an affinity between Plato and playwrights. The fragments of a papyrus from Oxyrhynchos dated to the middle or second half of the second century AD seem to corroborate the evidence from Albinos, Diogenes Laertios and the author of the *Prolegomena*. *POxy* xlv 3219 preserves a few scraps from what may in its original form have been a treatise on Plato and the dialogue. Although only two fragments are of adequate size to produce a fairly continuous text, this monograph had sections on the development of the Platonic dialogue (fr. 1), its *dramatis personae* and Plato's use of some of them as mouthpieces (fr. 2), dialogues with sympotic theme, or sympotic literature more generally (fr. 7), the relationship between dialectic and politics (fr. 11), and the method and principles of dialectics (frs 18–20). Of great significance is the theoretical stance adopted by this interpreter: so far as the evidence goes, the author builds on the picture of Plato the prose dramatist. He represents a tradition of reading the dialogues as philosophical dramas and bringing together Plato's philosophy and theatre.[10]

In particular, fragments 3–7 are concerned with the development of tragedy, especially with the increase in the number of actors (fr. 3.3; fr. 4.3–4; fr. 5.4). Diogenes Laertios draws a parallel between the completion of tragedy when Sophokles introduced

9 Cf. Nüsser (1991: 97): 'die Nähe des Dialogs zum Drama ist eine wesentliche Bemerkung Albins'.

10 The papyrus has been edited and excellently commented on by Haslam (1972) and (1977). Other discussions are found in Carlini and Montanari (1989); Nüsser (1991) 15–23; Tarrant (1993) 104–7 and (2000) 28–9.

the third actor and that of philosophy when Plato introduced dialectics after Sokrates had added ethics to his predecessors' physics (III 56; pp. 186–7). A similar analogy may conceivably be at work in the papyrus text. If so, it is tempting to see in the names of Dionysos (]νδιόνυσον[fr. 3.2) and Apollo (]απολλωκ[fr. 5.5), the patron-deities of tragedy and philosophy respectively.[11] It is also not unlikely that the possible reference to dinner-parties (]ειπνοι[fr. 7.6) belongs to a discussion of the dramatic settings of Plato's dialogues.[12] Moreover, the use of more than one character as mouthpiece for authorial views is attributed to Plato's concern with variety (ποικίλλειν fr. 2 col. ii (b) 5), a term later interpreters associated with theatrical writing – with a negative twist in the meaning missing from the author of our monograph (pp. 23–5).

But there are two points where it is explicitly stated that the dialogues are a piece of dramatic literature. In the section on characters, the reason given for Plato's choice to speak in the *Laws* through the Athenian Stranger and not in person is his intention to 'produce out-and-out dramatic dialogues' (fr. 2 col. i (a) 9–12).[13] It is plausible that the papyrus author believed that if Plato entered his dialogues as one of the characters, this would make the *Laws* less of a drama and himself less of a dramatist – the playwrights never put themselves on stage as a member of their plays' cast. The more so since Plato's commitment to writing prose drama is one of the cornerstones of the critical theory adopted in what remains of this monograph. In fact an even stronger claim is made. In the most recoverable fragment the text reads as follows:

> ἐ]ν τούτῳ κ[αὶ Σ]ώφρον[α] μειμησάμε-
> νος τὸν μιμογράφον κα<τὰ> τὸ δραμα-
> τικὸν τῶν διαλόγων· οὐ γὰρ πεισ-
> τέον Ἀριστοτέλει ὑπὸ τῆς πρὸς Πλά-

[11] Haslam (1977) 38. Cf. Haslam (1972) 30. [12] Haslam (1972) 31.

[13] I follow the restoration by Haslam (1972) 25 and (1977) 37: ἀλλὰ διαδραματι[κοὺ]ς ποιούμενος τοὺς διαλόγους [εἰσάγει εἰκό]να καὶ ἀνειδωλο[ποιεῖ τὸν ἀνώ]νυμον Ἀθηναῖ[ον]. His arguments in favour of the otherwise unattested διαδραματικούς are convincing and both Nüsser (1991) 17 and Tarrant (1993) 104 n. 32 follow him (the latter replaces εἰσάγει εἰκόνα with κρύπτει Πλάτωνα).

τωνα βασκανίας ε[ἰ]πόντι ἐν τῷ
πρώτῳ περὶ Ποιητικῆς καὶ πρὸ
Πλάτωνος γεγράφθαι δραματικοὺς
διαλό]γ[ους] ὑπ' [Ἀ]λεξαμενοῦ Τηνίου
(fr. 1 3–10 Haslam = *PCG* I Sophron Test. 4, 188).[14]

in this case he imitated Sophron the writer of mimes
as regards the dramatic form of the dialogues; indeed
we should not believe Aristotle when he said in the
first book of the *Poetics* out of malignity towards Plato that
dramatic dialogues have been written before Plato
by Alexamenos of Tenos

Here a conviction is expressed that Plato introduced the dramatic element in the genre of dialogue and hence was the first to write dramatic dialogues. The validity of Aristotle's claim that Alexamenos had composed dramatic dialogues earlier than Plato (fr. 3b Ross = 15 Gigon) is also challenged on the grounds of Aristotle's 'malice' towards his master (p. 50). Admittedly the author's argument raises a couple of questions. Aristotle does not make this claim for Alexamenos' dialogues; he just calls them *mimēseis*. It has been argued therefore that the author must have worked with a system of classification in which the terms 'mimetic' and 'dramatic' were interchangeable.[15] In addition, it is not absolutely clear what features Alexamenos' works had or lacked so as not to qualify as dramatic dialogues. Here are some plausible possible answers: (a) they violated the rule of authorial anonymity as Alexamenos appeared in them as a character in the manner of Aristotle; (b) they were reported dialogues and so the presence of a narrator reduces the dramatic element; (c) they were deficient in their ἠθοποιία as Alexamenos failed to portray his characters realistically unlike Sophron and, presumably, Plato.[16] All in all, however, there is no doubt that the papyrus author considered the Platonic dialogues as dramatic pieces very close to Sophron's mimes, which were texts intended for the stage.

[14] For a detailed discussion of the fragment see Haslam (1972) 18–24; Nüsser (1991) 18–22.

[15] Haslam (1972) 20–1.

[16] All three alternatives are discussed by Nüsser (1991) 19–21 who opts for the last one. Options (a) and (b) are found also in Haslam (1972) 22.

The nature, date and author of this monograph are unknown. It may have been a separate treatise or an introduction to Plato.[17] It is most likely a composition of the first or second century AD, although a Hellenistic or even late classical date cannot be precluded. On the other hand, an alternative dating between the end of the sceptical Academy (early first century BC) and the introduction of Thrasyllos' tetralogies (early first century AD) has also been suggested.[18] As for the author, it may be assumed that his reading of Plato as dramatist and the parallel three-stage development of tragedy and philosophy bring him close to the tradition established by Aristophanes of Byzantium. It has even been suggested that the author could have been Aristophanes himself.[19] Be that as it may, this interesting piece of Platonic criticism proves that an interpretation of Plato as a dramatic writer was established in literary theory long before the time of the first attested definitions. It also touches upon the following questions: (a) who were the authors who had paved the way for the development of Plato's prose drama? (b) who was the first to write dialogues featuring Sokrates? These questions bear on the prehistory and the immediate context of the Platonic dialogue, two themes discussed in the following sections.

Prose dialogue before Plato

If it is proper to claim that Plato, along with the other Socratics, marks the beginning of the prose dialogue as a distinct mode of literary communication, then a brief survey of the prehistory of this new genre is in place. This section comprises an examination of some occurrences of verbal exchange between two or more interlocutors in fifth-century prose literature. In most cases, they form part of a larger textual entity and so the dialogue form is subordinate. Nevertheless, as the first instances of a later developed

[17] As suggested by Haslam (1977) 29 and Nüsser (1991) 22, followed by Tarrant (1993) 104.

[18] These are the views of Haslam (1972) 34–5 and Nüsser (1991) 22–3 respectively.

[19] Tarrant (1993) 107.

tradition, these texts may be related to the possible origins of the dialogic mode.[20]

Ion and Stesimbrotos

The first authors to be dealt with are two islanders who flourished around the third quarter of the fifth century. Both followed the great Ionian prose tradition and left a versatile work, though preserved in fragmentary condition. **Ion of Chios**, in particular, was an exceptional case of a learned man who indulged in diverse intellectual activities, as he did not commit himself to any specific discipline. His work in verse includes elegies, dithyrambs, encomia, tragedies and satyr dramas. He wrote in prose an essay on the early history of his native land, recording the relevant mythical tradition (*Χίου Κτίσις*), as well as a philosophical treatise, *Triagmos* or *Triagmoi*, where, in the manner of the Presocratic thinkers, he speculates on the original constituents of the world, propounding a three-element theory.[21]

For the present purposes the relevant prose composition is the one known as *Stays* (*Ἐπιδημίαι*). Athenaeus preserves our only verbatim quotation from this work (13.603e–604d = *FGrHist* 392F6). There the author describes an incident with Sophokles as leading figure, which took place in a drinking party where he himself was one of the participants. The passages in direct speech are (a) Sophokles' remarks, towards the boy who served the wine, or the members of the gathering and (b) a record of a short exchange between the great tragedian and an Eretrian teacher over an issue of poetics.[22] The structure of the extract makes it possible that

[20] For the earlier stages of the development of the dialogue (in prose and poetry alike) see Hirzel (1895) I 2–67; Laborderie (1978) 13–51; Thesleff (1982) 56–60 [202–7] (with the bibliographical note in 56 n. 9 [203 n. 138] – page numbers in brackets refer to Thesleff 2009); Rutherford (1995) 10–16.

[21] Ion's extant fragments have been collectively edited by Blumenthal (1939) and, recently, Leurini (2000). They also appear separately, in *FGrHist* III B 276–83; *DK* I 377–81; *TrGF* 1 95–114; *IEG*² 79–82; *PMG* 383–6. The best available treatment of his life and work is to be found in the collection of essays edited by Jennings and Katsaros (2007). See also West (1985); Dover (1986); Bartol (2000); Dougherty (2009) 392–3.

[22] Here is the passage quoted in full (with the portions of direct speech underlined): Σοφοκλεῖ τῷ ποιητῇ ἐν Χίῳ συνήντησα, ὅτε ἔπλει πρὸς Λέσβον στρατηγός, ἀνδρὶ παιδιώδει παρ᾽ οἶνον καὶ δεξιῷ. Ἑρμεσίλεω δὲ ξένου οἱ ἐόντος καὶ προξένου Ἀθηναίων

neither the preceding nor the following paragraphs in the original were about Sophokles. As for the whole work – if one were permitted to generalise from a unique fragment – the pattern seems to consist in the succession of passages dedicated to the deeds or sayings of renowned persons. The unifying factor that guarantees textual cohesion is provided by the mere presence of the author in the anecdotes he writes down – although the narrative focuses on the people he met in every occasion.[23]

Stesimbrotos of Thasos is the other prose writer usually mentioned along with Ion. He wrote on subjects such as mythology or literary criticism but he is mostly known for his source-book of anecdotes concerning some of the major fifth-century Athenian statesmen, *On Themistocles, Thucydides and Pericles* (*FGrHist* 107F1–11). Whether the product of a wholeheartedly anti-Athenian pamphleteer or of a curious collector of political gossip, this work resembles Ion's in respect of its episodic structure. The

ἑστιῶντος αὐτόν, ἐπεὶ παρὰ τὸ πῦρ ἑστεὼς ὁ τὸν οἶνον ἐγχέων παῖς * * ἐὼν δῆλος ἦν εἶπέ τε 'βούλει με ἡδέως πίνειν;' φάντος δ' αὐτοῦ 'βραδέως τοίνυν καὶ πρόσφερέ μοι καὶ ἀπόφερε τὴν κύλικα'. Ἔτι πολὺ μᾶλλον ἐρυθριάσαντος τοῦ παιδός, εἶπε πρὸς τὸν συγκατακείμενον· 'ὡς καλῶς Φρύνιχος ἐποίησεν εἴπας «λάμπει δ' ἐπὶ πορφυρέαις παρῇσιν φῶς ἔρωτος». 'Καὶ πρὸς τόδε ἠμείφθη ὁ Ἐρετριεύς, γραμμάτων ἐὼν διδάσκαλος. 'σοφὸς μὲν δὴ σύ γε εἶ, Σοφόκλεις, ἐν ποιήσει· ὅμως μέντοι γε οὐκ εὖ εἴρηκε Φρύνιχος πορφυρέας εἰπὼν τὰς γνάθους τοῦ καλοῦ. Εἰ γὰρ ὁ ζωγράφος χρώματι πορφυρέῳ ἐναλείψειε τουδὶ τοῦ παιδὸς τὰς γνάθους, οὐκ ἂν ἔτι καλὸς φαίνοιτο. Οὐ κάρτα δὴ ≤καλὸν≥ τὸ καλὸν τῷ μὴ καλῷ φαινομένῳ εἰκάζειν.' ἀνγελάσας <δ'> ἐπὶ τῷ Ἐρετριεῖ Σοφοκλῆς 'οὐδὲ τόδε σοι ἀρέσκει ἄρα, ὦ ξένε, τὸ Σιμωνίδειον κάρτα δοκέον τοῖς Ἕλλησιν εὖ εἰρῆσθαι «πορφυρέου ἀπὸ στόματος ἱεῖσα φωνὰν παρθένος». οὐδ' ὁ ποιητής (ἔφη) ≤ὁ≥ λέγων «χρυσοκόμαν Ἀπόλλωνα»; χρυσέας γὰρ εἰ ἐποίησεν ὁ ζωγράφος τὰς τοῦ θεοῦ κόμας καὶ μὴ μελαίνας, χεῖρον ἂν ἦν τὸ ζωγράφημα. Οὐδὲ ὁ φὰς «ῥοδοδάκτυλον»; εἰ γάρ τις εἰς ῥόδεον χρῶμα βάψει τοὺς δακτύλους, πορφυροβάφου χέ[ρας καὶ οὐ γυναικὸς καλῆς ποιήσειεν ≤ ἂν≥.' γελασάντων δέ, ὁ μὲν Ἐρετριεὺς ἐνωπήθη τῇ ἐπιραπίξι, ὁ δὲ πάλιν τοῦ παιδὸς τὸν λόγον εἴχετο. εἴρετο γάρ μιν ἀπὸ τῆς κύλικος κάρφος τῷ μικρῷ δακτύλῳ ἀφαιρετέοντα, εἰ καθορᾷ τὸ κάρφος. φάντος δὲ καθορᾶν, 'ἀπὸ τοίνυν φύσησον αὐτό, ἵνα μὴ πλύνοιτο ὁ δάκτυλός σοι.' Προσαγαγόντος δ' αὐτοῦ τὸ πρόσωπον πρὸς τὴν κύλικα, ἐγγυτέρω τὴν κύλικα τοῦ ἑαυτοῦ στόματος ἦγεν, ἵνα δὴ ἡ κεφαλὴ τῇ κεφαλῇ ἀσσοτέρα γένηται· ὡς δ' ἦν οἱ κάρτα πλησίον, περιλαβὼν τῇ χειρὶ ἐφίλησεν. ἐπικροτησάντων δὴ πάντων σὺν γέλητι καὶ βοῇ ὡς εὖ ὑπηγάγετο τὸν παῖδα 'μελετῶ (εἶπεν) στρατηγεῖν, ὦ ἄνδρες, ἐπειδήπερ Περικλῆς ποιεῖν μέν ≤ με≥ ἔφη, στρατηγεῖν δ' οὐκ ἐπίστασθαι. ἆρ' οὖν οὐ κατ' ὀρθόν μοι πέπτωκεν τὸ στρατήγημα;' τοιαῦτα πολλὰ δεξιῶς ἔλεγέν τε καὶ ἔπρησσεν, ὅτε πίνοι. Τὰ μέντοι πολιτικὰ οὔτε σοφὸς οὔτε ῥεκτήριος ἦν, ἀλλ' ὡς ἄν τις ἦν τῶν χρηστῶν Ἀθηναίων.

23 Pelling (2007) 76–7. Cf. West (1985) 75; Dover (1986) 33. For the genre of the *Epidemiae* see Pelling (2007) 75–88. I follow him in translating the work as *Stays* rather than *Travels* or *Visits* (76).

use of direct speech is also well attested (F5). Since Stesimbrotos does not seemingly purport to write his memoirs the work lacks the autobiographical flavour of the *Epidemiai*. Nevertheless, the interest in the personalities' private lives, as exemplified in the selection and arrangement of the material, provides the common ground on which both compositions drew.

Admittedly, these writings are much closer to fourth-century historical and biographical treatises for which they may be thought to have paved the way. Moreover, especially in Ion's case, there is resonance with other traditional narrative genres, such as the circulation of the dicta of the Seven Wise Men, or even sympotic literature. On the other hand, the similarity between Athenaios' citation from the *Epidemiai* and some entries from Xenophon's *Memorabilia* is striking indeed.[24] The insertion of dialogic interchange may also be taken as a precursor to the technique of the reported dialogue, which was often employed by Plato and other Socratic writers. At the same time, Ion seems to have been the type of writer who would not abstain from experimentation in matters of literary production: one of his tragedies was titled *Great Drama* (Μέγα Δρᾶμα *TrGF* 19F15–7). One may be tempted to give Ion a place in the prehistory of dialogue, although it remains unclear still what this place could be.[25]

Presocratics and Sophists

Dialectic argumentation combined with eristic refutation was a formidable part of the Sophists' intellectual weaponry. No wonder then that those techniques came to be associated with the dialogic tradition. According to Diogenes Laertios, **Zenon of Elea** was considered to have been the first to write dialogues (III 48). But the attribution of the statement to some unknown or unnamed source (φασί) makes this a less than binding testimony. Nor does the evidence support such a view: in Zenon's extant fragments there is no

24 Compare the opening sentence of Ion's work with Xen. *Mem.* 3.2.1, 3.4.1, 3.5.1. Cf. also *Oec* 1.1.

25 Dover (1986) 34–5 goes so far as to consider Ion the inventor of the prose genre later developed by Plato and Xenophon. Cf. Hirzel (1895) I 36–8; Laborderie (1978) 41–2; Gera (1993) 6. For Stesimbrotos see *FGrHist* II B1 515–22 (fragments) and II B2 343–9 (commentary); Gera (1993) 4–5.

hint at a possible dialogic form for his book. The relevant tradition may well have originated from a wrong inference on the basis of Aristotle's assertion that Zenon was the inventor of διαλεκτική (Diog. Laert. IX 25 = *DK* 29A1). Whatever the meaning of this term, the reference must be related to his mode of philosophical activity and argumentation regardless of the form of his text.[26]

There is, however, one more tantalising piece of evidence that needs to be considered. In his commentary on Aristotle's *Physics*, Simplikios, one of the seven leading Neoplatonists who left Athens after 529, refers to Zenon's Millet Seed paradox, which Aristotle claims to have provided an answer for (*Ph.* 7.5.250a19). He then goes on to quote what he obviously takes to be Zenon's own formulation of the argument:

διὰ τοῦτο λύει [sc. Ἀριστοτέλης] καὶ τὸν Ζήνωνος τοῦ Ἐλεάτου λόγον, ὃν ἤρετο Πρωταγόραν τὸν σοφιστήν. 'εἰπὲ γάρ μοι', ἔφη, 'ὦ Πρωταγόρα, ἆρα ὁ εἷς κέγχρος καταπεσὼν ψόφον ποεῖ ἢ τὸ μυριοστὸν τοῦ κέγχρου;' Τοῦ δὲ εἰπόντος μὴ ποιεῖν 'ὁ δὲ μέδιμνος', ἔφη, 'τῶν κέγχρων καταπεσὼν ποεῖ ψόφον ἢ οὔ;' τοῦ δὲ ψοφεῖν εἰπόντος τὸν μέδιμνον 'τί οὖν', ἔφη ὁ Ζήνων, οὐκ ἔστι λόγος τοῦ μεδίμνου τῶν κέγχρων πρὸς τὸν ἕνα καὶ τὸ μυριοστὸν τὸ τοῦ ἑνός;' τοῦ δὲ φήσαντος εἶναι 'τί οὖν', ἔφη ὁ Ζήνων, 'οὐ καὶ τῶν ψόφων ἔσονται λόγοι πρὸς ἀλλήλους οἱ αὐτοί; ὡς γὰρ τὰ ψοφοῦντα καὶ οἱ ψόφοι· τούτου δὲ οὕτως ἔχοντος, εἰ ὁ μέδιμνος τοῦ κέγχρου ψοφεῖ, ψοφήσει καὶ ὁ εἷς κέγχρος καὶ τὸ μυριοστὸν τοῦ κέγχρου.' ὁ μὲν οὖν Ζήνων οὕτως ἠρώτα τὸν λόγον. (Simp. *in Ph.* 1108.18–28 Diels = *DK* I 29 A 29)[27]

In this manner [Aristotle] refutes also the argument of Zenon of Elea, which he applied when questioning Protagoras the sophist. 'Tell me Protagoras', he said 'is it the case that one millet seed or the ten thousandth of a seed makes a noise when it falls down?' When he replied that it does not, 'Does a *medimnos*', he said, 'of millet seeds make a noise or not when it falls down?' When he replied that the *medimnos* makes a noise, 'Well', Zenon said 'is there not a ratio between the *medimnos* of millet seeds and one millet seed or even one ten thousandth of a seed?' When he replied that there is, 'Well' Zenon said 'will the noises not display the same ratios between them? For the noises are equivalent to what makes them; and this being the case, if the *medimnos* of millet seeds makes a noise, so will the one seed and the ten thousandth of seed.' This is how Zenon presented the argument.

[26] Cf. *KRS* 278. For Zenon as a writer see Hirzel (1895) I 55–6; *HGP* II 81–2; *KRS* 263–5. Cf. Rutherford (1995) 11.

[27] For the Millet Seed argument see Barnes (1982) 258–60; Mourelatos (1987) 137–8; Wardy (1990) 317–27; Hagen (1994) 127–8 n. 450.

Evidently Simplikios knows of the paradox as part of a story depicting a cross-examination of Protagoras by Zenon himself. There is also no doubt that the extract, with its combination of directed and narrated speech recalls the manner of the reported dialogues of Plato and other Socratics. If Simplikios (a) quotes in reality from an otherwise unattested work by Zenon and (b) has not intervened in the text it seems that (c) Zenon must have composed a dialogic work of the narrated type. Not to be confused with the book Plato mentions in his *Parmenides* (127c–d), this work could have included, alongside the Millet Seed, the paradoxes of motion and that of place, as has already been suggested.[28]

As for (a) it must be admitted that in principle Simplikios could, in the early sixth century AD, have had direct access to Zenon's own words. The manner in which he introduces and rounds off the passage indicates that he had no qualms over its authenticity. The Millet Seed paradox had in any case been accepted as Zenon's by no less an authority than Aristotle himself. The Stagirite's extremely brief reference, however, is worlds apart from the dramatised version recorded by his commentator almost a millennium later.[29] This brings one to (b) and the possibility that Simplikios had introduced the persona of Protagoras, turning a succession of arguments into a small piece of drama. Aristotle for one does not involve Protagoras in the story at all. The suspicion of interpolation might be enhanced by the fact that the reader hears only Zenon's words whereas Protagoras' answers are always given in reported speech (τοῦ δὲ εἰπόντος, τοῦ δὲ φήσαντος). On this reading Simplikios must have also added the narrative framework (ἔφη, ἔφη ὁ Ζήνων) for the sake of the verisimilitude of his fiction.

This hypothesis clearly creates more problems than it sets out to solve. An experiment in dramatisation would go against common practice in philosophical commentary writing. It sounds quite unlike Simplikios in terms of his style and editorial practices.[30]

28 *KRS* 264–5.

29 διὰ τοῦτο ὁ Ζήνωνος λόγος οὐκ ἀληθής, ὡς ψοφεῖ τῆς κέγχρου ὁτιοῦν μέρος (Arist. *Ph.* 7.5. 250a19).

30 Cf. Wardy (1990: 320 n.30) 'Clearly Simplicius himself could never have fabricated the passage, since its vivid, natural writing stands out in sharp contrast with his own wooden, scholastic style.' Baltussen (2002) explains the reasons why Simplikios thought highly

It fails also to provide for a motive: there is no reason why Simplikios should give himself the trouble, since dramatisation adds nothing to the point he wants to make. As for Aristotle, his silence cannot be used as counter-evidence because he was not interested in giving more than the barest of information. It is reasonable to accept that the whole text from εἰπέ to κέγχρου is what Simplikios believed were Zenon's own words.

It is possible then that both (a) and (b) are valid. Even so (c) cannot follow from them. The parenthetical clauses are all in the third person singular, meaning that the narrator of the passage is not Zenon himself. If Zenon is also the author he apparently has composed a reported dialogue in which he appears in the action described but has assigned the role of the narrator to another character.[31] The most economical and natural hypothesis is that Simplikios' passage is an extract of a prose work that may be a dialogue in the manner of, say, Xenophon's *Oeconomicus* or *Symposium*, or a piece of (real or purported) autobiographical writing such as Xenophon's *Memorabilia*. In any case, Zenonian authorship is incompatible with the text as transmitted: either the dramatisation is a later interpolation or Zenon simply was not the author of the passages.

If the original work was indeed in dialogue form, and the author was a near-contemporary or even a student of Zenon's, who wanted to keep the memory of his master alive, then one might be able to talk of evidence for a fifth-century prose dialogue.[32] The passage is very short, isolated and decontextualised, so that any decisive answer for or against such a view may be impossible to attain. The structure of the episode and its apparent self-sufficiency point in the direction of anecdotal literature, of the type exemplified in

of direct quotations and would refrain from altering the original words of the masters of the past.

31 Alternatively one may suppose that ἔφην is what Zenon had originally written and this was somehow changed by the hypothetical 'dramatiser'. This would imply Simplikios' tampering with the text and therefore contradict premise (b).

32 On the basis of a testimony from Diogenes Laertios (8.56) Diels has tentatively suggested that Simplikios' extract comes from Alkidamas' *Φυσικός or Φυσικόν* (DK I, 254). But it is not known whether this work was indeed a dialogue and Alkidamas, an older contemporary of Plato's, wrote at a time when the dialogues of the Socratics were already under circulation. For his life and work see Muir (2001). Cf. also Edwards (2007a); N. O'Sullivan (2008); Rösler (2009) 436–7.

some writings of Ion of Chios or Stesimbrotos of Thasos (pp. 33–5), perhaps even more than to a piece of fiction with unified plot and developed characters.[33] On the present state of evidence this is as far as one can get.

Diogenes also provides the testimony that **Protagoras** was 'the first to start off the Socratic kind of arguments' (οὗτος καὶ τὸ Σωκρατικὸν εἶδος τῶν λόγων πρῶτος ἐκίνησε 9. 53 = *DK* 80A1). This might be interpreted as an indirect reference to dialogic writings. In addition, two of Protagoras' works had telling titles, namely *Καταβάλλοντες* (the alternative title to *Ἀλήθεια*) and *Ἀντιλογικοί*, the latter of which is said to have been plagiarised by Plato in his *Republic* (Diog. Laert. 3.37, 57). But none of these pieces of evidence indicates that Protagoras is a writer of dialogues. (a) Given that Diogenes does not speak of Σωκρατικοὶ λόγοι – the standard name for the dialogues written by the disciples of Sokrates – the most reasonable inference is that Protagoras was the first to employ some form of interrogative argumentation in his teaching, reminiscent perhaps of the Socratic elenchus. (b) Titles by themselves prove nothing: these works of Protagoras probably belong to the genre of ἀντιλογίαι. Linear succession of argumentative discourses lacking a conversational context does not constitute a dialogic text. (c) The point in the story of Plato's alleged plagiarism is the originality of his ideal state. There is nothing to suggest an identity *in form* between the two texts. It is not likely therefore that Protagoras wrote any dialogues.[34]

In the case of **Demokritos** we seem to find ourselves on slightly firmer ground. There is clear evidence that in one of his works he used dialogic interchange between the senses and the mind. According to Galen, Demokritos

> ἐποίησε τὰς αἰσθήσεις λεγούσας πρὸς τὴν διάνοιαν οὕτως· 'τάλαινα φρήν, παρ' ἡμέων λαβοῦσα τὰς πίστεις ἡμέας καταβάλλεις; πτῶμά σοι τὸ κατάβλημα.' (*DK* 68 B125)

[33] Muir (2001) holds that Alkidamas in his *Φυσικόν* 'was probably writing about [Zenon and Empedokles] from a biographcal point of view' (xviii). It is of course possible that the passage was extracted from a dialogue composed some time between the fourth century BC and the sixth century AD. Here even wild speculation cannot be of much help.

[34] For Protagoras see Hirzel (1895) I 56–7; *HGP* III 264 n.2; Laborderie (1978) 30–1. For the anecdote see Riginos (1976) 165 n. 3.

he presented the senses speaking to the intellect as follows: 'wretched mind, first you take the proofs from us and then you try to refute us? The refutation falls down to your discredit.'

The evidence from the introductory sentence, the personification of conceptual entities and the vividness of the senses' apostrophe indicate the degree of dramatisation demonstrated in this piece of direct speech. It would be interesting to know whether this passage was part of a continuous exposition or of a more extended sequence of exchanges in direct speech.[35]

Kritias was another versatile intellectual and writer. In the manner of Ion of Chios his literary production comprises both poetry and prose. A fragment from one of his prose works called *Ὁμιλίαι*, also preserved by Galen, records advice concerning intellectual improvement addressed to another person (*DK* 88 B40). It is unclear whether this advice is addressed to another character in the work or whether the implied 'you' is the listener/reader. His training as a tragedian may have facilitated the employment of dramatic techniques in his prose work. It is conceivable that the whole work consisted of a series of such advisory passages. But for the reconstruction of the form of the *Homiliae* speculation is the only available path.[36]

The advisory tone of Kritias' fragment is reminiscent of two other lost sophistic works, namely **Hippias**' *Trojan story* (*Τρωικὸς λόγος*) and **Prodikos**' *Horai* (*Ὧραι*) The former describes a conversation between Nestor and Neoptolemos held shortly after the end of the Trojan War; the latter contains the story of Herakles' choice at the crossroads between Arete and Kakia. Both these texts belong to the traditional genre of the *ὑποθῆκαι*, didactic works providing moral instruction. They actually seem to have been among the first ones of their kind in prose.[37] What is more important, their formal structure bears the marks of a dialogic

35 For Demokritos see Hirzel (1895) I 63–4. This passage may easily be related to the poetic tradition. Cf. Sapph. 114 L–P, Bacchyl. Fr. 18.

36 Galen's comments seem to suggest that the context of the quotation was a discussion on the opposition between the senses and the reason, as in the dialogic fragment from Demokritos. For Kritias' fragments see DK II 371–99; *TrGF* 1 170–84; *IEG*^{2} 52–6. Cf. Hirzel (1895) I 64–7; Tuozzo (2011) 70–90.

37 So Thesleff (1967) 56 [45–6].

pattern. Philostratos refers to Hippias' text as *Trojan dialogue* (*VS* 1.11.1 = *DK* II 86 A2.4), while Plato makes it clear that Neoptolemos had separate lines assigned to him (*Hipp. Mai.* 286a8). In fact the young warrior's question provides the *raison d'être* for the discussion. Similarly, one may reasonably suggest that Prodikos' work was a dialogue. According to Xenophon, who provides the fullest account (*Mem.* 2.1.21–34), the dramatic setting is there, Arete and Kakia are fully grown characters very impressively depicted, while a three-way elaborate dialogue is developed between them and Herakles.[38] The story then may be thought of as a piece of reported dialogue. Whether an identical pattern can be claimed for Hippias' work, namely that the discussion of Nestor and Neoptolemos was enclosed by a narrative frame, remains disputable.[39]

But the most striking example of a dialogic text in the sophistic corpus is the one found in the collection of antithetical arguments dated from around 400 BC and known as *Dissoi Logoi*. In the first pair of arguments that deal with good and evil (Περὶ ἀγαθῶ καὶ κακῶ) the writer temporarily abandons continuous exposition and resorts to the interrogation of a hypothetical supporter of the thesis that good and evil are one and the same thing (*DK* II 90 1.12–14). The short dialogue follows a triadic pattern: question by the examiner – answer by the interlocutor – an assertive statement made by the former (although the last question remains unanswered). Strikingly enough, all the answers are identical in form (πολλὰ καὶ μεγάλα). Despite this somehow *ad hoc* and monotonous tone, the passage remains a strong case for a late fifth-century application

38 The explicit addresses are: (a) Kakia to Herakles (23 and 29) (b) Herakles to Kakia (26) (c) Arete to Herakles (27 and 33) (d) Arete to Kakia (30). Kakia's address to Arete is hidden in her contemptuous remark on Arete's speech (29). In Xenophon's version Herakles does not address Arete but this may be inferred (a) on symmetrical grounds, as he has already spoken to Kakia and (b) on account of his decision to choose Arete, which could possibly have been given in direct speech. Whether in his narrative of the 'Choice of Herakles' Xenophon remains faithful to the actual wording of Prodikos' text remains an open question. Sansone (2004) answers in the affirmative, unlike Gray (2006) who remains sceptical and Dorion (2008) who argues for an extensive revision.

39 Thesleff (1982) 57 [203] argues for a narrative frame. Gera (1993) suggests that both works were written in dialogue form (51). Cf. also Hirzel (1895) I 59–63. For ὑποθῆκαι see Thesleff (1967) 56 [45]; Gera (1993) 51–2.

of the 'question-and-answer' technique, which was made famous by the Sokrates of the early Platonic dialogues.[40]

This feature leads to the question of the relationship of the writings of this section with fourth-century dialogic texts. Ion's possible influence on Xenophon's *Memorabilia* has already been mentioned (p. 35). Hippias' and Prodikos' works have been considered forerunners of the Socratic dialogue, but only in matters of content and intention *not* form, although it would be more cautious to restrict their alleged influence to Xenophon's *Cyropaedia*.[41] It is also tempting to suppose that Kritias exercised some form of influence on his younger nephew Plato.[42] As for the inserted dialogue in the *Dissoi Logoi*, its marginal position in the work and rather rudimentary structure and function make it less likely that it inspired future composers of dialogues. It is, however, an important piece of evidence because it shows that this type of dialogue was familiar among intellectuals at the time when the Socratics were writing their first works.

Historical works

Historiography is one of the first products of prose literary tradition. Sharing common thematic ground, it adopted and adapted methodological devices from epic poetry. A fundamental one was to allow the participants of an episode to speak on their own behalf, so that the listener may have first-hand experience about an individual's sentiments or thoughts. This device was taken up by the historians, who inserted pieces of direct speech in their own work. There is a certain thread linking the heroic ῥήσεις in Homer, the Debate on Government in Herodotos (3. 80–2), and the speeches of Nikias and Alkibiades in Thoukydides (6.9–23). Furthermore, one may pick up from the historical narrative passages which fulfil

40 The text has been edited by Robinson (1979) and recently by Becker and Scholz (2004). A reference to the Spartan victory in the Peloponnesian War (DK II 90 1.8) may plausibly be read as a *terminus post quem*. For date and authorship see Ramage (1961); Conley (1985); Robinson (2003); Becker and Scholz (2004) 16–17; Bailey (2008) 249–50. On its importance for the history of thought see Gera (2000); Barney (2006) 88–90.

41 Views held by Gaiser (1959) 61–4 and Gera (1993) 51–2, 54 respectively.

42 Cf. Thesleff (1982) 56–7 [203–4]. He also suggests that the *Homiliae* included dialogue where an interlocutor produced the definition of σωφροσύνη found in Pl. *Chrm.* 161b–c (57 n. 13).

the requirements of a dialogic text, such as Herod. 1. 8.1–13.2 (the Gyges story) or Thuc. 2.71–3 (Archidamos and the Plataeans exchange speeches). But their form is simply subsidiary to the general pattern. At best they may be considered reported dialogues. Yet their intrinsic dependence on the framing narrative conditions their function. Dialogue is not given any value *qua* dialogue.

Nevertheless, there seem to be a couple of instances where the dialogue form is apparently given some autonomy. Both occur in **Thoukydides**. In the third book there is a short discussion between an Akarnanian and an Ambrakiote herald (3.113.1–5). Apart from the vividness of the scene, the point of interest here lies in the structure of the passage: a narrative frames the conversation which bears the form of a reported dialogue (the usual pattern in historical works). But gradually the latter develops into a kind of dramatic dialogue owing to the abolition of the intermediary phrases that denote the change of the interlocutor. This shift, later to be used by Plato in his *Parmenides*, would indicate an interest on the part of Thoukydides on matters of textual form.[43]

The second passage is of course the famous Melian Dialogue (5.85–111). The setting is well known: Athenian and Melian delegates converse on the future of the island under the threatening presence of the Athenian fleet. After the first pair of speeches, accompanied by introductory entries (85.1, 86.1), there follows a proper dramatic interchange with the authorial presence temporarily suspended. It is not absolutely clear what led Thoukydides to this experimentation. In any case, his is the unique example of an indisputable use of dramatic composition in extant pre-Platonic Attic prose literature. Even if he did not affect the dialogic tradition directly, the value of his experiment should not be ignored.[44]

[43] It is noteworthy that the first exhange between the Akarnanian and the herald is given in reported speech (καί τις αὐτὸν ἤρετο . . . ὁ δ' ἔφη I 113.3) which turns into a narrated dialogue (ὑπολαβὼν δ' ὁ ἐρωτῶν εἶπεν . . . αὖθις δὲ εἶπεν ἐκεῖνος . . . ὁ δὲ ἀπεκρίνατο I 113.4) to be replaced in the middle of the story by a direct exchange of speeches. The episode of the Ambrakiote herald then has the following structure: narrative – reported dialogue – dramatic dialogue – narrative. For a narratological study of Thoukydides see Rood (1998).

[44] A kind of relation between the Melian Dialogue and Plato's works was acknowledged already in antiquity as indicated by Albinos' arguing against this view (*Intr.* 148.15–18). Cf. Nüsser (1991) 55–8. The latest reading of this self-contained dialogic episode

The Sicilian connection

Epicharmos

It may be useful at this point to bring into the picture another piece of evidence. In his life of Plato Diogenes Laertios quotes substantial extracts from the first out of the four books of the lost treatise *Πρὸς Ἀμύνταν* by the Sicilian historian Alkimos (3.9–17). There the author makes the surprising claim that some of Plato's central doctrines, namely the postulation of a dichotomy between a sensible and intelligible world or the participation of particulars in Forms, ultimately derive from thoughts that Epicharmos had expressed in his comedies. To support his argument Alkimos gives a paraphrase of a Platonic tenet followed by those verses which purportedly anticipated it. The point of this comparison is to show that Plato's indebtedness to Epicharmos was in reality a product of plagiarism. If Amyntas is to be identified with the student of Plato from Pontic Herakleia, and if Alkimos' voluminous work had him as a target, the anti-Platonic bias of the treatise seems a reasonable inference.[45]

According to the standard view, all six of these extracts are spurious and belong to the group of literary products that circulated in antiquity under the name of Epicharmos, collectively known as ψευδεπιχάρμεια (=pseudo-Epicharmean).[46] They have been suspected mostly on the grounds of their use of vocabulary and argumentation reminiscent of the ones employed by Plato.

is offered by Greenwood (2008) who views the historian as a precursor to Plato in incorporating dialogues and other speech genres (16). Cf. also Alker (1988); Morrison (2000); Price (2001) 195–204. On Thoukydides' influence on Plato see Rutherford (1995) 66–8 (with references); Hopkins (2007); Mara (2008).

45 See Dörrie (1987) 308–18; Goulet (1989). Cf. also Gigante (1953); Gaiser (1973). Cassio (1985) associates the composition of this polemical work with the internecine strife in Sicily between the supporters and the opponents of Dionysios II, Alkimos being on the tyrant's side (45). The accusation of plagiarism must have been in Diogenes' mind when writing that Plato has benefited a lot from Epicharmos τὰ πλεῖστα μεταγράψας, καθά φησιν Ἄλκιμος (3. 9).

46 Kassel and Austin in their recent edition of Epicharmos' fragments place these passages (*PCG* I 275–280) among the rest of the forgeries in the name of Epicharmos (*PCG* I pp. 138–73). Earlier editors include Jacoby (*FGrHist* IIIa 560) and Diels (DK I 23 B 1–6). The translation of *PCG* I 277 is mine.

Expressions such as θαυμαστὸν οὐδέν (*PCG* 279.1 ~ e.g. Pl. *Resp.* 3.390a5), οὐ γάρ (*PCG* 276.6, 277.4 ~ e.g. Pl. *Theaet.* 147b7) or, more tantalisingly, οὐδαμῶς (*PCG* 277.2) and πάνυ μὲν οὖν (*PCG* 277.1, 4) may understandably raise some eyebrows. It should be noted, however, that the Platonic connection may, under closer scrutiny, prove more of a construction on the part of Alkimos. If read by themselves, outside the context in Diogenes' account, only *PCG* I 277 would strike one as imitating the mode of the Platonic text in particular. As for the rest, they may look like pieces of philosophical dialogue (*PCG* I 275, 276) or monologue (*PCG* I 278, 279), though this alone cannot call into question their authenticity. The absence of their original context and the lack of sufficiently representative material from genuine Epicharmos are quite serious impediments. These 'philosophical' verses may or may not have been composed by the Syracusan comedian, but one needs something more than an alleged dependence on Plato to pass a safe judgement.[47]

For present purposes, however, the authenticity of these fragments is not so much of an issue. For even if they are not genuine, their significance lies in what they can tell about the expectations of the literary audiences in western Greece in classical times. Alkimos lived in the second half of the fourth century BC. This provides a *terminus ante* for their composition, even allowing for the unlikely scenario that some were forged by Alkimos himself.[48] The texts quoted by Diogenes are all in verse, most written in one of the characteristic metres of the Dorian comedy, namely trochaic tetrameter. As is the rule in the case of all (pseudo-)Epicharmos'

47 In a recent article Álvarez Salas (2007) argues convincingly in favour of the genuineness of all Epicharmos' fragments preserved by Alkimos. Similarly in his discussion of the fragments (*DTC*² 247–55) Pickard-Cambridge has no difficulty in considering all of them genuine, whereas Webster accepts the first two – then still undivided as in Diogenes (*DTC*² 254–5). Diels also seems to reject only one out of the whole lot (DK I 23 p. 193). Hordern (2004) is willing to accept the authenticity of fr. 279 (13 n. 41), whereas Kerkhof (2001: 65–78) cautions against any *a priori* athetisation of the fragments. For Epicharmos' life and works see *DTC*² 230–90 and Kerkhof (2001) 55–133.

48 A flourishing 'industry' of texts falsely attributed to Epicharmos is well attested for the same period (Athen. 14. 648d).

fragments, they all purport to come from a play.[49] If so, a performance context has to be postulated for the publication of these fragments, whether as parts of whole new plays or interpolations in existing comedies. The alternative route, that of the conscious contamination in the textual transmission, seems less satisfactory an answer given the pragmatics of the publication of literary texts in that period. Despite the lack of hard evidence, it is reasonable to assume that in the thriving theatrical culture of fourth-century Italy and Sicily productions of the celebrated local comedian would have their own share.

That the extracts from Alkimos' book originally reached the public through performance leads to some further considerations. Take for instance *PCG* I 277, the most 'Platonising' of all the fragments:

(A.) ἆρ', ἔστιν αὔλησίς τι πρᾶγμα; (B.) πάνυ μὲν οὖν.
(A.) ἄνθρωπος οὖν αὔλησίς ἐστιν; (B.) οὐδαμῶς.
(A.) φέρ' ἴδω, τί δ' αὐλητάς; τίς εἶμέν τι δοκεῖ;
ἄνθρωπος, ἢ οὐ γάρ; (B.) πάνυ μὲν οὖν. (A.) οὐκ οὖν δοκεῖς
οὕτως ἔχειν <κα> καὶ περὶ τἀγαθοῦ; τὸ μὲν
ἀγαθὸν τὸ πρᾶγμ' εἶμεν καθ' αὕθ'· ὅστις δέ κα
εἰδῇ μαθὼν τῆν', ἀγαθὸς ἤδη γίγνεται.
ὥσπερ γάρ ἐστιν αὔλησιν αὐλητὰς μαθὼν
ἢ ὄρχησιν ὀρχηστάς τις ἢ πλοκεὺς πλοκάν,
ἢ πᾶν ὁμοίως τῶν τοιούτων ὅ, τι τὺ λῇς,
οὐκ αὐτὸς εἴη κα τέχνα, τεχνικός γα μάν.

(A.) So, is there such a thing like aulos-playing? (B.) Definitely.
(A.) Is then aulos-playing a man? (B.) By no means.
(A.) Let me see, what about the aulos-player? What does he appear to be?
Is he a man or rather not? (B.) Definitely a man. (A.) Don't you then believe

[49] Even the existing fragments from the *Maxims* (*Γνῶμαι*) yield a continuous text in the form of a soliloquy (*PCG* I 244–8) rather than an accumulation of discontinuous verses from different sources in the manner of, say, *Γνῶμαι Μενάνδρου*. Diogenes might have such collections in mind when talking of *memoirs* (ὑπομνήματα) containing physical, ethical and medical doctrines (8. 78). A testimony that is possibly based on the tradition that Epicharmos had been a Pythagorean (see Balaudé 1999, 1003 n. 5; Burkert 1972, 289 n. 58. Incidentally Burkert tentatively accepts the authenticity of the fragments). That Epicharmos composed only comedies has been sufficiently shown (*DTC*[2] 243–5) and this is how fourth-century Greeks remembered him, if Plato's testimony is of any worth (*Tht.* 152e5).

that this would also be the case as regards the good?
The good is the thing by itself; but whoever happens
to learn and know this, he immediately becomes good.
Just as an aulos-player is the one who learned aulos-playing
or a dancer is someone who learned dancing or a weaver is the one who learned weaving
or in each and every one of those practices you want,
the practitioner himself could not be a craft, but a craftsman instead.

Here is a series of questions answered briefly in the affirmative or negative and leading to a final proof that whoever comes to know what good is does not necessarily become good himself. The structure of the argument, namely a number of premises followed by a conclusion supported by the accumulation of similar examples and the speaking roles shared by a dominant questioner and a cooperative interlocutor, indeed recalls the situation in a number of Platonic dialogues.[50] Their presence in a performance text means that an audience would not be surprised if they were listening to a 'sophisticated' argument from the stage. True, a dialectical exchange in a comedy is put to the service of parody, characterisation and the other requirements of the genre, so that its reception is conditioned in a way unknown to a philosophical work. The fact remains, however, that Plato's (near-)contemporaries, whether as members of large public audiences or of smaller private gatherings, must have been familiar with dialectical argumentation being presented to them in the course of the production of dramatic poetry.[51]

Mime

Whether any of these writings played some role in the development of the Platonic dialogue cannot be determined, not least because of the silence of the sources. The only prose genre that ancient literary theory recognised as relevant to Plato's compositions is the literary

[50] These elements also feature in *PCG* I 276 and, with some variation, 275. For a full discussion of this fragment see Álvarez Salas (2007) 46–57.

[51] This argument gains in probability if the fragments were genuine, thus coming from a play presented on stage. On the ability of the ancient audiences to cope sufficiently with the demands of theatrical communication see Revermann (2006a).

mime, the main fifth-century exponent of which is **Sophron**. His works are dramatic compositions featuring comic representations of scenes from everyday life. They are divided into 'male' and 'female' with respect to their subject matter and are written in the local Syracusan version of Dorian dialect, in a language full of proverbial phrases. As far as diction is concerned, their peculiarly intermediate status makes them particularly intriguing: though a poet, Sophron seems to have replaced verse with a kind of rhythmic prose.[52]

Sicilian mime would be the first instance of a genre employing the dialogue form on purely 'mimetic' grounds in the manner of theatrical diction, i.e. without any narrative frame. In this respect, mime provides a precedent for the Platonic dialogue. In fact, ancient tradition talks about Plato's admiration of Sophron while, at the same time, alluding to his literary debt to his Syracusan 'predecessor': we have seen that the author of *POxy* xlv 3219 states categorically that Plato wrote dramatic dialogues on the model of Sophron's plays (pp. 29–32). It is also tempting to associate Aristotle's remark that Plato's style is halfway between poetry and prose with Sophron's 'poetic prose' or 'prose poetry' (pp. 108–10). Admittedly, it is difficult to discern whether there is any kernel of truth in this tradition. There is always the possibility that it is a fiction prompted by Aristotle's juxtaposition of Socratic dialogues and mimes in his *Poetics* (1447^{b}). All in all, a direct influence of Sophron, whose *floruit* is placed at about 440–430 BC, on Plato is quite likely. Except for a similarity in the medium (prose

[52] Cf. Sch. in Greg. Naz. *Hymn VIII* 'οὗτος [sc. Σώφρων] γὰρ μόνος ποιητῶν ῥυθμοῖς τε καὶ κώλοις ἐχρήσατο ποιητικῆς ἀναλογίας καταφρονήσας' (Christ and Paranikas 1871, 29). The only relatively extensive extant fragment seems to confirm this testimony (*PCG* I Sophron fr. 4, 188). Hordern (2004) 15–16 questions the validity of this piece of evidence, on the assumption that the scholiast, who did know Sophron's works at first hand, fell victim to a tradition generated by a conflation of two Aristotelian passages: the association of Sophron's mimes with Platonic dialogues in the *Poetics* and the remark on Plato's style as halfway between prose and poetry in the *On the poets* (pp. 105–10). The latest edition of Sophron's text with introduction, translation and commentary is Hordern (2004), while the standard edition of testimonia and fragments remains *PCG* I 187–253. Cf. also Olivieri (1930) 169–233 (with commentary); MacDonald (1931) 79–113; Cunningham (2002a) and (2002b). For mime in general see Reich (1902); Cunningham (1971) 3–11.

dialogue) and possible parallels in characterisation little else may be said with certainty about its nature.[53]

The Socratic dialogue

Whether influenced by Sophron or not, when Plato was launching his literary career his affinities as an author came from a different context: he was expected to be seen as one of those associates of Sokrates who had undertaken to commemorate his life and teachings in their writings. In all probability other Socratics had already preceded him as writers of such texts – Antisthenes, Phaidon or Aischines are likely candidates. By the mid-fourth century BC these particular compositions, the first prose dialogues in Greek literature, had been recognised as a distinct literary genre under the name of 'Socratic discourses'. According to Aristotle the distinguishing element of these texts is the notion of imitation, as a Socratic dialogue purports to stand as a representation of scenes from the master's everyday life (pp. 105–8). The discussion in the *Poetics* may provide the basis for a definition of this new genre that would come close to the understanding of a contemporary reader. Socratic dialogue may be defined as the literary prose text that portrays Sokrates in action and in conversation at his encounters with a variety of interlocutors.[54]

53 Cf. MacDonald (1931) 142–58. Based on these similarities some scholars have followed MacDonald (1931) 143 in calling Plato's dialogues 'philosophical mimes' as, for instance, Klein (1965) 18. Cf. Clay (1994) 37–41. Hordern (2004) is reluctant to see any direct influence of Sophron's to Plato (26–7).

54 Influenced by the ancient testimonies on Plato's works Puchner (2010) produces an attractive definition of the Socratic dialogue: 'a dialogue in prose (rather than poetry) to be read aloud to small groups of listeners (rather than a large audience) based on the speech of individual characters (rather than a chorus) who engage in conversations on philosophical topics for the purpose of either giving instruction or accumulating knowledge' (21). Alternative definitions: Sykoutris (1937) 10 n. 2; Else (1957) 43; Clay (1994) 24–5. Ford (2008) traces convincingly the beginning of the Socratic *logoi* to the rhetorical culture of the fourth century and identifies character-drawing, *ēthopoiia*, as one generic feature that differentiates them from other argumentative texts. Rossetti (2007) puts forward the attractive hypothesis that during the first fifteen years after Sokrates' execution his followers as a group promoted dialogue-writing as a revolutionary communication formula, a 'trademark' for the new type of philosophy they stood for (20–5). See also Giannantoni (2005); Rossetti (2005); Vegetti (2006); Decleva Caizzi (2006) 122–5. In contemporary Platonic scholarship the term often denotes the so-called

Alexamenos

That the Socratic dialogue was recognised as a new genre is demonstrated in the various traditions about its inventor, the first Socratic who introduced this kind of prose text. The first three authors to be dealt with have all been claimed by some ancient source for the title of the πρῶτος εὑρετής. *POxy* xlv 3219 records the well-known tradition, repeated by Diogenes Laertios (3. 48) and Athenaios (11. 505c), that Aristotle claimed **Alexamenos of Teos** to be one of the first writers of literary dialogues. The passage from *On Poets*, quoted by Athenaios, makes it clear that Aristotle thought of Alexamenos' texts as pieces of literature comparable to Sophron's mimes (pp. 107–8). It is precisely their status as *mimēseis* that the papyrus author argues against (pp. 29–32). There is, however, an uncertainty as to whether the reference to these texts as τοὺς πρώτους γραφέντας τῶν Σωκρατικῶν διαλόγων implies that they were Socratic dialogues. Are we to suppose that Alexamenos was the first Socratic (?) to have composed in the new genre or that he was a dialogue-writer earlier than and unrelated to the Socratics and the Socratic literature?[55] On the present state of evidence a definite answer is not available and, therefore, it is impossible to form any idea on either Alexamenos or his writings. His twilight presence, however, casts its shadow on the Socratic literature.[56]

Simon

Another candidate is **Simon** the cobbler. Once again it is Diogenes who records the tradition (φασί) that Simon πρῶτος διελέχθη τοὺς λόγους τοὺς Σωκρατικούς (2.123). If the verb has the meaning of

early dialogues of Plato, believed to reflect more faithfully Sokrates' own doctrines (cf. the discussion in Rowe 2006b).

55 Kassel and Austin print a corrected text that favours the second alternative: οὐκοῦν οὐδὲ ἐμμέτρους <ὄντας> τοὺς καλουμένους Σώφρονος μίμους μὴ φῶμεν εἶναι λόγους καὶ μιμήσεις, ἢ τοὺς Ἀλεξαμενοῦ τοῦ Τηίου τοὺς πρότερον γραφέντας τῶν Σωκρατικῶν διαλόγους; (*PCG* I Sophron Test. 3, 187). The first alternative is favoured by Ford (2010) who accepts the transmitted text – except for the substitution of λόγων for διαλόγων (224–7) – for 'it is unwise to alter Aristotle's information about Alexamenus' (225).

56 On Alexamenos see Natorp (1894); Hirzel (1895) I 100–1; Narcy (1989); Clay (1994) 33.

'write in prose' (cf. *LSJ*[9] s.v. διαλέγω B 4) then an otherwise unknown artisan emerges as the progenitor of a literary genre. This testimony, however, ought to be treated with caution because of (a) Diogenes' disclaimer by attributing this piece of information to anonymous sources; (b) the presence of folk-literature elements in the relevant tradition: Simon's alleged encounter with Perikles seems to reproduce the folk motif of 'the sage and the king'; and (c) the absolute silence of the sources. These of course do not prove the tradition mistaken. Simon may have known and conversed with Sokrates and may even have been the first to deliver publicly and/or discuss his dialogues (if this is what διελέχθη means). But his legend may have grown less from his writings than his appearance as a character in literary works, as in Phaidon's *Simon* and the stories attached to him. Diogenes gives the titles of thirty-three short dialogues (2.122), but there is no way to find out anything about their content or authenticity. Simon the cobbler and his σκυτικοὶ διάλογοι remain a fascinating but unverifiable piece of ancient tradition.[57]

[57] Sellars (2003) offers a useful overview of the questions around Simon and his 'leather dialogues' (207–9). Li Volsi (2001) explains the identity in the titles of some Platonic dialogues with those attributed to Simon as Plato's reworking in his own fashion themes for the first time dealt with by the cobbler (220 n. 6). Cf. also Hock (1976). Clay (1994) believes that Simon is 'the true inventor of the Socratic dialogue in its purely mimetic and dramatic form' (32) – so incidentally Li Volsi (2001) 220 – though he bases his argument on the doubtful rendering of διελέχθη as 'write in dramatic form'. Brumbaugh (1991) also claims that Simon's dialogues were an early phase in the development of the genre. At the other extreme there are scholars who deny that Simon was a real person, like Zeller (1868) 210; Wilamowitz (1879) 187, who believed Simon was Phaidon's literary creation that took a life of its own; Kahn (1996) 10 n. 18. The opposite view has been taken by Hirzel (1895) I 102–5; Hobein (1927); Hock (1976). For the ancient testimonia on Simon see Sellars (2003) 207 n. 3. Archaeological findings have renewed the interest in this controversy. At the south-west corner of the Athenian Agora, in the courtyard of a private building, a number of iron hobnails and bone eyelet rings have been unearthed along with a cup-base bearing the inscription ΣΙΜΟΝΟΣ. The identification of the building with a shoemaker's house is certain. The possibility that the owner of the cup, the owner of the shop and the Simon of tradition were one and the same person presents itself as an attractive one. See the initial excavation report by Thompson (1954) 54–5, followed by a full treatment in Thompson (1960) who concludes that 'we have found the house of a shoemaker, who worked there from about 450 to 410 BC' (238). Cf. also Lang (1978) figs 12 and 13 with the accompanying text; Camp (1986) 145–7. The identification is considered plausible by Brumbaugh (1991); Goulet (1997) 122; Clay (1994) 32 n. 19 (with caution); Goulet-Cazé (1999) 365 n. 13; Navia (2001) 124. Sellars (2003, 208) remains sceptical.

Xenophon

A somewhat unexpected claimant is **Xenophon**. On the testimony of Diogenes Laertios he was the first to note down and circulate Sokrates' conversations under the title of *Memoirs*.[58] Given the relatively late date of Xenophon's Socratic works, it is highly improbable that this testimony would point to any priority of his as an author of Socratic dialogues in general. More plausibly, the new element that Xenophon brought to Socratic literature is associated with the form of the specific work mentioned in the text. Perhaps the autobiographical style of his *Memorabilia* was considered a novelty in contemporary prose writing – or so Diogenes, or his source, may have thought.[59]

Aristippos

Xenophon was only one out of a substantial number of Socratics who left dialogic texts featuring Sokrates as their leading character. But whether **Aristippos of Kyrene** should be counted among them is an open question. Prolific writer though he was, his status as a Socratic author appears rather elusive. Diogenes Laertios provides two lists of his works, among which is a book containing twenty-five dialogues written in Doric and Attic dialect (2.83). But the authenticity of his dialogues, especially the Doric ones, is very much disputed. Even if some of them were genuine, they may not have featured Sokrates as a character.[60] An argument in favour of Aristippos' authorship of Socratic dialogues may be grounded on (a) a passage in one of the so-called 'Socratic epistles', where it is said that Dionysios of Syracuse 'keeps him as the person in charge of the Socratic dialogues' (λόγων ἐπιμελητὴν τῶν Σωκρατικῶν κατέχει [sc. Ἀρίστιππον], *Socrat. Epist.* 9.1 =

[58] καὶ πρῶτος ὑποσημειωσάμενος τὰ λεγόμενα εἰς ἀνθρώπους ἤγαγεν, Ἀπομνημονεύματα ἐπιγράψας (2.48).

[59] According to Momigliano (1993) '[t]he fact that they [sc. the *Memorabilia*] combine a defense of Socrates with recollections of Socrates seems to speak for their originality' (53). That Xenophon was a latecomer in Socratic literature is maintained, among others, by Kahn (1996) 30 with n. 56 and Huß (1999) 18–25. For Xenophon as an author of Socratic dialogues see now O'Connor (2011). Cf. also Narcy (1997); Patzer (1999); Dorion (2006); Gera (2007); Narcy and Tordesillas (2008).

[60] As suggested by Clay (1994) 30 and Geffcken (1934) 33 respectively. Cf. *SSR* IV 157–8.

SSR IV A 222) and (b) a fragment in Syriac, from a supposedly lost – and unrecorded – dialogue, which depicts the discussion between Sokrates and someone called Herostrophos (*SSR* IV A 159). But these pieces of evidence provide weak support for such a thesis, because (a) nothing in the meaning of the word ἐπιμελητής suggests the notion of authorship and (b) the Syriac fragment is very likely a post-Aristotelian composition.[61] It seems plausible that Aristippos exercised his influence through his life rather than his writings.[62]

Eukleides

Eukleides of Megara is depicted as the founder and the leading figure of the Megarians, a philosophical school oriented towards issues associated with logic and the philosophy of language. He has been credited with the composition of six Socratic dialogues (Diog. Laert. 2.108). Interestingly enough, we hear of no other works of his. It seems possible then that he confined his literary product to the dialogue form (as was the case with Plato and, apparently, Aischines). Unfortunately, we do not possess any first-hand information about these texts. The titles themselves denote a certain preoccupation with favourite motifs of the Socratic literature. Three of them bear the names of well-known persons in the Socratic circle (*Aeschines*, *Crito*, *Alcibiades*), while the presence of the erotic element, possibly accompanied by an educative nuance, may be safely conjectured (*Erotikos*, *Alcibiades*).[63]

[61] Ryssel (1893) 175–8. Clay (1994) 31 n. 16 (although notice his reference to the dialogue as 'Aristippus' mysterious *Herostrophos*' 30).

[62] Mann (1996) 119. Kahn (1996) remarks that he was 'perhaps the only one [sc. among the prominent Socratics] who did *not* write Socratic dialogues' (15). For Aristippos' writings see *SSR* IV 155–68; Goulet-Cazé (1999) 181–3, 286–8; Döring (2011) 39–41. Cf. also Kahn (1996) 15–18; Decleva Caizzi (2006) 130–2; Wolfsdorf (2008a) 10–13.

[63] The testimonia on Eukleides may be found in *SSR* I 377–84. For his school and its doctrines see *HGP* III 499–507; Sedley (1977) 74–8; Döring (1989); *SSR* IV 41–60; Goulet-Cazé (1999) 198–201, 365–6 n. 14; Drodzek (2005); Decleva Caizzi (2006) 132–4; Döring (2011) 36–8. For his dialogues see Hirzel (1895) I 110–1; Rossetti (1980) 198–200; *SSR* IV 36–9; Kahn (1996) 12–5; Brancacci (2005).

Phaidon

Phaidon of Elis is also said to have founded a philosophical school at his home town, about which we know next to nothing. Irrespectively of any philosophical significance, his literary talent seems to have been much appreciated in antiquity. Of the dialogues attributed to him two were considered genuine by Diogenes Laertios, namely *Zopyros* and *Simon*. It was possibly in the former work that Sokrates' silenic features were first given a positive reading. The dialogue is about Zopyros, a Persian physiognomist, an expert in understanding people's characters from their physical appearance. His verdict that Sokrates' features pointed to a stupid and amorous person, though laughed at and protested at by the rest, is confirmed by Sokrates, who claims to have overcome these natural inclinations (p. 175 n. 51).[64] The latter dialogue is named after Simon the cobbler. Whether a real person or not, there can hardly be any doubt that Simon's portrait owed a lot to Phaidon's dialogue. The occurrence of σκυτικοὶ λόγοι among his spurious works suggests that Phaidon and Simon were somehow associated in the thought of the historians of philosophy.[65]

Antisthenes

The authenticity of both Eukleides' and Phaidon's dialogues had been disputed in antiquity by the Stoic Panaitios (Diog. Laert. 2.64). No such doubts, however, did ever cast their shadow on the writings of the next Socratic. **Antisthenes**, one of the oldest members of the Socratic circle, is said to have taught at Kynosarges

[64] That the power of love and its philosophical exploitation played a central role in this dialogue may be said to find some support by the only extant verbatim extract. There Zopyros narrates a story about a lion cub (λέοντος σκύμνον) which had been given as a present to the king's youngest son. When the animal grew up, it kept following the boy everywhere as a pet ὥστε οἵ γε Πέρσαι ἐρᾶν ἔφασαν τοῦ παιδὸς αὐτόν (Theon *Progymn*. 75.1–8, 33–4 Patillon–Bolognesi = *SSR* III A 11).

[65] Notably, the other claimant for the authorship of these dialogues, except for Simon of course, is Aischines, who is known to have composed a dialogue entitled *Phaedo* (Diog. Laert. 2. 105; Suda s.v. Αἰσχίνης = *SSR* III A 14. Cf. Goulet-Cazé 1999, 313 n.3). For Phaidon's writings see *SSR* I 491–3 (fragments) with IV 119–27 (discussion); Rossetti (1980) 183–98; Wolfsdorf (2008a) 14–5; Döring (2011) 33–6. For a reconstruction of his thought see Boys-Stones (2004), who provides a very useful overview of the secondary literature on Phaidon in notes 3, 4 and 5 (1–3).

and propounded doctrines similar to the ones the Cynics would later employ. For this reason he was often classified as their predecessor. His intellectual background as a sophist was expressed through the versatility of his interests and the diversity of his writings: philosophical treatises, works on Homeric interpretation, scientific monographs. As a Socratic, the author made use of myths (*SSR* V A 44), while the titles of some of his dialogues point to familiar figures of the relevant literature (*Aspasia*, *Menexenos*, *Alcibiades*, *Archelaos*). Although we have no information about their form, a description of Alkibiades that Antisthenes gives out of his personal experience (ὡς δὴ αὐτόπτης γεγονὼς τοῦ Ἀλκιβιάδου, Ath. 12.534c = *SSR* V A 228) may more naturally belong to a dialogue the author had himself introduced or narrated in the first person.[66] One may plausibly argue that Antisthenes, a prolific writer and an important intellectual figure in his own right, must have been a reference point for the other Socratics.[67]

Aischines

Another Socratic whose dialogues were accepted as genuine by Panaitios is **Aischines of Sphettos**. He did not found any philosophical school. Instead he gave private lectures and composed forensic speeches for professional purposes. Apart from these, he seems to have been a devoted writer of Socratic dialogues. With the exception of Plato and Xenophon he is the only other Socratic of whom we possess substantial literary remains. Perhaps he was the first one to introduce Aspasia as a positive figure in the namesake dialogue.[68] He may well have been the first exponent

66 So Kahn (1996) 33, who sees Antisthenes' influence on Xenophon on the use of this technique. On the other hand, *Alcibiades* seems to have been a dramatic dialogue (*SSR* V A 200).

67 The significance of Antisthenes in antiquity is demonstrated by the wealth of testimonia on his life and works, collected in *SSR* II 137–225 and commented on in *SSR* IV 195–411. On Antisthenes' thought see Rankin (1986); Navia (2001); Romeyer Dherbey (2001); Brancacci (2003); Mársico (2005); Prince (2006); Decleva Caizzi (2006) 126–30; Döring (2011) 42–5. For Antisthenes as a founder figure of the Cynics see Rankin (1986) 179–88; Brancacci (1997); Navia (2001) 89–122. His status as a writer of dialogues is discussed by Hirzel (1895) I 118–29; Kahn (1996) 4–9; Prince (2006) 78–80 who plausibly suggests that Sokrates was not his literary hero (84–5).

68 Antisthenes in his own *Aspasia* had presented a rather unfriendly picture of Perikles' consort (*SSR* V A 142–4).

of the stock-motif of Socratic love.[69] An experimentation with the dialogue form may also be inferred: (a) *Miltiades*, his first work, and *Alcibiades* were reported dialogues with Sokrates in the role of narrator (*SSR* VI A 76 and 43, 48 respectively) and (b) in the *Aspasia* he apparently employed a technique of 'bracketed reported dialogue', i.e. dialogue-within-a-dialogue in a narrative framework (*SSR* VI A 70).[70]

The Platonic dialogue

Plato the dramatist

The next question is how Plato fits into this context as a writer of dialogues. On the one hand, it may be safely assumed that other Socratics had preceded him: the sources name five individuals as the inventors of the new genre but Plato is conspicuously absent. On the other hand, his lifelong and exclusive commitment to producing texts featuring Sokrates places him in a class of his own. His fellow-Socratics had either (a) tried their hand in other genres as well (Aristippos, Antisthenes, Aischines, Xenophon) or (b) their literary output was relatively meagre (Phaidon, Eukleides) or (c) they wrote short dialogues (Kriton, Simon, Glaukon, Simmias, Kebes) some of which may not have had Sokrates as a character. The ancients were aware of Plato's special position and attempted to explain how he came to dominate the genre, even though he was not among its first practitioners. Diogenes Laertios holds that Plato brought the prose dialogue to perfection and deserves to be called its inventor as well.[71] This claim shows that Plato was thought to have revolutionised the Socratic dialogue and transformed it into something new, a peculiarly Platonic type of text. Admittedly, the

[69] Kahn (1994).

[70] Kahn (1996) 23 believes that *Aspasia* had the form of a direct dialogue between Sokrates and Kallias without a narrative frame. For Aischines' writings see *SSR* IV 585–96; Clay (1994); Rutherford (1995) 45–6; Kahn (1996) 18–29; Giannantoni (2001); Döring (2011) 27–33. Diogenes mentions as writers of dialogues also Glaukon (2.124), Simmias (2.124) and Kebes (2.125).

[71] δοκεῖ δέ μοι Πλάτων ἀκριβώσας τὸ εἶδος καὶ τὰ πρωτεῖα δικαίως ἂν ὥσπερ τοῦ κάλλους οὕτω καὶ τῆς εὑρέσεως ἀποφέρεσθαι (3. 48). For the short prose dialogue as a separate genre see Slings (1999) 21–34.

loss of the Socratic dialogues, except Xenophon's, has deprived us of direct comparison with Plato's works. But the agreement of the sources and the eventual identification of the prose dialogue with Plato's compositions prove the inadequacy of a classification that would ignore this distinction. Therefore, the term 'Socratic dialogue' is better reserved for the relevant works of the other Socratics, whereas the Platonic dialogue could be defined as the dialogic text written by Plato.[72]

It is worth considering what could have made Plato so exceptional an author compared to his fellow-Socratics. Two hypotheses are of particular inetrest. Thesleff (1982) makes the persuasive case that Plato was the first to introduce the dramatic dialogue in the Socratic literature. Whereas the narrated dialogue was available to and employed by authors like Aischines and Antisthenes,[73] prose texts in dramatic form do not seem to have existed before the fourth century BC. The only exception was the mimes, and the tradition that Plato borrowed this feature from Sophron may suggest that Plato was the first Socratic to write a prose dramatic text. If so, the dramatic dialogue at some point must have become a kind of 'trademark' of Platonic writing. That twenty-three out of the thirty-six dialogues of Thrasyllos' canon are in pure dramatic form may not be irrelevant after all. It is also tempting to see in the prologue of the *Theaetetus* a statement of (re)appropriation of that form. Thesleff then may not be far from truth when suggesting that 'the dramatic dialogue type intended for wider circulation was an innovation of Plato's Academy' (61 [208]).[74]

Another path is explored by Clay (1994). For him Plato is the first Socratic to reconstruct a recognisable historical setting for his dialogues. The provision of a context in time and space for the depicted action allows the author to play with his audience's

72 This distinction is not universally accepted, though. Rossetti (2007), for one, deems it unnecessary. For Plato's development from a minor Socratic to a creator of a new type of dialogue see Kahn (1981) and (1990); Clay (1994) 20–32 and (2000) 1–12; Prior (1997). Schofield (2008) offers an overview of the historical context in which Plato composed his works.

73 If the dialogues by Kriton, Simon and Glaukon were similar in form to Xenophon's *Memorabilia*, as suggested by Slings (1999) 25 (with n. 44), they would have been written in the reported form. In the present state of evidence any answer necessarily remains conjectural.

74 See the full discussion in 58–62 [204–9]. He is followed by Tarrant (1996) 136.

knowledge of history. Plato's characters argue for certain theses and ways of life, mostly unaware of the full meaning of their words and actions. It is this discrepancy between what Sokrates and his interlocutors stand for and what Plato and his readers know about their fate that characterises the Platonic dialogue. For Clay, then, Plato's innovation is that he 'exploited the ironies of the tragic poet in his dramatizations of Socratic conversations' (1994, 44).[75]

Although focusing on different aspects of Plato's literary art, both these hypotheses suggest that what made Plato the creator of a new type of dialogue was the dramatic qualities of his writings. Plato the prose dramatist had been a standard element of his reception throughout antiquity, with the dialogues themselves contributing immensely to the longevity of the image (as will be documented in Chapter 4). Given the premises of Athenian culture in Plato's time it is perfectly reasonable that his public would react to his dialogues as pieces of dramatic literature and, hence, related to the poets' plays. The composition of literary works full of argumentation and philosophical ideas would not strike them as particularly eccentric since playwrights did not refrain from either of these (obviously on a different scale and degree).[76] Moreover, theatre was the dominant mode of public discourse in classical Athens and it was soon to acquire a similar status all over Greece in the course of the fourth century and beyond.[77] No wonder if a writer of prose drama was engaged in a 'dialogue' with the works of the Attic theatre. It is conceivable that Plato appropriated the most powerful literary genre to promote his ideas as a philosopher-poet of his generation, in the tradition of Xenophanes, Parmenides and Empedokles.

In what follows, some points of contact between the Platonic dialogue and the works of Attic theatre will be briefly examined.[78] The first and most evident similarity is the very form of Plato's

[75] See also Clay (2000) 10–11. Kahn (1996) 34–5 argues that Plato created the 'realistic' historical dialogue.

[76] Kullmann (1986); Kaelin (1993).

[77] Easterling (1993) and (1997); Chaniotis (1997); Taplin (1999) and (2007); Kowalzig (2008).

[78] Puchner's (2010) excellent first chapter is the best available introduction to the theme of Plato the dramatist (3–35). See also Arieti (1991); Fendt and Rozema (1998); Gordon (1999) 63–92; Clay (2000) 3–40, 79–176.

compositions. In his dramatic dialogues, and those with a dramatic frame, the action is communicated through the words and deeds of the characters in the manner of plays. In the purely reported dialogues the narrator's voice brings the dialogue closer to the model of epic poetry and storytelling. Nevertheless, in these texts, the narrator is always identified early on as one more *dramatis persona* and he is a participant, active or silent, in the narrative he relays. The author himself is nowhere to be directly heard, but fragments and diffuses himself among his characters. The reader and/or the performer of the Platonic text impersonates not Plato but some member of the cast. Role-playing and authorial effacement are two defining elements in theatrical writing.[79] By composing prose dramas for more than half a century Plato signalled his presence as an alternative dramatist working in parallel with the city's poets. His fellow-Athenians would not have missed the association.

In view of the generic affinities, it would be interesting to bring Aristotle's *Poetics* into the discussion.[80] It may be noted that Aristotle's views on poetry seem to have been shaped out of a constant dialogue with Plato's theories. There is a strong possibility that his conceptual framework in the analysis of tragedy may not only be relevant to the poets' plays but also reflect his experiences as reader and composer of the prose drama that the Academy promoted. Out of the six constituent parts of tragedy (Arist. *Poet.* 1450^{a}9–10) plot (μῦθος) applies evidently to Plato's works as well, even though in most of the dialogues it is associated more with the outcome of the conversation than with any happenings that befall the characters. Thought (διάνοια) is an immediately recognisable common element: argumentation,

79 Both principles may be found outside dramatic poetry, as is the case with Bakchylides' dithyramb *Theseus* (fr. 18; cf. Campbell 1982, 440–2) and Sappho's lyric dialogue between a girl and the personified Virginity (114 L-P). For more examples and discussion see Herington (1985) 50–7. The difference is that in the case of drama these are sufficient and necessary conditions for any composition: there can be no play without role-playing and authorial effacement. On Platonic anonymity see the collected essays in Press (2000). Cf. also Kosman (1992); Cohn (2001); Laks (2004).

80 For a reading of Plato's dialogues in the light of the *Poetics* see Gordon (1999) 76–86; Westermann (2002) 30–46. A similar interpretation has been suggested for particular Platonic texts: Gomme (1958) for the *Crito*; Gilead (1994) 109–27 for the *Phaedo*; Erler (1998) for the frame dialogues of the *Timaeus* and the *Critias*; Howland (2008) 523–5 for the *Apology*.

constructions of theories, confrontation of ideas are found in abundance in Plato's dialogues. It is these ideas that reveal the type of life the interlocutors lead and Plato is a master of character-portrayal. His gallery of characters (ἤθη) boasts a collection of philosophers (Parmenides, Zenon, Eleatic Stranger), sophists (Protagoras, Hippias, Prodikos, Gorgias), playwrights (Agathon, Aristophanes), political and military leaders (Nikias, Laches, Alkibiades, Hermogenes). These characters may be as young as the boys Lysis and Menexenos (*Lysis*) or as old as Kephalos (*Republic*) and the three pilgrims in Crete (*Laws*). Their position in the social hierarchy may be as high as that of a priestess (Diotima) or as low as that of a slave (*Meno*, *Theaetetus*). There is also a variety in patterns of behaviour: the supportive and caring Kriton (*Crito*, *Phaedo*) may be contrasted with the angry and threatening Anytos (*Meno*). Moreover, it does not take many lines to create a memorable character, as the examples of Xanthippe (*Phd.* 60a5–6) and Agathon's doorkeeper (*Prot.* 314d) demonstrate.[81] Finally, and above all, there are the portraits of Plato's literary hero, Sokrates.

The element of diction (λέξις) is obviously a point where the plays and the dialogue are as far from each other as poetry is from prose. But a standard feature of Plato's text is the incorporation of theatrical diction in the form of quotations from plays. Dialogic characters often resort to passages from tragedians and comedians, along with Homer and the other poets, to support their argument or use them as tokens of a shared culture. The appropriation of this type of theatrical discourse takes one of the following forms:

(a) *Quotations*. The poetic text is cited verbatim or without significant alterations. It retains its textual autonomy as it is carefully distinguished from the dialogic context and is provided with recognisable signs of its generic identity (e.g. *Grg.* 492e10–11 = Eur. *TrGF* 5.2 F 638).
(b) *Citations*. The dramatic text has been incorporated into the structure of the dialogue, thus losing its textual autonomy. The extent

[81] The standard prosophographical study of the Platonic dialogues is now Nails (2002). An authoritative discussion of Plato's use of character-portrayal is found in Blondell (2002). Beversluis (2000) offers a defence of the dialectical integrity of some of Sokrates' interlocutors. Cf. also Coventry (1990); Blundell (1992) with a later version in Blundell (2002) 113–64; Frede (1996); Gordon (1999) 93–116.

of the changes involved determines the differentiation between the cited text and the implied original (e.g. *Resp.* 8. 550c4–5 = Aesch. *Sept.* 451+570). There is an obvious difference between these two patterns. The latter represents an advanced stage of intertextual interaction, where a conflation of separate modes leads to the emergence of a hybrid entity. Whereas in a quotation one may speak of recontextualisation of the dramatic extract *per se*, in the case of a citation the passage itself is in some sense rewritten, i.e. having its internal construction reformulated. Consequently the original poetic text, though still recognisable, is 'relegated' to the status of subtext.

(c) *Allusions*. In this case the reference to a dramatic work is made by indirect means. Instead of an autonomous quotation or an embedded citation, the name of a poet, a similarity in reasoning, a single word or a structural correspondence suffices to recall the play to the reader. The absence of the dramatic text from the texture of the dialogue serves as the distinguishing feature of this group. Examples of allusions are *Resp.* 6.522d1–5 (= Eur. *TrGF* 5.2. F 581) and *Lg.* 6. 757a5-b5 (= Eur. *Ph.* 535–6, 541–2).[82]

The case of the quotations is particularly interesting for an additional reason. When a character utters a passage from a play it looks as if the normal flow of the Platonic dialogue has been temporarily suspended and an 'alien' type of discourse is granted a place where it may be performed. Since the mode of delivery for, say, the iambics of tragedy is different from that of a prose text (p. 233 n. 169 passage (e)), it makes sense to suppose that the character assumes for a while the role of an extempore actor and delivers the tragic verses accordingly. This presumably is how Sokrates acts when, at the end of the second book of the *Republic*, he recites the longest quotation of dramatic text in the Platonic corpus (*Resp.* 2.383b2–9 = Aesch. *TrGF* 3 F 350). Similarly, the delivery of a line from Aischylos' *Xantriae* a little earlier (*Resp.* 2. 381d8 = Aesch. *TrGF* 3 F 168.17) would have been the one appropriate to the lyric dactyls of the line. It is very likely that Protagoras and Sokrates quoted Simonides' poem in the *Protagoras* mostly by

[82] For a list of the passages quoted from plays see Brandwood (1976) 991–1003 and Sansone (1996a) 61–7 (a complete index of the quotations from Euripides). For discussions of particular passages see Sansone (1996a) and (1996b). Plato's use of poetic passages in general is discussed by Halliwell (2000); Freydberg (2000). Whittaker (1989) comments on the semantics of quoting in antiquity.

singing (*Prot.* 339b1–3, c3–5, 341e3, 344c4–5, e7–8, 345c6–11, d3–5, 346c3–11).[83]

It would be pedantic to claim that Simonides' ode and, one may infer, other lyric passages correspond precisely to the musical parts (μέλος) of tragedy. Nevertheless, they indicate that a kind of musical performance was not completely absent from the dialogues. The same holds true for the visual element (ὄψις). Although not meant for public performances in the theatres of Athens, Plato's dialogues are no less equipped with the potential for performance and cater for viewers as well as listeners/readers. Plato shares with his fellow-dramatists the technique that allows the transition from the dramatic to the theatrical text, namely the incorporation of stage directions in the words of their *dramatis personae*.[84] All the necessary information for the visualisation of a particular scene is embedded in the remarks of the interlocutors (or the narrator in the case of the reported dialogues). This enables the listener/reader to visualise Charmides sitting between Sokrates and Kritias (*Chrm.* 155c4–5), Hippothales hiding himself from Lysis (*Ly.* 207c4–8), Sokrates refusing to cross the Ilissos (*Phdr.* 242b8). Exits and entrances of the characters as well as significant details of their appearance are signalled in the same way.[85] Plato sometimes underscores the deictic function of language that is one of the fundamentals of theatrical communication.[86] There are also some scenes that could very well be imagined on the stage: the episode of the angry doorkeeper and the choreography of the sophist's entourage in the *Protagoras* (314c–315b), the geometry lesson in the *Meno* (82b–85b), Aristophanes' hiccups in the *Symposium* (185c–e). It may be assumed

[83] The poem is almost exclusively referred to as ᾆσμα 'song' (339b4, 341a8, 343c7, 345d1). Only once (339d3) is it called ποίημα 'poem'. On Simonides' poem (*PMG* 542) see now Beresford (2008).

[84] Taplin (1977); Revermann (2006b) 320–5.

[85] Entrances: Anytos in the *Meno* (89e9–10), Theodoros with Theaitetos and the Eleatic Stranger in the *Sophist* (216a1–2). Exits: Euthyphron in the *Euthyphro* (15e3–4), Lysis and Menexenos in the *Lysis* (223b3–4). Details of appearance: Sokrates' shoes (*Symp.* 174a4) and garment (*Resp.* 1. 327b4), Prodikos' blankets (*Prt.* 315d5), Alkibiades' ivy crown (*Symp.* 212e1), Phaidon's long hair (*Phd.* 89b2–5).

[86] Some examples of *deixis* in Plato are *Ion* 537e4–7, *Prt.* 335d1, *Phdr.* 236e1, *Lg.* 1. 624a4. For a discussion on *deixis* see Elam (1980) 138–48.

therefore that Plato was much concerned with the theatre of his dialogues.[87]

Plato also appropriates a number of motifs of dramatic composition. The change in scenery is one of them. In no less than eleven dialogues the action takes place in more than one space.[88] The night setting for the opening of the action and the door-knocking scenes are similarly well-established elements of theatrical writing.[89] Silence is another motif that Plato uses effectively. One need only recall Kriton who sits silently at the side of sleeping Sokrates at the opening of the *Crito* (43b1–2), the absolute silence after the second proof for the immortality of the soul in the *Phaedo* (84c; cf. 95e) or the enigmatic presence of an almost completely silent, or silenced, Sokrates throughout the *Sophist* and the *Statesman*.[90] From a structural point of view, Plato redefines also the notion of the chorus. Although his dialogues formally lacked a chorus, in eight of them the conversation of the interlocutors is attended by an indeterminate number of bystanders.[91] As a rule they remain silent but they express their approval by laughter and applause (*Euthd.* 276d1–3, *Prt.* 334c7–8). For the most part they are unidentified individuals, but in three dialogues their names are given (*Phd.* 59b–c, *Prt.* 314e–315a, *Resp.* 1.327c, 328b), a feature shared with some comic and satyric choruses. Twice Plato

[87] For Plato's use of theatrical vocabulary see Louis (1945) 84, 209–10; Charalabopoulos (2000). Monoson (2000) examines the implications of the theatrical imagery in the *Republic* and the *Laws* (206–38). Boegehold (1999) collects the passages in which a gesture is implied (110–25).

[88] These are the *Phaedo*, *Theaetetus*, *Parmenides*, *Symposium*, *Phaedrus*, *Theages*, *Lysis*, *Euthydemus*, *Protagoras*, *Republic* and the *Laws*.

[89] Schofield (1992) 127; Charalabopoulos (2001) 154–8.

[90] Some more silenced characters: Meletos (*Ap.* 24d7); Lysis (*Ly.* 222a4); Ktesippos (*Euthd.* 286b7); Euthydemos (*Euthd.* 299c8); Sokrates (*Euthd.* 303a5); Protagoras (*Prt.* 360d6); Polos (*Grg.* 475d5–6); Gorgias (*Grg.* 515b3, c3–4). For Sokrates' silence (a) at the opening of the *Hippias Minor* see Blondell (2002) 122–4; Sales-Coderch (2007) 60–1; (b) throughout the *Sophist* and the *Statesman* see Gonzalez (2000); Blondell (2002) 386–96. Heath (2005) 259–314 reads silence as a powerful dialectical weapon for the interlocutors in Plato's dialogues, indicating less the absence of speech than the construction of an alternative non-verbal meaning – a point supported by modern communicative theory (cf. Acheson 2008). On silence in Greek antiquity see Montiglio (2000).

[91] In the *Phaedo*, the *Protagoras* and the *Symposium* there are two such groups for both the frame dialogue (*Phd.* 58d7–8, *Prt.* 310a, *Symp.* 172a) and the narrative. The other dialogues are the *Philebus*, *Charmides*, *Lysis*, *Euthydemus*, *Gorgias* and the *Republic*.

associates these Platonic 'choruses' with their dramatic counterparts (*Euthd.* 276d7–8, *Prt.* 315b1–8). Once again the parallel is an intended one.[92]

Dialogues with the genres of theatre

Throughout his long life Plato was producing dialogues by appropriating and transforming a variety of discourses, particularly the language of the tragic and comic poets. He was addressing his work to an audience educated in and by the theatrical culture and therefore sensitive to the poetics of drama. The presence of a dramatist who was not competing in the public festivals but went on building his own literary world in a silent dialogue with the playwrights would have hardly been left unnoticed.[93] Evidently the interplay between Plato's dialogues and the works of the Attic stage goes beyond the limits of a simple intertextuality. As a literary writer Plato has repeated one of the two original contributions of the first tragedians, namely the syncretism of genres. Dramatic poetry had integrated epic recital, lyric song and iambic trimeters into a new synthesis and developed into the all-embracing poetic literary genre of the classical period. The dialogues, it may be claimed, incorporate most of the existing types of discourse in verse and prose alike.[94] Plato consistently exposes the polyphony

92 For named choreuts in comedy and satyr play see Wilson (1977) and Sutton (1986a) respectively. The closure of the *Phaedrus* may offer one more structural parallel with theatre. Plato concludes his dialogue with Sokrates' praying to Pan (279b–c). A hymn to a deity or deities is found in the finale of plays like the *Eumenides*, the *Philoctetes* and the *Lysistrata*. The rhythmic prose of Sokrates' prayer may be taken as an indirect intergeneric reference. Interestingly, the beginning and end of the prayer seem to scan as follows: (a) Ὦ φίλε Πάν τε καὶ ἄλλοι ὅσοι τῇδε θεοί (b8) = — U U — U — (dod) / — — U — — U U — (ia ch) and (b) μήτε φέρειν μήτε ἄγειν δύναιτο ἄλλος ἢ ὁ σώφρων (c2–3) = — U U — — U U — U — — (2ch ia^) / — U — U — — (ith). For a discussion see Clay (1979); Gaiser (1989).

93 The city of Athens officially instituted the reperformance of old tragedies in 387/6 BC, although productions of Aeschylus' plays were staged well before the end of the fifth century (Lech 2008). According to tradition, Plato established himself and the performances of his own dialogues in the Academy at about the same period (388/7–384/3 BC). It is tempting to see some connection between the two events: while his fellow-citizens turned to the poets of old as sources of wisdom, Plato offered his own works as a better alternative.

94 For the syncretism of genres see Else (1965); Herington (1985) 144. The definitive study for the multiplicity of discourses in Plato's dialogues is Nightingale (1995). See also Thesleff (1967).

of his text, underlining thereby his advantage over the poets: by using prose he was able to 'absorb' a broader spectrum of discourses and therefore produce a fuller version of an all-embracing literary genre.

It is a reasonable assumption that Plato presented his own drama as an alternative to (and possibly a transcendence of) the theatrical one. Like plays, his dialogues became an institutionalised mode of discourse. Unlike plays, they were never sanctioned by the city of Athens as part of its official public performance policy but remained a defining feature of the community in the Academy. At the same time, Plato reflects on fundamental issues like man's position in his community and the world or the source of happiness, as tragedians and comedians do. His construct of philosophy as the best way of living seems to have been meant to address those questions that the playwrights had failed, in his eyes, to answer satisfactorily.[95]

Plato's appropriation of tragic, comic and satyric elements need not run contrary to the expectations of a fourth-century audience. That a dramatist would cross the generic boundaries to fertilise his own compositions was by then an established practice. Paratragedy was an essential feature of Aristophanic comedy, while some of Euripides' tragedies were filled with comic features. Euripides had also produced his *Alcestis* as the fourth play in his tetralogy instead of the usual satyr play in the Dionysia of 438 BC. Kratinos' *Dionysalexandros* and Timokles' *Demosatyroi* are two comedies featuring a chorus of satyrs while the latter comedian produced in 341 BC a satyr play called *Lycurgus*. Interestingly, Alkaios, a poet of Old Comedy still active in 388 BC, and Anaxandrides, a poet of Middle Comedy who won his first victory in 376 BC, each composed a play with the suggestive title *Κωμῳδοτραγῳδία* (*PCG* II 9–10 and 249–50 respectively). It is not unlikely that some contemporaries may have responded to Plato's experimentation in the context of these precedents. On the other hand, what may have struck them as unusual were the consistency and the extent

95 Nussbaum (2003) has perceptively stated that 'Plato's dialogues ought to be seen as they no doubt would have been received by their audience as rivals to the tradition of tragic drama' (229). For the difficulties of theorising on the genres of antiquity, with reference to tragedy, see Most (2000); Mastronarde (2010) 44–62.

of Plato's reflection on the relationship between the dialogic and the theatrical text. One possible dimension of the famous quarrel between philosophy and poetry in Plato could have been the legitimisation of the dialogue as the ultimate dramatic discourse in fourth-century Athens. That being the case, what has been suggested for Euripides may also apply to Plato, namely that '[h]e is not abandoning or corrupting a fixed genre, but exploring the potentialities of a living genre'.[96]

The relationship between the Platonic dialogue and the genres of theatre may be described as follows:

Dialogue and Tragedy

These two genres are the privileged interlocutors in this interplay of dramatic discourses. As the dominant theatrical genre and the authoritative poetic medium for the articulation of wisdom on human affairs tragedy stands simultaneously as the model for and the rival of Plato's prose drama. Tragedians deal with figures of the mythical past and, by recasting the traditional stories, they confront their audiences with the limitations of human existence; the power and restrictions of intellect and passions; slavery and freedom; knowledge and ignorance; justice and the foundations of the civic order; the relation of humanity to the divine/metaphysical world. Plato similarly tells stories about people of the past, albeit a very recent one, and he wrestles with these very same themes. His audience's knowledge of the fate of the historical figures he uses as characters allows him to exploit fully the device of tragic irony. Plato also appropriates the mode of tragic catharsis: his readers are invited to identify with Sokrates' interlocutors, share with them the suffering of dialectical defeat, and hence have themselves purged

[96] Mastronarde (2010) 54. Tragedy and comedy: Taplin (1986) and (1996); Silk (2000) 42–97; Lowe (2007) 23–9; Foley (2008). Comedy and satyr play: Ghiron-Bistagne (1991); Revermann (2006b) 103–4. Comedies with satyr choruses: Storey (2005); Revermann (2006b) 299–302 (*Dionysalexandros* as parasatyric comedy); Dobrov (2007); Bakola (2010) 102–12. Tragedy and satyr play: Sutton (1980) 159–79; Seaford (1984) 21–33; Voelke (2001) 389–412; Hall (2006) 142–69; Mastronarde (2010) 55–7. The function of satyr play in relation to the rest of dramatic genres is discussed by Seidensticker (1999) 32–9 and Griffith (2008) 73–9. The *Alcestis* as a prosatyric play is discussed in Slater (2005) and paratragedy by Rau (1967) and Silk (1993). For the osmosis of tragic and comic elements in fifth-century theatre see Medda et al. (2006). Cf. also Knox (1979); Zacharia (1995); Gregory (1999–2000).

of erroneous beliefs. Dialogue was evidently meant to supplant Tragedy as the ultimate σπουδαία ποίησις (*Resp.* 10.608a6–7).[97]

As the dialogue depicting Sokrates' last day, the ***Phaedo*** has been reasonably interpreted as an example of Platonic tragedy. The main theme is the life and death of the hero. The discussion on the immortality of the soul, in the context of his imminent execution, takes an ominously appropriate turn. The outcome of the debate will show whether Sokrates was right in leading his life the way he did (and, accordingly, in choosing the stance that led to his death), or whether he was deceived, his set of beliefs is unfounded and his whole life proved a lie. The eschatological myth may be seen as an answer to the traditional mythology that constitutes the backbone of epic and tragedy.[98] The emotional power of the narrative, the lament of the disciples (117c–d) and Sokrates' own words (ἐμὲ δὲ νῦν ἤδη καλεῖ, φαίη ἂν ἀνὴρ τραγικός, ἡ εἱμαρμένη 115a5–6) prove that Plato intended a direct comparison with tragedy.[99]

An eschatological myth also concludes another dialogue with tragic overtones, the ***Gorgias***. Sokrates' confrontation with the rhetoricians Gorgias and Polos soon develops into a passionate debate over which is the better life: Sokrates argues for the life of the philosopher who strives after truth, models himself on absolute

[97] Cf. Halliwell (1996) 'Plato's engagement with tragedy . . . is not simply an opposition but an active attempt to transform and overcome tragedy within a new philosophical writing' (338). Dialogue and Tragedy: Stella (1933); Kuhn (1941–2); Cameron (1978); Halliwell (1984); Anderson (1993); Hyland (1993); Nightingale (1995) 60–92. Plato and tragic irony: Gifford (2001) 43–52; Gordon (1999) 117–33. Plato and philosophical catharsis: MacCabe (2008) 92–109. Socratic irony: Vasiliou (1998) and (2002); Lane (2006) and (2011). On the vexed question of the triangular relationship between Socratic, Platonic and dramatic irony see Ferrari (2008); Wolfsdorf (2008b) 242–60.

[98] Cf. Murray (1999) 'Plato's concern is . . . to appropriate myth from the hands of the poets and construct new myths that will serve the interests of philosophy' (257). On the Platonic myths see now Partenie (2009). See also the comprehensive studies by Zaslavsky (1981); Moors (1982); Elias (1984); Brisson (1998); Coulloud-Streit (2005) and the relevant articles by Anton (1964); Findlay (1978); Annas (1982); MacMinn (1990); Fussi (2000–1); Kuch (2003); Weiss (2006); Benitez (2007); Brisson (2007); Speliotis (2007).

[99] *Phaedo* as tragedy: Wilamowitz (1920) I 326, 356; Gilead (1994) 2. Cf. also Rowe (1993) 1; Halliwell (1996) 339; Gallop (2001) and (2003); Kahn (2010). For *Phd.* 115a5–6 see Rowe (1993) 290; Halliwell (1996) 339; Sansone (1996a) 46–51. *Phaedo* as 'anti-tragedy': Kuhn (1941–2) I 25; Halliwell (1984) 58. *Phaedo* and the 'transposition' of tragedy: Vicaire (1960) 269–70. *Phaedo* and *Oedipus at Colonus*: Ghira (2004). *Phaedo* and *Alcestis*: Susanetti (2002). Cf. also the references in Mader (1977) 125 n. 438. The emotional aspect of the dialogues is examined by Blank (1993); Baumgarten (2009).

values and abstains from politics insofar as his involvement may lead him to committing unjust deeds. Kallikles, his third and most formidable interlocutor, argues for the life of the active politician who seeks power, models himself on the ideal of the absolute ruler as the embodiment of ultimate freedom and abstains from no means in his attempt to win over the popular approval. Once again Plato has signalled the metatheatrical character of his text. By means of the most extended and sustained instance of citation in the Platonic corpus (484e–486d) he establishes Euripides' *Antiope* as a subtext for the dialogue with Sokrates–Amphion competing with Kallikles–Zethos.[100]

The ***Crito*** offers a different paradigm. The case in which a relative, friend or comrade tries to persuade the hero to abandon an original decision that may lead to his self-destruction is a traditional motif. In the ensuing debate issues of honour, justice and wrongdoing come to the fore. Often the hero is pleaded with to yield on emotional grounds. The thematic affinity with the Embassy to Achilles in *Iliad* Book 9 would have hardly been missed by Plato's audience. Tekmessa's supplication to Ajax in Sophokles' *Ajax* and, probably, the stichomythia between Kreon and Menoikeus in Euripides' *Phoenician Women* may also provide possible subtexts. Sokrates' dream enhances the heroic-tragic context of the occasion. In addition, the silent *tableau* of the opening scene, Kriton's description of Sokrates' trial (45e), the image of Sokrates the refugee (53a, d) and, above all, the introduction of the personified Laws of Athens underline the theatricality of the dialogue.[101]

100 *Gorgias* as tragedy: Wilamowitz (1920) I 127; Rutherford (1995) 167. *Gorgias* as paratragedy: Trivigno (2009a). *Gorgias* and *Antiope*: Dodds (1959) 273–9, 79–93; Arieti (1993); Nightingale (1992) and (1995) 67–87; Tulli (2007); Tarrant (2008). On the eschatological myth and the *deus ex machina* of the play see Nightingale (1995) 73, 85 with n. 66; Trivigno (2009a) 85–7. On the dramatic qualities of the dialogue as a whole see Bosch-Veciana (2007). For the relationship between Plato and Euripides see Korres (1955); de Romilly (1984); Sansone (1996a).

101 *Crito* as tragedy: Gomme (1958) 49–51. Possible subtexts of the *Crito*: Greenberg (1965) 73–81 and Payne (1983) (*Iliad*); Gill (1996) 317 n. 302 (*Ajax*); Korres (1955) 10–2 (*Phoenissae*). Sokrates' dream: Kramer (1987–8). For Plato's use of dreams see Tigner (1970); Gallop (1971); Brillante (1996); Rotondaro (1998); Holowchak (2007). On the *Apology* as a kind of tragedy with an ongoing dialogue with Sophokles' *Oedipus Tyrannus* see Howland (2008).

Dialogue and Comedy

If Dialogue resembles Tragedy in assuming the role of the authoritative dramatic genre, many of its structures, techniques and motifs are borrowed from Comedy. Most importantly, Dialogue and Comedy were two classical literary genres able to transgress the boundaries and incorporate 'alien' modes of discourse.[102] Comic poets do not retell traditional stories: they put on stage contemporaries or near contemporaries instead. Similarly, Plato invents the plots of his dramas and his cast comprises not mythical but historical figures of the previous generation. The satire of social, intellectual and political celebrities is another point of contact. Furthermore, in a number of dialogues Sokrates exposes the apparent wisdom of the impostors and triumphs over the rest of his companions in the manner of the comic hero. The language and interaction of the interlocutors are closer to the world of comic than that of tragic characters. The dialogues are full of colloquialisms, word-play and coined terms. Plato's characters often resort to irony, ridicule and jokes, while laughter is a standard element in many works.[103]

A case in point is the ***Euthydemus***. Two pairs of brothers bewilder and finally refute their interlocutors by using fallacies and other eristic devices. Sokrates enters in a kind of mock-duel with them. The parody of proper dialectical investigation is evident throughout the dialogue, while the reversal of the roles of the victor and the defeated is an element of the plot. This *agōn* takes place in a relaxed atmosphere, full of comic spirit. This is the dialogue with the largest number of references to laughter (e.g. 273d1–2, 275e4, 276d1, 298e9, 300d3, 6) and, arguably, the most memorable relevant scene in the Platonic corpus (303b1–7). Finally, the five distinct parts of the dialogue might even be an allusion to the division of the comedies into five acts.[104]

102 Nightingale (1995) 191–2.

103 Dialogue and Comedy: Brock (1990); Howland (1993) 94–118; Nightingale (1995) 172–92. Laughter and humour in Plato: Rankin (1967); Mader (1977) 29–42; Wagner (1981); de Vries (1985); Shelley (2003); Halliwell (2008) 276–302. Colloquialisms and word-play: Tarrant (1946) and (1958).

104 *Euthydemus* as comedy: Michelini (2000); Palpacelli (2009). Cf. Collins (2004) 50–3. For the five-act division see Hamilton (1991); Poe (1999).

The ***Protagoras*** is another dialogue to be compared to a piece of comic theatre. One need only recall Hippokrates' rushing to Sokrates' house (310b), the angry doorkeeper (314c–e), the *tableau* of the three sophists with their followers inside Kallias' house (314e–316a) and Sokrates' cancelled departure (335c–d) to appreciate their theatrical potential. Interestingly, ancient interpreters had already recognised Eupolis' *Flatterers* as a possible subtext.[105]

Dialogue and satyr drama

The most important point of contact between Plato's works and the satyr plays is the confluence of the dialogic and the satyric in the character of Sokrates. His silenic features and his dominant presence make it almost inevitable that every Platonic dialogue, except for the *Laws*, is a new type of satyr drama featuring Sokrates, in most cases, in the role of Papposilenos (pp. 174–8). Another shared feature is a parallel response to to the political community. Unlike their tragic and comic counterparts, the characters of satyr drama by definition live in a world outside or, rather, before, the polis. Similarly, in most of the dialogues the polis and its institutions, though present, remain somehow marginalised or, alternatively, transformed: the community of the interlocutors has moved from the public domain to private spaces. The otherwordliness of the Platonic myths, most of which describe a primeval state of affairs (e.g. *Symp.* 189c–193d, *Plt.* 272b–274e), recalls the world of *illo tempore* inhabited by the satyrs. It may also be noted that Platonic dialogue, like satyr drama, combines tragic and comic elements.[106]

[105] Athenaios' testimony is telling; ὁ δὲ καλὸς αὐτοῦ Πρωταγόρας πρὸς τῷ καταδρομὴν ἔχειν πολλῶν ποιητῶν καὶ σοφῶν ἀνδρῶν ἐκθεατριζόμενον ἔχει καὶ τὸν τοῦ Καλλίου βίον μᾶλλον τῶν Εὐπόλιδος Κολάκων (11. 506f). The best available treatment of the *Protagoras* as comedy is found in a seminal study by Capra (2001). See also Casertano (2004); De Vita (2004); Capra (2005). Possible subtexts: Goldberg (1983) 328–35 (*Clouds*). For other dialogues as comedies see Diès (1927) I 316 (*Sophist*); Tessitore (1994) and Rivera (2007) (*Laches*); Capra (1998) and Trivigno (2009b) 32–4 (*Menexenus*). Petre (2009) makes the ingenious suggestion that the *Menexenus* replays Eupolis' *Demoi*: the funerary speech co-authored by the long-dead and textually 'resurrected' Aspasia and Sokrates answers the Athenian needs of Plato's time much better than Perikles 'resurrected' on the comic stage by Eupolis.

[106] Dialogue and satyr drama: Thesleff (1982) 124 [272–3] (*Euthydemus*, *Menexenus*); Chance (1992) 13 (*Euthydemus*); Arieti (1991) 118 (*Protagoras*).

The satyric aspect of the dialogues is alluded to in the ***Lysis*** by means of the following elements: the wrestling-school as a setting of the action, the erotic theme present throughout the work (Sokrates enters the gymnasium at the invitation of Hippothales who is in love with Lysis, 206d), the image of the elderly Sokrates as an associate of young promising men (223b5–7, a version of Silenos the *paidagōgos*), and, especially, the violent entrance of the drunken slave attendants of the boys (223a–b) who are explicitly compared to semi-divine creatures (ὥσπερ δαίμονές τινες, 223a2).[107]

A more significant reference is found in the ***Theaetetus***: Plato repeatedly draws attention to Theaitetos' likeness to Sokrates: both have the same satyr-like face (143e, 144d). A play on the meaning of the word πρόσωπον, 'face' as well as 'mask', is extremely intriguing in this context. Here, interestingly, Sokrates self-consciously assumes the role of the instructor (cf. his likening himself to an intellectual midwife 149a–151d). It is not unreasonable that Plato's original audience would have likened Sokrates to Papposilenos and Theaitetos to a young satyr. It may be of some significance that this version of the 'Sokrates/Silenos *paidagōgos*' occurs in the *Theaetetus*, a dialogue with a prominent metatextual character.[108]

Plato's dialogue as the fourth dramatic genre: the Symposium

Interestingly enough, the *locus classicus* for the imagery of the silenic Sokrates is, of course, the ***Symposium***.[109] It looks as though

[107] For comprehensive discussions of satyr drama see Griffith (2002); Harrison (2005). On the motifs of the genre see Chourmouziadis (1974) 44–9, 115–47; Sutton (1980) 145–59; Seaford (1984) 33–44; Seidensticker (1999) 28–32; Voelke (2001) 377–89.

[108] On the theatricality of the *Theaetetus* see Sallis (2004) 177–81. On the semantic connotations of the term πρόσωπον in Plato in the context of the related interplay between the theatrical and the philosophical see Romani (2006). The author argues that Plato exploited the theatrical connotations of πρόσωπον to develop a philosophically oriented genealogy of κεφαλή: the 'mask' of the actor as an inferior version of the 'head' of the philosopher (159).

[109] Here is a selective list of commentaries and studies on the *Symposium*: Sykoutris (1934); Rosen (1968); Dover (1980); Rowe (1998); Corrigan and Glazov-Corrigan (2004); Hunter (2004); Lesher et al. (2006); Sheffield (2006). See also Arieti (1991) 95–116; Blackenhagen (1992); Rutherford (1995) 179–205; Velardi (2000); Nussbaum

by composing this most self-referential text Plato was making an exemplary gesture to his fellow-citizens, establishing his own drama as the legitimate successor to the theatrical discourse. There are a number of pieces of evidence in favour of the hypothesis that the *Symposium* was intended as a paradigmatic dialogic text. To begin with, it is one of those dialogues intended for the general public as well as the members of the Academy. The topic, the dramatic setting, the rich characterisation and the variety of philosophies of life promoted in the various speeches indicate that the broadest possible audience was targeted. Second, the dialogue is published at a time when the Academy has been an established institution for some years.[110] Therefore Plato may legitimately present himself as another public voice of authority. That is why the *Symposium* demarcates Plato's position as a writer of dialogues in relation to his fellow-Socratics. Standard themes from the Socratic literature, such as the liaison between Alkibiades and Sokrates or the female teacher of erotics, are refashioned into Platonic motifs.[111] The similarities and differences between the Socratic and the Platonic dialogue are properly settled. Similarly, the incorporation of a number of 'alien' discourses (e.g. sympotic/erotic literature, encomia, mythology) points to the multi-generic character of Plato's texts.[112]

The *Symposium* seems to have been constructed as an embodiment of all three genres of theatre:

(a) It is a satyr, or rather, silenic drama (τὸ σατυρικόν σου δρᾶμα τοῦτο καὶ σιληνικὸν κατάδηλον ἐγένετο 222d3–4) with Sokrates the Wise Silenos initiating his younger associates into the mysteries of erotic

(2001) 165–99; Nichols (2004); White (2004) and (2008); Nehamas (2007); Crick and Poulakos (2008); Hyland (2008) 27–63; Avlonitis (2008); Sheppard (2008); Belfiore (2011).

110 The *Symposium* is usually dated to the period 384–379 BC after Dover (1965) 16. Cf. Dover (1980) 10; Rowe (1998) 11.

111 Kahn (1990) 297–9 and (1994). For Diotima as Plato's response to Aischines' Aspasia see Kahn (1996) 26 and (1994) 100 with n. 42. This appropriation on the part of Plato is a way to underline the similarities and differences between the Socratic and the Platonic dialogue.

112 For Plato's dialogue and its position in the sympotic literature see Martin (1931) 198–201, 294–8. For the *Symposium* and encomiastic discourse see Nightingale (1995) 110–30. On Plato's views on wine in general see Tecuşan (1990); Belfiore (2004).

desire. Sokrates, like the Eros he praises and the mythical satyrs, is the *daimōn* mediating between man and god.[113]

(b) It could have well been a comedy entitled, say, 'Banqueters'. The relaxed and friendly atmosphere results in a lot of laughter and ridicule among the symposiasts. The *kōmos* with its paraphernalia (food, drink, sex, flute-players) is there. Eryximachos' presence might allude to the role of the comic (false) doctor, while Aristophanes is the indisputable joker of the party as the hiccup episode and the grotesque fantasy of his myth prove.[114]

(c) Or it may be read as a tragedy with the title 'Eros Tyrannos': The fixed dramatic date of the dialogue (416 BC) allows the occasion to be seen in a tragic perspective. The twin scandals of the mutilation of the herms and the profanation of the Eleusinian Mysteries, in which some of the symposiasts were involved, and the disastrous Sicilian expedition loom largely over this festive gathering. Alkibiades will soon destroy his city, himself and his beloved Sokrates. His tyrannical behaviour and (future) punishment resemble the primeval men of Aristophanes' myth whose arrogance brought upon them the divine vengeance.[115]

The *Symposium*, then, exemplifies the new type of theatre featuring Sokrates as the new hero, the Platonic philosopher.[116] Plato

[113] Cf. Usher (2002). For an interpretation of Alkibiades' speech as see Sheffield (2001); Hunter (2004) 99–101; Reeve (2006). Sokrates as Silenos: Belfiore (1980) ; Colligne (1989) 91; Bonelli (1991) 87–104; Kofman (1998) 21–31; Clay (2000) 69–76. It is reasonable to suppose that whenever the *Symposium* was presented in the Academy this image would acquire special significance since the audience would have visual contact with the well-known statue of Sokrates (Clay (2000) 167–75).

[114] *Symposium* as comedy: Wilamowitz (1920) I 356; Mason (1979–80); Arieti (1991) 107; Luljak (1994); Rowe (1998) 8. For Aristophanes' *Banqueters* and *Clouds* as possible subtexts see Segoloni (1994) 111–93. A characterisation of Eryximachos is offered by Edelstein (1945); Rowe (1991). For Aristophanes as a comic hero see Avlonitis (1999). His speech is considered a comedy by Neumann (1966) and Nussbaum (2001) 171–3 while Dover (1966) describes it, surprisingly, as 'unsophisticated, subliterate folklore' (45). The hiccups are now discussed by O'Mahoney (2011). Cf. Lowenstam (1986).

[115] The *Symposium* as tragedy: Beck (2006) 317–40; Nails (2006). For the tragic dimension of the androgynes myth see Rosen (1968) 157–8; Allen (1991) 34–5. On the basis of the parallel images of man in the riddle of the Sphinx and the primeval men of the *Symposium* in terms of their representation as many-legged creatures Rokem (2008) claims Sophokles' *Oedipus Tyrannus* as an intertext for the story of the Platonic Aristophanes (245–9). For the scandals see Nails (2002) 17–20; Rosenbloom (2004).

[116] As Blundell (1989) insightfully remarks 'Plato's tragic hero was, of course, Socrates' (8). For Sokrates as hero see Eisner (1982); Irwin (1988); Schauer and Merkler (1992); Rankin (1993) 49; Loraux (1995) 167–77; Clay (2000) 51–9; Hobbs (2000) 175–262; Michelini (2003b) 47–9; Howland (2008) 526–9. MacCabe (2000) describes Sokrates as 'the tragi-comic figure whose death is often prefigured (e.g. *Meno*); sometimes anticipated (*Euthyphro*, *Theaetetus*) and once actually described' (11). For the construction of the philosopher in the *Symposium* see Hadot (2002) 39–51.

is careful to underline the metatheatrical nature of his drama by means of two interrelated themes. The first is the Dionysian-theatrical ambience of the occasion. Agathon's symposion is part of his celebration for his victory at a Dionysian festival. Moreover, the succession of speeches is referred to by Agathon in terms of theatrical contests (194a–c). The frequent references to Sokrates as a silen also add to the picture.[117] The second is the motif of the rivalry between Sokrates and the playwrights. There is the explicit contest of wisdom in the case of Agathon and Sokrates (175e) and an implied competition in the speeches of Aristophanes and Sokrates (212c). The two themes converge when Alkibiades-Dionysos declares Sokrates as the victor (213e). The paradox of the playwright who composes both tragedy and comedy states more explicitly what has been throughout a fundamental theme. The reader is invited to interpret Sokrates' victory over Agathon (primarily) and Aristophanes as the superiority of the Dialogue over Tragedy and Comedy, and Plato as the true poet who produces the ultimate drama that unites and transcends the three genres of theatre.[118]

It is worth attempting to demonstrate Plato's demarcation of his own prose drama by means of the following diagram:

	DIALOGUE	
TRAGEDY		COMEDY
	SATYR PLAY	

[117] Anton (1962/3); Sider (1980a); Usher (2002) 216–19.

[118] Bacon (1959); Patterson (1982); Clay (1983); Nichols (2004); Rokem (2008). Cf. also Jäkel (1992); Imbert (1993). On the conscious confrontation between the theatrical and the philosophical in the *Symposium* see Emlyn-Jones (2004) who calls the dialogue 'a dramatic commentary on the artistic issues later raised in "Republic" 2, 3 and 10' (405). Robinson (2004) puts forward the attractive hypothesis that the contest of wisdom between the dramatists, mostly Agathon, exemplifies the tension between the civic, institutionalised and the private, mystery cults of Dionysos (83–7). Duncan (2006), in turn, persuasively argues for Plato's Agathon as the embodiment of the seductive theatrical self, a figure defying classification that is set up as a foil to an equally ambiguous Sokrates who, however, remains true to his identity (47–57).

In this pattern the horizontal axis represents the world of the polis on which both tragedy and comedy draw for their discourse. The direction from left to right takes one from the traditional myth of the heroic past to the invented plots of a familiar present, from the high to the low. Satyr play stands in the middle of tragedy and comedy, for it shares elements with both the former (myth, characters) and the latter (laughter, licence) and, at the same time, below them, for it stands for a pre-political community. Dialogue displays a similarly middle position for the same reasons: it tells the stories of a heroised recent past featuring characters conversing with each other in a present setting. It also stands outside the horizontal axis, for it recreates a private space for a new community away from the public sphere of polis institutions. The figure of Sokrates the philosopher, both a doomed transgressor against the divine like a tragic hero and a successful manipulator of his fantasy world like a comic hero, in his capacity as the teacher of true wisdom, appropriates the image of wise Papposilenos, the satyric character *par excellence*. Platonic dialogue then is represented as a reversed satyr play, blending the seriousness of tragedy with the playfulness of comedy, which looks towards the future of a reformed political community.[119]

The question next arises whether Plato's drama is entirely different from theatre and makes the questions the latter poses obsolete. It seems very difficult to answer in the affirmative.[120] Take, for

[119] For Howland (1993, 31) the Platonic dialogue is a philosophical kind of drama, akin to the satyr play, that combines elements from epic, tragedy and comedy. Rokem (2008, 245) rightly suggests that for Plato 'the philosophical discourse has to align and integrate the performative practices of the tragic and the comic . . . in order to re-create its own fullness'. The ultimate failure of theoretical reflection exemplified in the *aporia* of Sokrates and his interlocutors has been variously associated with features of comedy: Duvoisin (1996, 364) argues for the inherent comic character of the dialectical method, whereas Miller (2008) focuses on the double-edged, tragicomic nature of the laughter at the expense of the interlocutors on the part of Plato's reader. On a reappraisal of Agathon's contribution to the philosophical arguments of the *Symposium* see Stern-Gillet (2008) and Sheppard (2008) who suggests for this dialogue an integration of the modes of epideictic rhetoric and drama.

[120] So does Nussbaum (2001) who speaks of Plato's anti-tragic theatre (122–35). For Plato as a tragic philosopher see Roochnick (1988) and (1990); Brogan (1991). On Plato as a kind of poet speaking about the norms and rules of his art see Erler (2003). Emlyn-Jones (2008) offers an illuminating discussion of Plato's reception of drama. According to Pradeau (2009) 'Platon aurait entrepris d'imposer au théâtre de la cité grecque la représentation du seul drame philosophique, afin de s'approprier sans ménagement cet

instance, the position of the new hero, the philosopher, in the world. Through him Plato advocates a new way of living, but at the same time he is very well aware of its limitations. In the *Symposium* Sokrates is called by both Agathon and Alkibiades ὑβριστής (175e7, 215b7), hardly an attribute of an unproblematic hero. The latter's speech questions the effectiveness of the philosopher's interpersonal communication with others, while it is also of the utmost significance that *almost never does Sokrates succeed in winning over an unwilling interlocutor.*[121] Far from denying the tensions of the theatrical world-view, exemplified, for instance, in the ambiguous relation of the hero with his own community, Plato embraces it.

In terms of metafictional poetics the fundamental polarity is that between theatrical and philosophical discourse. The hierarchical priority of the latter does not necessarily condemn the former to extinction. It should not be overlooked that Agathon remains crowned alongside Sokrates at the end of the dialogue – a possible indication that theatre is in a sense vindicated and has its own place in the Platonic world. This reading of the *Symposium* may surprise anyone familiar with Plato's unflattering remarks on theatre in a number of dialogues.[122] The more so since the (in)famous exile of the poets in the *Republic*, which is only partially and incompletely recalled in the *Laws*, should have left little doubt as regards the author's intentions. But a condemnation of mimetic art and dramatic representation pronounced by characters in pieces of prose drama should at least qualify its force and leave some room for a more complex interplay between philosophy and dramatic poetry. Significantly, such an alternative interpretation is supported by a

extraordinaire instrument pédagogique et politique qu'était la tragédie, et d'écarter de la sorte ses rivaux' (13).

[121] Blondell (2002) speaks very eloquently of what she calls the pedagogical failure of the elenctic Sokrates and rightly stresses its tragic overtones (126–7). Robertson (2009) attributes the inability of the Platonic speakers to understand each other not to the philosophical limitations of the Socratic method but to the dramatic purpose of characterisation (369).

[122] It is useful to compare here the opposite claims made by Robinson (2004), who believes that in the *Symposium* Plato approves of tragedy (94) and Emlyn-Jones (2004) who holds that Plato appropriates the mode of theatre to prove its inadequacy as a road to truth (405). On the strucrural polarities in the *Symposium* see the comprehensive discussion by Wardy (2002).

number of related passages from Plato's dialogues, as shown in the next section.

Platonic drama as self-reflective storytelling: the Republic

The first of these passages comes from the third book of the ***Republic***, embedded in the discussion that will eventually lead to the first censorship of poetry.[123] Having dealt with the content of the poetic compositions to be admitted in the ideal city (376d–392c) Sokrates moves on to the question of the acceptable literary form (392c–398b). At the beginning he puts forward his threefold division of literature in terms of the manner of presentation into pure narrative, drama and *mimetic* narrative, in essence a combination of the other two types. When Adeimantos professes lack of understanding, Sokrates clarifies his scheme by (a) commenting on and refashioning the introductory scene of the *Iliad* and (b) associating each of the three types with existing literary genres. By the end of this short explanatory 'lecture' Sokrates is able to articulate the great potential of literary form as educational force in explicit terms:

Τοῦτο τοίνυν αὐτὸ ὃ ἔλεγον, ὅτι χρείη διομολογήσασθαι πότερον ἐάσομεν τοὺς ποιητὰς μιμουμένους ἡμῖν τὰς διηγήσεις ποιεῖσθαι ἢ τὰ μὲν μιμουμένους, τὰ δὲ μή, καὶ ὁποῖα ἑκάτερα, ἢ οὐδὲ μιμεῖσθαι.

Μαντεύομαι, ἔφη, σκοπεῖσθαί σε εἴτε παραδεξόμεθα τραγῳδίαν τε καὶ κωμῳδίαν εἰς τὴν πόλιν, εἴτε καὶ οὔ.

Ἴσως, ἦν δ' ἐγώ, ἴσως δὲ καὶ πλείω ἔτι τούτων· οὐ γὰρ δὴ ἔγωγέ πω οἶδα, ἀλλ' ὅπῃ ἂν ὁ λόγος ὥσπερ πνεῦμα φέρῃ, ταύτῃ ἰτέον.

Καὶ καλῶς γ', ἔφη, λέγεις. (*Resp.* 3. 394d1–10)

This then is exactly what I was saying in the beginning, namely that we need to agree between us whether we should allow the poets to produce for us narratives by means of impersonation throughout, or to use impersonation in some parts and not in others, and what type of parts would belong to each group, or whether they should not impersonate at all.

[123] The latest introduction to the *Republic* is Santas (2010). The collected articles in Santas (2006) and Ferrari (2007c) offer a more comprehensive study. Fronterotta (2010) reviews the major themes in recent readings of the *Republic*. See also Kraut (1997); Ferrari (2003); Roochnik (2003); Rosen (2005); Rowe (2006a); Scott (2008); Meinwald (2011); Petraki (2011).

I guess, he said, that you wish to examine whether we will accept tragedy and comedy in the city or not.

Perhaps, I replied, perhaps much more than these are at stake; I do not really know yet, but in whatever direction the argument, like a breeze, may lead us, this is where we should go.

You speak nicely indeed, he said.

The crucial question according to Sokrates is the legitimacy of the status of direct speech in literary production. What makes this mode of discourse problematic is its dangerous potential in existential and moral terms: whenever it is employed the poet ceases to speak in his own person and acquires the identity of his fictional character (393a–b) – a device that verges suspiciously on deception. As founders of the ideal community therefore, Sokrates and the sons of Ariston are left with three options: (a) unconditional approval, (b) conditional approval and (c) rejection. Adeimantos, in turn, translates his interlocutor's ventures on literary theory into more practical terms: what in reality is at stake here is the admission of theatre into their city. His interpretation is the reasonable conclusion of Sokrates' line of thought, since tragedy and comedy have been singled out as poetic genres instantiated exclusively by means of direct speech (394c). As a result Adeimantos envisions for dramatic poetry a revised form of Sokrates' alternatives reducing the number of options to only two, namely (a) admission and (c) rejection.

Adeimantos' reformulation of the main objective in the ensuing examination does not raise any eyebrows. Sokrates' non-committal comment evidently does. In view of the taxonomy of literature he himself had just formulated he should have been expected to agree with Adeimantos' suggestion. The more so since his performance up to that moment has not prepared the reader for so hesitant a stance in the face of an ensuing discussion. It is the first time Sokrates replies with an indeterminate 'perhaps' (ἴσως), displaying a state of indecisiveness so far discernible only in his interlocutors' reactions.[124] More importantly, he produces in full earnest an admission of unqualified ignorance at this stage (οὐ γὰρ δὴ ἔγωγέ

[124] This is true for Thrasymachos (350b2), Adeimantos (371e11, 381e11, 499d9) and Glaukon (404a3, 583c3). On only one occasion in the whole of the *Republic* does

πω οἶδα). Unlike earlier disavowals of knowledge concerning the definition of the just (338c4–5, 354c1), his present disclaimer carries with it serious implications for the status of the dialogue at that particular moment. Sokrates confesses that he has neither control over the discussion nor a preconceived plan to implement; he is left at the mercy of the *logos* instead. This discussion on the rules of poetic composition is an open quest for a destination not yet revealed to any of the participants. Adeimantos' agreement (καλῶς . . . λέγεις) means that he realizes his understanding of that quest to have been rather restricted: something greater than the mere status of tragedy and comedy may after all lie ahead.[125]

There is hardly any reason to doubt Sokrates' sincerity at this point. An argument in favour of taking his words at face value is their agreement with a standard pretence of the dialogue, namely that the plot of the *Republic* unfolds almost above the interlocutors' heads. On at least two occasions the conversation takes an unexpected course contrary to Sokrates' intentions (357a, 449a–b), while earlier conclusions, initially presumed final, prove inadequate and the relevant discussion reopens much later – as is the case with the critique of poetry. It is all too natural therefore that Sokrates suspends his judgement on where this investigation will eventually lead. The nautical imagery says as much: he and his companions are likened to a captain with his crew who have lost control of their ship and are forced to sail to wherever the storm takes them. In the journey of the *Republic* navigation is not the prerogative of the captain-Sokrates but has been completely left in the power of the wind-*logos*.[126]

This simile is the first explicit manifestation of an intertextual *leitmotiv* that runs through the substructure of the dialogue and establishes the *Republic* as Plato's philosophical replay of the

Sokrates seem to react in a similar manner, when Adeimantos claims that the character of the timocratic man resembles that of his brother. The difference is that Sokrates there knows what he is talking about and has a position to defend (548e1–2). On the philosophical implications of the brothers' intervention in general see Weiss (2007).

125 On Socrates' disavowals of knowledge in the 'early' dialogues, *Republic* 1 included, see Wolfsdorf (2004b); Matthews (2006).

126 Plato famously likens an alternative way of argumentation to a 'second sailing' (δεύτερος πλοῦς) in the *Phaedo* (99c9–d1), the *Statesman* (300c2) and the *Philebus* (19c2–3). Cf. Benardete (1989); Yunis (2007a) 86–7.

Odyssey, a narration of the quest for the discovery of the just man and his city in prose designed to rival the archetypical epic about the adventurous return of the king of Ithaca to his home country. This subtext is constantly evoked in the *Republic* right from the *katabasis/nekyia*-motif of the opening scene (327a–b) and the imagery of the three waves in the middle section (457b, 457c–d, 472a) through to the Homeric resonances of the concluding myth of Er (614b–621d). Sokrates and the company in Kephalos' house take on the guise of Odysseus and his comrades and sail through the seas of narrative while fighting off storms on their way towards their destination. Unlike their Homeric counterparts, however, Platonic voyagers do not know in advance where they are supposed to go, since their own Ithaca will not be discovered until the very end. Most importantly, the whole crew reaches 'home' safely (cf. 621c), whereas in the epic Odysseus had been the only survivor.[127]

The invocation of the Homeric subtext is a piece of evidence that militates against an interpretation of Sokrates' words as replete with irony – otherwise the Odyssean guise would fail. His suspicion that much more than merely the admission of theatre lies behind the examination of the modes of literary discourse is about to be confirmed in the course of the discussion. Commenting on the second critique of current literature in Book 10 Sokrates calls it retrospectively an apology for the exile of poetry, a 'verdict' presumably passed at the end of the first critique in the third book:

> Ταῦτα δή, ἔφην, ἀπολελογήσθω ἡμῖν ἀναμνησθεῖσιν περὶ ποιήσεως, ὅτι εἰκότως ἄρα τότε αὐτὴν ἐκ τῆς πόλεως ἀπεστέλλομεν τοιαύτην οὖσαν· ὁ γὰρ λόγος ἡμᾶς ᾕρει. (*Resp.* 10. 607b1–3)

[127] For the motif of descent in the *Republic* see Seery (1988); Hyland (1993) 43–6; Rosen (2005) 19–21; O'Connor (2007) 59–76; Silverman (2007). Commenting on this motif Capra (2010) perceptively claims that '[f]rom a structural and metapoetic point of view, then, the very core of Homer's *Odyssey* provides Plato with a starting point for a new form of poetry' (202). On the *Odyssey* as subtext see Klonoski (1993); Howland (2005–6). Cf. Segal (1978); Hyland (1990); Freydberg (2007). Ferrari (2007b) calls the *Republic* 'Plato's philosophic *Iliad* and *Odyssey* combined' (xvi). Incidentally Planinc claims the *Odyssey* as a subtext of the *Phaedrus*, the *Timaeus* and the *Critias* (2003), while viewing Sokrates as the new Odysseus in the *Symposium* (2004). For the *katabasis* motif in the *Symposium* see Steel (2003). Finally Pender (2007) reveals intertextual affinities between (a) Hesiod's *Theogony* and the *Timaeus* (cf. Sedley 2010) and (b) Anakreon's and Sappho's songs and the *Phaedrus*.

Let then these words, I said, be our apology now that we remind ourselves of the topic of poetry, namely that we had every reason to exile her from the city since she is of such a nature; indeed it was the argument that forced us to do so.

In its conscious replaying of the '*logos*-the-leader' theme the last sentence is eloquent enough in relation to its intratextual predecessor. By making *logos* the driving force behind and the actual 'author' of the 'decree' against poetry Sokrates implicitly articulates the answer to his earlier hesitation to agree with Adeimantos' interpretation as to where their investigation on the educational expediency of direct discourse might lead. His reluctance to anticipate a prearranged end for their intellectual quest turns out to have been a true moment of 'prophetic illumination': the condemnation or acquittal of poetry does indeed seem to be a much larger issue than the public performance of one of its genres. Moreover, the theme of the ancient quarrel between philosophy and poetry, introduced at precisely this point (607b5–c8), by making use of the vocabulary of forensic discourse (cf. 607d6, 608a2) and leading to the 'official' closure of the discussion on literature (608 b4–10), confirms that here is the end of a journey begun quite some time earlier.[128]

The exile of poetry therefore is presented as the solution to Sokrates' riddle-like utterance in the third book. Yet his words there do not only serve a proleptic function but also stand for a striking instance of analepsis. Right at the beginning of Book 2 Plato's brothers launch their formidable attack on Sokrates' arguments in defence of justice in his discussion with Thrasymachos (357a–367e). At the conclusion of his devastating critique Adeimantos sums up the thrust of his thesis, namely that justice and injustice have to be judged by themselves, regardless of the prejudices of social convention (367a–e). Paradoxically, he declares himself a

[128] Interestingly, a similar expression about the argument as a driving force is found in the *Laws* (ἀλλ' ὁ λόγος ὅπῃ φέρει, ταύτῃ πορευώμεθα 667a9). The issue there is whether there is an art form better than choral and dramatic poetry. For the 'ancient quarrel' see now Most (2011) who takes it as a result of philosophical allegoresis by Plato of the ancient poetic utterances. Ford (2009) intriguingly considers what he calls 'Plato's war-story . . . at best a partisan interpretation of literary history, if not as an outright fiction' (631). Cf. Kannicht (1980); Giuliano (2000b); Levin (2001) 127–67; Rosen (2005) 352–76. On the influence of poetic discourse on Plato see Rorty (2008); Crotty (2009); Tanner (2010); Destrée and Herrmann (2011).

believer in justice and genuinely wishes for a refutation of his own critique (a8–b1). He openly admits that he builds as strong a case for injustice as possible so that its demolition may finally silence any potential detractors of justice. In other words, he plays the devil's advocate in order to condemn him. Adeimantos lays his cards on the table at the outset of his conclusion:

> Ταῦτα, ὦ Σώκρατες, ἴσως δὲ καὶ ἔτι τούτων πλείω
> Θρασύμαχός τε καὶ ἄλλος πού τις ὑπὲρ δικαιοσύνης τε
> καὶ ἀδικίας λέγοιεν ἄν, μεταστρέφοντες αὐτοῖν τὴν δύναμιν φορτικῶς, ὥς γέ μοι δοκεῖ. (*Resp.* 2. 367a5–8)
>
> These arguments Sokrates, or even much more than these,
> could Thrasymachos or any other evidently put forward in relation to justice and injustice, twisting the faculty of both in a vulgar manner, in my opinion.

It is on this occasion that Adeimantos utters a phrase that Sokrates will repeat later in his examination of the propriety of the mimetic element in poetry, slightly changing the order of the words (ἴσως δὲ καὶ ἔτι τούτων πλείω, 367a5 = ἴσως δὲ καὶ πλείω ἔτι τούτων, 394d7). It seems a reasonable inference therefore that these passages have been designed to be read in association, featuring the same pair of interlocutors who alternate at the receptive end of the communication. In both cases the speakers make it clear that there may be more to the picture than at first meets the eye. Adeimantos points out that advocates of the 'might-is-right' principle like Thrasymachos are able to mount a more powerful defence of injustice, implying that his own devastating arguments do not exhaust the arsenal of the detractors of the just life. Similarly, Sokrates hesitates to commit himself prematurely to defining the ultimate goal of his attempted reformation of existing poetry, in full awareness of the fact that the incoming argument cannot be narrowed down to the mere expediency of theatre as a social institution.

In terms of the architectonics of the *Republic* this duplicated phrase functions as a marker for a potential narrative route leading outside the particular context in which it is embedded. It looks as though the reader is invited to pause and think for himself how much more effectively Thrasymachos could have defended injustice, or what else beyond the public performance of tragedy and comedy could have been in the mind of a reformer of traditional poetry. The possibility of an alternative course creates momentarily a 'narrative void' meant to be filled with speculative constructions of fictional worlds. This 'window' lasts for a short while and the reader is quickly led back to the normality of a linear narrative on both occasions. The difference is that, whereas Adeimantos' remark in Book 2 is made in passing and left to oblivion, Sokrates in Book 3 makes out of the same phrase a 'prophecy' about to be fulfilled very much later when understood as such only in retrospect.

The cumulative effect of this delicate interweaving of passages from three different books is the uncovering of a self-reflective dimension for the status of the *Republic* as a narrative. A common thread uniting all three references is *the negotiation of boundaries*. Two out of three passages deal with the prospect and the range of the banishment of poetry from the ideal city: what was in the beginning tentatively suggested in relation to theatre alone (394d) was later vindicated as a justified conclusion now affecting the whole of poetic composition (607b). The earliest passage, on the other hand, forms part of a discussion on the intrinsic value of justice, irrespectively of the distorting influence of social conventions (367a). The question here is why a just life is worth living and preferable to an unjust one that only gives the impression of being just; or, to put it differently, the exile of injustice from men's private and public lives. The close association between these instances of boundary-formation is eventually brought forward in the coda that seals the section on the exile of poetry: there Sokrates tells Glaukon that becoming good or bad is so important an issue that one should not neglect justice or any other virtue in favour of the mesmerising and inflating effects of honours, wealth, political power or poetry (608b4–8).[129]

Interestingly, poetry and justice coexist also in the earliest passage. According to his own statement Adeimantos does not believe in what he has just argued for. His only reason for producing the

[129] Μέγας . . . ὁ ἀγών, ὦ φίλε Γλαύκων . . . <u>τὸ χρηστὸν ἢ κακὸν γενέσθαι</u>, ὥστε οὔτε τιμῇ ἐπαρθέντα οὔτε χρήμασιν οὔτε ἀρχῇ οὐδεμιᾷ οὐδέ γε <u>ποιητικῇ ἄξιον ἀμελῆσαι δικαιοσύνης</u> τε καὶ τῆς ἄλλης ἀρετῆς.

most competent case against justice available is his desire to see Sokrates demolishing even such a passionate defence (367b1–2). When he gets into the shoes of the spokesman of injustice he does not identify himself with this persona since his sympathies lie with the opposite 'camp'. Like his brother before him (cf. 358c1, c6–d3, 361e2), he assumes the role of Thrasymachos, but merely as a means to promote his own cause. Now, speaking in a voice different from one's own, or, to use a technical term, role-playing, is a distinctive feature of most poetic performances whether in the exclusive manner of tragedy (impersonation only) or the circumstantial one of epic (impersonation mixed with narration). Given that Homeric epic and tragedy in the *Republic* are treated as successive versions of one and the same poetic continuum, it may be argued that through the brothers' role-playing poetry is in a way put at the service of justice.[130]

This 'confession' that comes *after* the delivery of an 'encomium of injustice' has implications for any perception of the negotiated boundaries as inflexible or impenetrable constructions. Here is a follower of justice who wears the mask of a great opponent so successfully that his allegiances would have never been challenged had it not been for his revealing his true purposes (367b1). By emulating the lover of injustice and speaking passionately in her defence he turns the tables on the poets by displaying in action their corrupting influence on their public. Adeimantos' speech, therefore, is one more instance of a literary device that Plato is regularly applying in the *Republic*, namely a character acting out his own argument.

Significantly this technique is employed elsewhere in the context of the argument against poetry. On both occasions there seem to be implications for the status of the *Republic* and its characters, as the related passages are effectively self-reflective. When in Book 3 Sokrates, the guest at Kephalos' house, explains to Adeimantos

[130] From the beginning right up to the concluding section Plato reminds the reader that Adeimantos' defence is a continuation and culmination of Glaukon's speech (362d–363a, 363e, 367b). The 'role' of Thrasymachos therefore is divided between the two brothers in a manner reminiscent of a convention in ancient theatre, namely that occasionally more than one actor may share the part of a single character. As for tragedy's special relation to epic, suffice it to notice that throughout *Republic* 10 Homer is systematically refered to as a tragedian (595b–c, 598d, 605c, 607a).

that the direct discourse of dramatic poetry derives from epic narrative when the poet removes the passages between the speeches, at this point Sokrates the narrator omits precisely those passages from the narrative of the *Republic* (394b–c). The implication is that as a text this particular dialogue has intrinsic affinities with theatrical writing, a kind of prose drama surfacing occasionally from the enveloping narrative. Similarly, in Book 10 when Sokrates argues for the preferability of the life of reason, conscious of the insufficient persuasive power of a set of propositions as such, he resorts to a performative demonstration of his thesis, namely the story of a virtuous man who suffers a grave misfortune but remains emotionally undisturbed (603e–604d). It is this performance with its emphasis on affective discourse (courage, perseverance) that justifies the life of reason and not any argumentation based on impeccable logic.[131]

The appropriation of standard devices of performance literature stands therefore at the core of the identity of the *Republic* as *the* comprehensive philosophical narrative to replace all narratives. Sokrates is, then, right when he claims that the examination of poetry entails much more than the legitimisation of theatre. The ultimate goal is the establishment of the narrated Platonic dialogue as the new authoritative mode of storytelling. In view of their notorious quarrel the foundation of Kallipolis seem to define the domains of philosophy and poetry which are thought of as mutually exclusive. But the truth is that the *Republic* itself denies any fixed identities in both types of discourse and establishes the intrinsic continuum between philosophy and poetic myth and imagery.[132]

[131] The point about the sliding from narrative to dramatic discourse in 394b–c was made by Laird (1999) 68: his question whether this feature indicates that the *Republic* resembles drama may be answered in the affirmative. The importance of 603e–604d for the exposition of the limitations of reason has been brought out by Earle (2003) 386–90: the author rightly remarks that 'Socrates' own "prose" can be said to have already "shown" the benefit of mimetic performance in a way that his reason is yet to be able to "say"' (390). Saxonhouse (2009) takes this incommensurability as evidence for a democratic reading of the *Republic*.

[132] This is the main argument of Naddaff's (2002) thought-provoking study. Her 'paradoxical' concluding remarks are worth quoting in full: 'Socrates' censorship of poetry finally achieves its end: the censorship of censorship. Philosophers, like poets, are free to encounter any and all foreign sources. Liberated from the deadweight of unexamined prejudices while condemning the practice of unreflective and uncritical condemnation,

Platonic drama as self-reflective performance text: the Laws

In the *Republic* Plato challenges Homer by composing a better account of the man and his society than that of the poets – hence the narrated form of the dialogue and the mythological subtext of the storytelling. Having dealt with their leader, he decides to confront head-on the tragedians themselves in his second major composition, the *Laws*.[133] The absence of a narrator's voice and the dramatic setting in terms of time (daytime) and place (outside Attica) differentiate Plato's last work from its earlier counterpart and make it more immediately comparable to plays. A more significant point of deviation between the two dialogues for the present purposes relates to *metatextuality*: instead of the oblique, layered presentation of the *Republic* as philosophical narrative, the status of the *Laws* as self-reflective performance text is regularly invoked in so unambiguous a manner that the discussion of three elders in Crete during their pilgrimage in honour of Zeus, the legislative code of the would-be colony of Magnesia, and the text of the *Laws* are comfortably blended.

Poetry in prose

The most astonishing instance of metatextual reference is to be found in the discussion of the educational system for the new city (809e–812a). The Athenian Stranger doubts whether the literature currently in use is suitable for teaching schoolchildren. When Kleinias asks for an exemplary text (παράδειγμα 811b8) that the authorities may use as a criterion for the formation of an acceptable curriculum, he seizes the opportunity to put forward his original and unexpected suggestion:

the philosopher of the postcensorship age cultivates the desire to imagine all images of what philosophy is and could be' (134). Cf. also Ebert (2002); Soares 2004; Giuliano (2005); Meinwald (2011); Halliwell (2011).

133 For the first seven books of the *Laws* the running commentaries (in a German translation) by Schöpsdau (1994) and (2003) update and, ossasionally, supplant the standard work by England (1921). The classic study of the whole dialogue still remains the monograph by Morrow (1960). Recent discussions include Lamprellis (1995); Bertrand (1999); Benardete (2000); Lisi (2001); Bobonich (2002); Scolnicov and Brisson (2003); Laks (2005); Brisson and Pradeau (2006); Zuckert (2009) 51–146. For bibliography see Saunders and Brisson (2000).

ΑΘ. Τοῦ μὴ παντάπασι παραδείγματος ἀπορεῖν. νῦν γὰρ ἀποβλέψας πρὸς τοὺς λόγους οὓς ἐξ ἕω μέχρι δεῦρο δὴ διεληλύθαμεν ἡμεῖς – ὡς μὲν ἐμοὶ φαινόμεθα, οὐκ ἄνευ τινὸς ἐπιπνοίας θεῶν – ἔδοξαν δ' οὖν μοι παντάπασι ποιήσει τινὶ προσομοίως εἰρῆσθαι. καί μοι ἴσως οὐδὲν θαυμαστὸν πάθος ἐπῆλθε, λόγους οἰκείους οἷον ἀθρόους ἐπιβλέψαντι μάλα ἡσθῆναι. τῶν γὰρ δὴ πλείστων λόγων οὓς ἐν ποιήμασιν ἢ χύδην οὕτως εἰρημένους μεμάθηκα καὶ ἀκήκοα, πάντων μοι μετριώτατοί γε εἶναι κατεφάνησαν καὶ προσήκοντες τὰ μάλιστα ἀκούειν νέοις. τῷ δὴ νομοφύλακί τε καὶ παιδευτῇ παράδειγμα οὐκ ἂν ἔχοιμι, ὡς οἶμαι, τούτου βέλτιον φράζειν, ἢ ταῦτά τε διδάσκειν παρακελεύεσθαι τοῖσι διδασκάλοις τοὺς παῖδας, τά τε τούτων ἐχόμενα καὶ ὅμοια, ἂν ἄρα που περιτυγχάνῃ ποιητῶν τε ποιήματα διεξιὼν καὶ γεγραμμένα καταλογάδην ἢ καὶ ψιλῶς οὕτως ἄνευ τοῦ γεγράφθαι λεγόμενα, ἀδελφά που τούτων τῶν λόγων, μὴ μεθιέναι τρόπῳ μηδενί, γράφεσθαι δέ· καὶ πρῶτον μὲν τοὺς διδασκάλους αὐτοὺς ἀναγκάζειν μανθάνειν καὶ ἐπαινεῖν, οὓς δ' ἂν μὴ ἀρέσκῃ τῶν διδασκάλων, μὴ χρῆσθαι τούτοις συνεργοῖς, οὓς δ' ἂν τῷ ἐπαίνῳ συμψήφους ἔχῃ, τούτοις χρώμενον, τοὺς νέους αὐτοῖς παραδιδόναι διδάσκειν τε καὶ παιδεύειν. οὗτός μοι μῦθος ἐνταῦθα καὶ οὕτω τελευτάτω, περὶ γραμματιστῶν τε εἰρημένος ἅμα καὶ γραμμάτων. (*Lg.* 7.811c3–812a3)

ATH. For we are not in a complete lack of a model. Indeed now when I look upon the speeches we have gone through from dawn up until this very moment – as it seems to me, not without the inspiration of some god – they gave me the impression that they have been delivered in every respect much like some kind of poetry. Perhaps the feeling that came upon me is not surprising, namely my taking great pleasure in looking at our speeches brought together. Certainly compared to the majority of the speeches I have learned and read, uttered in poems or in prose like this, they appeared to me the best measured of all and entirely appropriate for the young to read. I could not suggest to the guardian of the laws and the educator any better model, as I believe, than this, i.e. to encourage the teachers to teach these to children, and as for other discourses that follow closely and resemble our speeches, if by any chance he happens to come across them when going through poets' poems and prose writings or prose utterances that have not been written down, all of which are akin in some degree to these discourses, by no means to neglect them but have them written down. First he should compel the teachers themsleves to learn and praise them and not work with the teachers who disagree but work with these who cast their vote for praise along with his and allow them to teach and educate the young. Let my story end at this point and in this manner, a story that has been told about schoolteachers and letters. (after Cooper 1997, 1478–9 with modifications)

In this lengthy reply the Athenian practically ordains the establishment of the *Laws* as the central text in the educational system, the one to define the canon of textbooks for use throughout the Magnesian schools. Designated as the culmination of the speaker's reasoning on the subject, this carefully constructed passage is articulated around the succession of two related themes: (1) the *Laws* as literature (811c6–d5) and (2) the *Laws* as legislation (811d5–812a1). The treatment of these themes in turn displays the same principle of bifurcation: (1a) the announcement of the literary status of the dialogue is followed by (1b) the favourable comparison of the Platonic text with the existing body of literature; similarly, (2a) the formation of a corpus of officially approved texts determines (2b) the criterion for the selection of teachers. The coda (812a1–3) confirms in the most unambiguous way that this section is meant to be read as the Athenian's authoritative word on the subject.[134]

One can hardly overestimate the multiple ramifications of the present self-contained section, which evidently bears the signs of a programmatic statement. To begin with, this is the first and only time in Plato that a character comments *explicitly* on the fictional status of the dialogic text as *literature*. This metadialogical reference is also significant in terms of the vocabulary employed. The Athenian Stranger looks upon (ἀποβλέψας) what has been discussed from early dawn up until well into the day. He goes on to step up the power of this metaphor by portraying himself as observing (οἷον . . . ἐπιβλέψαντι) his and his interlocutors' arguments in their totality (λόγους οἰκείους . . . ἀθρόους). A body of personified speeches in full view, especially if visualised as a long procession, may parallel the spatio-temporal movement of the characters of the dialogue themselves who talk as they walk from Knossos to the cave of Zeus on Mount Ida in Crete. At the same time this imagery oversteps the boundaries of literary fiction, invading the experience of the readers. For it is they who are capable of performing the very act implied in the imagery: they may literally look upon the discourses of the *Laws* in the form of written signs on papyri or even, synecdochically, in the form of the book-rolls themselves. The metaphor materialises both inside the text as visualisation and outside the text as actual seeing. The consequence of this temporary suspension of fictionality is that whatever is said in

134 For discussions of the passage see Robb (1994) 236–9; Bobonich (1996) 252–9; Adomenas (2001) 32–5; Schöpsdau (2003) 569–78; Mouze (2005) 305–17.

this section about the fictional conversation in Crete applies also to the text of the *Laws*.

This fleeting fantasy of 'the collected speeches' parade' is a far cry from a neutral fiction delivered by a detatched narrator: the Athenian frankly admits that he receives great delight and joy from this spectacle (μάλα ἡσθῆναι). His indulgence resembles that of any person who takes pride in the outcome of his performance, owing to his natural attachment to the work he accomplished. But here the self-congratulating feeling cuts deeper: it derives from a successful comparison of the fictional dialogue in the *Laws* with the existing texts both in poetry and prose (ἐν ποιήμασιν ἢ χύδην). Reviewing the content of his education (μεμάθηκα) and his readings from personal initiative (ἀκήκοα) the Athenian claims confidently that the discussion on Magnesia comes out second to none compared with what may be found in established literature. At a metatextual level this is a statement on Plato's part that his *Laws* enter the competitive environment of Greek literary production on an equal footing.

So much has been established by Kleinias' opening remarks. Significantly, the extreme pleasure experienced by himself as a viewer is described in terms of a powerful emotion forced upon a passive subject (οὐδὲν θαυμαστὸν πάθος ἐπῆλθε). Eliciting particular responses from its audience places the text of this dialogue alongside poetic genres like tragedy or comedy, each of which is credited with its own kind of pleasure. This focus on a specific reaction is one of the markers that associate the *Laws* with poetry. Another one is its inspirational status: the conversation between Kleinias, Megillos and their Athenian visitor seems to have been held under the auspices of the gods (οὐκ ἄνευ τινὸς ἐπιπνοίας θεῶν). In the wake of the best traditions of Greek poetry this prose work is self-proclaimed as a piece of divinely sanctioned literature, its characters ranking among those privileged individuals of a bygone, heroic time when men had a rather immediate access to divine wisdom.[135]

[135] *Pace* Sauvé-Meyer (2011) 398–9, it is difficult to read any irony into this reference to divine inspiration. The religious context of the *Laws*, since all three interlocutors are pilgrims to the cave sanctuary of Zeus on mount Ida (625b), suggests rather the non-ironic invocation of divine presence here.

The literary credentials of the Platonic dialogue allow the Athenian to assign it a central position in his reformational project. New cities need new texts for the formation of the character of their citizenry. The *Laws* is elevated to the status of the official textbook, the centrepiece of the educational policy, the yardstick for the (re)formation of the curriculum: only those like-minded (ὅμοια), kindred (ἀδελφά) texts that promote a similar world-view to that of the city founders will be taught in the schools of Magnesia. New texts need devoted interpreters to transmit the new message to the next generation: only those who believe in the truth of the officially approved works will be allowed to teach. In their recorded form the speeches produced by the three old pilgrims turn into the founding charter of a Cretan colony-in-speech under the auspices of the gods, taking on the features of a revered, divinely inspired, almost sacred text.[136]

By the end of the Athenian's narrative (μῦθος) on education the terms for the reception of this particular dialogue have been established. The *Laws* is the flagship of a new literary fleet, an alternative 'poetic' text intended for emulation by both the internal audience of the Magnesian citizenry and the external audience of Plato's readers. It is placed at the head of a new literary canon selected from the whole spectrum of written *and* oral literature to be memorised and recited in schools (810e–811a) – one may justly think of the Platonic dialogues as prominent members of the group. As a thoroughly self-referential lawcode that invites its (re)performance, the *Laws* constitutes a comprehensive prose dramatic text inviting any comparison with other 'kindred' works.

The tragedy of the real

It is indicative of Plato's masterly manipulation of audience response that he stages precisely such a contest a few pages on. The section of the educational policy concerning literature (809e–812a) and music (812b–813a) is followed by that on dancing and physical training (813a–817e), at the end of which special reference is made to the production of plays. In an uninterrupted narrative the

[136] Nightingale (1993); Adomenas (2001) 31–5. Naddaf (2000) argues that the laws of Magnesia were to be versified and performed as songs and dances.

Athenian argues in favour of comic performances provided that no citizen is involved in the acting business (816d–e). When it comes to tragedy, however, he opts for a more impresssive manner of argumentation by presenting an encounter between the authorities of the Cretan colony and the members of a wandering troupe (817a–d). As a fictional dialogue embedded in the dialogic fiction of the *Laws* this story recalls the familiar metatheatrical mode of 'play-within-a-play'. In combination with the arguments aired by the Magnesians, this interface produces an evocative context for the supersession of tragedy by (Platonic) philosophy as the authoritative literary discourse.[137]

This episode consists in two direct speeches of unequal length preceded by respective introductory sentences. At first the Athenian raises up the curtain for the scene to follow:

τῶν δὲ σπουδαίων, ὥς φασι, τῶν περὶ τραγῳδίαν ἡμῖν ποιητῶν, ἐάν ποτέ τινες αὐτῶν ἡμᾶς ἐλθόντες ἐπανερωτήσωσιν οὑτωσί πως· (*Lg*. 7.817a2–5)

As for our so-called serious tragic poets, if some of them were to approach and ask us again some such question as this:

The picture is quite clear: the speaker envisages a meeting with a group of tragic poets who are about to request permission for the production of their plays. But there appear a few words with an evident metalinguistic role since, if they were removed or, in the case of the verb, modified, the content of the sentence would have remained practically the same. Their presence qualifies the ensuing text as a story told not by a dispassionate third party but by someone with his own invested interests:

(a) ὥς φασι: the Athenian distances himself from the accepted truth of classical Greece that tragedy was the authoritative poetry of the

137 The latest and most comprehensive discussions of the passage are Laks (2010) and Sauvé-Meyer (2011). See also Mouze (1998); Benardete (2000) 216–23; Westermann (2002) 28–30; Schöpsdau (2003) 596–9; Mouze (2005) 332–54; Jouët-Pastré (2006) 139–54. From a narratological point of view, this passage is one more instance of *hypophora*, namely the introduction of imaginary speakers and/or addressees. The preludes to the actual legislation the Athenian addresses to the citizens of the future city are another example of the application of this figure of speech. For the role of the preludes see Bobonich (2002) 97–119; Pradeau (2005); Jouët-Pastré (2006) 159–64. Sauvé-Meyer (2011) perceptively recognises the structural analogy between these preludes and the choral odes in tragedies (396–7).

day, the legitimate successor to the Homeric epic, dealing with the ultimate questions of men's lives. A certain indeterminacy over the subject of the verb adds to the subversive tone of the parenthetical phrase: the high esteem of tragedians may reflect what the people believe or equally plausibly what the poets think of themselves – in which case an acceptable expression of professional pride may sound, to a less sympathetic audience, dangerously close to a sign of arrogance.

(b) ἡμῖν: an ethical dative by definition indicates a personal interest of the speaker and/or his addressee in the relevant action or statement (Smyth 1956, 342–3). This touch of intimacy suggests that as a group the three elders of the *Laws* may have some scores to settle with tragic poets – or so the Athenian thinks.[138]

(c) ἐπανερωτήσωσιν: the use of the compound form in a context where the simple verb is normally expected raises some eyebrows – unless, of course, the preposition makes a difference. 'To ask again or further' presupposes that an earlier question has not been satisfactorily answered or is used as a premise for the elaboration of an argument. It seems plausible that the tragedians are envisaged as having confronted again the magistrates of Magnesia before this present exchange.

Having prepared the field the Athenian brings the troupers onto the stage:

'Ὦ ξένοι, πότερον φοιτῶμεν ὑμῖν εἰς τὴν πόλιν τε καὶ χώραν ἢ μή, καὶ τὴν ποίησιν φέρωμέν τε καὶ ἄγωμεν ἢ πῶς ὑμῖν δέδοκται περὶ τὰ τοιαῦτα δρᾶν;' (*Lg*. 7. 817a4–6)

'Strangers, may we enter your state and country, or not? And may we bring along our poems with us? Or what is your policy on this point?'

This piece of direct speech is the only contribution of the theatre practitioners in the story. They request permission to visit the city on a regular basis (φοιτῶμεν) and stage their plays. The way they address the authorities of the city underlines their liminal and ambiguous status. Two of the usual translations of ξένος are 'stranger' and 'visitor'. From the point of view of a group of wandering artists any newly visited city is an unknown land whose

[138] Unless the Athenian suspends his identity as a philosopher when arguing for the laws of Magnesia, the intratextual identity of this collective 'we' seems to contradict Sauvé-Meyer's (2011) claim that 'it is not the philosopher but the legislator who lays claim to the title tragedian' (388).

people may welcome or chase them away. Both the newcomers and the citizens are 'strangers' to each other so their relationship has the potential to move across the border from animosity to partnership. By requesting permission to frequent the city the tragedians wish to depict themselves as 'visitors' who are no longer perceived by the community as an alien group but as a part of the city's fabric. For ultimately they may aim at being granted the status of a 'guest-friend', another meaning of the word ξένος. They ask for 'hospitality' and they bring their own gifts with them, their productions. If the Magnesians reply positively to the tragedians they will move gradually away from mutual alienation (strangers–strangers) towards the establishment of a hierarchical bondage (hosts–guests) and eventually to social symbiosis (guest-friends).

Poetry is what the tragedians are out to offer to their prospective new hosts. They hold their trade in high esteem and have every reason to believe they are offering their audience a great service by introducing them to the experience of theatre. The dative of advantage (ὑμῖν) signifies their self-confidence and their pride as bearers and distributors of the poetic truth. Small wonder they cap their appeal with a direct invitation to the authorities to announce their decision, probably in the expectation of a positive answer.

This reading reflects the tragedians' point of view, which does not coincide with that of the Athenian narrator who composed these lines for them. In fact, his dissociation from his 'characters' at this point has been embedded in the text. To begin with, he chooses to present a *summary version* (οὑτωσί πως) of what actual poets would have said in real-life circumstances. In place of a well-crafted speech they deliver a few lines in which they bluntly say what they ask for. This plain, almost rough, style may reflect the Athenian's wish to avoid the attractiveness of a more poetic rhetoric. Second, the tragedians' last sentence adds nothing substantial to their petition – if it were left out of the text the meaning would still have remained intact. The reference to the established rules of the community (δέδοκται) reminds the reader of the subordinate position of the poets. The mirroring of the same personal dative (ὑμῖν) with a different syntactical function serves a similar purpose: this time the poets' addressees are not the beneficiaries of the art of theatre but a collective decision-making body.

Finally, the phrase used for the introduction and dissemination of tragic poetry (φέρωμέν τε καὶ ἄγωμεν) sounds alarmingly self-defeating. In its reversed form (ἄγωμέν τε καὶ φέρωμεν) it would mean 'plunder'or 'destroy', as in the case of a wasted and looted land. This suppressed meaning opens the door for the unravelling of a 'dark' side in the poets' statement: the self-proclaimed champions and preachers of poetry may in reality prove its detractors and abusers. It looks as if the Athenian attempts to undermine his competitors' credentials by exposing them as impostors, pseudo-poets who harm true (hence the definite article) poetry – as if he needs to draw a sharp line between reality and illusion.

The tragedians have made their plea. Before responding to them the Athenian turns to his companions and invites them to join in his fiction:

τί οὖν ἂν πρὸς ταῦτα ὀρθῶς ἀποκριναίμεθα τοῖς θείοις ἀνδράσιν; ἐμοὶ μὲν γὰρ δοκεῖ τάδε· (*Lg*. 7.817a7–b1)

In view of this request what would then be the right reply for us give to these divine men? I believe we should answer as follows.

This address brings us for a moment back to the dramatic setting of the *Laws*. Kleinias and Megillos are ostensibly asked to think of a proper reply to the troupers. Their eloquent silence after the Athenian's question (we may envisage a pause there) gives him the opportunity both to finish what he started in his own terms (ἐμοὶ) and to do so on his interlocutors' behalf. His ensuing contribution in this untypical and unbalanced 'contest of speeches' is meant to function as a closure, his final word on whether and if so on what terms is tragedy to be performed in the Cretan colony. Hence the significance of accuracy (τάδε) down to the last detail: unlike the poets', his own speech is a full and precise 'transcript' of the Cretan authorites' final verdict.

For these reasons one is tempted to detect heavy irony in the tragedians' description as 'divine men' (θείοις ἀνδράσιν). Yet the context here suggests a more nuanced interpretation. If one were to accept Sokrates' testimony in the *Meno* that to call a man divine was a Spartan style of praise (99d9), Megillos for one would have no reason to doubt his companion's honesty. In the beginning of the *Laws* Tyrtaios was addressed as 'a most divine poet' (629b9) with no evidence of irony. Homer (*Phd.* 95a2) and Simonides (*Resp.* 331e6) are similarly acclaimed elsewhere in the dialogues. Owing to their privileged access to the world of gods, poets were traditionally highly esteemed as gifted individuals favoured by the divine. In this case the Athenian mostly complies with a well-established practice in ancient Greek society. But as soon as he switches to the direct speech this expression of praise will be a contested title between two competing groups of poets.[139]

The Athenian's reply to the tragedians' request in his capacity as the leading figure among the city's rulers is one of the most arresting images in Plato. It is divided into three distinct sections. The first one is the all too significant prelude:

'Ὦ ἄριστοι,' φάναι, 'τῶν ξένων, ἡμεῖς ἐσμεν τραγῳδίας αὐτοὶ ποιηταὶ κατὰ δύναμιν ὅτι καλλίστης ἅμα καὶ ἀρίστης· πᾶσα οὖν ἡμῖν ἡ πολιτεία συνέστηκε μίμησις τοῦ καλλίστου καὶ ἀρίστου βίου, ὃ δή φαμεν ἡμεῖς γε ὄντως εἶναι τραγῳδίαν τὴν ἀληθεστάτην. ποιηταὶ μὲν οὖν ὑμεῖς, ποιηταὶ δὲ καὶ ἡμεῖς ἐσμεν τῶν αὐτῶν, ὑμῖν ἀντίτεχνοί τε καὶ ἀνταγωνισταὶ τοῦ καλλίστου δράματος, ὃ δὴ νόμος ἀληθὴς μόνος ἀποτελεῖν πέφυκεν, ὡς ἡ παρ' ἡμῶν ἐστιν ἐλπίς.' (*Lg.* 7.817b1–c1)

'Best of strangers, we ourselves are poets of the best and most beautiful tragedy so far as it lies in our power. For our public life in its entirety has been constructed as a representation of the best and most beautiful of lives, which we strongly claim to be in fact the truest tragedy. So you are poets, we are poets, both in the same field, your competitors as artists and actors for the most beautiful drama, that it is only in the power of true law to produce, as we hope.'

The speech starts with an unexpected statement that changes the rules of the game and must have taken the tragedians off their guard. So far they might have believed that they had approached a newly founded colony in need of their services. It appears that this city has its own team of tragic poets, so the assumed vacancy does not apply and competition is inevitable. What is more, these poets happen to be the city's magistrates, who claim paradoxically that the genuine tragedy is not the one presented on stage but the other one experienced in everyday reality, as citizens lead

[139] The excessive praise of famous poets of the past in Plato should not be read as an unmistakable sign of ironic treatment without additional evidence. Those passages mentioned above must not be lumped together with others where humour and satire carry the day as, say, Sokrates' mock-praise of Ion at the end of the *Ion* (542b).

their lives performing their roles as scripted by their legislation. A theatre taken out into the streets, as it were, does not leave much breathing space for a theatre of the stage.

The element of surprise is a corollary of the paradox of the legislators-tragedians revealed in full glory at the opening of the speech. This paradox is founded on a sophisticated manipulation of the reality of literary production. Tragic poets compose plays to be enacted by actors on stage. The Magnesian rulers compose laws to be enacted by the whole citizenry in private and public. Both in their respective texts construct fictional worlds that purport to teach the truth about the meaning of life (τῶν αὐτῶν). Fictionality as representation is therefore the key feature shared by both compositions. This common ground allows the philosophers of the Cretan city to put on the mantle of tragic poets and prepare themselves for the competition with their colleagues.

The opening section of the Athenian's reply is essentially a manifesto for the Real Tragedy. The identification of its practitioners is followed by the definition of the new type of poetry and an admission of a professional rivalry between the Magnesian and the wandering tragedians. Naturally the accumulation of so many terms with theatrical overtones in so short a space guarantees the identity of the section (τραγῳδία, δρᾶμα, ἀποτελῶ). It is not an accident that the rhetoric of the passage is replete with elements such as: (a) repetition (καλλίστης . . . καὶ ἀρίστης, καλλίστου καὶ ἀρίστου, καλλίστου); (b) structural symmetries (ὃ δή φαμεν ≈ ὃ δὴ νόμος); (c) ring composition (τραγῳδίας . . . τραγῳδίαν); (d) instances of *anaphora* (ποιηταὶ μὲν ≈ ποιηταὶ δὲ) and wordplay (νόμος . . . μόνος). Evidently the manifesto displays many features of a formulaic text, a *credo* for the new tragic poet and his audience.

In terms of its immediate context the Athenian argues for the superiority of the philosopher-poets over their rivals on the strength of their awareness of the best available life men may aspire to. Both the object and the product of imitation are cast in the highest evaluative terms, namely *kalos kai agathos* in the superlative. It is the lack of this knowledge that prevents the poets of the stage from producing a true tragedy, to paraphrase the superlative of the original. Yet the Athenian never loses sight of the unbridgeable gap separating the model from its instantiations. The philosopher-poets of his city may depict the pattern of the ideal life only up to a point (κατὰ δύναμιν), while they will have always to hope that the result will be successful (ὡς ἡ παρ᾽ ἡμῶν ἐστιν ἐλπίς). Limitations of power and control condition their productions. As imitators they are not different in the practice of their art from their colleagues in the theatre. This is what makes them contenders for the first prize in the festival for the most beautiful drama (τοῦ καλλίστου δράματος).[140]

The affinity between the two groups is unexpectedly suggested by the Athenian himself already from the very first words of his speech. The address 'best of strangers' (ἄριστοι . . . τῶν ξένων) may be read in a number of ways as: (a) an expression of courtesy for a group of visitors; (b) an ironic praise that plays on the tragedians' bloated ego; (c) a soothing compliment before the delivery of the condemning blow; (d) an allusion to the well-known Homeric formula ('best of the Achaeans') associated with a number of Greek warriors at Troy (Achilles, Diomedes, Agamemnon). Although more than one option may be at work here (d) catches one's attention. Tragic poets systematically turned to the heroes of the *Iliad* and the *Odyssey* for their plots, while Homer was considered by literary critics their predecessor as the 'patriarch' of serious poetry. A traditional attribute of Homeric heroes would be a fitting title for those 'warriors' of the theatre, *qua* competitors at festivals, who follow in the epic poet's footsteps. So the Athenian may after all make a playful reference to the literary history of their art.

Intriguingly, the same phrase occurs only twice in the *Laws*. In both cases it is the Athenian who speaks to a group of interlocutors. Except for the tragic poets of a fictional future, the other addressees are Kleinias and Megillos, the co-founders of Magnesia in the fictional present of the dialogue (634c5). Both of them are among the philosopher-poets who compose real tragedies in the projected

[140] On the vexed question of *mimēsis* in Plato see the excellent studies by Giuliano (2005) 21–135 and Palumbo (2008). For the *Laws* see also Lisi (2004). On the *Laws* as a new type of tragedy see Kargas (1998); Mouze (1998) and (2005); Naddaf (2000) and (2007) 344–8; Gioia (2004); Panno (2007). Laks (2010) points out the resemblance of this passage with the definition of tragedy in Aristotle's *Poetics* (222–4).

future. The flexibility in the transition of characters between the narrative levels allows the Athenian to bring together these two groups of 'best of strangers' for an emblematic confrontation in an improvised story. Notably the Athenian, who is himself addressed as a stranger throughout the dialogue, is deeply involved in this competition as both the creator of the fictional *agōn* and its leading player for the Magnesian team.

That is why the reply to the visiting tragedians is predictably negative. That much is said in the central section of the speech. The verdict, though, has a coda: the tragedians of the stage may still have a chance if they can persuade the authorities of the quality of their plays:

μὴ δὴ δόξητε ἡμᾶς ῥᾳδίως γε οὕτως ὑμᾶς ποτε παρ' ἡμῖν ἐάσειν σκηνάς τε πήξαντας κατ' ἀγορὰν καὶ καλλιφώνους ὑποκριτὰς εἰσαγαγομένους, μεῖζον φθεγγομένους ἡμῶν, ἐπιτρέπειν ὑμῖν δημηγορεῖν πρὸς παῖδάς τε καὶ γυναῖκας καὶ τὸν πάντα ὄχλον, τῶν αὐτῶν λέγοντας ἐπιτηδευμάτων πέρι μὴ τὰ αὐτὰ ἅπερ ἡμεῖς, ἀλλ' ὡς τὸ πολὺ καὶ ἐναντία τὰ πλεῖστα. σχεδὸν γάρ τοι κἂν μαινοίμεθα τελέως ἡμεῖς τε καὶ ἅπασα ἡ πόλις, ἡτισοῦν ὑμῖν ἐπιτρέποι δρᾶν τὰ νῦν λεγόμενα, πρὶν κρῖναι τὰς ἀρχὰς εἴτε ῥητὰ καὶ ἐπιτήδεια πεποιήκατε λέγειν εἰς τὸ μέσον εἴτε μή. (*Lg*. 7. 817c1–d3)

Do not expect therefore that we would so easily grant you permission to fix your stage-buildings on the marketplace and put on stage actors with beautiful voices who speak louder than we do, and allow you to deliver your speeches in the presence of children, women and the rest of the population, although you do not profess the same ideas as we do on the same issues – on the contrary, in most of the cases, the exact opposite. We would have to be completely driven out of our minds, along with the entire city, if we allowed you to do the things we have just said before the authorities pronounce judgement on whether you have composed poems that are both sayable and suitable for public performances or not.

Here the Athenian explains the reasons why an *unconditional* permission for theatrical performances could not be granted. Tragedies promote a world-view that goes against the principles inculcated by the laws of Magnesia (ἐναντία τὰ πλεῖστα). If the citizenry were to engage as audiences with the plots of the plays they would have been dangerously disorientated, for they would have been forced to reconcile contradictory claims on very important issues (ἐπιτηδευμάτων). The authoritative discourse of the tragedy on stage would so interfere with the authoritative discourse of the tragedy offstage that people would start challenging the truth of their lives and social cohesion would collapse. To facilitate one's self-destruction would indeed be a sign of absolute madness (κἂν μαινοίμεθα τελέως). An officially approved production of a traditional tragic drama in a city like Magnesia is perceived as a threat, for although it could be incorporated into the structural patterns of the city, it could not be assimilated. It would essentially remain an 'alien' dramatic discourse undermining the dramatic discourse of the city it was meant to support. That is, not a play-within-a-play but a play-against-a-play. Besides, tragic theatre has an irresistible appeal of its own. Once exposed to it, audiences would have difficulty in denying its charm.

To give an example of the threatening power of the theatre the Athenian entertains very briefly the possibility of such a performance. By focusing on three moments in the process of a production he is able to evaluate its impact. The first moment is the troupe's admission into the city and their preparing the material infrastructure: they establish themselves in the heart of the city where the stage-building and any adjacent constructions are erected (σκηνάς τε πήξαντας κατ' ἀγορὰν). The realistic choice of the *agora* as a place for theatrical events carries with it a menacing symbolism: the centre of the polis has been temporarily (?) occupied by outsiders. The force implicit in πήξαντας, as though the tragedians stab the city's heart, adds to this unsettling thought. The second moment relates to the day of the premiere: the actors appear on stage and mesmerise the audience with their beautiful voices (καλλιφώνους ὑποκριτὰς εἰσαγαγομένους). The charm of their performance may lead the citizens to indulge in the spectacle and grow forgetful of the distinction between reality and fictionality while persuading themselves about the truth of the characters' arguments. By offering a more attractive, hence influential, mode of communication the tragedians, through their actors, may easily block any other official discourse and replace the local authorities as dominant public speakers (μεῖζον φθεγγομένους ἡμῶν). The politics of theatre is precisely what the third moment deals with. Here the tragic poets are envisaged delivering public speeches to the people of Magnesia, much as politicians do (δημηγορεῖν). But they are in a more privileged position because the theatre audience is broader than that of an assembly, as it includes all those excluded from the male citizenry (πρὸς παῖδάς τε καὶ γυναῖκας καὶ τὸν πάντα ὄχλον). The tragic poets target this segment of the population as more vulnerable to political manipulation.

A proof of the power of theatre as a means of persuasion is the Athenian's own practice. When asked to legislate on the place of tragic drama in Magnesia he invents a rudimentary contest of speeches in which he plays the role of both parties. He also redefines the notion of tragedy as imitative art by turning the life in his ideal city into a living performance of a 'sacred' text and himself into a master dramatist. His choices indicate an intention to beat the dramatists at their own game. So indeed does his version of the effect a production of tragedy would have had on the Magnesians. This version implies that the authorities are sufficiently familiar with theatre – a reply to the tragedians' earlier hint at the locals' lack of cultural sophistication. Theatrical imagery dominates this embedded narrative while the aural dimension is particularly emphasised. From the noises during the erection of the temporary wooden constructions to the beauty and strength of the actors' voices the sound of theatre is omnipresent. The uniqueness of the experience is further highlighted by the number of words that are found here but occur only once or not at all outside this present speech. καλλίφωνος (*hapax* in Plato); ἀντίτεχνος, δρᾶμα, πήγνυμι, δημηγορῶ (*hapax* in the *Laws*); σκηνή (twice in Plato); ὑποκριτής (twice in the *Laws*).

Throughout the second section the Athenian shows why the authorities should have a say in which plays, if any at all, will be produced in Magnesia. The third and last section of the speech contains the official reply:

νῦν οὖν, ὦ παῖδες μαλακῶν Μουσῶν ἔκγονοι, ἐπιδείξαντες τοῖς ἄρχουσι πρῶτον τὰς ὑμετέρας παρὰ τὰς ἡμετέρας ᾠδάς, ἂν μὲν τὰ αὐτά γε ἢ καὶ βελτίω τὰ παρ' ὑμῶν φαίνηται λεγόμενα, δώσομεν ὑμῖν χορόν, εἰ δὲ μή, ὦ φίλοι, οὐκ ἄν ποτε δυναίμεθα. (*Lg*. 7. 817c4–8)

And now, children of soft Muses, display first to the authorities your songs showing how they may compare to ours and, if it proves that your stories are either the same or even better than ours, we will grant you permission to produce your plays; but if not, friends, that we could never do.

The epilogue of this long speech is structurally marked out from the rest of the speech by the transitional οὖν and the double addresses that flank the main body of the text. In view of the preceding warnings about the dangers of theatre the verdict might be expected to be an outright rejection. Only the unconditional *a priori* approval of all tragedies is not an option. Instead the tragedians are offered a choice: they may either leave or persuade the authorities that their compositions are competent imitations of the ideal life. Since the rulers in Magnesia are themselves fellow-tragedians they are well-equipped to act as judges in a contest for the better representation of the values and principles of their community, i.e. the truest tragedy. Admittedly, this decision sounds more like an invitation for the composition of plays than a banishment of tragic poets.

One may object to this reading as too charitable towards the Athenian. He has so vividly depicted the potential threat of theatre that he surely would not change his mind seconds later. The choice he offers is merely a sham: the authorities would always turn down all applications, and no play would ever make it to the stage. The 'contest of songs' is a thinly veiled pretext for censorship. This objection, though, may be challenged on two accounts. First, the phrase the Athenian uses for the state approval of plays is 'to grant a chorus' (δώσομεν ὑμῖν χορόν). This is exactly the official term in classical Athens, and for the same reason. Terminology of this kind presupposes an institutionalised screening process resulting in rejections *and* approvals like the one in Athens. Besides the production of comedies in Magnesia required also a body of citizens to select the works to be performed.

More importantly *the Athenian needs theatre*. His own practice throughout indicates that he knows how to exploit the advantages of the dramatic discourse for his own purposes. His redefinition of the notion of tragedy as the imitation of the ideal life on- and off-stage is a novelty that turns the legislation of a city into a script for materialisation. For, if experiencing the truest tragedy is indeed the aspiration to realise on an everyday basis the paradigm of the best life, then the citizens of Magnesia are destined to live fully aware that they will never manage to embody their ideal, but, at the same time, lead one of the best lives accessible to human beings.

The composition and production of philosophical tragedies would have been a great help for these citizens.

This reading may find some support from the difference in the Athenian's mode of addressing the tragedians at the beginning and the end of the epilogue. At first, in full imitation of tragedy's high-flown diction he calls them 'children of soft Muses'. The reference to the Muses and the scansion of the opening words as a full hexameter shortened by one syllable (νῦν οὖν, ὦ παῖδες μαλακῶν Μουσῶν ἔκγονοι) allude once more to the Homeric origin of tragic poetry. The notion of softness is associated primarily with the senses, while in the field of aesthetics it denotes artistic products that owe their success mainly to the pleasure they give. It is possible that the Athenian has in mind a distinction he had made earlier in the context of choral poetry and dance between two types of artistic production, the pleasurable and the right one.[141] If so, the choice the tragedians are given is at the same time an invitation to follow the Athenian's lead and become 'children of the right Muse', just like the philosopher-poets of Magnesia.

For the affinity between these two groups runs through this section of the *Laws* as a *leitmotiv*. When the Athenian bids farewell to the tragedians by calling them friends (ὦ φίλοι), he assimilates them once more to his interlocutors in the dramatic fiction of the *Laws* (cf. 662b1, 689d4). Regardless of their admission in the city the tragedians of the Athenian's story are not called 'strangers' any more but 'friends'. Now it is they who have to make a decision. The final words of the speech (οὐκ ἄν ποτε δυναίμεθα) do not so much constitute a closure as invite those interested to compose true, philosophical tragedies.[142]

The model text that prospective compositions of the new drama will be tested aginst is of course the *Laws*. Systematically Plato reminds his reader that this dialogue is composed as a self-reflective performance piece. As a written text it is an imitation of

[141] The passage is worth quoting in full: ΑΘ. Καὶ τούτοις δὴ τοῖς τὴν καλλίστην ᾠδήν τε ζητοῦσι καὶ μοῦσαν ζητητέον, ὡς ἔοικεν, οὐχ ἥτις ἡδεῖα ἀλλ' ἥτις ὀρθή· μιμήσεως γὰρ ἦν, ὥς φαμεν, ὀρθότης, εἰ τὸ μιμηθὲν ὅσον τε καὶ οἷον ἦν ἀποτελοῖτο (668b). The verbal and conceptual parallels with the Athenian's reply to the tragedians are so striking that Plato must have encouraged the intratextual reference.

[142] On the use of friendship terms in Plato see Dickey (1996) 109–19.

the 'best and most beautiful' life instantiated by an ideal community in Crete. It is therefore the paradigmatic text for the new type of philosophical tragedy. Its dramatic form, the role-playing involved in the imaginary dialogues, the close identification between the different narrative levels, and its self-presentation as a body of legislation to be implemented suggest that Plato's *Laws* was a dialogue that invited its own performance.

3
PERFORMING PLATO

Preliminaries

If the argument of the previous chapter is valid and Plato presented an authorial identity as an alternative metatheatrical dramatist, the issue of the publication of his dialogues may need to be re-examined. True, Plato composed written works, which circulated in book-form and could be purchased by members of the reading public. But this was the case with most literary texts, regardless of their mode of delivery. So one is made no wiser as to whether the dialogues reached their audience only in this way. On the other hand, a Platonic dialogue is a prose dramatic text. And all fifth- and fourth-century drama, either in verse (Attic theatre, Sicilian comedy) or prose (Sicilian mime), was meant primarily for performance. The same holds true for the poetry of the period in general, while the aspect of oral delivery is similarly indispensable to some genres of prose literature, for instance forensic and deliberative speeches. It is reasonable then to wonder how Plato's production fits into such a context and whether the reception of his work is at all related to the contingencies of this performance culture. In other words, are Plato's dialogues the only classical dramatic texts intended *exclusively* for a reading public? Or was the element of performance of much greater importance for the reception of the dialogues than the majority of scholars would readily admit?

It is this possibility of a reading of the Platonic dialogue as a performance text which I set out to examine in this chapter. An ancient line of interpretation, attested already by Aristotle and documented in the works of Themistios, Demetrios, Dion and St Basil, associates Plato's work with poetical and prose performance genres. This leads to the question of the possible mode(s) of reception of the dialogue in its original context. Reading techniques and the institutionalised aspect of most literary production are of relevance here, as is the evidence for oral delivery of the dialogues.

The ancient record

Aristotle

In the introductory paragraph of the *Poetics* **Aristotle** outlines the objectives of his study while laying the foundations for the field of literary theory. He goes immediately on to offer a taxonomy of the poetic (and musical) genres distinguished on the basis of their medium, object and mode of representation. Rhythm, music and speech are considered the media through which *mimēsis* is achieved, employed either in themselves or in combination with each other. Examples of the arts that correspond to this classification are provided. In the case of those genres that have speech alone as their medium Aristotle makes the following remark:

ἡ δὲ [ἐποποιία] μόνον τοῖς λόγοις ψιλοῖς <καὶ> ἡ τοῖς μέτροις καὶ τούτοις εἴτε μιγνῦσα μετ᾽ ἀλλήλων εἴθ᾽ ἑνί τινι γένει χρωμένη τῶν μέτρων ἀνώνυμοι τυγχάνουσι μέχρι τοῦ νῦν· οὐδὲν γὰρ ἂν ἔχοιμεν ὀνομάσαι κοινὸν τοὺς Σώφρονος καὶ Ξενάρχου μίμους καὶ τοὺς Σωκρατικοὺς λόγους οὐδὲ εἴ τις διὰ τριμέτρων ἢ ἐλεγείων ἢ τῶν ἄλλων τινῶν τῶν τοιούτων ποιοῖτο τὴν μίμησιν. (1447a28–b13)

Both the genre that uses prose and the one that uses metres, whether mixing them together or employing one type of metre, have remained without a name up to now; for we could find no common designation for both Sophron's and Xenarchos' mimes and the Socratic dialogues; not even if one performed his mimesis by means of trimeters or elegiacs or the other similar metres.

This is an admittedly difficult passage on textual grounds and most of the first sentence is the product of scholarly emendation.[1] But

[1] The transmitted text runs as follows: ἡ δὲ ἐποποιία μόνον τοῖς λόγοις ψιλοῖς ἢ τοῖς μέτροις . . . ἀνώνυμος τυγχάνουσα μέχρι τοῦ νῦν. The word ἐποποιία has been rightly excised by Uberweg as an interpolated gloss. It contradicts the meaning of the sentence and is not found in the Arabic translation of the *Poetics*. The replacement of ἢ by <καὶ> ἡ and the change of τυγχάνουσα to τυγχάνουσι, followed by the necessary change of the adjoining adjective to plural (probably already in the Arabic translation), was suggested by Lobel (1929) 77 and accepted by Kassel in the OCT edition. Luckily for the present purposes the second part of the sentence does not present similar textual problems.

the main train of thought throughout the whole section (a28–b23) remains relatively clear. Aristotle draws attention to a gap in the terminology of literary criticism that reflects a weakness in the prevailing concept of poetry. There is no single name covering those mimetic writings composed in prose or in verse with no musical accompaniment. The reason for this omission is the popular misconception of the function of the poet. People identify poetry with writing in verse regardless of the content of the poems. This is wrong, since the real criterion is not the metrical form but whether the work is an instance of artistic imitation or not. The current nomenclature that attaches the title of 'poet' to any composer of texts in a single metre is merely a source of confusion. For it lumps together poets and versifiers alike while, at the same time, it fails to acknowledge those poets who employ either prose or any mixture of metres.

Before any comment on details it is important to realise the rationale of the passage as a whole. There is evidently a critical tone here and an intention to lay the foundations for a proper literary theory. Aristotle finds fault with the way people think about poetry in his time and points out its deficiencies. The fact that a branch of literature remains nameless means that it has not received its due recognition. Aristotle's remarks aim, then, at orienting his contemporaries to realising the existence of this ignored branch, namely mimetic prose and plain verse (i.e. unsung) writing. It is in such a context that any references to particular genres are to be understood. As members of the nameless class of prose imitation Aristotle mentions Sicilian mime and 'Socratic discourses'. He stresses the necessity for a common name for both these forms of prose literature.

On the basis of his formulation three inferences may be reasonably made. First, by the second half of the fourth century the set of texts that had Sokrates as the leading character had formed a separate literary genre. In this group, we may assume, Plato's writings featured prominently. Second, an affinity between these two literary forms is postulated. There is also the implication that their common elements will cease to be obscured when their nature as subdivisions of a larger class is realised. Third, this mimetic prose literature is associated with literature in spoken verse as two classes using unadorned speech as a medium for imitation (or divisions of one class if the reading of the manuscripts is maintained). Both are parts of the poetic art by virtue of being imitations. Poetry is not confined only to verse compositions but encompasses prose texts as well. Consequently mimetic prose writers may legitimately be called poets.

This passing reference in the *Poetics* provides a late fourth-century context for Plato's work. It is significant that the reference occurs in a digression in which Aristotle reflects on the nature of poetry and redefines the relevant theoretical framework. The introduction of the notion of a poetry dissociated from the musical element is itself a rather innovative suggestion. In a similar vein the abolition of the formal aspect as a criterion for poetry opens the door to the incorporation of prose compositions into poetic literature. According to the new taxonomy, Plato (and the other Socratics for that matter) could be considered a poet. More precisely, he is rather a prose dramatist in the wake of Sophron and Xenarchos. And the fact that mime was a performance genre makes the association more than interesting. Whether or not Aristotle envisaged in this section the development of a musicless drama, as has been suggested,[2] it is true that at least in terms of literary theory he thought of the dialogue in the context of other poetic, mainly dramatic, performance texts.

Aristotle evidently insisted on this generic association between the mime and the 'Socratic discourses'. He seems to have repeated this point in his three-volume dialogue *On Poets*.[3] In a fragment preserved by Athenaios, Sophron's mimes in rhythmic prose and Alexamenos' prose dialogues are both considered instances of mimetic literature:

Ἀριστοτέλης δ' ἐν τῷ Περὶ Ποιητῶν οὕτως γράφει· '<u>οὐκοῦν οὐδὲ ἐμμέτρους τοὺς καλουμένους Σώφρονος μίμους μὴ φῶμεν εἶναι λόγους καὶ μιμήσεις ἢ</u>

[2] Else (1957) 60–1. Kurke (2006) identifies this nameless genre with mimetic prose (11–12) and suggests that 'the *Sôkratikoi logoi* of Plato and Xenophon are to the mimes of Sophron and Xenarchus as tragedy is to comedy' (42, n. 27).

[3] For the fullest treatment of Aristotle's dialogues see Laurenti (2003). Cf. also Gigon (1987) 218–54. The extant fragments of the *On Poets* may be found in the standard collections of Rose (1886) 76–81, Ross (1955) 67–72 and Gigon (1987) 263–7. For an attempted reconstruction see Rostagni (1926–7). A full discussion is to be found in Laurenti (2003) 389–95.

τοὺς Ἀλεξαμενοῦ τοῦ Τηίου τοὺς πρώτους γραφέντας τῶν Σωκρατικῶν διαλόγων;' (Ath. 11. 505c = 72b Rose = 69, 3b Ross =15 Gigon = *PCG* I Sophron Test. 3, 187)

Aristotle in his *On Poets* has writen the following: 'Are we then not to hold that the so-called mimes of Sophron, themselves metrical in form, are mimetic prose nor are those of Alexamenos of Teos, the first Socratic dialogues ever to be written?'

Once again we confront a passage that is notoriously difficult because of textual uncertainties.[4] Although the exact wording of the original may be a matter of conjecture, the general meaning of the extract seems clear enough: both writings ought to be recognised as belonging to the same genre of 'prose imitations', despite their apparent dissimilarity. Sophron's literary mimes (μιμήσεις) were also prose compositions (λόγοι), while Alexamenos' dialogues (διάλογοι) qualify equally as artistic imitations (μιμήσεις). In other words, in this popular and influential dialogue Aristotle argues for a thesis he wholeheartedly endorses in a more theoretical work such as the *Poetics*. The recognition of the Socratic dialogues as poetic, i.e. literary, compositions remained a constant in his thought.

So far the evidence presents Aristotle's reflections on Socratic literature in general without any explicit reference to Plato.[5] This silence, however, may very well be accidental, owing to the fragmentary nature of the material. At any rate there is a testimony that records what Aristotle believed about the Platonic dialogue in particular. In a section composed of various testimonies on the dialogues **Diogenes Laertios** writes:

[4] I am following Gigon in printing the manuscript text, although I differ from him in construing the sentence as a question (after Bernays in Gulick 1933, 267 n. *d*). In an attempt to make better sense of the transmitted text scholars resorted to a number of corrections. For instance, the addition of ὄντας after ἐμμέτρους (Kaibel) or the suggested transposition ἢ μὴ μιμήσεις τοὺς (Jahn). Emendations that substantially affect the meaning of the extract are the change of πρώτους to προτέρους (Meineke following Dobree) and the substitution for διαλόγων of the variants διαλόγους (Bake), λόγων (Susemihl, Ford) and λόγους (Natorp). Kassel and Austin in *PCG* I accept Kaibel's addition of ὄντας and rewrite the last phrase as follows: τοὺς πρότερον γραφέντας τῶν Σωκρατικῶν διαλόγους. For a discussion see Narcy (1989); Laurenti (2003) 391–2; Ford (2010) 224–7.

[5] Although it is extremely unlikely that Aristotle was speaking of Socratic dialogues without thinking *primarily* of Plato's works. For a different view see Ford (2010) 226–7.

φησὶ δ' Ἀριστοτέλης τὴν τῶν λόγων ἰδέαν αὐτοῦ [sc. Πλάτωνος] μεταξὺ ποιήματος εἶναι καὶ πεζοῦ λόγου. (3. 37 = 73 Rose = 4 Ross = 862 Gigon)

Aristotle says that the style of his [sc. Plato's] writings lies between a poem and a prose text.

Here is a piece of evidence free from the textual ambiguities of the previous passages, though still raising some questions of its own. First, Diogenes does not purport to give a verbatim quotation and so the statement may stand for anything from a sentence in the original recast in indirect speech to an impressionistic summary of the content of a larger whole. Accordingly, we lack any positive information about the context of the fragment, i.e. the kind of writing (treatise or dialogue) it comes from, its immediate textual surroundings and the nature of the discussion in which such a remark would be in place.[6] Third, the abruptness and the 'self-contained' character of the extract suggest the question of whether this reflects Diogenes' own view only or echoes earlier scholarly tradition.

These reservations notwithstanding, the significance of the testimony should not be underestimated. Aristotle, according to Diogenes, pronounced a judgement on Plato's writings as pieces of literature, assigning them on stylistic grounds an intermediary place between poetry and prose. It seems reasonable to suppose that this reference was somehow conditioned by the tenets of literary theory. The comment then on the formal aspect of Plato's texts suggests an attempt at generic demarcation. Though written in prose, their literary form (ἰδέα τῶν λόγων) undermines the conventional polarity poetry/prose as they claim for themselves the role of a genre mediating between these two modes of composition (μεταξὺ).[7] It is this uniqueness of Plato's diction that Aristotle

[6] Most scholars have assumed, quite reasonably, that here we have another extract from the dialogue *On Poets* (e.g. Laurenti 2003, 390). Gigon (1987), more cautiously, places it among those of unknown origin (796).

[7] That the word ἰδέα, as a literary term, usually bears this meaning is well attested (cf. Arist. *Poet.* 1449^{b}8, 1450^{b}34; Isoc. *To Nicocles* 48; Dion. Hal. *Lys.* 16; Ath. 11. 505c). It is noteworthy that Isokrates, in a discussion on the kinds of prose writing, uses exactly the same phrase, though in the plural, in the sense of *prose literary genres* (*Antid.* 46.2). Interestingly, one of the genres mentioned is the works of those who have dealt with the question-and-answer form (περὶ τὰς ἐρωτήσεις καὶ τὰς ἀποκρίσεις γεγόνασι), the so-called ἀντιλογικοί – a possible allusion to Plato as a writer of dialogues.

stresses by setting him apart as an author of a separate, innovative mode of writing. In other words, Plato's own use of the dialogue form is in all probability implied here as the distinguishing marker of his style. The overall result would be his association with the poets no less than the prose writers, since his affinities lie equally with both.[8]

Themistios

We cannot know whether and to what extent the above remark affected the reception of the Platonic dialogue. But it was evidently taken up by later generations and became a point of reference in the relevant tradition. Diogenes Laertios is not our only witness to that. An extremely interesting parallel occurs in a speech by **Themistios**, a philosopher-orator of the fourth century AD. The author defends himself against the accusation of introducing new ways and of degrading philosophy. He is rebuked for lecturing in public on serious philosophical matters, in pursuit of the applause of the people rather than the reasoned discussion of his colleagues, and, in general, for behaving in the manner more of a sophist than of a philosopher. In an attempt to prove that he follows an established tradition, Themistios launches on a brief survey of the philosophers from Thales to Aristotle, focusing on their contributions in relation to their predecessors (*Or.* 26.317a–320a). This is how he closes the section on Plato:

πρὸς δὲ καὶ ἕτερα πάμπολλα ἐπεισηνέγκατο καὶ εἰσήγετο, λόγου ἰδέαν κερασάμενος ἐκ ποιήσεως καὶ ψιλομετρίας, τοὺς ἐρωτῶντας καὶ ἀποκρινομένους καὶ διηγουμένους, ὑφ' ὧν κατεχόμεθα ἅπαντες ἄνθρωποι καὶ αἰρόμεθα ἀπὸ τῆς γῆς. (*Or.* 26. 319a)

Moreover, he brought in a great many other features and, in particular, having created a style mixed of poetry and prose he introduced characters who ask

[8] There is a very good chance that Aristotle's reflections on the Platonic dialogue were related to the discussions in the Academy on the subject. Since the dialogue *On Poets* and the first draft of the *Poetics* were probably written between 360 and 355 BC (Düring 1966, 49–50), one wonders whether considering Plato a poet in prose was not an interpretation endorsed and promoted by Aristotle's teacher himself. On Aristotle's works see now Anagnostopoulos (2009).

questions and provide answers and give narratives, by which all of us people are possessed and lifted from earth.[9]

Although there is no marker of an intertextual reference, the similarities in phrasing with Diogenes' version indicate that both authors share the same source. Themistios' dependence on Aristotle is further confirmed by his idiosyncratic use of the very rare term ψιλομετρία, introduced in the *Poetics*.[10] There are, however, two points of difference that preclude the possibility of mere copying from Diogenes. First, the style of the Platonic dialogue is considered a combination of poetic and prose elements. Though perfectly compatible with Diogenes' account – they almost describe the same thing from a different perspective – the idea of a mixed style suggests the milieu of literary theory.[11] The immediate context supports this view. For in Themistios, and this is my second point, Aristotle's remark is not an isolated piece of evidence, but has been incorporated in a discussion of Plato's stylistic innovations. In fact, the dialogic form of his writings, with the division into dramatic (ἐρωτῶντας καὶ ἀποκρινομένους [sc. ἄνδρας]) and narrated (διηγουμένους) dialogues, results from a special rearrangement of the traditional modes of composition. Themistios sounds pretty certain: to him, the employment of dialogic characters is a novelty (εἰσήγαγε) that exemplifies the particular nature of the Platonic text as a mixture of poetry and prose.

The last point may lead to the following questions: (a) is the explicit association of Aristotle's fragment with the peculiarities of the dialogue form Themistios' own contribution, or does it reflect

9 On Themistios' life and work see Vanderspoel (1995); Penella (2000) 1–50.

10 In fact this word occurs *only* in these two texts in extant literature. It may very well have been Aristotle's coinage. In the *Poetics* the term evidently stands for 'poetry unaccompanied by music' ($1448^{b}11$). If we take for granted that the meaning needed for the Themistios passage is 'prose' there remain three answers: (a) The transmitted word is a mistake for a term denoting prose such as ψιλολογία (so Kan in Downey and Norman 1971, 131); but the uniform textual tradition at this point makes this a rather weak solution. (b) The word in Themistios' time had acquired this new meaning; this, however, was an exceptionally rare term, hardly ever used in criticism, and it seems improbable that Themistios was the innovator. (c) Themistios was recalling the passage from the *Poetics* and confused the meaning of ψιλομετρία with that of the neighbouring word λόγους which obviously means prose literature.

11 See, for example, Plato's discussion of poetic styles in *Republic* 3 or the tripartite division of the Platonic dialogues mentioned by Diogenes Laertios (3.50).

an older tradition? and (b) could this line of thought be traced back to Aristotle himself? On the present state of evidence any conclusive answer must be unattainable. Themistios has indeed embedded in his speech a number of passages from earlier authors in an attempt to establish his own status as the most recent member of a respectable cultural lineage.[12] The nature of the allusion, owing to its rephrasing or utilisation in another context, does not allow a distinction between the successive layers of interpretation. In the present case the lack of a reference to Aristotle by name and the loss of his dialogue *On Poets* leave little room for speculation on the original context of the extract. Therefore we cannot know whether Themistios acted as an innovator or an inheritor.

Either way, the real significance lies in the very fact of the reference itself. An author of the Christian era chooses to round up his selective, concise tribute to Plato's contribution to philosophy with an appraisal of his literary talent. The innovation he praises is the employment of dialogic characters either as interlocutors or as narrators, which he sees as the result of a conscious experimentation with the standard modes of writing. All these details testify to the longevity of this line of interpretation that associates Plato with his literary predecessors. Plato the poet in prose had become a traditional image with a history of its own.

Demetrios

The viability of this image is confirmed in a subtler way and from a different perspective by the next piece of evidence. **Demetrios** is the author of a text that seems to be the earliest extant work on literary criticism after Aristotle. His treatise *On Style* (*Περὶ ἑρμηνείας*) is generally considered a product of the late Hellenistic period (first half of the 1st cent. BC). The section dealing with the features of letter-writing (223–35), one of the writer's original contributions to literary theory, starts off with a stylistic comparison between letters and dialogues. In an attempt to correct Artemon's

12 The most conspicuous instance is Philosophy's exhortation to mankind, actually a slightly modified version of Sokrates' similar speech in the *Clitophon* (*Or.* 26. 320d–321c ~ *Clit.* 407b–408b). See Slings (1999) 87–8.

theory that the letter and the dialogue share essentially the same stylistic features (223), Demetrios points out the different requirements for the composition of each genre. He argues that the style of a letter is more formal than that of a dialogue which purportedly represents improvised conversations (μιμεῖται αὐτοσχεδιάζοντα 224). In support of his thesis he offers two examples. The first is a passage from Aristotle's letter to Antipater demonstrating the 'sophisticated' nature of letter-writing (225). The second refers to the conversational style of the dialogue exemplified in the opening of Plato's *Euthydemus*:

Καὶ λύσεις συχναὶ ὁποῖαι <αἱ τοῦ διαλόγου> οὐ πρέπουσιν ἐπιστολαῖς· ἀσαφὲς γὰρ ἐν γραφῇ ἡ λύσις, καὶ τὸ μιμητικὸν οὐ γραφῆς οὕτως οἰκεῖον ὡς ἀγῶνος, οἷον ὡς ἐν τῷ Εὐθυδήμῳ· "τίς ἦν, ὦ Σώκρατες, ᾧ χθὲς ἐν Λυκείῳ διελέγου; ἦ πολὺς ὑμᾶς ὄχλος περιειστήκει"· καὶ μικρὸν προελθὼν ἐπιφέρει· "ἀλλά μοι ξένος τις φαίνεται εἶναι ᾧ διελέγου· τίς ἦν;" ἡ γὰρ τοιαύτη πᾶσα ἑρμηνεία καὶ μίμησις ὑποκριτῇ πρέποι μᾶλλον, οὐ γραφομέναις ἐπιστολαῖς. (226 Marini)

Yet a series of abrupt sentence breaks such as <suit the dialogue> does not suit the letter. Abruptness in writing causes obscurity, and the imitation of conversation is less appropriate to writing than to oral debate. Take the *Euthydemus*: "Who was it, Socrates, you were talking to yesterday in the Lyceum? There was certainly a large crowd standing round your group." And a little further on he adds: "I think he was a stranger, the man you were talking to. Who was he?" All this sort of style in imitation of reality suits an actor better; it does not suit letters since they are written. (after Innes 1995, 483, with minor changes)

Here is a revealing passage in view of the explicit connection of Platonic with dramatic diction. Drawing on the familiar distinction between the *graphic* and the *agonistic* styles of compostition,[13] Demetrios finds an example of the second type in the very first words of a Platonic dialogue. It is clear from the context that the *Euthydemus* is treated as a text intended for performance rather than reading. The critic in fact says precisely as much when remarking that the way these lines have been constructed is more

[13] He has himself introduced these two types of diction a little earlier: Ἐναγώνιος μὲν οὖν ἴσως μᾶλλον ἡ διαλελυμένη λέξις, ἡ δ' αὐτὴ καὶ ὑποκριτικὴ καλεῖται· κινεῖ γὰρ ὑπόκρισιν ἡ λύσις. Γραφικὴ δὲ λέξις ἡ εὐανάγνωστος (193 Marini). This distinction was formulated for the first time in the third book of Aristotle's *Rhetoric*: ἔστι δὲ λέξις γραφικὴ μὲν ἡ ἀκριβεστάτη, ἀγωνιστικὴ δὲ ἡ ὑποκριτικωτάτη (1413^{b}8–9). Cf. Marini (2007) 253–4.

suitable for delivery by an actor. To put it differently, on that particular occasion Plato is believed to have worked in a manner very close to that of the dramatists and composed a text that displays the principle of performability like those produced on stage.

To this interpretation the following objection may be raised. It is not necessarily the case either that the world of theatre is specifically evoked here or that any particular reading of the *Euthydemus* as a text appropriate for the stage is meant. A brief look at the language used both in this passage and in the section on the disjointed style (192–4) shows that Demetrios is heavily dependent on Aristotle's discussion in the *Rhetoric* (3. 1413^b3–1414^a7). There actors and orators are treated interchangeably as practitioners of the art of histrionics (cf. 1413^b16, 21) while the conclusions reached apply equally to a stage performance and a public speech. Demetrios' use of the opposition γραφή / ἀγών seems derivative from the comparison of rhetorical with non-rhetorical texts mentioned by Aristotle (1413^b15–17), with ἀγών meaning in both cases the speakers' public confrontations.[14] The concluding remark should also be read in a similar way. The reference to ὑποκριτής is not to be interpreted exclusively in theatrical terms. The word may stand for the orator as well as the actor (*LSJ*[9] II.2). Moreover, the whole phrase may be simply a rephrasing of the opposition between the two types of diction, as the pair ὑποκριτῇ/γραφομέναις indicates.[15] Demetrios merely says that the kind of sentence breaks exemplified in the opening of Plato's dialogue should be better reserved for public speeches not for written compositions.[16] There is no reason for supposing that any connection between the diction of Plato's dialogues, or the *Euthydemus* in particular, with theatre is implied.

The objection above is reasonable but rests ultimately on a couple of misconceptions. The first concerns the conclusions drawn from the pairing of actors and orators in Aristotle's *Rhetoric*. It

[14] Translators seem to agree: Innes (1995) 483 translates ἀγών as 'real debate' following Rhys Roberts (1902) 263, while Marini (2007) uses 'dibattiti' (125).

[15] It is probable that Demetrios drew on Aristotle's characterisation of the *agonistic* style as ὑποκριτικωτάτη (1413a9) and his persistent use of terms from the same word-family throughout the section.

[16] For example, Innes (1995) translates ὑποκριτής with 'oral delivery' (483) and Marini (2007) with 'recitazione' (127).

was standard practice for the theorists of rhetoric in antiquity to mention these professionals together, especially when commenting on the features of delivery (ὑπόκρισις). The reason was that the orator resorted to some basic acting techniques whenever he gave his speech. This continuum between the theatrical and the oratorical performances signified the priority of the histrionic model: the public speaker assimilated himself to an actor delivering a (prose) monologue. Given the structural affinities between forensic oratory and theatre it is not difficult to realise that, in matters of *delivery* (ὑπόκρισις), the theorists thought of the speech in terms of stage performance. Similarly, to call the orator a ὑποκριτής was evidently a secondary development, based on the histrionic quality of the orator's delivery. In other words, in many a theoretical discussion of the delivery of a public speech the element of theatrical performance is not only present but also predominant.[17]

This leads to my second point, namely the precise meaning of Demetrios' reading of the *Euthydemus* passage. Throughout the section Aristotelian influence is, for one thing, plainly evident.[18] In fact, it provides the context for the proper understanding of the terminology applied. It has been persuasively shown that Aristotle's use of the word *agōn* and its cognates in the discussion of diction in the *Rhetoric* suggests not contest or debates but the aspect of performance.[19] The classical distinction between the *graphic* and the *agonistic* styles amounts to a differentiation between the texts composed primarily for reading and those intended for public performance.[20] Demetrios' oppositional pair γραφή / ἀγών reflects a similar taxonomy, with the letter and the Platonic dialogue as representative texts of each group. The author has no doubts that the style of the Platonic passage he cites, with its abrupt sentence breaks (λύσεις), is one appropriate for texts meant

[17] On the common ground between forensic oratory and theatre see Hall (2006) 353–92; Duncan (2006) 58–89. For an interesting theory on the adoption of ὑποκρίνομαι and its cognates for the theatrical vocabulary see Svenbro (1999) 54–6.

[18] For Demetrios' relation to Aristotle and early Peripatos in general see Innes (1995) 315–20.

[19] Sifakis (1997–8) 26–7.

[20] As Sifakis (1997–8) remarks, in connection with Aristotle's postulation of γραφική and ἀγωνιστική types of diction, 'the adjective *agonistic* in this context does not mean *antagonistic* but "*hypocritic*", i.e. histrionic and theatrical' (25). Gavrilov (1997), less persuasively, thinks of a distinction between silent reading and reading aloud (71 II ii).

for staging rather than reading out.[21] In the eyes of a late Hellenistic literary critic, therefore, the *Euthydemus* stands out as a piece of performance literature.

Another indication is found in the symmetrical structure and almost identical meaning of the sentences framing the quotation from Plato. Demetrios practically repeats himself almost word for word: imitation (τὸ μιμητικόν ~ μίμησις) is rather appropriate (οὕτως οἰκεῖον ~ πρέποι μᾶλλον) not for a written text (γραφή / γραφομέναις) but for a performance act (ἀγών / ὑποκριτῇ). The notion of imitation refers back to the earlier description of a dialogue as a type of mimesis (224). This brings to mind Aristotle's classification of the 'Socratic discourses' alongside Sophron's mimes as examples of prose dramatic literature (pp. 105–8).[22] Demetrios evidently views the *Euthydemus* as a drama sharing elements of diction with the works of stage. His remark that Plato has composed a passage suitable for delivery by an actor is pretty telling.

This emphasis on the pragmatics of histrionics, furthermore, suffices to disprove an alternative, non-theatrical meaning for the ὑποκριτής, namely that of someone answering in a conversation, an interlocutor. Though in agreement with the etymology of the noun, this rendering is otherwise unattested. More importantly, according to this reading, the *hypokritēs* mentioned would be none other than Kriton, the speaker of *Euthd.* 271a1–5. The use of the word as a technical term for the character in a play or dialogue is similarly unparalleled, while running contrary to the reasoning of the section which contrasts different modes of presentation of the texts, i.e. performance *vs* reading.[23] It is also suggestive that on the other three occasions in which the noun is used in the *On Style* (58, 195 twice) there can be no doubt that Demetrios has the stage

[21] Earlier on the disjointed style has been treated as characteristic of the actors' delivery, as a quotation from Menander makes clear (193–4; cf. also 271).

[22] Note that the only other occurrence of τὸ μιμητικόν in *On Style* (in fact an emendation from the manuscripts' τιμητικόν) is found in a discussion of the so-called 'Socratic', i.e. dialogic, type of writing, exemplified in the works of Aischines and Plato (298).

[23] By one's accepting the variant manuscript reading γραφομένῳ for γραφομέναις the sentence acquires an attractive balance as the actor, the producer of the performance text (play/dialogue), is contrasted with the author, the producer of the written text (letter).

actor in mind.[24] That the ὑποκριτής of § 226 is also an actor is a reasonable and unsurprising conclusion.[25]

There is an additional piece of evidence demonstrating that Demetrios saw close connections between Plato's dialogues and theatre. In his discussion of the figure of prosopopoeia he quotes from Plato's *Menexenus* (246d) with the following comments:

Ὥσπερ ἐν τῷ ἐπιταφίῳ Πλάτων τό· "ὦ παῖδες, ὅτι μέν ἐστε πατέρων ἀγαθῶν <···>" καὶ οὐκ ἐκ τοῦ ἰδίου προσώπου λέγει, ἀλλ᾿ ἐκ τοῦ τῶν πατέρων· πολὺ γὰρ ἐναργέστερα καὶ δεινότερα φαίνεται ὑπὸ τῶν προσώπων, μᾶλλον δὲ δράματα ἀτεχνῶς γίνεται. (266 Marini)

This is what Plato uses in his Funeral Speech [sc. the figure of prosopopoeia], "Children, that you are the sons of brave men <···>" He does not speak in his own person but in that of their fathers. The personification makes the passage much more lively and forceful, or rather it really turns into a drama. (after Innes 1995, 503)

The Platonic text cited records the opening words of the speech which the dead warriors are imagined to address to their children. This is an instance of the familiar technique of personification. A character, usually Sokrates, lends temporarily his voice to an absent, dead or imaginary person (or, in one case, a personified argument), who then delivers a speech and/or engages in a debate with the interlocutors.[26] The effectiveness and emotional power of this authorial technique are duly acknowledged by the critic. More significantly, he recognises this type of personification for what it is, a particularly impressive *coup de théâtre*. Assuming the 'identity' of another person and delivering words that belong

[24] In fact, in all these instances Demetrios allows his reader to take a glimpse of the actors' performance on stage. The first talks about actors who add superfluous exclamations to their lines, evidently for the purposes of a more emotional style of acting (58). The other two come from a special section on theatrical writing, mentioning a couple of stage directions in Euripides' *Ion* (195). The actor who plays the leading role is envisaged acting out the scene of Ion's chasing the swan away from Apollo's temple.

[25] So Chiron (1993) 64; Hathaway (1969) 40 n. 5.

[26] This technique may be interpreted as an elaborate and more sophisticated version of the figure of the *hypophora*. Except for the deceased fathers of the *Menexenus* other celebrated imaginary characters in the Platonic corpus are the personified finale of the *Protagoras* (361a–c), Protagoras himself (*Tht.* 166a–168c), the wily lover (*Phdr.* 237b–241d), the visiting *thiasos* (*Lg.* 7. 817a) and, the most famous of all, the laws of Athens (*Cri.* 50c–54d). Cf. Tsitsiridis (1998) 372–3; Szlezák (1999) 100–2; Trivigno (2009b) 41–4.

simultaneously to both the physical and the nominal speaker constitutes the essence of role-playing. This effacement of the self is precisely what gives the essentially theatrical character to this scene, in which Sokrates becomes the mouthpiece of those Athenians who fell in battle (supposedly) speaking to their (imaginary) children.

Demetrios' comment betrays a high degree of theoretical engagement with the poetics of Plato's text. The introduction of role-playing is what really turns (ἀτεχνῶς γίνεται) Sokrates' funeral speech, a continuous, expository text (with τὰ λεγόμενα implied subject of the verb) delivered by the speaker in his own person, into a sequence of characters' utterances, i.e. a dramatic text (δράματα).[27] This is the meaning of the last sentence if one takes Sokrates as the subject of λέγει, on the evidence of the *Menexenus*. There is a further implication, however, if Plato is also meant, as the syntax makes possible. If (a) speaking through characters (ὑπὸ τῶν προσώπων) defines theatrical writing and (b) Plato nowhere in his works speaks in his own person (οὐκ ἐκ τοῦ ἰδίου προσώπου λέγει), then the inference that the Platonic dialogues are themselves an example of theatrical texts is not an unwarranted one. Sokrates' role-playing in the *Menexenus* reflects Plato's practice as an author. Demetrios' comment may hint at a larger theoretical framework for the interpretation of Plato the prose dramatist.

There remains one question worth asking, namely whether the remarks on the affinity between Plato and the dramatists were somehow associated with these particular dialogues. The dead warriors' address in the *Menexenus*, as a speech within a speech, could have been presented as an 'autonomous' piece in its own right, perhaps assigned to a different speaker than the rest of the funeral speech. The *Euthydemus*, on the other hand, is a more straightforwardly theatre-oriented text. The main part of the dialogue, a narration of Sokrates' encounter with the brothers

[27] That role-playing is the distinguishing mark of δρᾶμα is confirmed by Demetrios' two other uses of the word: one time for Sophron's mimes (156), following the standard way of referring to these works, while the other for the *Iliad* (62), presumably because Homer allows his characters to speak in direct speech (cf. Innes 1995, 391 n. b, who, surprisingly, characterises the mime and the Platonic dialogue non-dramatic genres).

Euthydemos and Dionysodoros, is composed of distinct episodes interrupted by conversational interludes. This is possibly modelled on the similar structure of the tragedies and, at least from late Aristophanes, comedies – later to be crystallised in the five-act rule of New Comedy. The comic elements in the plot, the delineation of characters, especially the two brothers, and the abundant use of irony, parody and laughter bring the dialogue very close to a kind of 'Platonic comedy' (p. 69 with n. 104). Consequently I would like to put forward the following suggestion: when Demetrios claims that role-playing turns *Menex.* 246d into a drama or that the opening lines of the *Euthydemus* could have come from the mouth of an actor, he may indirectly reflect reading and/or performance practices of the Academy at the time. If Demetrios was writing in Athens in the decades before or after 100 BC,[28] he may have been acquainted with Philo of Larissa and his students and thus possessed information lost to us. This is admittedly no more than a speculation but, I hope, not an unfounded one.

Dion

Demetrios spoke about the dramatic qualities of Plato's dialogues as a literary critic. **Dion of Prusa the Chrysostom**, in turn, an orator and philosopher of the first Christian centuries (AD 40–*c.*110), was a producer and performer of literary texts, whose relation to the great figures of Greek literature was coloured by his self-presentation as their successor. In one of his most famous speeches, the *Borystheniticus* (*Or.* 36), he tells the story of his visit to Borysthenes, a city at the north coast of the Black Sea, and his conversations with local friends. Living at the fringes of the Greek world and not often being visited by intellectuals, they are more than eager to make the best of Dion's visit. A respectable old man called Hieroson asks him to share with them his views on the heavenly city (24–7) – thus allowing Dion to expound the Stoic doctrine on the common bondage of the universe under the law of Zeus (28–38).

[28] Chiron (1993) xxxvi. Marini (2007) suggests a date in the second half of the first century AD (16). Cf. Dihle (2007).

Hieroson prefaces his request with an explanation of why he has picked up this particular topic. He declares himself to be Plato's admirer, therefore he would like to hear a lecture on a Platonic theme delivered in an equally Platonic style (27). This is how he formulates his statement of loyalties in an expressely apologetic tone:

Ὁμήρου δε, ὡς οἶσθα, ἐρασταὶ [sc. ἐσμέν] καί τινες οὐ πολλοὶ Πλάτωνος· ὧν δὴ κἀμὲ ὁρᾷς ὄντα, ἀεί ποτε ἐντυγχάνοντα τοῖς ἐκείνου ὅπως ἂν δύνωμαι· καίτοι ἴσως ἄτοπον βαρβαρίζοντα τῶν ποιητῶν μάλιστα τῷ ἑλληνικωτάτῳ καὶ σοφωτάτῳ χαίρειν καὶ συνεῖναι, καθάπερ εἴ τις μικροῦ τυφλὸς τὸ μὲν ἄλλο φῶς ἀποστρέφοιτο, πρὸς αὐτὸν δὲ τὸν ἥλιον ἀναβλέποι. (26.6–11 Russell)[29]

As you know, we are lovers of Homer and some of us, not many, of Plato; one of whom you see in front of you, namely myself, always willing to read his writings as much as I can. Although it may sound weird that I, whose language is full of barbarism, take pleasure in and consort with the most Greek and the wisest of poets, as if someone whose sight has been impaired keeps away from every other source of light but looks up at the sun itself.

That Plato and Homer would be singled out as the most popular authors hardly raises any eyebrows. But that Plato would be considered not just a poet but the greatest of all is indeed a strange claim to make.[30] Evidently a way to explain both the paradoxical nature of the utterance and the factual mistake involved is for the passage to be read in its context. The speaker is a self-proclaimed partisan, a leading member of the tiny pro-Platonic faction, living in a city dominated by supporters of Homer. It is only to be expected that he would take the chance to eulogise his author while delivering a blow to the pride of his opponents by challenging one of their 'articles of faith'. For the title of the greatest among the Greek poets had universally and unquestionably been Homer's rightful prerogative since classical times. When describing Plato in these

[29] I follow the text from the edition with commentary by Russell (1992). Dion's life and work: Desideri (1978); Jones (1978); Swain (2000); Moles (2005) with bibliography (136–8); Gangloff (2006); Klauck (2007); Nesselrath (2009). On the *Borysthenitticus* see Russell (1992) 211–47; Trapp (2000a) 214–19; Nesselrath (2003); Gangloff (2006) 145–53.

[30] It is true that ποιητῶν is a scholarly emendation. But the manuscripts' πολιτῶν is in itself hardly defensible and the correction gives a perfectly sensible sentence and has the additional merit of palaeographic economy, since only two letters need to be changed. For the arguments defending his text see Russell (1992) 224.

terms Hierophon does nothing short of moulding the *persona* of the philosopher out of that of the poet. In view of this battle of the literary camps there is no paradox whatsoever. Far from being a slip of the tongue on the part of someone with an incomplete knowledge of Greek, calling Plato a poet was the ultimate blow: by means of this intentional 'mistake' Homer is by a sleight of hand eliminated from the picture and supplanted by Plato.

A closer look at the architectonics of the passage in full may prove that the *lapsus* is a deliberate one. There is an unmistakable air of a programmatic statement about it. The contesters are there from the start: the names of Homer and Plato open and close the first sentence respectively (26.6), so that there is no doubt left to those present on what is at stake here, namely the prize for the best author in Greek literature.[31] In fact, however, Homer is only mentioned right at the beginning and gets completely erased afterwards.[32] The scene will be dominated by his younger rival in a variety of modes. The 'Platonisation' of Hieroson's discourse will of course culminate later on in the request itself: not only does he ask for a lecture that would be comparable to the *Timaeus* and the *Republic* in terms of their subject (περὶ δὲ τῆς θείας εἴτε πόλεως εἴτε διακοσμήσεως φίλον σοι καλεῖν 27.16), he also expects the lecturer in his oral performance to imitate Plato's freedom of style (ὡς δύνασαι ἐγγύτατα τείνων τῆς τοῦ Πλάτωνος ἐλευθερίας περὶ τὴν φράσιν 27.17–19). Even his final remark that their familiarity with Homeric language makes it easier for his fellow-citizens to understand Plato (27.20–1), ostensibly a compliment to the poet, could be construed by a staunch supporter of the philosopher's superiority as a thinly veiled value-judgement that knowledge of Homer is commendable mostly as preparatory for Plato.

Hieroson himself seems to have been such a person, as may be concluded from the construction of his self-image in the passage quoted above. Although he does not exclude himself from

[31] Ancient criticism regularly associated Plato with Homer, especially in terms of style (Blondell 2002, 30 n. 85; Gangloff 2006, 148).

[32] In other words, Hieroson prefigures in his speech the much-wished-for replacement of Homer by Plato hinted at by his little mistake. The name of Homer resurfaces at the very end of the Borysthenite's request, in the manner of *Ringkomposition*, once again in association with Plato (27.21). The message is clear: Homer exists in Hieroson's discursive world only as a shadowy figure, incapable of an independent life.

the 'lovers' of Homer (ἐρασταί), he proudly declares himself a member of the select few who had moved a step further and 'have fallen in love' also with Plato. He is always on the lookout for Plato's offspring (τοῖς ἐκείνου) and tries to 'make love' to them (ἐντυγχάνοντα) as best as he can, while at the same time admitting that to derive pleasure from his having intercourse (συνεῖναι) with Plato is strange (ἄτοπον) for someone who is neither a (proper) Greek nor a barbarian (βαρβαρίζοντα).[33] He rounds off his brief moment of self-presentation by likening himself to a man with impaired eyes who does not refrain from looking straight at the sun. To put it differently, by speaking of his admiration for Plato and his experience from reading his works in erotic terms and by introducing the imagery of the conversion to the true light, Hieroson combines a number of Platonic motifs from the *Symposium* and the *Republic* and recasts himself as a latter-day Sokrates, an *atopos* philosopher who makes love to the Form of the Beauty, an ex-prisoner who has left the cave and fixed his gaze at the Form of the Good.

It is in the middle of such a Platonising context that the phrase 'the most Greek and the wisest of the poets' acquires its new beneficiary. In a replay of the famous quarrel between philosophy and poetry Plato replaces Homer and turns into the king of the poets. This means that he is accepted as the best authority for guidance in life by a man who wanted both to retain his Hellenism and to pursue his quest for wisdom. But in the present context this wisdom is culturally determined and may be identified with one constituent element of Greek identity. As a member of a city at the edge of the Greek world that has to fight permanently for its survival,[34] Hieroson realises the need for an authoritative educator in the Greek way of life on both the personal and the communal level and strongly believes that Plato is the best candidate from the great men of the past. That is why he calls him a poet and considers him Homer's successor and superior.

[33] The erotic connotations function of course as a subtext given that most of these terms have non-erotic first meanings: for example, ἐντυγχάνω was mostly understood as 'to read' in Dion's times.

[34] That the Borysthenites live under the constant threat of Scythian invasion is a motif that runs throughout the text (cf. 4–7, 15–16, 27.14–15).

It is time to move from the fiction to the reception, or from the discursive to the dramatic level of the *Borysthenitícus* and start wondering what was Dion's purpose when he put into Hieroson's mouth Plato's apparently false classification among the poets. Dion's familiarity with the Platonic dialogues is so well documented, not least by the passage under discussion itself, that explaining away the evidence as insignificant is not an option.[35] It may be the case that he would like to remind the reader of the poetical features of Plato's texts.[36] Indeed the reference to his freedom of style and his affinity with Homer in language seem to point in this direction. Yet the question remains: what was the reason for bringing to the fore Plato's poetical *persona* in that particular oration? I suspect that an answer is likely to be found in the cultural politics of Dion's time. Living under the Romans Dion had to negotiate, reconstruct and reaffirm Hellenism and explore its boundaries.[37] As an educated Greek with powerful connections, a public speaker and popular philosopher, he was responsible for the preservation of his cultural tradition. He has assumed therefore the role of earlier educators of the community (poets, lawgivers, philosophers) and has a concern for the proper reception of all the major figures of the past. That is why in the *Borysthenitícus*, an oration with particular emphasis on issues of identity, he emphasises the rift between Homer and Plato so that he may later heal it. Dion the narrator detaches himself from Hieroson's partisan attitude and claims both authors as his intellectual ancestors and sources of inspiration (cf. 29.5). When he openly calls Plato a poet, then, he wishes to bridge a gap that was still kept open and to reclaim him for a larger section of Greeks than the students of philosophy alone.[38]

For our present purposes it is important to notice that there is no hint in the text that the notion of Plato the poet would take Dion's

[35] For Plato's presence in Dion's orations see Trapp (2000a). On Dion and Homer see Gangloff (2006) 154–64; Kim (2008) 601–4.

[36] Russell (1992) 224. [37] Swain (1996) 187–241.

[38] Cf. Trapp (2000a): 'the Plato [Dio] uses in his discourses is mainstream Plato, the works most familiar to rhetorical education and the cultivated general public' (238). In a similar vein, Maximos of Tyre undertakes in his *Or.* 4 to prove the continuity or essential identity in doctrines about the gods between the poetry of Homer and Hesiod and the major philosophical schools except for the Epicureans. See Trapp (1997) 31–3.

audience by surprise. No explanation is offered nor is any objection raised. It is a fair inference that the author of the *Borystheniticus* draws on a tradition, well established by his time, of associating Plato with poetry and treating his dialogues as pieces of dramatic literature. The evidence from the oration seems to add one more testimony for the survival of that stream of Platonic reception that viewed Plato as a prose poet, a successor to Homer and the playwrights, in the first Christian centuries.

St Basil

It is perhaps impossible to know whether Dion would have thought of the comic elements of Plato's dialogues when attributing him the title of the 'wisest of the poets'. But the next author leaves no doubt that he considers Plato a writer of a really merciless and powerful comedy. In a letter to Diodoros, later bishop of Tarsos, at the time presbyter of Antioch, which is dated to AD 372 or 373, **St Basil** comments on two books composed and sent to him by his addressee. The largest of them seems to have comprised substantial portions of a dialectical interchange in direct speech, if not itself written in dialogue form. This led St Basil to a meticulous critique of dialogue-writing, underlining the difficulties involved in the drawing of successful and functional characters. To stress the demanding literary skills expected from a writer of dialogues, he refers Diodoros to the various styles of some ancient practitioners of the genre:

Ἐκεῖνο πάντως συνεῖδέ σου ἡ ἀγχίνοια ὅτι καὶ τῶν ἔξωθεν φιλοσόφων οἱ τοὺς διαλόγους συγγράψαντες, Ἀριστοτέλης μὲν καὶ Θεόφραστος, εὐθὺς αὐτῶν ἥψαντο τῶν πραγμάτων, διὰ τὸ συνειδέναι ἑαυτοὺς τῶν Πλατωνικῶν χαρίτων τὴν ἔνδειαν. Πλάτων δὲ τῇ ἐξουσίᾳ τοῦ λόγου ὁμοῦ μὲν τοῖς δόγμασι μάχεται, ὁμοῦ δὲ καὶ παρακωμῳδεῖ τὰ πρόσωπα, Θρασυμάχου μὲν τὸ θρασὺ καὶ ἰταμὸν διαβάλλων, Ἱππίου δὲ τὸ κοῦφον τῆς διανοίας καὶ χαῦνον, Πρωταγόρου τὸ ἀλαζονικὸν καὶ ὑπέρογκον. Ὅπου δὲ ἀόριστα πρόσωπα ἐπεισάγει τοῖς διαλόγοις, τῆς μὲν εὐκρινείας ἕνεκεν τῶν πραγμάτων κέχρηται τοῖς προσδιαλεγομένοις, οὐδὲν δὲ ἕτερον ἐκ τῶν προσώπων ἐπεισκυκλεῖ ταῖς ὑποθέσεσιν· ὅπερ ἐποίησεν ἐν τοῖς Νόμοις. (135.1.20–32 Courtonne)[39]

[39] I follow the text and take the variant readings from the apparatus of Courtonne (1961) 49–51. For the letter 135 see also Deferrari (1928) 306–11; Kustas (1981) 260 n. 147;

That is what you in your sagacity know well, that of those pagan philosophers who composed dialogues, Aristotle and Theophrastos dealt with their subject in a straightforward manner, because they were themselves aware they lacked the Platonic graces. Plato, however, having command of his prose at the same time he fights with their doctrines and he satirises their characters, namely reproaching the rash and reckless Thrasymachos, the intellectually vain and frivolous Hippias, the arrogant and boastful Protagoras. But whenever he brings into his dialogues unnamed characters, he has these answering questions for the sake of clarifying the topic, but he brings nothing else from their characterisation to the discussions. This what he did in the *Laws*.

This is evidently a highly significant piece of evidence not only for the history of literary criticism,[40] but especially for the reception of Plato in early Byzantium. St Basil's digression to the writings of the 'non-Christian philosophers' amounts to a succinct summary of some principles of Platonic interpretation current in the late fourth century AD. The construction of the passage demonstrates that these comments were not simply the expression of personal preferences of an individual reader. The use of technical vocabulary and the content of the section imply instead a coherent system of critical theory on the genre of dialogue, presumably a common currency among the rhetorical and philosophical schools of the day. At the same time, the matter-of-fact reference to the poetics of the Platonic dialogue in the course of a personal correspondence means that it was considered customary for an educated Greek from the eastern part of the Empire to be well acquainted with Plato and his writings (συνεῖδέ σου ἡ ἀγχίνοια).[41] In fact, Diodoros, himself an emulator of the philosopher in authorial

Rousseau (1994) 44. The alternative dates have been suggested by Fedwick (1981) I:13 (after 7 September 372) and Deferrari (1928) 306 n. 1 and Courtonne (1961) 49 (arguing for 373). For St Basil's life and work see Fedwick (1981); Gain (1985); Rousseau (1994) and (2008); Chadwick (2001) 331–47; Webb (2008b). For Diodoros see Jülicher (1903) 713–14.

40 Cf. Deferrari (1928) 306 n. 1. That the letter was considered an instance of literary criticism is indicated by the full title preserved in the manuscript tradition: Διοδώρῳ πρεσβυτέρῳ Ἀντιοχείας περὶ τοῦ πῶς χρὴ συντάσσειν τὰς βίβλους.

41 Basil himself was so well versed in Plato that he emulated him by using his attack on the sophistry as a model for his own struggle with heresy: he attempted to discredit his Arian opponents by portraying them as sophists fighting against the true philosophy of Orthodoxy (Boyarin 2008, 222–3). For Basil as a student in Athens see Rousseau (1994) 27–60, while the educational institutions and practices of the fourth century are discussed by Cameron (1998).

terms, should be expected to be particularly knowledgeable about his predecessor's literary production.[42]

This passage comes in the middle of the criticism of Diodoros' longer work. It may be inferred from the letter that both compositions were polemics against Arians (1.5–6; 1.15–16; 2.15–16).[43] Diodoros had evidently attempted not only to refute his opponents' theses but to attack them personally as well (2.6–7), presumably by sketching satirical portraits of them. St Basil challenges the expediency of such a technique and criticises the author's poor performance precisely in matters of characterisation. In his view the abuse of parody, especially when direct speech is involved, disrupts the flow of the argumentation and weakens the vehemence of the intended refutation (1.15–19). On the basis of a distinction between the ideas themselves (τὰ πράγματα 1.10; 2.7) and the characters who stand for them (τὰ πρόσωπα 2.5,8), he moves on to offer some advice for a successful characterisation, useful for Diodoros' future literary attempts (2.12–14). He accepts the introduction of characters for personal invective only if it contributes to the moral education of the reader (2.2–3). This requirement is met when the butt of satire is a named individual, notorious for his insolent behaviour, who speaks in character (2.3–6). But in the case of an anonymous interlocutor (ἀόριστον . . . τὸ διαλεγόμενον 2.7–8), resisting any possible identification, this device is out of place. Diodoros then must have introduced either (a) well-known

[42] The literary form of Diodoros' works cannot be determined with certainty. Kustas (1981) takes both as dialogues (260 n. 147). The letter explicitly speaks in terms of a possible dialogic form only for the largest one: the text is described as διαλογικαῖς χάρισι κεκομψευμένον (1.11–12), featuring γλυκύτητας . . . διαλεκτικάς (1.16–17) with one of its characters referred to as διαλεγόμενον 'interlocutor' (2.8). The shorter work is also decribed in similar terms as including 'the objections of the opponents (τῶν ὑπεναντίων) and the replies to them' (1.5–6). On the other hand, the previous phrase need mean no more than the arguments of the opponents were presented, not the opponents themselves as characters. Furthermore, the supposed dialogic parts of the second work are said to be 'inserted in between' (1.15), a phrase that tells against a dramatic writing – though perfectly compatible with a narrative dialogue. All things said, the overall tone of the letter suggest that at least one of Diodoros' books was written in dialogue form, even if hard evidence is difficult to find.

[43] Diodoros was one of the leaders of the orthodox in Antioch. See Rousseau (1994) 290, 305 n. 149. On St Basil's theology in relation to ancient Greek philosophy see now Hildebrand (2007); Delcogliano (2010). For a survey of the orthodox and heretics in the fourth century see Chadwick (1998).

Arians who did not speak in character or (b) unidentifiable, perhaps fictional, figures, or (c) both. His mistake was that he failed to achieve the expected conjunction between character and speech.[44]

It is in this context that St Basil assumes for a while the role of the historian of literature. His immediate aim is to remind his friend how difficult it is to be an articulate expounder of ideas and a competent literary artist at the same time. Aristotle and Theophrastos, aware of their limitations as authors, were wise enough to focus on the content of their writings (αὐτῶν ἥψαντο τῶν πραγμάτων).[45] But Plato stands apart from the rest, in a class of his own, as the unsurpassed virtuoso of dialogue-writing.[46] The reason is that he was the only one capable of harmoniously combining doctrinal refutation (τοῖς δόγμασι) with personal invective (τὰ πρόσωπα). To put it in modern jargon, the philosophical and literary aspects of his dialogues form a unity.[47] St Basil's theorising on the proper use of named and unnamed characters is modelled on Plato's practices in dialogues like the *Protagoras* and the *Laws*. The message behind this brief 'lecture' on Platonic interpretation is this: if Diodoros wishes to include satirical portraits in his dialogues, let him be taught the proper lessons from the master himself.[48]

Plato is eulogised because of his unparalleled talent in refuting his opponents by argumentative and literary means. Given the immediate concerns behind the composition of Letter 135 it comes as no surprise that it is the satirical aspect of his artistry that is being emphasised: since Diodoros wrote dialogue(s) to refute his

44 Cf. Kustas (1981) 'What Basil is asking for is a special union . . . of ethos and logos' (260 n. 147).

45 For Aristotle as a wrtiter of dialogues see Gigon (1987) 248–53.

46 As Courtonne (1961) rightly remarks, 'Basile veut faire des dialogues de Platon une catégorie supérieure, un sommet auquel ne peuvent atteindre les œuvres littéraires du même genre' (50 n. 1).

47 St Basil here seems to anticipate the modern schools of interpretation who read Plato's dialogues as both philosophical and literary works.

48 Cf. Hirzel (1895) 'Für die Griechen war das klassische Vorbild Platon' (II 375). Interestingly, only a decade before Diodoros, Apollinarios the younger, in response to Julian's edict according to which Christians were banned from teaching pagan literature, had composed dialogues containing the basic truths of the Gospel and the Apostolic teachings, in imitation of Plato (Sokrates *Eccl. Hist.* 3.16.16–19 Hansen). For the Greek writers of dialogues in early Christian literature see Hirzel (1895), II 366–75; Edwards (2007b) 134–6; König (2008) 102–6.

opponents, so Plato is assumed to have done the same. The text makes it clear that the image of 'Plato the caricaturist' is expressed in terms of theatre, in particular comedy, criticism. The selection and taxonomy of the Platonic characters underline the parallel with the roles from the comic stage. St Basil speaks of 'Thrasymachos the reckless', 'Hippias the fool' and 'Protagoras the boastful', in the best tradition of comic typology. His choice of these particular interlocutors may also not be unrelated to the dramatic qualities of *Republic* 1, *Hippias Major* (and *Minor*) and the *Protagoras*. More indicative, however, is the language he uses to describe Plato's role as a satirist: Πλάτων . . . παρακωμῳδεῖ τὰ πρόσωπα. The Church Father employs a very rare verb that is used only three times elsewhere in extant literature. It occurs twice in the ancient scholia on Aristophanes meaning 'to parody'.[49] The direct reference to paratragedy in both instances is a proof that the verb was a familiar *terminus technicus* among the critics. The only literary author, except for St Basil, who uses the word is Athenaios. Interestingly, he does so while introducing a quotation from Aristophanes' *Triphales* (*PCG* III.2 556), in which the comedian laughs at the linguistic peculiarities of the Ionians.[50] Admittedly there is no sign of paratragedy in the quoted fragment. But the rarity of the verb, the conciseness of his sentence and, above all, the Aristophanic context suggest that Athenaios was drawing on, or even paraphrasing, the work of commentators. It is also not improbable that St Basil intended an implicit analogy between Aristophanes and Plato. At any rate, in a discussion of Plato's style, he uses a term associated, so far as our evidence goes, exclusively with the criticism of comedy. In combination with the 'comic' reading of some Platonic characters, this is an important testimony for the reception of Plato in the late fourth century AD.[51] In other words, to view Plato as an author who had a great deal in common

[49] The texts are (a) Sch. Ar. *Aves* 842a, 132 Holwerda: μήποτε δὲ παρακωμῳδεῖ τὸν Εὐριπίδου Παλαμήδη οὐ πρὸ πολλοῦ δεδιδαγμένον and (b) Sch. Ar. *Ranae* 688, 295b Dübner: ἔθος δὲ ἔχουσιν οἱ κωμικοὶ παρακωμῳδεῖν τοὺς τραγικούς. There is a good possibility that these scholia reflect the work of Hellenistic grammarians.

[50] καὶ Ἀριστοφάνης Τριφάλητι παρακωμῳδῶν πολλοὺς τῶν Ἰώνων (12. 525a).

[51] Significantly, at about the same period a mosaicist created an illustration of the *Phaedo* in the midst of scenes from the comedies of Menander in Mytilene (pp. 238–55).

with playwrights may still have been a living tradition in early Byzantium.

A letter to an ambitious writer of dialogues by an admirer of Plato, who happens to be one of the towering figures of the Greek Church, seems a convenient point for concluding a presentation of a relatively unnoticed area of ancient literary criticism. The passages discussed so far may be seen as the extant fragments from what could once have been a fuller picture of *Plato the prose dramatist*. A number of remarks by Aristotle suggest that, already in the fourth century BC and, possibly, among the members of the Academy, the Platonic dialogue was considered a literary genre, akin to poetic compositions despite its prose form. The evaluation of Plato as a rather *sui generis* stylistic reformer who writes a kind of non-verse poetry remained a constant feature of his reception down to Themistios' time (fourth century AD). At the same time, the testimonies of Demetrios, Dion and St Basil confirm that the association with the world of theatre and its poetics had a continuous presence in Platonic interpretation throughout antiquity. This tradition may have originated during Plato's lifetime, when his dialogues were written and read in their original context of a performance culture that permeated the production and publication of most of classical literature. It is time to take a closer look at that context.

The pragmatics of publication

The performance of literature

Any attempt to reconstruct the mode or modes of reception of Plato's works by his contemporaries requires an overview of the conditions of composition, presentation and dissemination of literary texts during the late fifth and fourth centuries BC. This in turn hinges on the models of communication between the author and his public that were available at the time. This relationship necessarily must be examined in the light of specific developments in Greek cultural history that fundamentally changed the community's perception of literary production. Of importance here is evidently the question of the transition from a predominantly oral to a (more) literate society, with the corollary theme of the introduction of silent reading as an alternative reading technique.

The interaction between orality and literacy in archaic and classical Greece has been a major theme in the scholarly agenda of the last decades. The introduction of the alphabet and the appearance of the first inscribed artefacts, the erection of legal, funerary, dedicatory and other inscriptions of a public and private nature, the use of documents for administrative purposes and the building of archives, the proliferation of school education and the establishment of the papyrus-roll as a medium for the dissemination of knowledge: all these demonstrate the gradual dependence of the ancient Greeks, particularly the Athenians, on the written word from post-Homeric times onwards. The period from the mid-fifth to the mid-fourth century, in particular, stands out as the turning point in the development of a literate culture. There occurs an increase in the number of attested schools as well as in the representation of school scenes on Attic vases. Written documentation becomes conspicuous in more spheres of public life (e.g. lawcourts, ostracism, Metroon). The rise of the sophistic movement generated a significant boost in book-culture. The book-trade was emerging as a growing activity with papyrus-rolls being dispatched as far as the Black Sea region (Xen. *An.* 7.5.14). The literary evidence points also to an increased familiarity with the 'technology' of literacy on the part of the citizenry. The tragedians often employ metaphors from writing and reading, and compose passages in which illiterate characters describe letters (Euripides' *Theseus TrGF* 5.1 F 382, Agathon's *Telephus TrGF* 1 39 F 4, Theodektas *TrGF* 1 72 F 6), while the comedians go a step further and put these letters on stage (Kallias' *Grammatical Theory* or *Alphabet Tragedy PCG* IV Test. 7, 39). Prose writers comment on the respective advantages and disadvantages of the written word (Alkidamas' *On the Writers of Written Speeches*, Plato's *Phaedrus*) and allude to their own status as authors (Isokrates' *Panathenaicus*). The inescapable conclusion then seems to be that an author of that period would address a public that found itself in the process of adopting a new role and exploring the possibilities of alternative ways of appreciating literature, those made possible by the establishment of book-culture.[52]

A consequence of this sophistication would have been the emergence of the solitary reader and silent reading. As texts circulate in written form their reception becomes independent of the constraints of a particular communal context. The purchaser of a book has the liberty to choose the time, place and manner of his 'listening to' the author and may repeat the process at will. Neither of these options is open to the listener of a song, speech or lecture as oral performance is by definition a linear, time-bound, unique event. This dissociation from the collective 'here and now' would favour a sense of an exclusive relationship between the reader and the text that, in turn, facilitated the adoption of silent reading as a technique appropriate for the privacy of a book-owner. As is normal for transitional stages, the new habits of reading alone and/or silently would have developed in the shade of the time-honoured ones of reading aloud and in company. In fact, the evidence for the new technique is so scarce that scholars have for long doubted that silent reading was ever a normal practice before the Middle Ages. One of the most enduring doctrines of scholarship has been that this technique was a rare phenomenon in antiquity, applied only in exceptional circumstances. It was considered such a defective method of reading that its occurrence caused amazement and called for special comment. A number of studies, however, have demonstrated the untenability of such an extreme view. The ability

[52] The essays edited by Johnson and Parker (2009) offer an illuminating starting point on the subject, supplemented by Nagy (2009) and Rösler (2009). The standard studies for orality and literacy in ancient Greece are Harris (1989); Thomas (1989) and (1992); Robb (1994); Johnson (2000a). Cf. also Detienne (1988); Kullmann and Reichel (1990); Worthington (1996a) and (1996b); Morgan (1999); Tarrant (1999); Watson (2001); Ford (2003); Pownall (2007); Wilson (2009); Eidinow and Taylor (2010). On literacy in general see Torrance and Olson (2009). The change from an oral mentality to one dominated by the written word in Classical Greece has been argued for in the most dramatic terms by Havelock (1963), (1982) and (1986). For a critical review of his theories see Nails (1995) 139–57. For book-production and readership see Knox (1985a); Johne (1991); Kutash (2007) 1–9 (technical writings); Sandin (2007) 221–5 (tragedies); Battezzato (2009). The iconography of book-rolls and vases has been studied by Immerwahr (1964) and (1973); (2007) and (2008) respectively. For Kallias' comedy see Rosen (1999); Ruijgh (2001); Slater (2002); Smith (2003).

to read in silence is in fact embedded in the very process of learning to read and write. It would be difficult to imagine that texts of a private nature or technical manuals had as a rule to be read aloud. Far from the abnormal practice of the standard theory, silent reading seems to have constituted an alternative, more private and leisurely way of appreciating a written text. It could very well be viewed as complementary to the communal experience of listening to a text being orally delivered.[53]

This debate reveals the dangers of approaching the subject with oversimplified models of the absolute victory of the written over the oral and their mutual incompatibility. Recent scholarship has rightly stressed the significance of the particular cultural contexts in discussions of literacy. The belief that the introduction of writing in any pre-literate society will lead to a specific type of changes is a clear instance of 'technological determinism'. The notion of an ahistorical 'literate mentality' that replaces, to the point of extinction, an oral one seems too much modelled on the experiences of the early modern West. Significantly, these experiences played a major role in the reconstruction of the consequences of literacy in ancient Greece. Alphabetical writing was instrumental in opening up new opportunities for storing and transmitting knowledge in post-Geometric societies. But the adoption of the new technology does not mean that pre-literacy methods became obsolete. The Greek world for long displayed features of 'residual oralism', a state in which writing is used in the service of the spoken word. Patterns of orality, in fact, never ceased to manifest themselves in the public and private life of the Greeks. Therefore, instead of viewing the fourth century as a time when the written texts finally

[53] As Gilliard (1993) rightly remarks 'the predominance of orality does not mean exclusivity, either in writing or reading' (694). The founding study for the thesis in favour of an exclusively oral character of reading in antiquity is Balogh (1927). He was followed, among others, by Clark (1931) and Achtemeier (1990). Knox (1968) was the first to challenge this view. Among the supporters of the presence of silent reading in classical Greece are Svenbro (1987); Gilliard (1993); Gavrilov (1997) with a useful overview of the evidence; Burnyeat (1997); Svenbro (1999). For a brief summary of the debate see Battezzato (2009) 6–18; Johnson (2010) 4–9. Although one should in principle avoid the identification between the solitary and the silent reader (Gilliard 1993, 692 n. 22) there is no doubt that a classical Athenian would have been less prone to read silently in the presence of others than in solitude.

won the day, it is more accurate to speak of a period of greater interaction between the old and the new.[54]

The composition and dissemination of literature brings out this phenomenon brilliantly. Written texts were certainly available from early on but their function was largely more that of a companion to the oral presentation of the relevant work. The majority of literary production of the classical period was meant for performance in the presence of an audience at public or private ceremonial gatherings. The recitation of Homer and epic poetry was a standard feature of the Panathenaia and other festivals. Choral lyric was sung and danced in honour of victors of the Panhellenic Games and at religious festivities. Monody, elegy and iambos were heard mostly in more private occasions, such as a symposion, a wedding, a funeral. The increasing impact of theatrical performances on audiences all over Greece hardly needs mentioning. Not only poetry but a number of prose genres were also intended for public performance. The three types of oratory comprised speeches delivered in the Assembly, public ceremonies and the courts. Herodotos is said to have given readings of his *Histories* at Olympia (Luc. *Herod.* 1), although its length precluded any performance of the work as a whole. Sophists like Gorgias and Hippias were famous for their oratorical displays. Nor should one forget the omnipresence of elements of discourse like the maxim and the apophthegm that point to the oral poetics of traditional wisdom. All in all, the diffusion of literature in the communities of classical Greece was channelled primarily through the mechanism of an all-pervasive performance culture.[55]

[54] For most of the argument of this paragraph see the excellent discussion in Thomas (1992) 1–28 and 88–93, building and elaborating on Thomas (1989) 15–30, 45–60. For the term 'residual oralism' see Robb (1994) 99–101. Significantly the reading of a prose literary text remained a performance act during the Christian centuries (Johnson 2000a; Cavallo 2007; Jeffreys 2008, 835; Papalexandrou 2010, 113–16; Johnson 2010). On the origin and dissemination of the alphabet see Lemaire (2008); Willi (2008); Luraghi (2010); Woodard (2010).

[55] Thomas (1992) 113–27; Wallace (1995) 202. Performance of (a) non-dramatic poetry: Herington (1985); Gentili (1988); Nagy (1989) and (1996); Edmunds and Wallace (1997); (b) iambos: Carey (2009); Rotstein (2010) 229–78; (c) elegy: Faraone (2008); Aloni (2009); (d) Herodotos: Thomas (1993) and (2000) 257, 269; Johnson (1994a); Rösler (2002); Scott (2005) 4–5; (e) traditional wisdom: Martin (1993); Russo (1997).

It is legitimate to wonder how texts like Plato's dialogues would fit into this pattern of institutionalised performance literature. Platonic scholarship, as a rule, is either indifferent or else reluctant to raise the question. So far as it becomes an issue at all, the manner in which the author Plato communicated with his contemporaries is usually taken for granted as one unrelated to any model of oral presentation. The reasons are not difficult to surmise. Plato was a prose writer, therefore more dependent on books and readers for his publicity than any of the poets. In general, it is the prose texts that are more associated with the 'book-culture'. As well as displaying their competence as oral performers the Sophists contributed immensely to the promotion of the written text as a means for disseminating ideas. Only one generation younger than Herodotos, Thoukydides seems to have written for a public more permanent than the audience of a public reading (1.22.4), while the later historians followed his lead. Isokrates stands apart from the orators of his time as his compositions were meant for a reading public (cf. *Philip* 25–6). Many prose writings, such as medical treatises or theoretical manuals (τέχναι), obviously addressed themselves to a specialised public and would not be so well accommodated in a performance context. More significantly, Plato wrote philosophy. Owing to their content these types of texts put a considerable demand for attentiveness and meditation on the reader. Their proper understanding requires rather the thinker-friendly conditions of privacy. It is not accidental that the Presocratics, almost in their entirety, became known primarily as authors: Anaxagoras was considered the first one to have his book circulated in the market (Diog. Laert. 2.11). In any case, by the time Plato enters the field a growing reading public has been established, as people could appreciate literary (and non-literary) texts alike outside the context of a single performance. The conclusion would be that fourth-century Greeks came into contact with the dialogues mostly as we do today, namely as private readers.[56]

For Isokrates the author and his readers see Usener (1994) 74–119; Bons (1993); Goldhill and von Reden (1999) 277–83. Worthington (1996b) focuses on the revision of those speeches intended for a reading public.

56 Sophists: O'Sullivan (1996). Thoukydides: Yaginuma (1995); Morrison (2007). Hornblower (1987) has suggested that sections from Thoukydides may have been read out in

This conclusion, however, ignores the importance of the oral dimension in the dissemination of the prose written text. The emergence of silent reading and the growth of the book-trade should not allow one to forget that reading aloud remained the common reading technique in antiquity. Writers often assume that (parts of) their work will be recited. Thoukydides' statement that his composition may not be so much of a delight for the ear (ἐς . . . ἀκρόασιν 1.22.4) indicates as much. Isokrates gives directions for the proper recitation of his speeches (*Antid.* 12). The oral aspect of reading is witnessed in the use of the verb ἀκούω in the sense of 'read'. Similarly, orality permeated the manner in which a work became known to the public. The publication of a work mostly meant that the author read his text aloud to a group of listeners and then allowed, or already arranged for, copies of his manuscripts to be distributed among those interested. It follows that the circulation of the written texts would ultimately go back to a performance act. It is not difficult to see some sophistic or medical writings publicised in this way. Presocratics who wrote in prose may have given public readings of their works, as Zenon had purportedly done (Pl. *Prm.* 127c–d). It may be inferred, then, that the aspect of performance was not the prerogative of poetry alone, but that the dissemination of prose texts, not least the philosophical ones, involved some degree of oral delivery.[57]

symposia (29 with n. 65). For the thesis that the early philosophical texts were not as a rule intended for the general public see Thesleff (1990). Anaxagoras' book is discussed in *KRS* 355–7; Nieddu (1984) 240–3; Thesleff (1990) 117 with n. 35. On early literary prose see now Granger (2007) 412–17; Bers (2010) 455–63.

57 Thomas (2003). Cf. Kelly's (1996) division of classical prose literature into '"public"... written for performance to large communal audiences in public spaces, and "private"... for personal presentation to small select groups in private houses' (152). A very good discussion on what a publication of a work in antiquity meant is found in van Groningen (1963) and Kelly (1996) 149–54. The meaning of ἀκρόασις as a testimony to oral performances is accepted by Hornblower (1991) 60, 61 (whereas Gomme in *HCT* I 139 remains sceptical). The prose usages of ἀκούω are examined by Schenkeveld (1992). For the oral dimension of Isokrates' texts see Hudson-Williams (1949); Usener (1994) 47–73. The same topic with regard to oratory in general is studied by Gagarin (1999). According to Diogenes Laertios Protagoras read his *On the Gods* in the house of Euripides or Megakleides (9. 54). Interestingly, the author of the *Dissoi Logoi*, a sophistic text possibly of *c*. 400 BC, alludes to the occasion of the original presentation of his work (ἔπειτα τοὶ ἐξῆς καθήμενοι αἰ λέγοιμεν "μύστας εἰμί" DK II 90.4.4). Lloyd (1979) has argued for public debates on medical topics in the presence of a lay audience in the late fifth or early fourth century BC (92–3). Cf. Thomas (1993) 231–7. The publication of the works of the Presocratics is neatly discussed by Thesleff (1990).

The performance of philosophy need not always be of a unique type, namely a reading in an *ad hoc* meeting of like-minded individuals. It may occasionally take the more traditional form of an address to a communal gathering in public or more private spaces. This was the case with the three Presocratics who expressed themselves in the medium of poetry and, as a result, communicated their ideas through rhapsodic recitation. Xenophanes (*c*.570–*c*.475 BC) composed epic, elegiac and iambic poetry which he himself performed as a wandering bard in various contexts, including the sympotic environment (Diog. Laert. 9.18 = *DK* 21 A1, Ath. 11.462c–f = *DK* 21 B1). Parmenides (*c*.515–after 450 BC) presented his vision of the Paths of Truth and Opinion in a single hexameter poem in the tradition of Homer and Hesiod (Diog. Laert. 9. 22 = *DK* 28 A1). Empedokles (492–432 BC) produced two epic poems, *On Nature* and *Purifications*, nominally addressed to his lover Pausanias and his fellow-citizens from Akragas respectively. The second one was delivered at the Olympic Games by a professional rhapsode, while Empedokles may have frequently recited his poetry himself (Diog. Laert. 8. 60–3, 66 = *DK* 31 A1, Ath. 14. 620d = *DK* 31 A12). By adopting the dominant mode of public discourse of the time, these thinkers were evidently assuming for themselves the role of the authoritative voice(s) in the community in their capacity as performers of wisdom. Consequently, their works were intended for a general audience and their publication was primarily a matter of poetic (re)performance. Their 'choice' of poetry instead of prose may have been a conscious attempt to subvert and transform the inherited poetic truth with the new philosophical one. Alternatively, it may be anachronistic to speak in terms of a choice because poetry was the normal mode of making one's ideas known to large audiences and, therefore, the default setting for all three. In either case, these philosophers-poets prove that down to the fifth century BC philosophical discourse could be accommodated in the existing patterns of performance culture along with the rest of production in verse or prose meant for a wider public.[58]

[58] See in general *KRS* 163–7, 240–2, 281–4; Nieddu (1984) 227–36; Long (1985a); Thesleff (1990) 114–16. Parmenides: Floyd (1992); Granger (2008). Empedokles:

The interplay between oral presentation and written circulation should also be taken into account in any discussion of the importance of the reading public in antiquity. A case in point is the postulation for the fourth century BC of a literary production exclusively for readers. The evidence is found in the third book of Aristotle's *Rhetoric*. Commenting on his taxonomy of diction (λέξις) the author states that the *agonistic* style is the one employed by the playwrights and favoured among the actors. He then offers the folowing bit of information:

βαστάζονται δὲ οἱ ἀναγνωστικοί, οἷον Χαιρήμων (ἀκριβὴς γὰρ ὥσπερ λογογράφος), καὶ Λικύμνιος τῶν διθυραμβοποιῶν. (3. 12, 1413b12–14)

Yet poets whose plays are suitable for reading *are* read and circulated. Chaeremon, for instance, who is as finished as a professional speech-writer; and Licymnius among the dithyrambic poets. (after Rhys Roberts 1984, 2256 with revisions)

It is important for a proper evaluation of the testimony to bring into the picture the pragmatics of publication in classical times. Evidently Chairemon and Likymnios are singled out because of their special relation with their public. The question is what makes them different from their fellow-poets. One interpretation has it that both write catering for the needs of (silent) readers rather than those of listeners/spectators. Aristotle's vocabulary apparently supports this view: the verb used to denote the popularity of the poets (βαστάζονται) brings to mind enthusiastic readers holding book-rolls under their cloaks, not unlike Phaidros in the Platonic dialogue which bears his name (Pl. *Phdr.* 228d). That Chairemon was aware of the status of his plays as written texts is proved by the acrostic ΧΑΙΡΗΜ[– found in a fragment (*TrGF* I 71 F 14b), possibly from the *Centaur*, an experimental drama written in a variety of metres (Arist. *Poetics* $1447^{b}20$–4, Ath.

Casertano (2007); Wolfsdorf (2009). Xenophanes: Granger (2007); Faraone (2008) 116–26. The 'paradox' of a philosopher-poet has elicited two opposite answers by Wright (1997) and Osborne (1997). Wright (1997) offers some evidence for the development of certain themes and imagery from Homer and Hesiod to Parmenides and Empedokles (9–22). Cf. also Havelock (1966); van Groningen (1971); Hershbell (1983). For the dispute in favour of Parmenides the religious mystic or the rationalistic thinker see Gemelli Marciano (2008); Granger (2010). On the supposed oral/poetic character of the prose employed by the Milesians and, especially, Herakleitos see the divergent views of Kahn (1983) and Robb (1983a). Cf. Osborne (1997) 28–31; Kahn (2003) 155–8.

13.608e). It could then be argued that both Chairemon and Likymnios belonged to the new type of ἀναγνωστικοὶ ποιηταί, who were not writing for the stage and the orchestra but for the privacy of the solitary reader. In this case Chairemon's plays would have been genuine closet dramas.[59]

According to an alternative interpretation, however, Aristotle's testimony should be read in a less rigid manner. There is nothing in the text to warrant the conclusion that these poems were not supposed to be performed. Their popularity as written texts does not mean that people could access them in no other way. In fact, inscriptional evidence proves the contrary. A production of Chairemon's *Achilles Thersitoktonos* was presented at a festival at Dodone, some time in the third century BC (*TrGF* I DID B 10). Furthermore, the context in the *Rhetoric* suggests that Aristotle thinks of diferent kinds of composition not modes of reception. Chairemon is compared to professional speech-writers not because they addressed only a reading public – not all of them did – but because his style of writing displayed exceptional accuracy and clarity, a feature usually expected from a prose author not a poet. In addition, it would be difficult to envisage that a fifth-century poet like Likymnios would write exclusively for readers. It follows that ἀναγνωστικός may mean simply a poet whose works lend themselves to reading. Chairemon and Likymnios could be equally appreciated by a reader as well as a listener/spectator. The passage from the *Rhetoric* therefore cannot be used as a testimony for the presence of a group of poets whose works became known through books only.[60]

59 Lucas (1968) 109 on 50b18; Harris (1989) 86. Rhys Roberts (1984) translates ἀναγνωστικοί as 'meant to be read' (2256). On the evidence for the existence of *Lesedrama* in Hellenistic period (works by Cynics and Sceptics, Ezekiel's *Exagoge*) see Zwierlein (1966) 134–55. Lesky (1983) uses this term for the tragedies of Diogenes the Cynic and Timon of Phleious (400), while Jacobson (1983) takes the stage production of Ezekiel's play for granted (4). Cf. Long (1985b) 637–8. For Chairemon see *TrGF* I 215–27; Collard (1970); Brown (1996). For Likymnios see *PMG* 386–8.

60 The translation of the extract in Cope and Sandys (1877) exemplifies this view: 'At the same time the poets that can be read (that write to be read as well as acted or rhapsodised) become pocket-companions or favourites' (III 146–7). Among the adherents of this reading are Pfeiffer (1968) 29; Xanthakis-Karamanos (1980) 6–8 (see 7 n. 2 for the bibliography up to then); Lesky (1983) 400; Knox (1985a) 14 and (1985b) 343–4. Sutton (1986b) translates as 'dramatic texts especially worth reading' or 'worth reading more than writing' (5 n. 9).

There is also a third possible interpretation that gives a new twist to the notion of a special type of literature. Allan (1980) has suggested that it is a mistake to translate ἀναγνωστικός as 'suitable for reading' (245). The adjectival form suggests an active rather than a passive sense while the reference is to an activity by the poet not the reader. Aristotle does not distinguish between groups of texts as such but between modes of publication. Ἀναγνωστικὸς ποιητής is someone who, instead of putting on productions of his plays or dithyrambs, reads out his works himself to a group of listeners. A number of passages in the *Poetics*, where it is stated that tragedy may achieve its effect without actors (1450^{b}18–19) but merely through acquaintance with the text (1462^{a}12–13), are interpreted as evidence for public readings (246–7 n. 7). According to Allan, Chairemon was a playwright who wrote recitation-drama, a type of play scholars usually associate with Seneca.[61]

Admittedly the *Rhetoric* passage is open to a number of different readings. In view of the premises of classical culture, however, it would be safe to remark that Aristotle's mention of *anagnōstikoi* poets is in itself an inconclusive piece of evidence for the emergence of a kind of poetry exclusively intended for silent reading. Chairemon's plays were staged a century later, so they could hardly have been intended only for reading or recitation in their own time. Moreover, the passages from the *Poetics* ought not to be interpreted as providing the theoretical support for non-theatrical tragedies.[62] The circulation of written copies of plays did not supersede, but supplemented the theatrical production. This recognition of the double nature of dramatic poetry as both a performance and a written text in the fourth century may be safely inferred from Aristotle's remark. Poets have become aware that the audience of the play is the potential readership of the 'published' copy. Similarly, readers would assume that

[61] Allan (1980) 244–6. For Seneca as a composer of *Rezitationsdrama* see Zwierlein (1966); Pratt (1983) 33–4. That Seneca's plays were intended for the stage is maintained by Sutton (1986b) 5–6; Rosenmeyer (1993) 236; Hine (2000) 39–42. For a discussion of the alternatives see Fantham (1982) 34–49, who herself favours the solution of the pure *Lesedrama*, i.e. silent reading (48–9); Pratt (1983) 15–34.

[62] Cf. Halliwell (1986): 'Aristotle should not be paraphrased as advocating the superiority of reading to performance' (341). See also Hunter (2003) 218–19.

the dramatic text they came across was in principle a script for performance.[63]

Publishing the Platonic dialogue

Let me now return to Plato. The discussion so far has not come up with a sufficient reason for the assumption that individual reading was the exclusive means for the dissemination of his works. Given the cultural premises of the time it is perfectly expected that a philosopher, active in the first half of the fourth century BC, would communicate his compositions by means of oral presentation. There is nothing surprising in the idea that his contemporaries could listen to or even watch a Platonic dialogue as well as read it. The performance context of the literary production makes the notion of a performed dialogue almost inevitable. Plato's works are representations of what certain individuals say and do in given settings and, as such, would classify along with the rest of *mimetic literature*. Since a type of performance was the norm for most classical literary genres, it would seem odd to make Plato an exception.[64]

There is one more element that adds to Plato's claims to the title of an author of performance texts. The institutionalised aspect of ancient Greek literature is a well-known fact. Poetry and most prose works were publicised in established gatherings of the community (as a whole or in its groups), carefully defined in space and time, be it a religious festival, a trial or a symposion. The authors worked inside a fixed set of conventions and with the expectations of a particular audience in mind. This referentiality and the attachment to public or private institutions is a standard

63 So Johnson (2000a) 620. Interestingly, modern theory seems to focus on reading as a performing art. The basic thesis of a recent monograph by Kivy (2006) is precisely that literary texts are analogous to musical scores, hence appreciated through performances enacted by (silent) readers. According to the words of a reviewer the author's 'compelling presentation of the case for a performative element in literature may serve to awaken us to the significance of such aspects of literary experience' (Davies 2008, 91).

64 The more so since even prose philosophical works were read in the presence of an audience. Blondell (2002) thinks it is plausible 'to envisage most of Plato's works as occasionally performed, probably by a single narrator, whether for Academy members or a wider audience, but also available in the Academy to be read and studied as texts' (25).

feature of all performance genres. In this respect, Plato's decision to move permanently into the area of the grove of Akademos takes on an additional perspective. The founding of a community of like-minded individuals under his guidance offered an alternative to civic institutions. It also provided the context for the development of new types of discourse. The prose dialogue naturally comes to mind as the genre associated with this philosophical community. Plato's output consists almost entirely of dialogues. A number of his students also emulated him (Aristotle, Speusippos, Herakleides of Pontos). It should also be noted that the majority of the pseudepigraphic texts in the Platonic corpus may be of Academic origin. The evidence suggests that the prose dialogue was an institutionalised mode of written discourse in the Academy. It then makes sense to suppose that an intended public for Plato's works, though by no means the only one, comprised the members of his own school. The significance of the dialogues for the construction of a shared identity and their role as paradigmatic literary compositions are beyond any doubt. By establishing himself in the Academy Plato created an institutional framework for the cultivation of a new genre. That his school would prove the ideal environment for the performance of his dialogues may come as no surprise.[65]

If the Academy played a key role on the lines I have suggested it would be interesting to have some information on how Plato introduced the dialogues to his associates. The silence (or lack) of

[65] For the topography of the Academy see p. 258 n. 1. On the creation and the evolution of the Academy as an institution, especially in the early formative period, see now Watts (2007). Earlier accounts comprise Cherniss (1945); Armstrong (1953); Lynch (1972) 54–63; Glucker (1978) 237–46; Isnardi Parente (1986); Baltes (1993); Ostwald and Lynch (1994) 602–16; Jones (1999) 227–34; Hadot (2002) 55–76. For Plato's students as authors of dialogues see: Bos (1989) (Aristotle); Dillon (2003) 34–9 (Speusippos); Fox (2009) (Herakleides). The case for the Academic origin of the doubtful and spurious dialogues has been made by Souilhé (1930) viii–ix; Müller (1975) 12–21; Thesleff (1982) 91 [239]. That Plato addressed his works to the members of the Academy is maintained by Thesleff (1982) 83 [230–1], 100–1 [249–50]; Miller (1995) 239–43. See also Usener (1994) 207–8, whereas Hershbell (1995) 29–30 remains sceptical and Morgan (2003b) holds that Plato aimed his dialogues at a panhellenic audience (192). Robb (1994) 235–6 suggests that the dialogues were used as 'paideutic textbooks' in the Academy (cf. Depew 2007, 144). For the public of the dialogues in general see Blondell (2002) 25–8 and Thesleff (2002) who argues that Plato's dialogues were not meant for the general public. On the contrary, a wide reading public is envisaged by Yunis (2007b) 9–15 and Rossetti (2007) 17.

the relevant evidence is particularly deplorable. Out of the whole range of anecdotal material only a few testimonies may be found to relate to Plato's personal interaction with his public.[66] Incidentally, none of them may be safely associated with the first publication of a dialogue to an Academic audience. The story about Sokrates' reaction after having been acquainted with the contents of the *Lysis* is attested by Diogenes Laertios and the anonymous author of the *Prolegomena to Platonic Philosophy*. The juxtaposition of both passages shows clearly both the potential and the limitations of such anecdotes:

Φασὶ δὲ καὶ Σωκράτην ἀκούσαντα τὸν Λύσιν ἀναγιγνώσκοντος Πλάτωνος, "Ἡράκλεις," εἰπεῖν "ὡς πολλά μου καταψεύδεθ' ὁ νεανίσκος." (Diog. Laert. 3. 35)

They say that when Sokrates heard Plato reading out the *Lysis*, "Herakles!" he said "how many lies this young man tells against me."

συγγράμματα ἐξέθετο [sc. Πλάτων], ἃ ἔτι ζῶντος τοῦ Σωκράτους εἰς χεῖρας αὐτοῦ ἦλθον. Τὸν γὰρ Λύσιν διάλογον ἦν γεγραφώς· ᾧ ἐντετυχηκὼς ὁ Σωκράτης φησὶ τοῖς ἑταίροις αὐτοῦ· 'Οὗτος ὁ νεανίας ἄγει με ὅπη θέλει καὶ ἐφ' ὅσον θέλει καὶ πρὸς οὓς θέλει'. (Anon. *Prol.* 3.35–9 Westerink)

He [sc. Plato] made known to the public some texts which as Sokrates was still living came to his hands. He had just composed the dialogue *Lysis*. After having read this work Sokrates tells his companions: 'This young man leads me wherever he wants, for as long as he wants, to whatever audience he wants.'

If taken at face value, the above extracts provide valuable information for the pragmatics of publication of the Platonic dialogue. Diogenes' version, in particular, looks like a snapshot from the *Lysis* 'premiere': a youthful Plato has just finished reading aloud his new or, possibly, first dialogue with Sokrates sitting among the audience, who then expresses his (playful?) indignation at the way the young writer has portrayed him. There is nothing in the story itself that could strike one as blatantly untrue. For example, though nowadays not a commonly held view, the possibility that Plato started his literary career before Sokrates' death cannot be in

[66] There were stories about the influence some dialogues had upon their readers: the *Phaedo* led Kleombrotos of Ambrakia to committ suicide (Callim. *A. P.* 7. 471 = 23 Pfeiffer = 53 Gow–Page), while the *Republic*, the *Gorgias*, and the *Apology* won over to philosophy Axiothea, a Corinthian farmer and Zenon the Stoic respectively (Them. *Or.* 23. 295c–d). See Riginos (1976) 180–5; Gow and Page (1965) II 204–5.

principle excluded.[67] The *Lysis*, a narrated dialogue, is a suitable text for oral presentation as the reader would in practice identify with the narrator. More importantly, the description of the mode of the dialogue's publication accords well with a fifth-century date: the author reads from a manuscript to a group of listeners who may comment during the ensuing discussion.

Unfortunately the grounds for attributing historical accuracy to the story are difficult to establish. The fact that this episode is for the first time mentioned in a writer of the Imperial period, though not damaging in itself, does not speak strongly in favour of its authenticity either. Diogenes refers to it without citing any source, as a piece of received knowledge (φασί). The decisive argument against its historicity, however, is that it bears the marks of a *topos*: Sokrates' reaction is similar to that of other figures who had been used as characters by Plato, namely Gorgias and Phaidon (Ath. 11.505e). All three have supposedly denied that they had been faithfully depicted in the dialogues. These stories, which effectively accuse Plato of distortion of truth, belong to a standard strand in the anti-Platonic literature. Since in Diogenes Sokrates explicitly calls his young disciple a liar (καταψεύδε[ται]), this anecdote may well be such a fabrication.[68]

At this point it would be interesting to compare the two passages. The *Prolegomena* preserves in a sense an updated version of Diogenes' story. Plato disappears from the scene and so does the idea of oral presentation. From a dialogue read aloud the *Lysis* turns into a circulated manuscript (συγγράμματα ἐξέθετο), which Sokrates reads, presumably in solitude (ἐντετυχηκώς). His remarks are addressed to some unnamed associates (τοῖς ἑταίροις). Both changes betray the influence of the parallel story told about Gorgias.[69] Such fluidity tells against the reliability of the story, as the *Prolegomena* version comes closer to the experiences and

67 An examination of the evidence in antiquity with an overview of the relevant literature is offered by Heitsch (2002). The author, like Sider (1980b) before him, concludes that Plato could have composed some dialogues while Sokrates was still alive; in a later article Heitsch (2003) claims that *Ion* and *Hippias Minor* were among those works. For the opposite view see *HGP* IV 54–6; Thesleff (1982) 24–5 [170–2]; Kahn (1996) 2.

68 See Riginos (1976) 55, 93–4. Cf. Thesleff (1982) 148 n. 102 [296 n. 408].

69 Λέγεται δὲ ὡς καὶ ὁ Γοργίας αὐτὸς ἀναγνοὺς τὸν ὁμώνυμον αὐτῷ διάλογον πρὸς τοὺς συνήθεις ἔφη 'ὡς καλῶς οἶδε Πλάτων ἰαμβίζειν' (Ath. 11. 505d).

expectations of its readers. On the other hand, Diogenes evokes a fifth-century cultural milieu in matters of publication. Given that individual reading was no less of an established convention in the third than the sixth century AD, Diogenes' 'anachronism' might reflect a version of the episode from an earlier phase of its history. Perhaps the presence of the *Lysis*, not so obvious a choice for exposing Plato's maliciousness, might indicate a touch of authenticity. Even so, it must still be doubtful whether a true story lies behind the legend.

In any case, these passages tell nothing about Plato's activity in the Academy. The second piece of evidence looks more promising in this respect. This time Diogenes is the only source and he names as his authority Favorinus, a writer active in the first half of the second century AD. The passage occurs in a section containing miscellaneous testimonies on Plato's dialogues and it comes immediately after Aristotle's remark about the intermediary position of Plato's style between poetry and prose:

τοῦτον [sc. Ἀριστοτέλη] μόνον παραμεῖναι Πλάτωνι Φαβωρῖνός πού φησιν ἀναγιγνώσκοντι τὸν Περὶ ψυχῆς, τοὺς δ' ἄλλους ἀναστῆναι πάντας. (3. 37)

Favorinus says somewhere that it was only him [sc. Aristotle] who remained in his seat when Plato was reading out his dialogue *On Soul* [i.e. *Phaedo*], whereas everybody else had got up and left.

The extract is tantalising in its simplicity both for what is said and, especially, for what is omitted. The situation appears rather straightforward. Plato is giving an unsuccessful reading of the *Phaedo* with Aristotle alone from the original audience staying until the end. The story has a strong dose of exaggeration that verges on comedy while its main purpose evidently is to give a picture of Aristotle as the loyal disciple. Both features suggest the possibility of an invention promoted by Peripatetic authors.[70] The issue of authenticity aside, it is not easy to define the type of occasion envisaged. Aristotle's presence proves that the Academy had already been founded. But it is not clear who the listeners were. Although it would be attractive to suppose an audience of students and associates, their behaviour is difficult to justify in an

70 Riginos (1976) 180.

intramural context. Similarly, the nature of Plato's reading cannot be determined either. Unlike the *Lysis*, the *Phaedo* is not a dialogue presented for the first time to the public. Instead of delivering the dialogue from beginning to end,[71] Plato is more likely to have used extracts for commentary and annotation. The occasion then could be a lecture on the *Phaedo*.

This conclusion gains some support from the third testimony. For the motif of the disillusioned audience that abandons the speaker is possibly borrowed from the story about Plato's unfortunate lecture on the Good.[72] The story is later attested in Themistios (*Or.* 21.245c–d) and Proklos (*In Prm.* 127C, 688.4–18 Cousin) but the earliest source is Aristoxenos. In the introduction to the second book of his *Elements of Harmony* the author suggests that the reader should be informed in advance about the subject matter of a discussion. In support of his claim he cites the counter-example of Plato's ill-received lecture:

> Καθάπερ Ἀριστοτέλης ἀεὶ διηγεῖτο τοὺς πλείστους τῶν ἀκουσάντων παρὰ Πλάτωνος τὴν περὶ τἀγαθοῦ ἀκρόασιν παθεῖν. προσιέναι μὲν γὰρ ἕκαστον ὑπολαμβάνοντα λήψεσθαί τι τῶν νομιζομένων τούτων ἀνθρωπίνων ἀγαθῶν οἷον πλοῦτον ὑγίειαν ἰσχὺν τὸ ὅλον εὐδαιμονίαν τινὰ θαυμαστήν· ὅτε δὲ φανείησαν οἱ λόγοι περὶ μαθημάτων καὶ ἀριθμῶν καὶ γεωμετρίας καὶ ἀστρολογίας καὶ τὸ πέρας ὅτι ἀγαθόν ἐστιν ἕν, παντελῶς οἶμαι παράδοξόν τι ἐφαίνετο αὐτοῖς· εἶθ' οἱ μὲν ὑποκατεφρόνουν τοῦ πράγματος οἱ δὲ κατεμέμφοντο. (*Harm.* 30–1 da Rios)[73]

> Just as . . . Aristotle always used to describe what happened to most of those listening to Plato's lecture on the Good. Each one had come believing that Plato would talk about one of those things commonly considered goods, such as wealth, health, bodily strength, in a word some kind of marvellous happiness. But when the lecture was discovered to be about mathematics and numbers and geometry and astrology and in conclusion that there is one good, it must have seemed to them, I assume, completely strange. That is why some tended to despise it but others openly to disparage it.

This is indeed a valuable testimony because there are convincing grounds that it records a historical fact. Recorded by Aristoxenos

71 Allan (1980) 250.

72 Riginos (1976) 180; Dörrie (1987) 282; Brisson (1999) 418 n. 1.

73 The most comprehensive discussion of Plato's lecture *On the Good* is Gaiser (1980) with full bibliography up to then (35–7). For later references see Dörrie (1987) 74–8, 278–85; Sedley (2007) 269–71.

as a story he had often heard from Aristotle, who was an eyewitness (Simpl. *In Ph.* 453.28–30 Diels), the narrative may be considered basically authentic. From the point of view of the performance of the dialogues the following remarks are in place. It is clear that the occasion was not an internal affair: Plato spoke in a public place, presumably in the area of the gymnasium of the Academy,[74] to a large audience. The choice of the subject suggests that the appeal to the general public was intended. It would be interesting therefore to know the precise manner of Plato's delivery. The standard interpretation is that he gave a lecture (ἀκρόασις) exposing the basic principles of his philosophy. Alternatively, the possibility that Plato gave not a lecture but a reading of a more literary composition cannot be ruled out either.[75] In this case, Aristoxenos would describe an occasion at which the audience disapproves of a writer's work at the moment of its public presentation.

The ancient tradition has not preserved enough information on how Plato's dialogues reached their public. This is one of the reasons why any evidence from the dialogues themselves gains a special significance. Although the reading of books is an activity illustrated in Plato's dialogues (*Prm.* 127c–d, *Phdr.* 230e), there is one exceptional occasion at which the text read is the dialogue itself. In the introductory section of the *Theaetetus* (142a–143c) the reader is informed that the following conversation between Sokrates, Theodoros and Theaitetos is a written reconstruction by Eukleides of the original encounter, based on Sokrates' own testimony. The text is read aloud by a slave from the author's manuscript to him and his friend Terpsion. Eukleides has already described in detail the stages his work went through before reaching its present finished form (142d6–143a5) and given his reasons for turning Sokrates' narrative into a triangular conversation between the interlocutors (143b5–c5). Reasonably enough, these remarks may be taken as reflecting Plato's authorial practices and

74 Düring (1957) 389; *HGP* V 424. Themistios has Plato speaking in Piraeus (245c).

75 So Ryle (1966) 24 who claims that this failure was the reason why this text was never issued in book-form. The word ἀκρόασις may mean both 'lecture' and 'recitation' (*LSJ*⁹ s.v. II 2). True, Simplikios' testimony that Aristotle, Speusippos, Xenokrates were some of those who took notes of what Plato was saying clearly points to a lecture not a recitation. But Simplikios may have mistaken separate works by Plato's students entitled *On the Good* for notes of the lecture – as Gaiser (1980) points out (9).

decisions. It is tempting therefore to find in the frame dialogue of the *Theaetetus* evidence for the mode of composition and publication of Plato's dialogues. The idea of an official 'premiere' in the Academy and its nuances are worth exploring further.[76]

It should be noted right from the start that the opening section of the *Theaetetus* has a strong metatextual character. The interplay between the oral and the written, tacitly assumed in every classical literary production, occupies a central place as the mechanics of dialogue writing get exposed. Eukleides' text is Sokrates' narrative made readable script. The final product is a combination of memory (ὑπομνήματα 143a1, ἀναμιμνησκόμενος a2), verification (ἐπανηρώτων τὸν Σωκράτη a3–4) and revision (ἐπηνωρθούμην a4). This authentication by Sokrates points to an implicit comparison with the *Symposium*, the text of which is similarly given the Socratic *imprimatur* (173b4–6).[77] The difference is that the transmission of Aristodemos' story remained oral throughout (like the narratives of Phaidon and Antiphon in the *Phaedo* and the *Parmenides* respectively), whereas Eukleides refused to rely on the word of tradition (οὔκουν . . . ἀπὸ στόματος 142d6) and resorts to the medium of writing instead. Writing, though, invokes reading: the story remains in a latent state waiting for the reader to relay it. The act of reading restores the oral dimension of the original occasion. Now, the fiction of Socratic conversations to be re-enacted by the reader is an apt description of Plato's own works. What the slave reads has of course been authored as much by the character Eukleides (in the world of the *Theaetetus*) as by Plato (in the world of the reader of the *Theaetetus*).[78] For these reasons the conclusion inevitably follows that, by dramatising the moment a Socratic dialogue is delivered to an audience, Plato commented on his own relationship with his readers. In this context it is safe to infer that

76 For a discussion of the frame dialogue see Alrivie (1971); Harrison (1978); Howland (1998) 39–51; Velardi (2000) 133–6; Westermann (2002) 25–30; Morgan (2003a) 102–7; Stern (2008) 1–31. For the *Theaetetus* see Bostock (1988); Burnyeat (1990); Polansky (1992); Casertano (2002); Sedley (2004); Stern (2008). Cf. also Palumbo (2000); Reitz (2003); Grazzini (2007); Lee (2008).

77 On the authentication of the narrative of the *Symposium* see now Hunter (2004) 20–9.

78 In Howland's (1998) words 'the dialogue is Plato's writing of a slave's reading of Euclides' transcription of his remembrance of Socrates' narration of his conversation with Theaetetus' (10).

reading aloud was a way of presenting a prose dialogue perfectly compatible with the expectations of a fourth-century public. The oral performance of Plato's dialogues may be taken for granted.[79]

The next question is how much else may be read into the prologue of the *Theaetetus* in relation to the dialogue's own mode(s) of publication. Evidently Eukleides' description of how he wrote his work cannot be factually valid for Plato's text.[80] Similarly, it is reasonable to assume that the audience for a Platonic dialogue would normally comprise more than one person. Other features of the setting are more ambiguous as regards their supposed relationship with an 'official premiere' in the Academy. The act of reading qualifies for a kind of 'premiere', since Terpsion has never before listened to his friend's composition (143a6–7). Moreover, the relaxed atmosphere of a private dwelling (b2–3) may owe something to the meetings at Plato's house. On the other hand, the use of a slave as reader does not necessarily suggest Academic practice.[81] In addition, the fact that the historical Eukleides was himself a writer of Socratic dialogues (p. 53) indicates that this prologue raises the possibility of intertextuality. It seems therefore that the fiction of the *Theaetetus* represents one possible type of performance of a Platonic dialogue, without any explicit reference to a specific occasion.

There is one section, though, that touches directly upon authorial technique in a way that leaves no doubt that the production

79 That the dialogues were read aloud is maintained by Robb (1994) 233; Hershbell (1995) 39; Waugh (1995) 61, 73; Rowe (2007a) 50; Irwin (2008) 75; Worman (2008) 159.

80 The *Theaetetus* must have been written at any time after the battle of Corinth of 391 BC, in which Theaitetos is said to have lost his life (Nails 2002: 275–7). For Plato writing before Sokrates' death see p. 143 n. 67. For an alternative prologue recorded by an ancient commentator see Bastianini and Sedley (1995) 268 (text): III 28–34; 486 (commentary).

81 Allan (1980) 248–9. His argument against the thesis that a slave was assigned the role of a reader in the Academy rests on his claim that to read 'connoted, for philosophers at least, a public reading with commentary' and so 'readers of books who added introductory sentences, made extracts, and participated freely in discussion were not *servants*' (249). But this does not apply to the *Theaetetus*, because the reading envisaged there was a continuous, uninterrupted oral rendering of the words of the dialogic characters. Thesleff (2007) is closer to the truth when interpreting the term ἀναγνώστης in the context of Plato's Academy, as a reader specifically trained for the delivery of dramatic manuscripts (78). As he states in his most recent publication 'the dialogues were read aloud by a single person (usually Plato or someone well acquainted with the text) to selected audiences' (2009, xvi).

and reception of Plato's dialogues were targeted. Before letting his slave start the reading, Eukleides explains that his text includes only the words of the interlocutors. He decided to excise the portions of Sokrates' narration between the speeches so as to avoid producing a cumbersome and complicated written version:

ΕΥ. Τὸ μὲν δὴ βιβλίον, ὦ Τερψίων, τουτί· ἐγραψάμην δὲ δὴ οὑτωσὶ τὸν λόγον, οὐκ ἐμοὶ Σωκράτη διαλεγόμενον ὡς διηγεῖτο, ἀλλὰ διαλεγόμενον οἷς ἔφη διαλεχθῆναι. ἔφη δὲ τῷ τε γεωμέτρῃ Θεοδώρῳ καὶ τῷ Θεαιτήτῳ. ἵνα οὖν ἐν τῇ γραφῇ μὴ παρέχοιεν πράγματα αἱ μεταξὺ τῶν λόγων διηγήσεις περὶ αὑτοῦ τε ὁπότε λέγει ὁ Σωκράτης, οἷον "καὶ ἐγὼ ἔφην" ἢ "καὶ ἐγὼ εἶπον," ἢ αὖ περὶ τοῦ ἀποκρινομένου ὅτι "συνέφη" ἢ "οὐχ ὡμολόγει," τούτων ἕνεκα ὡς αὐτὸν αὐτοῖς διαλεγόμενον ἔγραψα, ἐξελὼν τὰ τοιαῦτα. (143b5–c6)

EUCLIDES: This is the book, Terspion. You see, I have written it out like this: I have not made Socrates relate the conversation as he related it to me, but I represent him as speaking directly to the persons with whom he said he had this conversation. (These were, he told me, Theodorus the geometer and Theaetetus.) I wanted, in the written version, to avoid the bother of having the bits of narrative in between the speeches – I mean, when Socrates, whenever he mentions his own part in the discussion, says 'And I maintained' or 'I said', or, of the person answering 'He agreed' or 'He would not admit this.' That is why I have made him talk directly to them and have left out these formulae. (after Cooper 1997, 159)

Possible intertextual allusions to Eukleides' literary preferences aside, the association with the typology of Platonic prose is unmistakable. This privileging of the dramatic over the narrated form is usually interpreted as a stylistic manifesto and, consequently, a chronological indicator: Plato here dispenses with the narrative form, superbly demonstrated in the *Republic*, never to make use of it again; therefore no narrative dialogue is to be dated later than the *Theaetetus*.[82]

Whether a programmatic statement of stylistic changes made by Plato the author or not, Eukleides' remarks reveal themselves as identity markers when read in the narrower context of cross-textual poetics: they define the place of the *Theaetetus* in the company of the *Phaedo*, the *Symposium* and the *Parmenides*. These works comprise a subgroup linked by the common theme of the preservation and perpetuation of the memory of Sokrates. In all four

[82] See for instance *HGP* V 64; Rutherford (1995) 274.

the action is presented through a character other than Sokrates. But each is given a distinguishing formal feature. The *Phaedo* and the *Symposium*, both composed of a narrative preceded by a frame dialogue, diverge in the finale: only the *Phaedo* returns to the opening setting by means of an address to the narrator's interlocutor (ὦ Ἐχέκρατες 118a15). The *Parmenides*, lacking as it does a frame dialogue, starts as a thorough narrative by Kephalos which is silently dropped in the second part. Its formal structure is that of the previous works reversed: a dialectical interchange in a narrative framework.[83]

The *Theaetetus* stands apart from the remaining three dialogues of the group as the only fully dramatic text from beginning to end. Unlike the *Phaedo* and the *Symposium* the frame dialogue does not lead to the familiar storyteller's speech. Unlike the *Parmenides* the conversation between Sokrates, Theodoros and Theaitetos is not part of any narrative context. Eukleides' and Terpsion's words are similarly recorded unmediated. The voice of the living narrator is nowhere to be heard. The only narrator mentioned has been dead for some years now (τὸν Σωκράτη 143a3). After the prologue there is indeed a living voice present but that belongs to a reader. As such it reproduces a written script instead of (re)creating an oral text from memory. Certain consequences follow from this 'death of the narrator'. There is some marked discontinuity between the two recorded conversations of the *Theaetetus*. If the narration functions as a constant reminder of the distance between the temporal levels, dramatisation creates the illusion of bringing the past into the present. As soon as the slave starts reading the spatiotemporal constants of the opening scene (Megara, 391 BC) are permanently suspended, to be replaced by those of the performed text (Athens, 399 BC). The only link between the two realities, namely the book (βιβλίον 143b5, c8), is only a visual not a verbal sign, soon to turn into performance. The act of reading conceals itself: the reader vanishes behind the speeches he delivers, while the author, having renounced any authoritative voice in his text, as that of a narrator

83 For a discussion of these dialogues as a group see Johnson (1998); Bonzon (1988) 206–10; Clay (1992) 118, 124–5. It should be noted that the *Parmenides* is the only purely narrated dialogue of the group.

would have been, takes on the role of a listener and 'disappears', one more member of the silent audience.[84]

The withdrawal of both the author and the reader, the transformation of the written into an oral/aural text and the effacement of the act of reading owing to the dramatic form of the dialogue are features reminiscent of the principles of theatrical writing. This impression is confirmed by no less a person than Plato himself. In the third book of the *Republic* Sokrates accepts three types of literary form: the narrative, the mimetic and the mixed style (392a–398c). Mimesis (μίμησις), defined in constrast with pure narration (ἁπλῆ διήγησις), is discussed as if it is derived from the mixed style as follows:

Μάνθανε τοίνυν, ἦν δ' ἐγώ, ὅτι ταύτης [sc. ἁπλῆς διηγήσεως] αὖ ἐναντία γίγνεται, ὅταν τις τὰ τοῦ ποιητοῦ τὰ μεταξὺ τῶν ῥήσεων ἐξαιρῶν τὰ ἀμοιβαῖα καταλείπῃ.

Καὶ τοῦτο, ἔφη, μανθάνω, ὅτι ἔστιν τὸ περὶ τὰς τραγῳδίας τὸ τοιοῦτον. Ὀρθότατα, ἔφην, ὑπέλαβες. (394b3–8)

Then also understand that the opposite occurs when one omits the words between the speeches and leaves the speeches by themselves.

I understand that too. Tragedies are like that.

That's absolutely right. (after Cooper 1997, 1032)

The association with *Tht.* 143b5–c6 is too obvious to ignore. The verbal parallels lead to the conclusion that Eukleides in the *Theaetetus* acts precisely like the hypothetical τὶς of the *Republic*: he has removed (ἐξαιρῶν b5 ~ ἐξελών c5) what comes between the speeches (τὰ μεταξὺ τῶν ῥήσεων b4 ~ αἱ μεταξὺ τῶν λόγων διηγήσεις c1–2), leaving thus only the dialogic parts (ἀμοιβαῖα b5 ~ οἷς ἔφη διαλεχθῆναι b7).[85] In the *Theaetetus* the dialogic

[84] On the meaning of the distinct temporal levels see Bonzon (1988) 215–16 (narrated dialogues); Harrison (1978) 123 (*Theaetetus*). For the impression of immediacy conveyed by a dramatic dialogue see Clay (1992) 117. For a philosophical explanation of the use of these dramatic frames see Johnson (1998) 588–97. Morgan (2003a) makes the interesting suggestion that one function of the prologue in the *Theaetetus* is to problematise the fictiveness of Plato's dialogues, namely to raise questions about their authority as pieces of literature that present themselves as faithful records of conversations (104–5).

[85] Cf. Murray (1996) 172 on 394^{b}5.

replaces the mimetic/theatrical style as the one opposed to narration. The transition from the narrative to the dramatic form produces both theatre (cf. *Resp.* 394c2) and dialogue.[86]

This generic affinity does not apply only to the fictional work of the character Eukleides but refers to the whole of the *Theaetetus*. In fact the frame dialogue is rich in theatrical motifs. Take for example the opening lines. The two interlocutors enter the scene each from different directions, namely the fields (142a1) and the port (a6), in a manner reminiscent of the use of *parodoi* in theatre. Eukleides can tell by Terpsion's appearance that his friend had spent his day in the countryside. The latter's remark that he had been waiting for some time (a2) suggests that some action must be envisaged before the characters utter their first lines.[87] But the really striking *coups de théâtre* are:

(a) *The abrupt change of scene*: the two friends move from some unspecified place in the city (not the agora) to Eukleides' house (ἀλλ' ἴωμεν 143b2). Because of the absence of any narrative framework the relevant information has to be extracted from the utterances of the characters in the form of stage directions (τουτί 143b5; λαβὲ τὸ βιβλίον καὶ λέγε c8), as in the case of plays.

86 The replacement of the theatrical with the dialogic may be inferred from Eukleides' balanced and antithetical phrase: οὐκ ἐμοὶ Σωκράτη διηγούμενον ὡς διηγεῖτο, ἀλλὰ διαλεγόμενον οἷς ἔφη διαλεχθῆναι (143b6–7). The construction of the narrative form as the matrix out of which the dramatic one is produced both in verse and prose (theatre and dialogue) reflects an evolution of Greek literary genres from Homeric epic to drama and, finally, to Platonic dialogue. Therefore Plato establishes himself firmly as a legitimate heir to that tradition and may challenge the tragedians and their leader, namely Homer (*Resp.* 595b–c, 602b, 607a; *Tht.* 152e), by composing purely mimetic dialogues like a playwright as well as mixed ones like an epic poet (for the *Republic* as a Platonic *epos* see Howland 1993; Cerri 2002). In a sense, Plato puts Homer on stage since he effaces the authorial presence and allows the narrative to be delivered by a character, embedding it in the contours of a theatrical performance. The narrator then in any reported dialogue assumes the *persona* of a messenger, tragic or comic, or a rhapsode, in which case the tripartite pattern Plato–narrator–audience responds to the traditional Homer–rhapsode–audience. This double 'filtering' of the narrated story, through a fictional narrator, may serve also pedagogical purposes: according to Capra's (2003) attractive and persuasive theory it allows Plato to depict a panorama of actions and arguments the reception of which in a dramatic dialogue might have influenced the reader in the wrong way.

87 The very first lines of the *Theaetetus* look as if copied from the opening scene of the *Crito*: 'ΕΥ. Ἄρτι, ὦ Τερψίων, ἢ πάλαι ἐξ ἀγροῦ; ΤΕΡ. Ἐπιεικῶς πάλαι' (142a1–2) ~ 'Σω. Ἄρτι δὲ ἢ πάλαι; ΚΡ. Ἐπιεικῶς πάλαι' (43a9–10). It is clear that Kriton has entered the cell and been watching Sokrates in silence for some time before his friend wakes up. It is reasonable to assume that a similar stage direction is implied in the *Theaetetus* passage as well.

(b) *The slave's role-playing*: Given the conventions of antiquity and Plato's own testimony the reading of a dramatic dialogue would be very close to acting.[88] The reader is required to adjust his delivery to suit the needs of the character he impersonates each time. Eukleides and Terpsion watch, and listen to, a one-man performance based on the fundamental theatrical principle of role-playing.[89]

One wonders whether this *rapprochement* between dialogical and theatrical writing has any implications for the performance of Plato's text. The *Theaetetus* offers a model: the reader of the dialogue will read aloud from his manuscript impersonating successively Eukleides, Terpsion and the slave who in turn impersonates Sokrates, Theodoros and Theaitetos. This sounds a little complicated but a skilled performer could meet the challenge.[90] An alternative would be a dramatised performance divided between three readers taking up the various roles. In this case the characters in both the frame and the main dialogue would be enacted by the same group of performers. They could read from a script or recite by heart or fully enact the characters in the manner of a dramatic performance – as was the case in later centuries (pp. 197–226).

The last point may prove particularly useful for any discussion of the original publication of Plato's dialogues. These texts must have become known to the fourth-century public through *all* the modes

[88] Sokrates' description of the two opposed types of reader/reciter/performer in the *Republic* proves the theatricality of any act of delivering a literary text: ὁ μέν μοι δοκεῖ, ἦν δ' ἐγώ, μέτριος ἀνήρ, ἐπειδὰν ἀφίκηται ἐν τῇ διηγήσει ἐπὶ λέξιν τινὰ ἢ πρᾶξιν ἀνδρὸς ἀγαθοῦ, ἐθελήσειν ὡς αὐτὸς ὢν ἐκεῖνος ἀπαγγέλλειν . . . ὅταν δὲ γίγνηται κατά τινα ἑαυτοῦ ἀνάξιον, οὐκ ἐθελήσειν σπουδῇ ἀπεικάζειν ἑαυτὸν τῷ χείρονι (396c5–d5); Οὐκοῦν, ἦν δ' ἐγώ, ὁ μὴ τοιοῦτος αὖ, ὅσῳ φαυλότερος ᾖ . . . πάντα ἐπιχειρήσει μιμεῖσθαι σπουδῇ τε καὶ ἐναντίον πολλῶν . . . καὶ ἔσται δὴ ἡ τούτου λέξις ἅπασα διὰ μιμήσεως φωναῖς τε καὶ σχήμασιν, ἢ σμικρόν τι διηγήσεως ἔχουσα; (397a1–b2).

[89] Ryle (1966) speaks of the reading as 'a single *diseur*'s multiple impersonation' (29). The theatrical character of the prologue is superbly discussed by Vegetti (1988) 410–13 who remarks that 'le *Théétète* produit un effet de "théâtre dans le théâtre" car les deux protagonistes du dialogue originaire . . . sont aussi les spectateurs du dialogue représenté dans la lecture, pièce dont Euclide est également l'auteur' (411).

[90] Tarrant (1996) suggests that Plato read out his dramatic dialogues in person, providing any information about the setting orally before the reading (144). It follows that the framework of the narrative dialogues was added to the text after the original presentation in the manner of implicit stage directions. Tarrant then seems to believe that the texts Plato used in his premieres were in dramatic form. Cf. Thesleff (2007). Yamagata (2005) associates the dialogue form with an expected oral performance of his texts on Plato's part when concluding that 'we can interpret the format of the dialogue as Plato's invitation to performance' (124).

of presentation available at the time. The context of the reception was in most cases what favoured a particular mode over the other. Silent reading, reading aloud and dramatisation may all have been employed on various occasions and for different purposes. The cultural conventions of classical Athens make it virtually certain that a public presentation of a dialogue would constitute an act of performance: whether performed by a lonely reader of a script or a group of acting performers the element of role-playing would be present. In fact, the very nature of the dialogues as pieces of dramatic literature, their inherent theatricality and the norms of the period suggest dramatisation as a normal mode of persentation as was the case with all the other classical dramatic genres (Attic theatre, Sicilian comedy and mime). I find it hard to believe that for almost fifty years Plato would have never attempted a full production of any of his dialogues.[91]

[91] For the theatricality of Plato's dialogues see Moulinier (1967); Mathieu (1988). On the evidence of the *Theaetetus*, Blondell (2002) makes the surprising suggestion that 'even the "direct" dialogues were performed by a single narrator in Plato's own time' (24). She seems to have been misled in identifying an occasion for private reading with an institutionalised performance of authoritative texts, as must have been the case with Plato's dialogues in the Academy. I sympathise rather with her more qualified comment in the next sentence: 'Plato composed different works for performance in different contexts, by different performers or for different audiences on different occasions' (24).

4

PLATO'S 'THEATRE'

The fragments

Preliminaries

If Plato's dialogues were the performance texts envisaged in the previous chapter it would be reasonable to ask whether there are any vestiges of this aspect of his works surviving from antiquity. This is what I set out to examine in this chapter. The reader is presented with a variety of material, literary, archaeological and philological, which may reveal an unsuspected dimension of the reception of the Platonic dialogue. Admittedly, since these pieces of evidence are miscellaneous, distributed over a great span of time, and reflect a diversity of contexts, their meaning is more often than not a matter of interpretation. On the other hand, it is precisely this openness, this richness of contextual frameworks, this variety of discursive modes that implies a persistent, alternative tradition of Platonic interpretation. This tradition seems, one might say, to tell the unknown story of Plato the playwright.

The first piece of evidence is an artefact at the New Acropolis Museum, formerly exhibited at the National Archaeological Museum in Athens (NM 257): a Hellenistic marble copy of a bronze orginal statue-group dated not later than the 370s and possibly as early as 440/430 BC. It was excavated in the vicinity of the Theatre of Dionysos and may have stood there as a choregic monument. It represents Papposilenos in his fleece-like coat carrying over his shoulder little Dionysos who, in turn, holds a tragic mask. Surprisingly, Papposilenos' face bears a striking resemblance to Sokrates', especially the ones belonging to the more 'silenic' portraits (Type A), rather than those of the more conventionalised appearance of the model citizen (Type B). The portraits of the latter type seem to have derived from an official statue at the Pompeion, made by Lysippos, whereas Type A representations have been traced back to an earlier privately sponsored work, in all probability to be identified with a bust of Sokrates made by Sotes and erected by Plato and his associates in his Academy, the existence of which is confirmed by a new reading of *PHerc* 1021. In view of the preceding evidence it seems probable *that the Sokrates of the Academy must have been modelled on the Papposilenos of NM 257*. It may be further argued that the association of the first ever representation of Sokrates with a monument evidently emblematic of the world of the stage was a conscious decision on the part of Plato. By giving his Sokrates the persona of the Old Silenos, tutor of gods and heroes at the Theatre of Dionysos, he claims that the real teacher of wisdom is the father-figure of his philosophical community at the Academy.

Another link with the world of the theatre is suggested by the taxonomies of the Platonic dialogues in antiquity. The most influential was a creation of Thrasyllos, a first-century AD polymath with a keen interest in Plato. He arranged the dialogues in groups of four, thus dividing the whole corpus into nine tetralogies. For such a division he claimed Plato's authority, on the grounds of Plato's imitating the tragedians, who competed at the festivals with a set of four plays (Diog. Laert. 3.56); a claim that became part of the inherited wisdom well into Byzantine times (Anon. *Prol.* 24–5). Thrasyllos seems to have intended to improve on an earlier incomplete arrangement in trilogies suggested by Aristophanes of Byzantium, the great Hellenistic scholar. The appeal to Plato could very well be part of his scheme to outdo the trilogists at their own game. For it is to be expected that the proponents of the trilogic taxonomy would point to the tragic trilogies as the model Plato had in mind when publishing his works. But since the tragedians actually staged four plays (three tragedies *plus* the satyr drama), their opponents could claim that Plato must have followed the pattern of tetralogies as more faithful to the pragmatics of the theatre. In other words, both trilogists and tetralogists believed they were reconstructing Plato's original division on the assumption that he was influenced by the practice of the dramatists of the stage. On the basis of the evidence from the dialogues themselves, which suggests of groups of three or four (e.g. the triad *Theaetetus–Sophist–Statesman*, or Thrasyllos' first tetralogy), and the interest of Plato's associates in the taxonomy of his texts, the association with theatre may have been a tradition familiar to the early Academy.

It is an author of Thrasyllan sympathies who seems to provide the earliest extant evidence for the performance of a Platonic dialogue. A papyrus fragment of the second century AD preserves a few lines from a treatise on the *Theaetetus* that may date as far back as the first century AD. There the author mentions that the *Cratylus* was performed first among the dialogues of the second tetralogy with the rest of them following suit. The terminology employed recalls presentations with the involvement of music. At the same time, this practice is said to have been a normal practice in Plato's Academy. Although one would wish for more text to have been preserved, this information may prove a valuable contribution to the reception of Plato's dialogues as performance texts.

Next stop are two works of the Roman period. In the seventh book of his *Sympotic Questions* Plutarch records the speeches of the participants at a banquet at Chaironeia on what is the preferable type of sympotic entertainment. There an unnamed sophist suggests that every type of performance should be banned from symposia and replaced by the productions of Plato's dialogues, newly introduced to Rome at the gatherings of a selected few (711B–C). These are said to have been dramatic presentations where each actor delivered his lines by heart with the appropriate modulation of his voice and movement. Since this multi-volumed text dates from between AD 100 and 116, these productions must have appeared in Rome around or before that period. Almost a century later we may assume that such performances had become familiar so that they could be parodied. In Athenaios' *Deipnosophists*, dated in the period AD 193–7, Larensis, a Roman official and host of the gathering, is complaining about other hosts' habit of making their cooks recite most of the *Timaeus* while bringing in the dishes (9.381f–382b). In view of the presence of dinner theatre in symposia throughout antiquity and the evidence from the *Symposium* and the *Protagoras* for the rules of proper gathering, it is worth considering the possibility that these productions may not have been just Roman novelties but vestiges of a tradition ultimately traceable as far back as Plato's Academy.

A third-century AD papyrus from Oxyrhynchos is the next piece of evidence to be considered. *POxy* xiii 1624 contains fragments from the *Protagoras* with a number of corrections and alternative readings introduced by a second hand later in the century. Although all marks in the papyrus may be taken as critical signs, a particular cluster of dots and strokes in col. XLIV, fr. 25 ii, lines 2–4 [590–2] has led at least one scholar to explain them as possible traces of musical notation. An examination of this hypothesis leads one to the pragmatics of oral delivery of literary texts in the first Christian centuries and the accompanying notation. The recitation of Platonic passages either by schoolchildren in intercity competitions or competent performers in Neoplatonic schools is a possibility. Given the demands placed on a reader of any good piece of literature, it is natural for him to get some help from an 'ekphonetic' notation, similar to the one later used for the recitation of Gospels in Church. There is nothing inherently implausible in the idea that Plato's *Protagoras* could have lent itself to such an oral performance.

The trip through the evidence for the discovery of 'Plato the playwright' ends in Mytilene, where a late Roman villa was excavated in the early 1960s. The villa is called the House of Menander because its *triclinium* is decorated with mosaics featuring scenes from Menander's comedies. The mosaics of that room, datable in all probability to the period AD 350–75, have been deployed in a T-shaped arrangement. The evidently programmatic upper zone comprises two outer panels illustrating the portrait busts of Menander and Thaleia, the patron Muse of Comedy, which flank one three-actor scene from Act II of the *Plokion* and, surprisingly enough, a representation of Sokrates with Simmias and Kebes. The presence of these particular individuals and the fact that they are depicted as having a conversation suggest that here is an illustration of Plato's *Phaedo*. Since this is the only mosaic of the *triclinium* unrelated to Menander its inclusion calls for some explanation. According to one hypothesis the Sokrates panel, along with comedy scenes, was originally part of an illustrated edition of Menander and his plays and book-illustrations of such an edition were copied by the Mytilene mosaicist. Another answer brings cultural politics into the picture: the patron of the villa, a member of the pagan intelligentsia, commissioned a scene from the *Phaedo* featuring Sokrates flanked by associates in conscious imitation of the iconographical pattern of Christ in the middle of two apostles in order to commemorate his own executed Master. The merits of these theories notwithstanding, the visual politics displayed in the delicate combination of similarities and differences between the Sokrates panel and the rest of the mosaics (pattern, attire, gestures, colours) points rather to a conscious juxtaposition of two kinds of dramatic literature, probably performed in that very room as part of the sympotic entertainment. In this case, the mosaic provides the visual equivalent to the literary testimonies of Plutarch and Athenaios.

In sum, the reader is invited to see in these pieces, from the statue of Sokrates in the Academy (fourth century BC) down to the mosaic of Sokrates in Mytilene (fourth century AD), something like the extant fragments of Plato's lost 'theatre'.

The statue

The visitor to the New Acropolis Museum, while approaching the ramp on his way to the upper floors, is confronted with an elegant and intriguing statue-group (NM 257, fig. 1). On his left-hand side, next to a votive relief of theatrical masks, there stands a Papposilenos carrying over his left shoulder the child Dionysos, who holds in his right hand a tragic mask. The work is a marble copy of Hellenistic times, possibly second century BC. The date of the original is disputed (p. 166 n. 21). Moreover, the lower part of the mask, Dionysos' head, and Papposilenos' right arm (from the elbow), left leg (halfway from the calf) and right leg (from the knee) are missing. Nevertheless, the complex gives the viewer a pretty clear impression of the original.[1]

[1] Stampolidis (1982–4) offers the most thorough examination of this sculptural complex and the iconographical issues it raises. For other discussions see the complete lists in his notes 1 and 2 (123). The first full description of the group, accompanied by an excellent drawing, is provided by Pittakis (1839). For other illustrations see Choremi-Spetsieri (2009) 254–5 (detail of the upper half); 100–1 (view of the room with findings from the area of the Theatre of Dionysos).

Figure 1. Papposilenos and child Dionysos, marble statue. Hellenistic copy of an original, bronze, second half of 5th cent. BC.

This is an interesting piece on more than one account – not least because of its associations with a number of modes of discourse. For a start the world of the theatre especially is evoked. The adult member of the group evidently testifies to that. For the sculptor has been particularly careful to point out that the hairy body of his statue is in fact the χορταῖος χιτών, the fleece-like coat worn by old Silenos in satyr drama (as the edge of the sleeve on the left wrist makes clear).[2] The features of the face lack any ostensibly non-human element[3] and the garment that is worn over the theatrical costume is the proper civic dress and a token of civilised life. Both of these elements suggest a character distanced from the wild, lascivious, revelling creatures of cult.[4] Here is the image of a figure intrinsically linked with the stage. This link is further supported by the presence of Dionysos himself and his wearing of boots, visible only on Dionysos' right leg behind Papposilenos' back, a possible allusion to stage footwear.[5] Above all, however, the unmistakable token of theatre is the mask. Held by the god in an almost frontal position it identifies him as the patron-deity of dramatic performances.[6] Besides, the group was excavated in the vicinity of the Theatre of Dionysos, a public space dedicated to the worship of the god and the appropriate place for the display of festival-related monuments and offerings.[7] There is every reason to believe that the original was erected somewhere in that area. All these factors lead to the conclusion that, from the very first

[2] For this type of costume see *DFA*² 238. According to Simon (1989) it was first used by Sophokles in the middle of the fifth century (395–7). For illustrated examples see *LIMC* VIII 2 Suppl. Silenoi 20b, 90, 97, 107a.

[3] The absence of the equine ears and tail is more than telling. An old Silenos with a horsetail is less likely to qualify for a stage character (cf. *LIMC* VIII 2 Suppl. Silenoi 17). On the other hand, one may point to Papposilenos' strangely shaped ears as vestiges of his non-human origins. If, however, Stampolidis (1982–4) is right in holding that Silenos was wreathed (127) it is worth considering whether these 'ears' are more suggestive of ivy leaves.

[4] By wearing a garment a satyr or silen is somehow vested with a role in the context of the polis, as he momentarily moves away from his familiar wilderness. For representations of silens wearing garments see *LIMC* VIII 2 Suppl. 41a–43a.

[5] *DFA*² 204–8.

[6] There is no particular reason for considering the mask a later addition (cf. Stampolidis 1982–4, 140). It is almost certainly a tragic mask, but there is some uncertainty about whether it represents the young god (Webster 1956, 42, 81; *MITS*² 11) or a female figure of the 'Elektra' type (Stampolidis 1982–4, 140).

[7] Cf. Travlos (1971) 537–9; Kalligas (1994).

moment of its exposure to the public eye, the Athens statue-group stood for a visual statement in honour and on behalf of the world of theatre.

A closer look may give an idea of how powerful this statement may have been. Here is a composition that recasts traditional material in a concise 'programmatic' image and epitomises developments in the field of performance arts. The viewer is invited to apprehend the nature of the intimate relationship between the two figures. The wise old man of the myth reappears in his new guise as the educator of the young Dionysos – a role traditionally associated with the centaur Chiron, another marginal mythical creature.[8] The Silenos of NM 257 however has taken the decisive step towards his incorporation into a human context. He assumes the image of παιδαγωγός, a social persona with which every Athenian was acquainted. But the vocabulary of civic discourse is not the only one appealed to here. The old servant who was responsible for the upbringing of the young hero was also a familiar character in drama, whose importance was gradually growing.[9] In a word, the semi-bestial member of the Dionysiac *thiasos*, the wise educator of the young god, the old *paidagōgos* of everyday life, all these merge into and are supposed to be read under Papposilenos, a predominantly theatrical creation.[10]

This confluence of discursive worlds is exemplified in the treatment of the most conspicuous elements of the complex: *the faces*. Each one must have defined in some sense the three vertical axes in which the group may be roughly divided. The viewer would not fail to fix his gaze on the upper part, where an arrangement in a close geometrical pattern results in a powerful concentration of faces. Placed at the highest level, as befits a god, is Dionysos. Unfortunately the head is missing, so any attempt to reconstruct his semantics would be mere guesswork. The only certain assumption

[8] For the traditional figure of the 'wise Silenos' see Davies (2004); Easterling (2009) 161–4. There are a number of fifth-century vase-paintings of the child Dionysos with Silenos. See *LIMC* III 2 Dionysos 686, 691, 692; Gaspari and Veneri (1986) 480–1.

[9] Green (1999).

[10] Cf. Simon (1986) 1106. The object Papposilenos once held in his right hand (now lost) adds to the polysemy of the scene, whether it is the *thyrsos* of the Dionysiac reveller (as in fig. 686 on n. 270) or, more probably, the stick of the educator (as in the figs of n. 265).

relates to his size: as a child's head it would have been smaller than the other two. It is also not unlikely that the god looked at the viewer in the same way as Papposilenos.[11] But nothing in fact can be said about exactly how the god fitted into the facial vocabulary of the group, a loss all the more regrettable since we miss the significant top corner of this triangle of faces.

Luckily enough we get some help from the extant faces, placed at the same level next to each other. On the left side the eye meets the bodiless face of a mask with the features of a young hero or heroine. As it is suspended from the god's hand with the line of hair reaching to the back of the neck it looks like a severed head. This head, though, does not belong to any individual. For the missing body is that of the actor who impersonated the relevant role. A tragic mask outside the confines of the performance stands for a lifeless artefact which, nonetheless, instantiates different types of experience (myth, performance, extra-theatrical reality). Not unlike an isolated fragment itself, its reading requires the viewer to bring in elements from the broader picture. Moreover, as an indispensable factor of theatre practice the mask soon came to function as a, if not *the*, standard reference to dramatic performances.[12] Its presence in this group helps to put little Dionysos in the right perspective as the future patron of theatre. The signalling of this attribute of the god by means of his holding a mask reflects a decisive moment for the reception of theatre in Athens, given that this is one of the earliest extant representations of the artefact in free-standing sculpture.[13]

The face of the mask is evidently to be read in association with the one on its left. Papposilenos' face is the only one attached to an adult male body. It also occupies the centre of the arrangement.

[11] This inference is based on two principles of the work, namely (a) frontality, as the statue seems to have been designed on a one-dimensional basis, to be looked upon mainly from the front, and (b) the lack of any ostensible engagement between the two figures (cf. Stampolidis 1982–4, 133).

[12] Green (1994) 77–85 has shown us how the status of masks developed from frightening objects to familiar stage props. In an excellent article Calame (1986) reflects on the tragic mask as the 'gate' between intersecting worlds and the semiotics of (re)presentation and concealment. For a rationalistic interpretation of the function of the mask as mainly a theatre prop see Halliwell (1993). On the role of the mask in Old Comedy see Wiles (2008).

[13] Cf. Bieber (1917) 80; *MITS*^{2} 32–8.

The juxtaposition of the mask and the silenic face not only invites but also necessitates their complementary interpretation. The artisan seems to have worked with antithetical pairs: the youthful, rather feminine[14] complexion of a beardless face with long hair side by side with the manly face of an old, bald and bearded silen. Age and sex apart, the main difference refers to the inherent contrast between the features of a mask and those of a person. At this point, however, an unconditional acceptance of an opposition in black-and-white terms appears disturbingly insufficient. On the one hand, there can be no doubt that Dionysos' tutor *does not wear a mask*. The vividly depicted features of an old man's face and the lack of any sign betraying the presence of a mask speak decisively in favour of this view.[15] Nonetheless, it is precisely the type of face that renders itself open to ambiguity. Satyrs were quite often depicted in vase paintings with frontal faces, a feature shared with the representations of the Gorgoneion and Dionysos' ritual masks.[16] The association with this particular type of iconography may well explain the early appearance in art of satyr masks. In general, classical Athenians tended to recognise a strong affinity of a satyr's face with its double on a mask and were receptive to comments on the interplay between the two.[17] It is also noteworthy that, even in representations of stage silens, the vase-painter suggests the theatrical milieu, as a rule, by other means (e.g. loincloth) and not by indicating that there is an actor wearing a mask: the stage prop and the actor's face fuse into a new reality, namely the stage satyr's face.[18] In view of these conventions in visual arts

[14] The similarity with the mask of a heroine, possibly Elektra, on a Lucanian lekythos of the third quarter of the fourth century is too striking to be ignored (*IGD* 44 fig. III.1,7).

[15] Both points well brought out by Stampolidis (1982–4) 125.

[16] Korshak (1987) offers a survey of the material in the archaic period (see 5–11 for satyrs). See also Mackay (2001) 25–6.

[17] I have in mind a fragment from Aischylos' satyr drama *Theoroi* or *Isthmiastae* (*TrGF* 3 78a, 5–17). In this choral ode the satyrs comment on how the masks they are about to give as offerings to Poseidon look exactly like themselves. On this highly suggestive passage see Green (1994) 45–6.

[18] On this fusion of face and mask see the perceptive remarks by Bérard and Bron (1989) 142–3 in relation to the Pronomos vase. This conforms to the tendency of vase-painters to blur the differences between the satyrs of myth and their theatrical counterparts. Hedreen (1992) has shown the difficulty of distinguishing between the two (105–17, 138) and further suggested that actual performances may lie at the origin of the silenic iconography in general, not only in relation to the stage silens (156–61, 179–80). See also Hedreen (2007).

it becomes increasingly difficult to accept the silenic head simply as a human foil to the inanimate artefact. For it is precisely a stage satyr's head. *Papposilenos' face is a mask brought to life.* A hybrid of the performance world, it reflects a merging of different identities: the mythic/Dionysiac, the theatrical and the civic (by virtue of its human-like features). It also stands in a somewhat intermediary position in relation to the divine face on its left and the lifeless imitation of a human face on its right. Incidentally, each of the three faces corresponds to the three age groups of mankind, even though none of them belongs to a human being.

In short, the statue-group NM 257 gives a panorama of the world of the stage. Tragedy and satyr drama, close associates in more than one respect, are placed under the protection of Dionysos. The god is, in turn, introduced to his new domain by a competent tutor: a traditional teacher of wisdom, an 'indigenous' inhabitant of this very world who, as a marginal figure, touches upon other realities as well. The sculpture is rich in allusions as if the artist wished to project to his public an image instantiating the spell of theatre. In the wake of relevant stylistic arguments it seems reasonable to suppose that the original either belonged to or, more attractively, was itself a choregic monument.[19] If this is correct, there is a serious possibility that the group stood at the entrance to Tripods Street, a civic space dedicated to the commemoration of performance culture.[20] In this case, the postulated association of this group, and other statuettes of the same iconographical type, with a lost satyr play, Sophokles' *Dionysiskos*, falls neatly into place: the original might have celebrated the poet's victory with the tetralogy in which *Dionysiskos* was the concluding play.[21]

[19] The latter alternative suggested by Stampolidis (1982–4) 141. The adduced parallel with the Athena-Marsyas group is a point in favour of this hypothesis. Cf. Wilson (1999) 60–2.

[20] The excavator's phrasing about the location of the finding, 'πλησίον τοῦ Διονυσιακοῦ Θεάτρου' (Pittakis 1839, 282), leaves enough room for speculation. For discussion and reconstruction of the area around the Theatre of Dionysos see Korres (1980) 14–8, with figs 1 (12) and 2 (17). For the importance of Tripods Street in the social life of ancient Athens see Spetsieri-Choremi (1994).

[21] Stampolidis (1982–4) 142–4. See also his discussion on the late fifth–early fourth-century terracotta figurines representing Papposilenos with child/infant Dionysos (130–3, with a list of these figurines in 131 n. 37). The derivation of this type from Sophokles' play had already been suggested by Webster in *MITS*^{2} 148. This attractive hypothesis

There is, however, one detail that I have so far refrained from mentioning, a feature that would strike a modern viewer as perhaps the most paradoxical of all: *the undisputed resemblance that Papposilenos' face bears to well-known portraits of Sokrates*. The really remarkable fact is the degree of similarity, to the point of assimilation. Had it been found out of context, anyone familiar with the numerous busts and statuettes of the philosopher would hardly hesitate to count old Silenos' head among the examples of Socratic iconography.[22] Given that there seems to be no recorded parallel of so close a link,[23] the question naturally arises: why does this Papposilenos wear Sokrates' face?

A first step towards the solution of this riddle would be to establish how 'Socratic' Silenos' face is, or, to put it differently, how it fits into the typology of the representations of the philosopher. Scholarly consensus has it that Sokrates' portraits are divided into two main types: type A has more 'silenic' features, while type B conforms more to the representations of the proper citizen.[24] A close look at the extant portraits in the round shows that Papposilenos has more affinities with the following heads: (i) Villa Albani, Rome 1040 (esp. in the size of baldness, the eyebrows, the flesh around the eyelids, the high cheekbones); (ii) Staatliches Museum, Berlin 298 (note the curve of the eyebrows, the length and shape of the beard, the lengthy hair, the pattern of wrinkles);

brings in the vexed question of the chronology of the original. For it suggests that this statue-group may after all be a work of the fifth instead of the fourth century. So Stampolidis (1982–4) 143, who uses it as a further support for his thesis for a date around 440/430 BC (138, 141; he has already given a summary of the alternative suggestions, 124). His arguments, based on stylistic and iconographical evidence (130–41), such as the 'monumentality' of the composition, its relation to the terracotta statuettes, similarities to fifth-century figures, are very persuasive, though not conclusive (cf. Voutiras 1994, 158 n. 104). For instance, the mask seems to point to an early fourth-century date (*MITS*[2] 32). Even the link with Sophokles may tally with a later date if one postulates a reperformance of the play. Alternatively, it is not inconceivable that the supposed fourth-century choregos had copied the statue of the original production. All in all it may be concluded that (a) it would be difficult to move the lower limit much later than the first half or, rather, third of the fourth century BC and (b) the case for a date in the second half of the fifth century is a forceful one.

[22] Save only for its strange ears as pointed out by Stampolidis (1982–4) 158.

[23] This is evidently the only classical Papposilenos who recalls Sokrates. Even its immediate relatives, the terracotta figurines, due to their mask-like faces, point more to a stage character, a caricature than to an actual person (cf. *LIMC* III 2 Dionysos 689).

[24] Richter (1984) 199. For an illuminating summary of the present state of affairs see Rolley (1999) 299–300. Cf. also Beard and Henderson (2001) 235–7.

(iii) Capitoline Museum 3 (cf. the wrinkles, the eyebrows); (iv) Hermitage, St Petersburg, inv. 2348 (esp. in the wrinkles and the thick, unkempt beard).[25] Now these heads may be evenly distributed among the types, as (i) and (ii) belong to type A while (iii) and (iv) belong to type B.[26] Despite the difficulties inherent in a comparison between copies, Papposilenos' head evidently shares common elements with *all* of these heads. It follows that it could not be assigned exclusively to any of the two iconographical types.[27] There is also a combination of characteristics that are usually identified separately in the portraits of each group.[28] This feature may be traced back to the original sculptures of the classical period.[29] A proper understanding of how, if at all, these original statues related to each other might bring us closer to an explanation of this tantalising resemblance between this Silenos and Sokrates.[30]

[25] For a commentary see Richter (1965) I 111 no 3, figs 458, 460 (i); 111 no. 7, figs 461–3 (ii); 112 no.5, figs 484–6 (iii); 114 no. 22, figs 505–7 (iv). One may add to this list figs 459 and 511. For a complete survey of the iconography of Sokrates the standard work is still Richter (1965) 109–19, figs 456–573 (with Richter 1984, 198–204). For an excellent survey of Sokrates' images from antiquity up to the present see Lapatin (2006). Cf. also Blome (1999); Geiger (2007) and Mainz (2007).

[26] Head (i) is hard to classify: Richter (1965) I 111 no. 3 takes it as a variant of type A, while Rolley (1999) 299 opts for type B.

[27] Stampolidis (1982–4) 158 thinks it closer to the type B portraits, providing as an example the Albani head (fig. 19b. In line 6 read Πίν. 19 for Πίν. 18).

[28] A case in point is Papposilenos' ears, if this is what they are. One of the strongest distinguishing marks between the two types is the treatment of the ears: visible in A, covered by the hair in B (for possible exceptions see Richter 1965 I, figs 464–6 and 500–1, respectively types A and B, partial visibility; figs 502, 531 type B, complete visibility). Now the silen's ears are clearly visible, as in type A, but look as if they are somehow attached to a head of an otherwise type B hairstyle.

[29] Alternatively, one might attribute this confluence to the second-century copy as a result of the copyist's mixing distinct features of Socratic iconography while tampering with the original head. One could point to the well-known similarities in the representations of silens and Sokrates in the Hellenistic and Roman periods, arguing that the sculptor was following the artistic conventions of the time. It is impossible to prove or disprove such a hypothesis. But it does not seem likely that a copyist would be allowed to deviate significantly in reproducing a public and, apparently, popular work of art. Moreover, I cannot see how differently Papposilenos could have looked in a late fifth- or early fourth-century context. Therefore I am inclined to believe that the likeness to Sokrates was, in one way or another, there from the beginning.

[30] There is one question that may reasonably come up in this respect. If type A is the more 'silenic' portrait of the two, then why does not the most 'Socratic' of the silens have an unambiguously type A face? The answer lies in the inapplicability of the intended identification. The face of a mythic creature resembling a man does not *coincide* with the

The assumed existence of two fourth-century originals has provided the main rationale behind the classification of the portraits. Type B heads are thought to originate from what had until recently been the only statue of Sokrates attested in the literary sources. Diogenes Laertios devotes more than one-third of the second book of his *Lives* to Sokrates. There he records the ways in which the Athenians expressed their remorse for the execution of the philosopher. They are said to have closed the gymnasia, condemned Meletos to death and the rest of the accusers to exile and erected in the Pompeion a bronze statue of Sokrates, the work of Lysippos.[31] Archaeological findings apparently confirm this piece of doxographical tradition: the basis of a statue, dated to the fourth century BC, has been unearthed next to the south door of the Propylon. The association with the Lysippean work seems temptingly attractive.[32] A head from Terme, Rome (inv. 1236) is thought to come close to that of the original, while the posture of the body and the configuration of the statue as a whole are possibly reflected in the marble statuette of the British Museum (inv. 1925).[33] As for the chronology, a date *c*.350–330 BC has been considered the most likely.[34]

Despite scholarly consensus Diogenes' testimony does not seem beyond suspicion in itself. The real problem lies in the context of the testimony. For the information about the bronze statue belongs to a passage full of literary motifs. The suppression of social activities, the harsh punishment of the culprits, their rejection by the rest of the community and the public act of retribution are standard elements of the story of the hero who is unjustly condemned, not infrequently by his own kinsmen. This impression is further backed up by Diogenes' interpretation of Sokrates' execution as one more instance of Athenians' maltreatment of 'men of letters'

face of that man. Iconography is not photocopy. Inevitably there is a lot of subjectivism in deciding which type is more 'silenic' (cf. Voutiras 1994, 160).

31 Ἀθηναῖοι δ' εὐθὺς μετέγνωσαν, ὥστε κλεῖσαι καὶ παλαίστρας καὶ γυμνάσια. καὶ τοὺς μὲν ἐφυγάδευσαν, Μελήτου δὲ θάνατον κατέγνωσαν. Σωκράτην δὲ χαλκῇ εἰκόνι ἐτίμησαν, ἣν ἔθεσαν ἐν τῷ Πομπείῳ, Λυσίππου ταύτην ἐργασαμένου (2. 43).

32 Hoepfner (1976) 107, 124.

33 Schefold (1997) 174–7. For an alternative, though less likely, reconstruction of the original as an image of a seated Sokrates see Richter (1965) I 116.

34 Cf. Richter (1965) I 110; Schefold (1997) 174; Zanker (1995) 353 n. 30. Walters (1925) 259 dates the London statuette about 300 BC.

(Homer, Tyrtaios and Aischylos are mentioned by name). His belief that Euripides in his *Palamedes* criticises his fellow-citizens for their action, despite the chronological impossibility it entails, falls neatly into the picture of the suffering intellectual.[35]

To this literary argument a historical one may be added. The erection of an honorary statue in one of the most important religious and civic centres implies Sokrates' incorporation into public life as a celebrated figure of the past. So elevated a ranking for the convicted Athenian, however, is not a very likely development in mid-fourth-century Athens, a city that aspired to a dominant role in Greek politics and in which the political motivation of Sokrates' trial was still a reality strongly felt (cf. Aeschin. 1.173). It seems more at home in the milieu of post-classical times, when Athenian cultural superiority was consciously cultivated as a compensation for the loss of political power and when most of the city's flourishing philosophical schools pleaded allegiance to Sokrates and his teachings. For all these reasons Diogenes' narrative is very probably less of a historical document and more of a free composition of literary conventions.[36]

Does the probably fictional character of the passage *necessarily* invalidate the testimony for the existence of a statue at the Pompeion in the fourth century BC? There is no way to give a final answer. On the one hand, the information may be completely fictitious and a statue of Sokrates may have never existed. More plausibly, it may well have been erected in the Hellenistic or Roman period, and local legend could attach to it the famous name of Lysippos for 'patriotic' purposes. On the other hand, there is no

[35] For the image of the victimised poet in ancient Greece see Compton (2006) 1–189. Interestingly, Sokrates as a scapegoat figure shares important features with Aesop who was similarly unjustly condemned. See Compton (2006) 154–65; Clayton (2008).

[36] Voutiras (1994) 137–46 offers the most sustained argumentation in favour of this thesis. He concludes a persuasive discussion by holding that under this story of the Athenians' repentance there lies 'keine echte historische Überlieferung, sondern vielmehr ein rhetorischer Topos' (144). He suggests, plausibly enough, that the narrative is an example of Socratic 'hagiographical' literature, a phenomenon reflecting the mentality of the Athenians of the Roman era, who projected to classical times 'ihre eigene Verehrung des Anführers (und einzigen Märtyrers) der Philosophie' (145). Arguing from the silence of the sources he does not believe that a state-sponsored statue of Sokrates ever existed and, therefore, denies the validity of the current typology of Sokrates' portraits. Cf. also Henderson (1996) 342–4.

reason in principle why a piece of historical evidence should not be transmitted alongside fictional elements. In this case there are only two periods in the latter half of the fourth century in which the public rehabilitation of Sokrates could have taken place: either between the years 338 and 324, when Lykourgos was responsible for the restoration of Athenian self-esteem, or 317–307, when the Peripatetic Demetrios of Phaleron was running the affairs of his native city.[37] Both periods fall into the limits of Lysippos' career. In view of these conflicting alternatives one had better suspend judgement on the matter. A late classical statue of Sokrates at the Pompeion remains a historical probability, not a fact.

On the basis of Diogenes' testimony, type B portraits of Sokrates have been traced back to the Lysippean statue. The reverse development took place in the case of type A portraits. Differences in iconography have led experts to assign a group of heads to a separate type and assume the existence of a second statue with which these heads may be associated. In contrast to the state-sponsored work of Lysippos, this statue must have been a product of private initiative, an offering by Sokrates' friends in commemoration of the deceased master. It has been dated to the first decades of the fourth century, although nothing is known about either where it

[37] At first glance Lykourgos seems the most attractive candidate. He is famous for having bronze statues of the three tragedians erected in some unidentified public space ([Plut.] *Vit. X Orat.* 841F). He is also known to have studied at the Academy and been on friendly terms with Xenokrates, the head of the school at the time ([Plut.] *Mor.* 841B and 842B–C respectively). There is nothing surprising then if he decided to erect Sokrates' and the tragedians' statues at the Pompeion, as a visual statement epitomising Athens' cultural hegemony (cf. Mitchel 1970, 209 n. 197 cited by Zanker 1995, 353 n. 30; Harris 1992, 642–3). Lykourgos' political affiliations, however, weaken his credentials. As a leading member of the anti-Macedonian 'party' he may not have been so willing to honour a person who, as late as the 300s, was considered by Demochares and his like an unpatriotic figure alongside the rest of the philosophers (cf. Ath. 5. 215c, 11. 508f, 13. 610f). It takes a politician more sympathetic to philosophers and with greater strength of will to ignore opposing views for the sake of such a politically charged gesture. Demetrios of Phaleron was such a man. Himself an associate of Theophrastos, he had every reason – and the means owing to Kassandros' support – to restore Sokrates in Athenian civic life. His *Apology of Socrates* most probably replies to the accusations by Demochares in his speech in support of Sophokles' proposal for the closure of the extant philosophical schools (see Gottschalk 2000, 374–6; L. O'Sullivan, 2008, 395 n. 5). Demetrios then is a more attractive candidate than Lykourgos for having honoured Sokrates with a state statue (cf. also Vogt 1999, 85). The question remains an open one (cf. Dillon 2006, 104, 202 nn. 57–59; Lapatin 2006, 113).

was set up or who made it. On the evidence of an attested posthumous statue of Plato by Silanion it has been suggested that the supposed original of type A portraits was also a work by him and was placed in the Academy.[38]

The existence of a privately sponsored statue of Sokrates has so far been no more than a plausible hypothesis. Recent reassessments of the readings of a papyrus from Herculaneum, however, seem to provide literary evidence that confirms this thesis. *PHerc.* 1021 preserves a section from Philodemos' *The ordering of the philosophers* (*Σύνταξις τῶν φιλοσόφων*), a history of the Hellenistic philosophical schools. In the papyrus fragments the author presents in chronological order a doxographical account of the heads and other eminent members of the Academy from Plato up to and including Philon and Antiochos (early 1st cent. BC).[39] Early on in his discussion of Plato, Philodemos quotes frequently from Philochoros' *Ἀτθίς*, a work in seventeen books on the history of Athens from mythical times to around 261 BC.[40] One of these extracts reads as follows:

ἐ[ν] τῶι πέ[μ]|πτωι· 'καὶ ἀνέθε[σε]ν εἰκό[να] | Σ[ω]κράτους, π[ρόσω]πον [χαλ|κ]οῦν, ἐφ' ὧι ἐπιγέγραπται· | "[Σ]ώτης ἐπόη[σ]εν". τ[ὰ] κῶ|[λα..]υς ἐπιγέγρα[π]ται [ὀ|ν]όμ[α]τα συχνὰ. (*PHerc.* 1021 Col. II 12–18 Speyer)

. . . in the fifth: 'And they put up an image of Socrates, a bronze bust, on which was written: "Sotes made it". On the sides . . . there were inscribed numerous names (words?). (after Speyer 2001, 85)

The significance of this testimony is as great as the preserved text is lacunose. Col. II is in need of restoration in a number of places but there are a few points that may be put forward with some degree of certainty. The fragment is part of a discussion of

38 Richter (1965) I 112 (with caution); Schefold (1997) 45, 126.

39 Col. II has been excellently edited and fully commented by Speyer (2001). His text is the product of the most recent autopsy of the papyrus. For another reconstruction of the column see Voutiras (1994) 154–5. Dorandi (1991) offers the latest edition with commentary of the whole papyrus (cf. also Méndez and Angeli 1992, 249–52). For the latest treatment of Philodemos' *Syntaxis* and an attempt to read it in the context of his other works see Clay (2004).

40 *FGrHist* IIIb 328, 97–160 (text) and IIIb 1 328, 220–595 (commentary) provides a full survey of Philochoros' life, works and fragments. Recent literature on individual fragments includes O'Sullivan (2001); Fornara and Yates (2007). On Philodemos see Sider (1997); Fitzgerald et al. (2004); Tsouna (2007).

Plato's paramount importance for the dissemination of philosophy and other branches of knowledge and his beneficial effect on his students and associates (Coll. I–Y). In this discussion Philodemos utilises a number of earlier sources: an excerpt from Dikaiarchos' *Περὶ Πλάτωνος* (around 300 BC) is followed by possibly three more from Philochoros' work. Nothing is known about the first one except that it may be used to bring out a disagreement between these two authors on Plato (II 6 ff.).[41] The third extract records the year of Plato's death and his age at the time (II 35–8). In both cases Philodemos refers to the sixth book of the *Atthis*.[42]

Our passage comes in between and is the only one derived from the fifth book. Although a strong marker like 'he says' (cf. II 36) is missing, the wording makes it highly likely that a verbatim quotation is meant – although it is very difficult to point out where this quotation actually stops. In this extract Philochoros mentions the dedication of a bronze bust and the name of its sculptor. A recent autopsy of the papyrus has confirmed that the name mentioned is that of Sokrates.[43] An inscription on the base attests that this is a work of Sotes, an otherwise unknown artisan.[44] This is the strongest evidence against the identification of this statue with the one mentioned by Diogenes Laertios. In all probability it is the earlier of the two. It must have been erected before 360/59 for it to be mentioned in the fifth book of the *Atthis*.[45] Granted this, it is rather improbable that its dedication reflected the will of the Athenian people, as was allegedly the case with Lysippos' work. Although it was intended for public display, we are dealing

41 Φιλόχο|ρος ἐν τῶι τῆς Ἀτ[θίδ]ος ἕ|κτωι παρέ{ι}παι[σε]ν ἐπιγε|λῶ[ν· 'τ]αῦτ' ἀνα[κτᾶται ὥσ]|π[ερ π]αραξύων τ[ὰ π]άντα μη[δ]ὲ | [λαμ]βάνων [ὁ] Π[λάτ]ων η.. | [. . .] εἰδὼς (II 6–11 Speyer). The editor translates as follows: 'Philochorus joked laughingly in the sixth book of the Atthis: "He, Plato obtains that all more or less in passing, and does not take it . . . knowing . . . ".' We cannot know whether Philochoros is here quoted or simply paraphrased. For the possible meaning of these lines see Voutiras (1994) 148 n. 64.

42 Dorandi (1991) 30–1, 86–7.

43 Speyer (2001) 90–1, who offers conclusive arguments against a reference to Isokrates as an alternative emendation would have it (cf. also Dorandi 1991, 212; Méndez and Angeli 1992, 250–1).

44 The suggestion that this image is a bust created by Sotes is made by Speyer (2001). Before that, scholars used to speak of a statue and identified its sculptor as Boutes.

45 In that book Philochoros narrates the events between 403/2 and 360/59 or, less likely, 357/6 BC (see *FGrHist* IIIb 1 252, 254).

with an act of private initiative. A few lines below there is a similar reference to a bronze inscribed bust, somehow related to a sanctuary of Muses:

ἀναθή||[σ]ειν Ἀθ[ήνη]σ[ι]ν [εἰ]κόνα πρό|σωπον χαλκοῦν,
[ἐφ' ὧι ἐ]π{ε}<ι>γέ|γραπται· "τοῦ[το] τὸ
ἀνάθη|μα..[..]περιλυ[.].πεν ἀ|πολουν[. . . .]
α[.]ινε[. . . .]πο|.ωι παρ[ὰ τ]ὸ μουσεῖον, ἀλ[λ]ὰ Κολλυτεὺς
ἦν τῶν δή||[μ]ων. (II 26–34 Speyer)

that he has ordered to put up at Athens an image, a bronze bust, on which was written: "This image . . ." . . . besides the Museion, but he [sc. Plato] was from the demos Kollytos. (after Speyer 2001, 85)

If this second image is to be identified with the bust of Sotes then we may have some evidence for its original whereabouts, presumably the well-known shrine consecrated by Plato in the Academy.[46] In any case it is evident that Philodemos quotes from the fifth book of Philochoros' *Atthis* passages that are associated with the activities of the Academics. According to the tradition, Plato established himself as a teacher in the Academy not long after his fortieth birthday. It may be suggested therefore that a statue or, rather, bust of Sokrates made by Sotes was erected in the area of the Academy, in a place appropriated by Plato and his associates, as a private offering at a date between 387 and 360 BC.[47]

46 There is uncertainty as to the exact location of the sanctuary. The sources are not quite clear about whether the *mouseion* established by Plato is to be found in the public ground of the gymnasium (so, for instance, Wycherley 1962, 4) or whether it was part of his private property nearby (so Dillon 2003, 10). He may very well have founded a sanctuary in both places. It is also not known whether the altar of the Muses in the Academy mentioned by Pausanias (1. 30. 2) pre-dated Plato. For a judicious survey of the evidence and some suggested answers see Billot (1989) 743–4, 781–2, 785–6, who opts for the *mouseion* in Plato's house or garden as the likeliest place for the erection of privately sponsored statues. She cites the parallels of the Graces dedicated by Speusippos (743) and Silanion's Plato offered by Mithridates (785).

47 Voutiras (1994) holds that both references to a bronze image relate to the same artefact and, convincingly, finds a connection between the founding of Plato's school, the consecration of the sanctuary of the Muses and the statue of Sokrates, and therefore dates Sotes' work to the late 380s or 370s (155–6). Speyer (2001), on the other hand, leaves it open whether the reference here is to the same bust or to a second one, a copy of the first, dating by implication the production of the original bust shortly after Sokrates' execution (94–5). Now we may safely dispense with the ingenious but incorrect suggestions that the represented figure was either Apollo (Gaiser 1982, 98) or Plato himself (Rolley 1999, 299).

Granted the soundness of the argument so far, there follow a number of interesting points for the construction of Sokrates' iconography. First, we may safely dispense with the received opinion that the sculptor of the original of the type A portraits is Silanion. Second, we seem to have documentation for what was so far assumed on iconographical criteria: the existence of an early statue antedating the Lysippean one by some decades. This could have possibly been the earliest portrait of the philosopher. Third, the private nature and the personal tone of such a 'gesture' seem also to have been confirmed. Long before any official rehabilitation was under its way, at a time when Sokrates was for many Athenians a deservedly convicted 'enemy of the people', Plato's dedication of the statue reminded everyone that the spirit of the master lived on in the groves of the Academy; and that the students and friends frequenting the gymnasium and his garden were inspired by the life and teachings of the midwife's son. Outside the walls of the city another community is determined to keep the memory of that convicted citizen alive. The outcast had turned into a founding figure.

It is in this context that the genesis of Socratic iconography may be properly understood. As the Academy statue was the first of its kind there was no precedent to provide a helpful parallel. A portrait from life was obviously out of the question, while it is quite unlikely that the comic masks would be of any help.[48] Sotes was about to create an image that would depend heavily on the patron(s)' ideas on the matter. That is why the decision for

[48] Sokrates appears on stage in a number of comedies (Aristophanes' *Clouds*, Ameipsias' *Connus*, Eupolis' *Flatterers*). It is a reasonable assumption that, as a rule, the mask-maker was not meant to achieve a life-like resemblance to the actual person. If necessary, the reproduction of some striking feature(s) would be enough since the characters were usually identified by name. For the use of portrait-masks on the fifth-century comic stage see Dover (1968); Welsh (1979); Olson (1999). A story preserved by Ailianos (*Var. Hist.* 2. 13) might indicate that portrait-masks had been used for Sokrates all along. Indeed, there have been recorded some, admittedly doubtful, examples of masks of the 'Sokrates' type dating from the last quarter of the fourth century BC: see *MIMC*[3] 16; (AT 128) 183; (KT 16) 189; (UT 11) 201. Given the conventional nature of Sokrates' caricature in comedy, however, it is not clear how far we may speak of a real portrait here. In the conclusion of his discussion on the Sokrates of the *Clouds* Dover (1968) hits the mark: 'the result of [the mask-maker's] attempt to portray a real person would resemble what he had often done before in portraying fictitious characters' (28).

an appropriation of basic elements from Silenic iconography is all the more telling. Admittedly one may think that this transition was less abrupt than normally believed. There have been found, for instance, late fifth-century images of Silenos with features that later became associated with Sokrates.[49] It may also be the case that the frequent references to his unpleasant physical appearance in comedy and the Socratic literature had also to some extent prepared the ground.[50]

This impression, though, is only partially justified. For we lack the necessary evidence to reach some conclusions as to how far this process of 'assimilation' was underway before Plato. It is not impossible that it was in his writings that the new image either originated or else was fully developed.[51] As for the relation to actual satyric representations, figures like the one on the coin from Katane evidently could not have served as a model. In the Academy statue the grotesque features of the traditional imagery have been sufficiently 'tamed' resulting in a humanised appearance. This may be due to a number of reasons (not necessarily incompatible with

[49] Such as the drachma coin from Katane dated around 410 BC (*LIMC* VIII 2, p. 773 fig. 180).

[50] Sokrates' satyr-like ugliness was a *topos* in his followers' works (cf. Plat. *Tht.* 143e, *Phd.* 117b, *Symp.* 215a–b; Xen. *Symp.* 4.19, 5.9). Zanker offers an attractive hypothesis for the development of the Socratic imagery: the comedians' impoverished intellectual is taken up by Sokrates' enemies and detractors, who were the first to liken him to the satyrs, owing to the connotations of a base nature that such a comparison implied. Sokrates' friends answer back by adopting the new image and giving it a positive content (Zanker 1995, 32–9). Cf. MacLean (2007) 78–82.

[51] The loss of the Socratics' writings, except those of Plato and Xenophon, makes it very difficult to prove or disprove this view. On the present state of evidence there is one text outside the Platonic corpus in which the new theme may have appeared for the first time, namely Phaidon's *Zopyros*. The dialogue features the namesake intellectual who introduced into Greece physiognomics, that is the science of recognising character through a careful examination of physical appearance. In an extensive fragment the story is told that Alkibiades and the rest laughed at Zopyros when he said that Sokrates' features betrayed a stupid, immoral, licentious man. But Sokrates himself confirmed the truth of this remark, claiming that he was able to overcome his deficient nature only through philosophy (the testimonies are to be found in *SSR* I C 49). The story of Zopyros has been recently discussed by MacLean (2007) 68–75 and Boys-Stones (2007) 22–33, who both accept the authenticity of Phaidon's dialogue, unlike Trapp (2007b) 59 n. 42. For a thorough discussion of the fragments and the related passages see Rossetti (1980) 183–98. For the relevance of another Socratic work, Antisthenes' *On the Sophists* or *Physiognomonikos* see Rossetti (1980) 187 n. 10. On physiognomy in antiquity see Vogt (1999) 45–107; Boys-Stones (2007).

each other). Up to a point this reworking is expected when one makes the portrait of a human being. It may also indicate a will to avoid the negative connotations of a satyr-like appearance by bringing in some 'unmistakable features of propriety'.[52] Or this combination of satyric and human elements was already there in that artefact from which Sotes was inspired for his own statue. For it seems all the more likely that *the Sokrates of the Academy could have been modelled on the Papposilenos of the Theatre of Dionysos*.[53]

This adaptation must surely reflect a deliberate decision to associate Sokrates with those figures that exercised an authority over the collective consciousness of the community. On such a reading, Sokrates shares with satyrs an ambiguous position as a not quite human creature at the margins of society. Much more significantly, the choice of that particular statue-group as a model amounts to a powerful statement on the part of the Academics. By making Sokrates a direct descendant, in terms of iconography, of the dominant figure of that group, the artist implicitly provided a context for the reception of his work. Papposilenos the Dionysos-bearer is the wise old man, the repository of ancient wisdom, the teacher of young Dionysos. At the same time, he is a creation of the stage, a meeting point of on-, off- and beyond-stage realities, part of a work invoking and commemorating theatre. Both these aspects are meant to be read in and through Sokrates' portrait. Here is also a wise old man whose teachings will educate those young men frequenting the Academy. They will come to know him and the story of his life through his character in the dialogues of Plato. A couple of decades after his death, Sokrates returns to the world of the living as a 'mythological' and literary hero for the local community of friends. This Papposilenos, a *persona* created by and disseminated through the writings produced in the Academy,[54]

[52] Zanker (1995) 36. [53] Stampolidis (1982–4) 159.

[54] Those readers of Plato familiar with both statues would not have missed the implied reciprocity between the faces of Sokrates and Silenos. As Worman (2008) remarks, 'Plato's dialogues consistently portray Socrates as a humorous, irreverent, *silenos* figure' (154). This tallies well with Hadot's (1974) characterisation of Sokrates as a figure who 'devient donc un *prosopon*, c'est-à-dire un interlocuteur, un personnage, un masque donc, si l' on se souvient de ce qu'est le *prosopon* du théâtre' (55).

is a teacher of a new kind of wisdom that brings (young) men to realise their potential not for theatre but for (Plato's) philosophy.[55]

NM 257 was a popular choregic monument placed in one of the most charged civic spaces. The decision to use its Silenos as a model for the first statue of Sokrates erected in a private enclosure at the other end of the network of the city had itself very influential ramifications. The Academy's 'Silenos' set the tone for all the future representations and it must have been the starting point for the Lysippean version.[56] Sokrates the wise teacher in the familiar guise of Silenos the Dionysos-bearer is an image open to a variety of potential readings.[57] In due course the artists brought Socratic and silenic iconography even closer to the point of confluence.[58] In this they must have been helped by literary portraits such as

[55] A particularly apt statement if the portrait is seen in the context of Plato's promotion of his school. In view of the supposedly near-contemporary date of Plato's *Symposium* and Phaidon's *Zopyros*, Voutiras (1994) makes the ingenious suggestion that '[d]ie gleichzeitige Beschäftigung zweier Sokratiker mit der Physiognomie des Meisters könnte sehr wohl mit der Errichtung der Porträtstatue des Butes [sic] in Verbindung stehen' (160 n. 115). Cf. Giuliani (1997) 21–5.

[56] For the Pompeion statue as a refashioning of Sokrates in the role of the proper citizen in contrast to the Academy, one that promoted the image of the 'daemonic', anti-conformist intellectual see Zanker (1995) 58–62. The author has also suggested that a relief of the first century BC from Pompeii featuring Sokrates, Eros and Diotima (?) might give some idea of Sokrates' body in the lost original (36–8; Richter 1965 I, fig. 564). Even if less reliable in other aspects (e.g. the protruded belly), the mantle and the stick may be safely considered part of the original attire. In this way, Sokrates' appropriation of the role of the παιδαγωγός would be immediately recognised.

[57] It is worth mentioning that this motif is one of those that acquired a new life in the Christian centuries of Hellenism as it appears in the representations of St Christophoros. In an icon from Patmos dated in the years 1630–40 the saint crosses a river holding in his right hand a long staff that miraculously produced leaves at its top, while he has on his left shoulder the child Christ (hence the saint's name, Χριστοφόρος = Christ-bearer). The intriguing detail is that, although the composition in general follows Western models, the staff that sprouts (a reminiscence of *thyrsos*?) is a feature peculiar only to the Greek lives. See Chatzidakis (1977) 167–8 on fig. 144. Cf. also Stampolidis (1982–4) 158 n. 167.

[58] See Schefold (1959). A case in point is a terracotta lamp from Knidos of the late first–early second century AD (Bailey 1974, pl. 86 figs 1–3). It represents a seated Sokrates, as is shown by the inscribed name of the philosopher at the back of the chair, with a book-roll in his left hand wearing the χορταῖον, the costume of Papposilenoi in satyr drama! Bailey (1974) thinks the lamp was made for fun, 'to mock a revered and immortal philosopher and sage' (427b). From the opposite direction, one may mention a silen's head on a silver oinochoe from Philip's Tomb in Vergina *c.* 336 BC (Andronicos 1984, 152–3, figs. 115–16). The gentle, humanised face, unlike any other found in the Tomb, is strongly reminiscent of Sokrates.

the one found in Plato's *Symposium*. There seems to be evidence for a tendency to uncover a deeper meaning in this metaphor for the development of Plato as philosopher and the symbolism of his relationship with his teacher.[59] All in all, Sotes' work was the visual manifestation of the spirit Plato wished to breathe into his city. The Academy had a new hero: his face that of a Silenos, his voice that of Plato.

The taxonomy

Diogenes Laertios' *Lives of the Philosophers* is a comprehensive history of Greek philosophy up to the Roman period. The third book, which is devoted to Plato, includes a lot of information on his life and works, not all of it equally reliable. Immediately before the detailed description of the canon of nine tetralogies the author cites Thrasyllos' conviction that a tetralogical classification goes back to Plato himself:

59 *POxy* i 105 is a will of Pekusis from the reign of Hadrian (AD 117–138) who leaves as sole heirs his daughter and wife. The will is signed by the testator himself and six witnesses. The entry for the last one reads as follows: Διονύσιος Διον[υσ]ίου τ[ο]ῦ Διογένους ἀπὸ τῆς αὐτῆ[ς] πόλεως μαρτ[υ]ρῶ | [τῇ τοῦ Πεκύσιος διαθήκῃ, καὶ εἰμὶ] ἐτῶν τεσσαράκοντα ἕξ, οὐλὴ παρὰ κρόταφον δεξιόν, καὶ ἔστι μου ἡ σφραγὶς Διονυσοπλάτωνος (ll. 19–20 Grenfell–Hunt). The representation on this seal is a mystery. Most of the rest of the seals, belonging to the testator and the other witnesses, bear images of divinities, namely Dionysos (l.14), Sarapis (l.15), Harpokrates (l.18), the peculiar Diogepasto (l.16) and perhaps Ammon(?) (l.13. Cf. Grenfell and Hunt 1898, 173 note on l.14). The only apparent exception is that of the fifth witness: the name, lost but for the last two letters (. . . μη), was accompanied by the attribute φιλ[ο]σόφου (l.19. It may point to an image either of a philosopher or a god with this title). Sogliano (1902) has ingeniously suggested that the image was that of Plato with the costume and the attributes of the bearded Dionysos. He goes on to show how a reading of the dialogues and particularly the *Symposium* may have fostered the idea of an intrinsic relation between Plato's philosophy and Dionysiac religion. This idea, summarised in the equation 'Sileno sta a Socrate, come Dioniso a Platone', became popular and found its artistic expression in Alexandria in a new iconographical type by refashioning Plato's image in the guise of the god of wine. If Sogliano is right, here is the next step, following on Sotes' precedent: as Sokrates had been modelled on Silenos' image, it was natural that his disciple, soon to acquire a semi-divine status, should appropriate the features of the old silen's young student (cf. Milani 1903). For possible archaeological evidence lending some support to the hypothesis see Gabrici (1903) 371. Miller (1978) develops some fascinating thoughts on the relationship between Silenos, Dionysos and Christ and the imagery of the Great Teacher in Greek tradition. For the relationship between Dionysos and Christ and, in particular, a possible Dionysiac literary subtext in the *Acts of the Apostles* see Moles (2006).

Θράσυλλος δέ φησι καὶ κατὰ τὴν τραγικὴν τετραλογίαν ἐκδοῦναι αὐτὸν τοὺς διαλόγους, οἷον ἐκεῖνοι τέτρασι δράμασιν ἠγωνίζοντο (Διονυσίοις, Ληναίοις, Παναθηναίοις, Χύτροις) ὧν τὸ τέταρτον ἦν Σατυρικόν· τὰ δὲ τέτταρα δράματα ἐκαλεῖτο τετραλογία. (3. 56 Markovich)

Thrasyllos claims that he [sc. Plato] presented his dialogues on the model of a tragic tetralogy, because they competed with four plays – at the Dionysia, the Lenaia, the Panathenaia, the Chytroi – of which the fourth was the satyr play; and the four plays were called a tetralogy.

Diogenes' own composition dates from the first half of the third century AD. It is pretty certain, though, that the section 3.56–61 has been extracted directly from a work by Thrasyllos, presumably an introduction to the writings of Plato.[60] Therefore it is Thrasyllos, a court philosopher and polymath of the early first century AD, who is to be credited with the statement that Plato presented his dialogues in groups of four on the model of the tragedians' competing with four plays in the dramatic festivals. If Thrasyllos is indeed preserving an authentic story, Plato's dialogue with his contemporary theatre goes deeper than previously thought.

The idea that Plato was the author of tetralogies had a long history in Platonic studies. It recurs in two later authors, both of whom ultimately draw on Thrasyllos. Theon of Smyrna, a Platonist of the second century AD, is believed to have written an introduction to Plato that included a section on the classification of the Platonic corpus. In his encyclopaedic work *al-Fihrist* (= The Catalogue) the tenth-century Arab intellectual Ibn al-Nadīm produced an epitome of Theon's study. There we read:

Theon said: 'Plato arranged his writings for reading. Each group consisting of four books, he called a tetralogy'. (593–4 Dodge)

Since we are presented here with an apparently verbatim quotation, there is a strong possibility that we come closer to the original text. If this is the case, it is instructive to note that Theon, himself a tetralogist, claims a similar arrangement for Plato, as Thrasyllos had done earlier. Unlike him, however, he dispenses altogether

60 Cf. Mejer (1992) 3571; Göransson (1995) 80. Diogenes' use of excerpts: Mejer (1978) 16–29. Diogenes as a historian of philosophy: Warren (2007). Manuscript tradition and the reception of Diogenes' text: Dorandi (2009). For Thrasyllos as an author of an introductory work see Tarrant (1993) 19; Slings (1999) 22 n. 37; Carlini (2003) 27.

with the analogy with the dramatists. In fact, he thinks in terms of books and reading public rather than 'productions' and audience. As Theon in his extant work quotes Thrasyllos frequently, it is a reasonable guess that he adopted a modified version of his predecessor's claim, a version more compatible with his theory that a proper taxonomy is an implicit reading order. This suppression of the theatrical element is more likely due to Theon's reinterpreting the Thrasyllan testimony than indicative of an independent branch of tradition.[61]

That a theatrical context was intrinsically associated with the argument for tetralogies is evidenced by our second passage. The tenth chapter of the *Prolegomena to Platonic Philosophy* (pp. 26–9) is devoted to the taxonomies of the Platonic dialogues. The author mentions three systems of classification before giving an account of the 'true order' (τὴν ἀληθῆ τάξιν 26.1 Westerink), the standard Neoplatonic division in twelve dialogues. The section of the tetralogies begins as follows:

> ἐκ δὲ τῶν τετραλογιῶν οὕτως· κατὰ τετραλογίαν φασὶν ἐκδεδόσθαι αὐτῷ τοὺς διαλόγους κατὰ μίμησιν τῶν τραγικῶν καὶ τῶν κωμικῶν, οἵτινες διὰ τεσσάρων δραμάτων ἠγωνίζοντο τὸν αὐτὸν ἐχόντων σκοπόν, ἐν δὲ τῷ τελευταίῳ εἰς ἡδονὴν κατήντων. (24.25–25.1 Westerink)

> This is the reason for the tetralogical taxonomy: they claim that he presented his dialogues in tetralogies imitating the tragedians and the comedians, who competed with four plays sharing a common theme, while in the last one they arrived at pleasure.

Although no names are recorded, the exact correspondence with Diogenes' wording leaves no doubt that the well-known testimony was clearly intended here. The use of φασίν indicates that this claim had been dissociated from Thrasyllos' name and become part of the tetralogists' collective 'arsenal'. It also maintained its status as the 'founding myth' of any similar arrangement for more than five centuries. Of particular interest is the way in which the Byzantine teacher elaborates on the tradition and produces his own interpretation of Thrasyllos' text. There are four points at which

[61] Cf. Dunn (1976) 61–2, 76 nn. 18, 19, Tarrant (1993) 12. On Theon's introduction see Dellatre Biencourt (2010). For a reconstruction of his tetralogies see Tarrant (1993) 58–72. On Ibn al-Nadīm and his *al-Fihrist* see Stewart (2007) and (2009).

his version deviates from Diogenes' quotation – all instances of later accretion: (i) Plato's models were not only tragedians but comedians as well; (ii) he is said to have followed that pattern 'in imitation' of these poets; (iii) the four plays of the tetralogy shared a common purpose; (iv) the last play had a joyful character.

These differences reflect a reformulation of Thrasyllos' argument from an unfriendly viewpoint, because, if Diogenes is right, much is read into the original text that is simply not there. The addition of the comedians is inappropriate and may be simply considered a temporary slip on the part of the lecturer or the student-copyist.[62] It surely indicates the tendency in the tradition to associate Plato with dramatic poetry as a whole, not only tragedy. The remaining three points, however, are clear cases of deliberate overinterpretation. That Plato modelled himself on the tragic poets is a basic premise for the tetralogical thesis. It is also true that some tragedians, such as Aischylos, wrote tetralogies with a common theme and that the lightest member of the group, the satyr play, was staged last. But neither Thrasyllos nor any other like-minded taxonomist seems to have claimed that each and every Platonic tetralogy was supposed to feature one subject and comprise dialogues of the same character (e.g. political, ethical, elenctic). Similarly, Thrasyllos had ingeniously spoken of the satyr drama in terms of the fourth not the last play. Significantly, it is precisely these three revised formulations that provide the Byzantine scholar with the arguments for the rejection of the tetralogical classification. Plato could not have emulated the tragedians in writing tetralogies for the following reasons: (a) since he rejected them as makers of imitations, he could not have himself involved in a process he so much disliked; (b) the *Phaedo*, the last dialogue of the first tetralogy, is the exact opposite of a satyr play; (c) the dialogues of the first tetralogy are not of the same character and they lack a common purpose.[63] Here is, then, a repetition of

[62] Mansfeld (1994) takes this as an interpolation to an earlier version (60 n. 104). When the same claim is repeated a little later, the reference to comic poets is omitted (25.26–7 Westerink).

[63] Οὐκ ἀποδεξόμεθα δ' αὐτοὺς λέγοντας αὐτὸν κατὰ μίμησιν τῶν τραγικῶν τὸ τῶν τετραλογιῶν εἶδος ἐπιτηδεῦσαι· αὐτὸς γὰρ διαβάλλων αὐτοὺς λέγει εἴδωλα εἰδώλων γράφειν. Καὶ ἄλλως ἐστὶν δεῖξαι ὡς οὐ μιμεῖται αὐτούς· ἐκεῖνοι γὰρ τὸ τελευταῖον εἰς

Thrasyllos' testimony through the biased lens of philosophical, mainly Neoplatonic, exegesis.

Scholars have admittedly been eager to adopt this dismissive stance of certain ancient Platonists and reluctant, therefore, to take Thrasyllos' testimony at face value.[64] The grounds for suspecting the historical accuracy of the citation may be based on the following objections. First, the author seems to confuse plays with festivals and indiscriminately to attribute dramatic performances to all the major Athenian festivals. This carelessness in composition throws into doubt the rest of the information as well. Second, Thrasyllos lived four centuries after Plato. The chronological distance, combined with the apparent silence of the earlier sources, makes it less likely that Plato's practices and intentions would be faithfully reported in this work of Roman times. Third, following from that and possibly hitting the mark, one may have to call into question the objectivity of the reference. This is not so much the case of a dispassionate reader who records a neutral piece of information, since Thrasyllos was a partisan of the tetralogical arrangement. By showing that Plato had resorted to the same principle he would win the day for his taxonomy. In the absence of hard evidence he could very well appeal to a convincing fiction. For all these reasons there is always the possibility that the story that there were Platonic tetralogies, fashioned in direct imitation of the tragedians' ones, is no more than a Thrasyllan invention.

These objections pose real problems. Only a careful reading of Diogenes' text and related passages may lead to a proper evaluation of the testimony and, accordingly, establish whether it should be ignored as misleadingly useless or not. As the latter half of § 56 is practically a verbatim quotation (as implied by the use of ἐκεῖνοι for referring to the tragedians, evidently already mentioned earlier in the original), it is safe to assume that here is to be found a piece of Thrasyllan taxonomical thought. What really strikes the

ἡδονὴν καταντῶσιν, <u>οὗτος δ' ἐν τῷ Φαίδωνι</u>, τελευταίῳ ὄντι τῆς πρώτης τετραλογίας, <u>οὐκ εἰς ἡδονὴν κατήντησεν, ἀλλ' εἰς τελευτὴν τοῦ Σωκράτους</u>· οὐκ ἄρα καλῶς λέγουσιν εἰς τετραλογίας ἐκδεδόσθαι τοὺς διαλόγους αὐτοῦ. Καὶ ἄλλως <u>ἄλλος ἐστὶν ὁ σκοπὸς</u> ἐν τῷ Εὐθύφρονι καὶ ἄλλος ἐν τῇ Ἀπολογίᾳ καὶ ἄλλος ἐν τῷ Κρίτωνι καὶ ἄλλος ἐν τῷ Φαίδωνι (25.25–36 Westerink).

64 For example Chroust (1965) 43 n. 3; Barnes (1991) 127 n. 49.

reader in this extract is the repetitive emphasis on the number four: τετραλογία (twice), τέτρασι, τέταρτον. The author goes to great lengths to explain the nature of a tragic tetralogy and he keeps on pressing his point that it is the production of the fourth play that makes the difference. In this context it may be expected that he would not have presented a list of four festivals unless he had reasons to believe in its accuracy. The addition of the Panathenaia and the Anthesteria may in fact be less arbitrary than at first seems. Plays were evidently performed in classical times in the third day of the Anthesteria, called Χύτροι. The sources speak of comic contests but they are silent about tragedies. There is also epigraphic evidence for the production of a new tragedy in the Panathenaia in the first century AD.[65] It is not inconceivable then for a writer of Roman times to have read anachronistically back to Plato's time practices from subsequent centuries.

Nevertheless, the awkward manner of the reference causes justifiable suspicions. The names of the four festivals, inserted parenthetically in the text, break up the normal flow of the sentence by intervening between the relative and the main clauses. Moreover, they add a piece of information that nothing in the preceding phrase had prepared the reader for, since there had been no mention of festivals that called for any explanation. This reference distracts from and potentially damages the main point of the argument, not least because of the unnecessary confusion it introduces. I cannot see how the author himself could have been responsible for that careless piece of writing. More plausibly, a reader of that particular work, mesmerised by the 'numerological' associations of the text, may have thought that the addition of four festivals would strengthen and complete the thesis in favour of the analogy. The names would have originally appeared as *marginalia*, a kind of explanatory comment on δράμασι, and have later found their way into the main text.[66] If, then, the reference to the festivals is in

[65] The relevant documents are a passage from the *Life of Lycurgus* mentioning a law about the contest in the day of the Chytroi ([Plutarch] *Vit. X Orat.* 841F) and a fragment from an agonistic inscription (*IG* ii^2 3157 ll. 4–5). See *DFA*^{2} 16 and 56 respectively.

[66] So Dörrie (1990) 339, followed by Göransson (1995) 80. Dörrie himself thinks that the interpolator must be either Thrasyllos or Diogenes. In my view, Diogenes has no reason to tamper with the transmitted text since he is not particularly interested in favouring

fact a later interpolation, a major block to Thrasyllos' reliability is removed and the first objection loses much of its force.

The question whether a contemporary of Augustus could have access to accurate information about the 'editorial' habits of the founder of the Academy is a legitimate one. But in a sense it misses the point. For a start, to discredit a testimony merely on the grounds of considerable lapse of time is equivalent to an outright dismissal of the power of tradition. It is to be expected that stories about the Master as a teacher and writer were transmitted from one generation of Academics to the next, part of the cherished collective memory of the School. Since the closure of the Academy antedated Thrasyllos by less than a century, it is not inconceivable that he drew for his information about Platonic tetralogies on centuries-old Academic lore. More to the point, the demand for a claim based on indisputable evidence mistakes the testimony for what it may not be. We are not dealing with a fragment from a history on Plato's life and writing in the best tradition of *Quellenforschung*. Evidently the main reason for the reference is to lend authoritative support to a particular classification of the Platonic corpus. The point is that whoever favours a tetralogical arrangement is simply following a pattern first laid down by Plato himself. But Thrasyllos does *not* claim that he has discovered what the original classification was, *nor* does he present his own taxonomy as a reconstruction of the Platonic one (Tarrant 1993, 12 with n. 27). He does not therefore have to produce a record of Plato's tetralogies. All he needs for his purposes is the minimal thesis that Plato *could* have followed the example of the tragedians when presenting his works.

It is precisely the attractiveness of the latter possibility that casts so much doubt on the historicity of the testimony. The story serves too well the cause for tetralogies to be unconditionally true. Thrasyllos seems to have resorted to some kind of wishful guesswork, a piece of evidence *ben trovato* because difficult to disprove. This is a plausible explanation. Its weakness, though, is that it fails to give the context its due, so that too much is read into Diogenes'

the tetralogical classification. The modification was probably generated in the history of reception of Thrasyllos' study, during the two centuries that separate him and Diogenes.

passage and, possibly, in the wrong direction. Here it is essential to distinguish the real import of Thrasyllos' claim. Significantly he finds it apposite to refer to the competition of the tragic poets as providing the model for Plato's mode of 'publication'. The stress on the institutional framework of the production of plays (ἠγωνίζοντο) suggests that he may have something else in mind than the mere circulation of manuscripts. There is no hint here at a complete edition by Plato of his literary output for the reading public. The analogy with the festivals points rather to the manner in which the dialogues were presented to an audience. They are envisaged as pieces of performance literature.[67] It is more than telling that the argument for the tetralogies is founded on the affinities between Plato and the dramatists *and not the other way round*. Thrasyllos is convinced that his taxonomy remains faithful to the original state of affairs because this is how the tragic poets, and by implication Plato, used to work. When he mentions the τραγικὴ τετραλογία he focuses exclusively on the number four, while not explaining why a convention from the world of stage should have any bearing on his topic. It follows that the interpretation of the dialogues in theatrical terms was something with which his readers were not unfamiliar. Therefore it is hardly likely that Thrasyllos *invented* the story of Plato the emulator of the tragedians. Contrariwise, he makes the best out of it for his own purposes: Plato the tetralogist was the offspring of an established hermeneutic tradition.

On the other hand, it is plain that the case for a tetralogical arrangement had to be persuasively constructed. The main argument is that Plato had followed in the tragedians' footsteps when presenting his dialogues. Thrasyllos makes it clear that this affinity is reflected in his own taxonomy in at least three ways. According to Diogenes he placed at the head of his classification the tetralogy that contains the common subject, namely an exemplary life

[67] The inadequacy of translating ἐκδίδωμι with 'to publish' and the need for a performance-oriented reading of the extract have been perceptively remarked by Tarrant (1993) 12 n. 25. Mansfeld (1994) follows suit when arguing that 'Thrasyllus was thinking of premières, or a sort of vernissage, or a more or less public reading . . . The idea behind this will be that (most of) *the dialogues are dramatic in a technical sense*' (61, italics mine).

of the philosopher.[68] On one reading this principle of thematic coherence applies only to the group composed of the *Euthyphro*, the *Apology*, the *Crito* and the *Phaedo*. It is beyond doubt that these dialogues form a dramatic unity and are the best candidates for what an original Platonic tetralogy would look like 'in action'. An alternative view, supported by a more natural rendering of the sequence of the words, would have it that the philosopher as the paradigmatic hero is the unifying theme that runs through the whole corpus. In this case, the first group would function as a distinct, introductory unit.[69] The concept of the odd-member-out is the second point of contact with drama. Just as the poets competed in the Dionysia with three tragedies and a satyr play, Thrasyllos' first tetralogy comprises three works depicting the trial, imprisonment and death of Sokrates and a dialogue with a related but on the whole less tense atmosphere. Significantly, that dialogue, the *Euthyphro*, comes first, as was precisely the case with the staging of satyr plays in the Dionysia of 341–339 BC.[70] A last, but definitely not least, indication is the use of ὑπόθεσις in the sense of the theme of the dialogues. The word had been used as a technical

[68] πρώτην μὲν οὖν τετραλογίαν τίθησι τὴν κοινὴν ὑπόθεσιν ἔχουσαν· παραδεῖξαι γὰρ βούλεται ὁποῖος ἂν εἴη ὁ τοῦ φιλοσόφου βίος (3.57).

[69] The crux lies in whether the article is to be taken with the noun or the adjective, meaning that the first tetralogy has 'the subject common' or 'the common subject' respectively. The first reading is favoured by Dörrie (1990) 340 and Brisson (1992) 3711, who wonders, however, whether other tetralogies might each have a common theme. Proponents of the second reading include Dunn (1976) 77–8 n. 26 and Tarrant (1993) 66, 91.

[70] As attested in the *didaskaliai*-inscriptions for these years (*IG* ii^2 2320 I.16). Cf. *DFA*^{2} 109, 124. True, the distribution of production does not follow the fifth-century pattern of tetralogies: there is only one performance of satyr play, evidently outside the competition, while the tragedians are competing with two tragedies each. A tetralogist, however, could have used similar evidence to support a classical pedigree for his taxonomy. If Tarrant's reconstruction is correct, then Theon of Smyrna, a tetralogist of the second century AD, seems also to have applied the principle of putting the different dialogue first in the group. Here the criterion was a philosophical one: inconclusive, aporetic works in doctrinal tetralogies. Similarly, in Thrasyllos' scheme one dialogue seems to belong to a different philosophic class than the other three (though only in two cases is this dialogue placed first). It is possible then that 'the odd man out, analogous to the satyr play was . . . part of the very theory of tetralogies' while there may be some truth in the claim that 'the "satiric" dialogue of a tetralogy [has] a fairly obvious introductory purpose' (Tarrant 1993, 71; cf. 67–72). The lack of a fixed position for satyr play in post-classical productions might be reflected in Thrasyllos' distribution of the 'odd' dialogue in various places inside a tetralogy. For a new piece of evidence that sheds more light on this taxonomical pattern see Sedley (2009).

term by the Alexandrian grammarians to denote the plot of a play, a use that goes back to Aristotle's student Dikaiarchos of Messene in the late fourth century BC.[71]

One of these grammarians is known to have favoured an alternative taxonomy. Immediately after the description of the Thrasyllan tetralogies, Diogenes turns to an arrangement of the Platonic corpus in groups of three. Five trilogies are mentioned while the rest of the dialogues are said to have been left without any particular ordering. Aristophanes of Byzantium (*c.*257–180 BC) is singled out as the most notable exponent of this taxonomy.[72] Two features of this arrangement in particular need to be noted. First, it is for the most part based on literary criteria. Cross-references and compositional affinities between the dialogues determine the membership in each group. The point is to bring together those works that share the same cast and/or subject matter or centre on the last days of Sokrates. Since the justification of this arrangement derives from an interpretation of clues provided by the texts themselves, Plato is presented as the ultimate authority for these trilogies.[73] Second,

[71] Δικαιάρχου τινὰς ὑποθέσεις τῶν Εὐριπίδου καὶ Σοφοκλέους μύθων, οὐκ ἄλλο τι καλοῦντες [sc. ἡμεῖς] ὑπόθεσιν ἢ τὴν τοῦ δράματος περιπέτειαν Sext. Empir. *M.* 3.3 = Dicaearch. fr. 78 Wehrli. This passage makes it clear that this meaning was alive in the second century AD. Cf. Pfeiffer (1968) 193–6; Haslam (1975) 152–6; Rusten (1982) 359–64.

[72] Ἔνιοι δέ, ὧν ἐστι καὶ Ἀριστοφάνης ὁ γραμματικός, εἰς τριλογίας ἕλκουσι τοὺς διαλόγους (3.61). There follows a list of the trilogies: 1. *Republic*, *Timaeus*, *Critias*; 2. *Sophist*, *Statesman*, *Cratylus*; 3. *Laws*, *Minos*, *Epinomis*; 4. *Theaetetus*, *Euthyphro*, *Apology*; 5. *Crito*, *Phaedo*, *Letters*. As for the other works we are told that they have been arranged individually (τὰ δ' ἄλλα καθ' ἓν καὶ ἀτάκτως 3.62). On Aristophanes' classification see Alline (1915) 78–103; Müller (1975) 27–32, Dörrie (1990) 334–7 (with bibliography). For his composition of ὑποθέσεις, introductory summaries to plays, see Pfeiffer (1968) 192–6. Schironi (2005) presents new evidence for an Alexandrian edition of Plato by Aristophanes, which in turn formed the basis for Aristarchos' grammatical and philological commentary.

[73] *Ti.* 17c–20c, 27a–b and *Tht.* 210d provide the grounds for the establishment of the first and fourth trilogy respectively. The two last trilogies taken together offer a panorama of Sokrates' encounters in the period shortly before his death. The *Letters* fill in the required sixth position partly because they offer one more paradigm of the philosophic life (cf. Tarrant 1993, 106 n. 36). The identity of the cast and the dramatic occasion points to an underlying continuity between the *Sophist* and the *Statesman*. The place of the *Cratylus* in the second trilogy is justified if Aristophanes identified this dialogue with the *Philosopher*, a work announced in *Plt.* 257a as a follow-up of the *Statesman* but apparently never written (so Baltes in Dörrie 1990, 336 n. 2). The third trilogy comprises those dialogues with a legal content and a Cretan connection. The only oddity here is the intermediary position of the *Minos* that interrupts the natural sequence *Laws*–*Epinomis*.

this taxonomy is an incomplete one. Only fifteen dialogues are included while the rest are left unclassified, presumably because of the lack of sufficient textual evidence for ordering them into groups. The fact that more than half of Plato's works do not comply with the required criteria makes it doubtful that the principle of the trilogic arrangement was meant to have a complete application throughout the corpus.[74]

There has been considerable discussion about which one of the two classifications, that in trilogies or that in tetralogies, antedates the other.[75] Whatever the answer may be, there can be little doubt that Thrasyllos considered his own taxonomy a superior alternative to those available up to then. In particular, he seems to have intended to supplant the standard Hellenistic arrangements in trilogies with his tetralogical one, presented as a more satisfactory pattern on all grounds. The great advantage is that Thrasyllos offers a complete taxonomy: each one of the works that were believed to come from Plato's hand was allotted a place in one of the nine new groups. Significantly, the new arrangement incorporates the previous one in a smooth, almost 'surgical' manner. The first, second and third trilogies are transferred lock, stock and barrel to the eighth, second and ninth tetralogies respectively (the only difference being the transposition of the *Cratylus* at the head of the group and the *Minos* before the *Laws*). The first tetralogy emerges from the last two trilogies if taken as a unity and 'pruned' of the first and last works. These, however, are added to the second

[74] The partial nature of the arrangement calls for some explanation. One answer may be that only fifteen dialogues were known to Aristophanes at the time, while the rest were supplemented as they became available over the years (Tarrant 1993, 205). Alternatively, it may derive from Aristophanes' own critical judgement: the grammarian classified only those works that he considered worth reading and included in an anthology for the general public (Chroust 1965, 35 with n. 3). Or it may simply reflect the limitations of the principle applied: the trilogies were composed of the only dialogues that were, or could be made to be, linked together on literary criteria. I find the last explanation slightly more convincing.

[75] The issue of priority has usually centred on whether Aristophanes revised a previous tetralogical ordering or composed his groups out of the blue. Diogenes' use of the verb ἕλκουσι is frequently cited in support of the former view. It is taken to suggest that the exponents of trilogies violated some earlier taxonomy. Among the proponents of an Old Academic tetralogical order are Wilamowitz (1920) II 324–5; Erbse (1961) 219–21; Pfeiffer (1968) 196–7; Philip (1970), who offers the most sustained case; Slings (1999) 220 n. 394 (with caution). Cf. also Dunn (1976) 75 n. 15 and Mansfeld (1994) 62 n. 109.

and third trilogies, turning them into tetralogies: the *Theaetetus* before the *Sophist* (and after the repositioned *Cratylus*) and the *Letters* at the conclusion of the ninth group and the whole classification. In other words, not only are the trilogies fully absorbed into the new scheme; they are treated so that they retain a certain degree of 'independence'. The very same fifteen works arranged by Aristophanes have been used to form four tetralogies without any external insertion (other than the unavoidable addition of a dialogue to reach the required number of sixteen titles). The trilogies are to be found more or less preserved and easily recoverable in the first, second, eighth and ninth Thrasyllan groups.[76]

This is more than an attempt at rendering the earlier arrangement obsolete. It is a powerful *statement of continuity*. By beginning and ending his own taxonomy with a slightly revised version of a time-honoured order, Thrasyllos declares his full acceptance of the tradition and presents himself as walking on the same path all the way to the end. He shares the same basic principles with Aristophanes but offers a much more apposite division of the corpus. A similar story is told by the pattern of thought displayed in the rearrangement of the trilogies. The assignment of the *Minos* as the opening work of the last tetralogy removes the dialogue from its former embarrassing position. The establishment of the first tetralogy with its exemplary thematic unity brought together the *Apology* and the *Crito*, cancelling their unnatural rift in the previous division. Dissociated from the Sokrates' trial-and-death group, the *Theaetetus* is attached to the *Sophist* and the *Statesman* on the basis of the continuity between their *dramatis personae*. In this way the second Thrasyllan group comprises a more natural trilogy than the corresponding one in Aristophanes. The place of the *Cratylus* at the head of the group, before the *Theaetetus*, may be explained by an implicit link between the stage directions found at the end of the former and the beginning of the latter.[77]

[76] Müller (1975) 30–2; Mansfeld (1994) 90 n. 146. Slater (1986) believes that 'some sort of dramatic unity appears to be intended' (158).

[77] At the denouement of the *Cratylus* the eponymous philosopher is ready to leave for the fields: (Σω.) νῦν δέ, ὥσπερ παρεσκεύασαι, πορεύου εἰς ἀγρόν· (440e4). The very first information given in the opening words of the *Theaetetus* is that Terpsion, one of the two interlocutors of the frame dialogue, has returned from the fields: ΕΥ. Ἄρτι, ὦ Τερψίων, ἢ πάλαι ἐξ ἀγροῦ; ΤΕΡ. Ἐπιεικῶς πάλαι. (142a1–2).

Similarly, the selection of the *Clitophon* as the additional dialogue to supplement the *Republic*-group is based on some structural affinities between the short dialogue and the first book of the voluminous work.[78] In all these cases it is the literary aspect of the dialogues that guides the ordering. Thrasyllos develops his model on the lines of Aristophanes, but surpasses him by showing that it is groups of four, not three, that form the proper taxonomical unit of the corpus. To put it briefly, the tetralogic classification is intentionally presented as an amendment of the trilogic one,[79] as the ultimate taxonomy based on literary criteria.

In antiquity the systems of classification of the Platonic corpus were divided into two classes, the 'dramatic' and the 'philosophical' ones.[80] The former were more text-oriented, stressing affinities on a formal level, the latter related to the manner of the argumentation and the presence or absence of doctrines, more attuned to the needs of the specialist reader and therefore appropriate for the pedagogical purposes of the philosophical schools. The evidence for this division is once again provided by Diogenes Laertios. In his discussion of the character classification, an arrangement of the dialogues according to their philosophical disposition, he feels the need to insert the following comment as if in a footnote:

Οὐ λανθάνει δ' ἡμᾶς ὅτι τινὲς ἄλλως διαφέρειν τοὺς διαλόγους φασί (λέγουσι γὰρ αὐτῶν τοὺς μὲν δραματικούς, τοὺς δὲ διηγηματικούς, τοὺς δὲ μικτούς) ἀλλ' ἐκεῖνοι μὲν τραγικῶς μᾶλλον ἢ φιλοσόφως τὴν διαφορὰν τῶν διαλόγων προσωνόμασαν. (3.50 Markovich)

[78] Twice in this little dialogue Thrasymachos is depicted as Sokrates' rival for the education of the young Kleitophon (406a3, 409c7). He will prove the fiercest of Sokrates' interlocutors in *Republic* 1 (335b–354c).

[79] So Alline (1915) 117; Hoerber (1957) 13–14; Dörrie (1990) 337; Tarrant (1993) 103–7; Mansfeld (1994) 63. It is implied that there was no tetralogical arrangement prior to Aristophanes and he therefore did not revise any traditional model. See Solmsen (1981) 106; Brisson (1992) 3714 n. 434; Dörrie (1990) 336; Göransson (1995) 81 n. 1. Tarrant (1993) 13–17 offers a thorough refutation of the 'Academic tetralogies' thesis. Cf. Gregory Snyder (2000) 257 n. 23.

[80] On the philosophical classifications see Nüsser (1991) 101–74; Tarrant (1993) 31–72; Mansfeld (1994) 74–89; Göransson (1995) 87–104; Opsomer (1998) 27–33; Reis (1999) 53–104. For a useful overview of the reading order and the arrangement of Plato's dialogues see Gregory Snyder (2000) 94–9, featuring a comparative table with the major taxonomies (97); Westermann (2002) 16–25; Altman (2010a), (2010b). On the significance of Thrasyllos' classification for the philosophical edification of the reader see Dunshirn (2008).

We are not unaware that some claim that the dialogues are divided in a different manner – they call some of them dramatic, some narrative, some mixed – but those critics made the classification of the dialogues according to criteria suitable for tragedy rather than philosophy.

Here is an alternative ordering of Plato's works based on differences in the pattern of composition. The action of a dialogue may be presented either through the words and deeds of the interlocutors only in the manner of plays, or the voice of a narrator as in epic, or a combination of both.[81] By juxtaposing a 'dramatic' and a 'philosophical' taxonomy Diogenes makes the nature of the distinction clear as he invites the reader to compare the respective examples. Of special importance is the nomenclature employed. The use of the word τραγικῶς as a collective term applicable to the principles of those taxonomies irrelevant to philosophical purposes is telling. The fact that a more neutral word, say φιλολόγως, was not used shows that the division had been drawn with the traditional interpretation of the Platonic dialogues in theatrical terms in mind.[82] Such a polarised distinction may have been promoted by some passages in the dialogues in which tragedy (or poetry) and philosophy are depicted as uncompromising rivals.

Thrasyllos' tetralogies and Aristophanes' trilogies were most prominent among the examples of the 'dramatic' type. Their association with theatre was evident since they presented Plato as a follower of the tragedians. This point is also supported by the context in which Diogenes mentions the tetralogical classification. The reference to Thrasyllos, his testimony on Plato's tetralogies and his own classification come immediately after the remark about the parallel development of tragedy and philosophy:

81 There appears some uncertainty as to which dialogue should be grouped under the 'mixed' class. See the discussions in Sluiter (2000) 192–6; Ebert (2003). On the importance of Plato's tripartite scheme for the scholiastic tradition see Nünlist (2009) 94–115.

82 There appears to be some differentiation in the reception/interpretation of texts between the φιλόλογοι and the φιλόσοφοι and some mutual animosity by instances of quarrels of these two groups in Athenaeus (see Lukinovich 1990, 266 n. 14 for the relevant passages). For the meaning of the terms from Plato to Plotinos and the development of an oppositional pair see Pepin (1992). For the existence of two alternative ways of reading Plato in the second century AD, the 'philosophical' and the 'literary' ones, see de Lacy (1974) 6–8.

Ὥσπερ δὲ τὸ παλαιὸν ἐν τῇ τραγῳδίᾳ πρότερον μὲν μόνος ὁ χορὸς διεδραμάτιζεν, ὕστερον δὲ Θέσπις ἕνα ὑποκριτὴν ἐξεῦρεν ὑπὲρ τοῦ διαναπαύεσθαι τὸν χορὸν καὶ δεύτερον Αἰσχύλος, τὸν δὲ τρίτον Σοφοκλῆς καὶ συνεπλήρωσεν τὴν τραγῳδίαν, οὕτως καὶ τῆς φιλοσοφίας ὁ λόγος πρότερον μὲν ἦν μονοειδὴς ὡς ὁ φυσικός, δεύτερον δὲ Σωκράτης προσέθηκε τὸν ἠθικόν, τρίτον δὲ Πλάτων τὸν διαλεκτικὸν καὶ ἐτελεσιούργησε τὴν φιλοσοφίαν. (3.56)

As in the old days of tragedy initially it was only the chorus who had a part, but later Thespis invented a single actor so that the chorus might rest for a while and Aischylos introduced a second one, and Sophokles a third and thus brought tragedy to its completion, likewise the discourse of philosophy was initially of only one type, namely physics, then Sokrates added ethics as a second type, and Plato added dialectics as a third type, and thus he brought philosophy to perfection.

This extremely interesting piece of evidence weaves tragedy and philosophy into a common texture as their evolution towards their natural end is described in a similar way. Both evolutionary models seem to come from Aristotle (*Poet.* 1449^a9–19 for tragedy, *Topics* 105^b19–25 for philosophy) and the tripartite division of philosophy into physics, ethics and dialectics is found in the Old Academy. The latter could very well be the milieu in which the interpretation of Plato's 'affair' with the tragedians had its origins. Interestingly, the passage seems to presuppose an evolutionary model of a history of literature, one in which tragedy is superseded by philosophy as a less developed form of intellectual activity – one further instance of the post-theatrical character of Plato's philosophy.[83]

The papyrus fragment

Thrasyllos' main argument for his tetralogical arrangement was his belief that he was following a practice introduced by Plato himself. The same claim for upholding the Platonic tradition is evidently made by the author of a work very recently discovered in the findings from Oxyrhynchos. *POxy* lxxiii 4941, a single fragment of a papyrus dated to the second century AD, contains a

83 Sluiter (2000) 194. The Academic provenance is postulated by Hadot (1979) 206. Brisson (1992) holds that the passage is more influenced by Stoicism (3709). Cf. Hadot (1979) 211–12. A similar analogy is claimed by the author of *POxy* xlv 3219 in a work to be dated possibly before Thrasyllos' time. See Haslam (1977) 38.

few lines from what appears to be the introduction of a commentary on the *Theaetetus*. In the extant fifteen lines the author speaks of the dialogues of the second tetralogy (*Cratylus*, *Theaetetus*, *Sophist*, *Statesman*) in the expected canonical order and explains that the unifying theme of the particular group is the acquisition of philosophical knowledge. His views place him so firmly in the Thrasyllan tradition that his identification with the first-century AD tetralogist remains a possibility to be considered.[84]

[. . . . . .]ηδουσ[. . . .με]θοδικ[. . . .]μα
[. . . .].μενοσ̣[..ἀρ]μοστὴν περὶ τῶ(ν)
[. . . .]ατ̣ων [πραγμ]α̣τείαν παρεχομέ-
[..προ]ή̣ιδετο [γὰρ ὁ Κρ]ατύλος, τὴν περὶ ὀ-
[νομάτ]ω̣ν [ὀ]ρθότητος δ̣[ιδασκ]αλίαν περι-
[. . . . .]· ἑξῆς δὲ τούτωι̣ [ὁ Θεαίτ]η̣τ̣ο̣ς οὑτοσί̣,
[κα]ὶ̣ μ̣ὲ̣ν̣ δὴ ἐπὶ τῶι Θε[α]ι̣[τ]ή̣τωι [ὁ Σο]φιστής
[τ]ε καὶ Πολ̣[ι]τικός, τὴν ὁριστικήν τε κ[αὶ τὴν
[δ]ι̣[α]ι̣ρετικὴν μέθοδον διδάσκοντες,
[ἀν]αμφιλόγως μὲν ἐκεῖνοι, ὁ δὲ Θεαίτη-
[τ]ο̣ς ἀμφιδόξ[ως, ἐπεὶ] καὶ βούλεται περὶ
[ἐ]π̣ιστήμης ἐ̣[κεῖ πλά]ν̣ας ἀνασκευάζω(ν)
[δε]ῖ̣ξαι τὰ̣ [ἐπὶ τῶι ἀ]ν̣δρί, τῶν τρι̣[ῶ]ν δια-
[λόγ]ω̣ν τὴ[ν ἐκ τῆς] μ̣νημονεύσεως ἀνά|[πτυξιν

. . . methodical . . . provide a harmonized study about. . . . For the *Cratylus* used to be sung as a prelude, [bringing in] (his) teaching on correctness of names. Directly after it comes this (dialogue), the *Theaetetus*, and, following upon the *Theaetetus*, the *Sophist* and *Statesman*, which teach the methods of definition and division. They do so transparently, whereas the *Theaetetus* does so ambiguously, since he also aims there, in eliminating errors about knowledge, to demonstrate those points that bear upon the individual man (Theaetetus), with the three dialogues [showing that] the unfolding, as a result of memory process, [of innate concepts] . . . (after Sedley 2009, 67)

For the present purposes what is really intriguing about this new discovery is the claim the author makes when commenting briefly on the philosophical content of each one of Plato's works. He writes that the *Cratylus* 'was sung first' among the dialogues of the tetralogy, implying that the rest of the group would follow

84 The papyrus has been edited and commented upon by Sedley (2009). I owe special thanks to the editor for bringing this piece of evidence to my notice and sending me a draft of his edition ahead of its publication.

suit. By using the third singular imperfect indicative of προᾴδομαι (l. 4), a rare verb associated with the world of music, he seems to have a rather clear idea of what he is reporting. This imagery is significantly sustained throughout the section, for the implied verb in the following sentences may be the appropriate type of the simple form ᾄδομαι (ll. 6–8) – that is, the *Theaetetus*, the *Sophist* and the *Statesman* 'were also sung' after the *Cratylus* in this order. Apparently the unknown author could have been convinced that at least four of Plato's texts were performed in the past much like their poetic counterparts in theatrical and musical festivals.

Perhaps a certain degree of caution is commendable here. Leaping to hasty conclusions, especially in view of the inconclusive nature of the evidence, might threaten to falsify any argumentation that builds on shaky ground. Fourteen damaged lines do not quite qualify for the safe interpretative context required for a reading that in effect rests on a partially reconstructed word. True, but caution need not mutate into, or provide an alibi for, critical defeatism. The reconstruction of l. 4 seems convincing beyond reasonable doubt. *Ēta* is the best reading for the uncertain letter before *iōta* (see the *apparatus criticus* in Sedley 2009, 66), revealing the deciphered word as a form of the verb for singing. Its subject is certainly Κρ]ατύλος and the word-order suggests the verb as the opening word of the sentence. The damaged beginning of the line leaves enough space for both the final letters of the participle in the line above (possibly a masculine singular ending like -νου or -νος) and the first ones of the verb. The preposition πρό fits the bill perfectly because it explains the adverb ἑξῆς (l. 6): the *Cratylus* has to open the series of performance for the rest to follow. As for the lack of adequate contextual support due to the size and the physical condition of the fragment, one may respond that the correctness of προῄδετο is all that the initial hypothesis requires.

On the other hand, the minutiae of palaeography may prove not so decisive a factor here. Even if προῄδετο is what was originally written, there are alternative interpretations available. Nothing in the text compels us to think of actual singing, whereas the immediate context points rather in the opposite direction. The preceding three lines contain phrases such as 'harmonised study' (ἁρ]μοστὴν . . . [πραγμ]ατείαν) or, more conjecturally, 'song of the method' (με]θοδικ[ὸν ἆισ]μα) that defy any literal rendering but form part of a musical metaphor that includes the contested verb as well (Sedley 2009, 69 on ll. 1–4). Besides, the verb in the passive voice as impersonal (ᾄδεται) often means 'it is said/rumoured/widely known'. A similar rendering may be conjectured for the compound form so that it may be translated as 'was read/studied/taught first'. In this case, the structure of the second tetralogy would be praised as a fitting arrangement for the teaching of the philosophical method in terms of an accomplished musical composition and the metaphor was simply carried over to the ordering of the dialogues. The Thrasyllan milieu of the treatise makes the sustained use of musical imagery in a discussion on Platonic dialogues a serious likelihood.

This second objection stands on solid ground. The metaphor is there and without additional material it is impossible to state conclusively whether there is more to the musical vocabulary than a mere figure of speech or not. But such evidence as exists seems to favour the 'maximalistic' approach. The key piece is again προᾴδω. In its extant, relatively few, occurrences it is often used as a technical term for singing in advance in actual performances. Every time it occurs in comparisons or metaphors it never fails to recall its musical provenance. Unlike the simple verb, it lacks an impersonal form with a semantic field extending outside the musical context. That is why it does not need to be part of a musical imagery to convey the relevant milieu. In full knowledge of these particular connotations, our author must have deliberately used the term to inform his readers that the dialogues of the second tetralogy were used as set performance pieces.[85]

[85] With one exception all extant occurrences of προᾴδω are found in post-classical authors. The exception is Aeschin. 2.163.1–2, where the word is meant as a technical term – interestingly interpreted by the scholiast as denoting rehearsal (Sch. Aeschin. 354.95 Dilts). Polydeukes, an author of the second century AD, uses it in his discussion of the parabasis to distinguish the performance of the ode from that of the antode (*Onom.* 4.112.7 Bethe). A couple of centuries later Synesios compares his composing an opening section of a speech to 'singing the prelude song' (προᾴσας . . . μέλος *Calv. Enc.* 4.22 Aujoulat). Other Byzantine authors speak of psalms that ought to be recited before the prayers at the beginning of meals (ψαλμὸν προᾴδεσθαι Pallad. *Hist. Laus.* 32.6.8

There remains one last point to be considered, namely the usefulness of this testimony as a source of historical data. Granted that the author speaks of an oral presentation of the *Cratylus* and the rest of the dialogues, the question arises whether one may draw any valid conclusions for the reception of Plato at the time of the composition of the treatise – let alone any earlier period. To begin with, the fragment allows one fairly safe inference: the author believes the performance of the dialogues to have been a regular practice in Plato's Academy. The use of the imperfect in προῄδετο indicates an action that kept on repeating itself, presumably as a means for the presentation of the dialogues. Plato also looms large in the text as the man who brought all four dialogues together to serve specific philosophical purposes (ll. 11–14; the logical subject of βούλεται in l. 11 being Plato; cf. Sedley 2009, 70). Finally, as seen in the previous chapter, Thrasyllos had attributed the tetralogical arrangement to Plato's emulation of the theatrical tetralogies. For all these reasons it may be assumed that the author could very well mean that the *Cratylus* 'was sung as a prelude' to the tetralogy since Plato's time.

Whether he was right is a moot point. On the present state of evidence it is almost impossible to know for certain. Hence the significance of this newly discovered scrap of papyrus for Platonic studies. If my reading above is not very far away from the truth, then a writer of an introduction to the *Theaetetus* informs his readers that some Platonic dialogues were performed in the Academy at the time of Plato. More importantly, this is not an isolated piece of evidence but belongs to a tradition that may reach as far back as the classical period. Whether it comes from the first or the second century AD this testimony adds another piece of evidence for Plato's reception as a prose dramatist who took advantage of all the tropes of theatre at his disposal for the presentations of his dialogues, performances included.

Bartelink) or of David, the author of the psalm, who prophesies the eventual salvation of the Gentiles (τὴν τῶν ἐθνῶν σωτηρίαν προᾴδει Theodor. *Interpr. In Psalm. PG* 80.861.31). Significantly, in the latter instances it is the performative nature of the Old Testament Psalms that explains both the use of the term and its extended meaning.

The dinner theatre

Plutarch

Both Thrasyllos and the author of the new *Theaetetus* treatise postulate a Plato who followed the tragedians' practice when making his work known to the public, i.e. that he staged productions of his dialogues. But it is not until some decades later that we hear of something of the sort. In the seventh book of his *Sympotic Questions* Plutarch mentions a discussion that took place at a banquet at Chaironeia on the theme of the appropriate kinds of sympotic entertainment. One of the guests expresses his preference for a new type of production. Here is to be found the earliest extant *literary* testimony for actual dramatic performances of Plato's dialogues:

οὐδὲν μελλήσας ἐκεῖνος ἔφη τἆλλα μὲν ἐπὶ τὴν θυμέλην καὶ τὴν ὀρχήστραν ἐξελαύνειν, εἰσάγειν δὲ τὸ νεωστὶ μὲν ἐν Ῥώμῃ παρεισηγμένον εἰς τὰ συμπόσια μήπω δ' ἀναλάμπον ἐν τοῖς πολλοῖς. 'Ἴστε γάρ' εἶπεν 'ὅτι τῶν Πλάτωνος διαλόγων διηγηματικοί τινές εἰσιν οἱ δὲ δραματικοί· τούτων οὖν τῶν δραματικῶν τοὺς ἐλαφροτάτους ἐκδιδάσκονται παῖδες ὥστ' ἀπὸ στόματος λέγειν· πρόσεστι δ' ὑπόκρισις πρέπουσα τῷ ἤθει τῶν ὑποκειμένων προσώπων καὶ φωνῆς πλάσμα καὶ σχῆμα καὶ διαθέσεις ἑπόμεναι τοῖς λεγομένοις. Ταῦθ' οἱ μὲν αὐστηροὶ καὶ χαρίεντες ἠγάπησαν ὑπερφυῶς, οἱ δ' ἄνανδροι καὶ διατεθρυμμένοι τὰ ὦτα δι' ἀμουσίαν καὶ ἀπειροκαλίαν, οὕς φησιν Ἀριστόξενος χολὴν ἐμεῖν ὅταν ἐναρμονίου ἀκούσωσιν, ἐξέβαλλον· καὶ οὐ θαυμάσαιμ' ἂν εἰ τὸ πάμπαν ἐκβαλοῦσιν· ἐπικρατεῖ γὰρ ἡ θηλύτης.' (711B–C)

he replied without delay that they should drive the rest away to the stage and the orchestra and introduce a form of entertainment recently imported to Rome, but not yet brought to the knowledge of the many. 'You know', he said, 'that some of Plato's dialogues are narrated, others dramatic. Slaves are taught the lightest of these dramatic ones and recite them by heart. They act in accordance with the personality of the characters and modulate their voices and posture while the staging follows the spoken words. Men of rigorous education and culture loved these productions immensely, but the unmanly and those with pampered ears due to their ignorance of culture and beauty, those who, as Aristoxenos says, vomit bile whenever they hear the enharmonic scale, attempted to banish them; and I would not be surprised if they eventually banish them altogether; effeminacy wins the day'. (after Minar 1961)

This is a rich passage that raises a number of issues and necessitates a careful reading of the expressed or implied statements.

First there is the unambiguous dramatised nature of this type of entertainment. The vocabulary used leaves the reader no room for considering the possibility of a recitation or any other non-dramatic mode of presentation.[86] The dialogues are performed by slaves (παῖδες), who do not read aloud from a script but deliver their lines by heart (ἀπὸ στόματος). Oral delivery in the absence of a written text was the standard manner of presenting plays and other verse (and prose) compositions to the public until late in antiquity – and beyond. More significantly, it is emphatically stated that this delivery is accompanied by ὑπόκρισις: the performers are supposed to modulate their voices (φωνῆς πλάσμα) and vary their posture (σχῆμα) in accordance with their utterances so that the character of the dialogue's *personae* may be appropriately rendered (ἤθει τῶν ὑποκειμένων προσώπων) and the staging follow the signs of the text (διαθέσεις ἑπόμεναι τοῖς λεγομένοις).[87] The sentence is so replete with technical vocabulary that one is reminded of rhetorical manuals. In fact, Plutarch's words bear a striking resemblance to a definition of *hypokrisis* found in Longinos' *Art of Rhetoric*, a work of the third century AD.[88]

Role-playing is one element that these performances of Plato's dialogues share with theatre productions. Special training and rehearsals is another: the slaves are thoroughly taught (ἐκδιδάσκονται) how to act out the dialogues. This training evidently addresses

[86] Cf. Frazier and Sirinelli (1996) 222 n.178; Lakmann (2000) 283.

[87] There is some uncertainty on what exactly σχῆμα stands for here. On the basis of the analogy with rhetorical usage 'posture' is a likely rendering (cf. Long. *Rh.* 311.15–17 Spengel). Similarly, Minar (1961) translates as 'gestures' (79). Frazier and Sirinelli (1996) tentatively suggest that it is related to the appearance of the body, having cited Losfeld's interpretation of it as a feature of the voice (222 n. 178). From a more stage-oriented point of view, Lakmann (2000) makes the attractive hypothesis that the word refers to the attire of the performers ('entsprechende Kleidung' 283). The performance context also suggests that διαθέσεις have less to do with oral delivery than the staging of the dialogues (cf. Hero *Aut.* 20.2; the plural there may point to different productions).

[88] As Lakmann (2000) 284 was the first to point out. The definition goes as follows: 'Υπόκρισίς ἐστι μίμησις τῶν κατ' ἀλήθειαν ἑκάστῳ παρισταμένων ἠθῶν καὶ παθῶν καὶ διάθεσις σώματός τε καὶ τόνου φωνῆς πρόσφορος τοῖς ὑποκειμένοις πράγμασι (310.21–4 Spengel). As Longinos is unlikely to have borrowed his technical vocabulary from some very obscure source, Plutarch, too, draws probably on standard rhetorical theory on oral performance intended for orators and actors alike (cf. Lakmann 2000, 283). Longinos himself urges the orator to emulate the best tragic and comic actors in matters of ὑπόκρισις (311.19–23 Spengel). See Hall (2006) 369–73.

both verbal and non-verbal aspects of performance.[89] The theatrical mode is further confirmed by the kind of texts presented. For this is not the case of a production of all Plato's dialogues indiscriminately. The selection is based on the division between narrated (διηγηματικοί) and dramatic (δραματικοί) dialogues.[90] In the former the action is presented through the voice of a narrator, in the manner of epic, whereas in the latter through the utterances of the characters, in the manner of plays. This feature alone made the works of the second group the obvious candidates for staging. Then the group of suitable texts is narrowed down to those 'lightest' (ἐλαφροτάτους) among the dramatic dialogues. Although the precise meaning of a 'light dialogue' here may be elusive, one ought to think of works without complex structure and, perhaps, with a relatively cheerful character, less demanding therefore in terms of production and more at home in the context of a social gathering.[91] It is clear that these Platonic dialogues were treated as pieces of theatre and their presentation was constructed on the model of stage performances.

A second point relates to the novelty and context of these kinds of performances. We are told that the production of Platonic dialogues is a recent development in Rome (νεωστί). Now the

89 Although not explicitly stated, it is reasonable to suppose that the slaves were trained by professional actor-directors who also supervised the rehearsals.

90 Plutarch provides the earliest extant testimony for this type of classification. In its standard version a third type is added, the mixed dialogues. The division derives from Sokrates' taxonomy of literature in the third book of the *Republic* (392d5–6). Other ancient testimonies for the classification are found in Diog. Laert. 3.50; Anon. *In Theaet.* 3.38–9 Bastianini and Sedley; Proklos *In Remp.* 1.14.27–9 Kroll. For more ancient sources see Haslam (1972) 20–1. Cf. Nüsser (1991) 177–204 (with a collection of the relevant passages); Göransson (1995) 84 n. 1; Lakmann (2000) 281–3.

91 Minar (1961) translates τοὺς ἐλαφροτάτους as 'the most lively' (79). Teodorsson (1989–96) rejects this and suggests 'light/easy/facile (to learn)' instead (III, 110, with reference to other passages in Plutarch). Similarly, Frazier and Sirinelli (1996) render 'les plus faciles' (48). Lakmann (2000) 238 takes it as a reference to dialogues that were easier to learn by heart or more suitable for staging rather than less difficult to understand. Perhaps the adjective is used here in the sense of 'easy to learn, produce and follow', indicating a notion of appropriateness from the viewpoint of the performers, the director and the audience at the same time. The length of the dialogue and the simplicity of the scenery (and props) could have been two factors affecting the selection. The notion of a light-hearted text may also be at work (cf. Plutarch's use of the adverb in 616D). Among the dialogues that would fulfil these criteria one could name, for instance, the *Ion*, *Alcibiades* and *Second Alcibiades*, *Hippias Major* and *Minor*, the *Minos*, the *Theages*, the *Menexenus*, the *Phaedrus*.

Sympotic Questions, one of Plutarch's last works, is a voluminous project, possibly written over a long period of time. Internal evidence indicates a date of composition in the period between 99 and 116 AD.[92] If Plutarch had really sent to Sosius Senecio, the addressee of the whole work, each of the books 4–9 separately,[93] the seventh book would have been composed at a late stage within this period. There is, however, no way to be more precise on the dramatic date of the gathering at Chaironeia. The discussion described in questions 7 and 8 lacks any chronological indication. Question 5 mentions an episode dating as far back as 83 AD, in fact, the earliest attested dramatic date throughout the work.[94] The fact that question 6 points to the milieu of the years AD 90–100 shows that Plutarch compiles material from different chronological layers even in neighbouring questions of the same book. The adverb νεωστί is the only piece of information to go by – not very useful in the present circumstances.[95] In the face of this indeterminacy it may be safe to conclude that Rome first became acquainted with productions of Platonic dialogues at symposia some time in the four decades before and after the turn from the first to the second century AD (definitely before 116).

We are also told that these productions were put on at banquets (συμπόσια), presumably in the context of the after-dinner entertainment. This was an indispensable feature of elite social gatherings throughout antiquity, as the host was expected to offer his guests a variety of musical happenings and spectacles. In Imperial Rome the performers included, among others, trumpeters, acrobats, conjurors, dancers, mime and pantomime actors. Troupes of such artists were actually owned by rich Romans and used for private performances. A significant part of this sympotic entertainment was the presentation of tragedies and comedies in

[92] Jones (1966) 72–3. Fuhrmann (1972) dates it to the second decade of the second century (xxvi).

[93] As suggested by Teodorsson (1989–96) I 38 on 612E; II 237 on 686E.

[94] Frazier and Sirinelli (1996) 9, 11.

[95] The interpreter should be aware that time is a relative notion and, to some extent, a cultural construct. Plutarch has himself notoriously written that the bronze statue of Demosthenes was dedicated by the Athenian people shortly after the politician's death (ὀλίγῳ ὕστερον, *Dem.* 30.5), even though the event actually took place more than forty years later (cf. Richter 1965, II 216).

the form of either a recitation of selected passages, say messenger or *agōn* speeches, or, possibly, a performance of a whole play. The works of theatre were equally accessible through the public space of the stage and orchestra and the more confined space of a private dwelling. It was then all too natural for Plato's dialogues to be given a treatment similar to that of other dramatic compositions.[96]

A third point concerns the reception of this new type of theatrical venue. At the time of the meeting at Chaironeia these productions were little more than an experiment, indulged in by a few pioneering individuals and not yet turned into a familiar spectacle. The private nature of the performances and their recent addition to Rome's cultural – or, preferably, night – life account for the fact that most people were not familiar with them (μήπω δ' ἀναλάμπον ἐν τοῖς πολλοῖς). But it is clear from the text that another factor may have also been responsible for this state of affairs. For the productions of the dialogues are said to have elicited a mixed response from their first audiences. Unconditional admirers found themselves on the defensive against an ever-growing opposition by those who had expressed their disagreement vehemently, even attempting to ban the productions. The latter group was apparently a majority (ἐπικρατεῖ) and a fear is expressed that they may succeed in their objective. In fact, the voice of this opposition is to be heard immediately after the end of the passage: performances of Plato should be banned because a dinner-party was the least appropriate context for the presentation of the dialogues.

[96] In an important article Jones (1991) discusses the phenomenon of visual entertainment in ancient symposia. He coins two terms: 'dinner-theater' for describing 'both that which is specifically intended to be watched, as opposed to being heard, but also that which is appropriate to the public spaces of the theater and to a lesser extent of the amphitheater'; and 'theater-dinner' for those 'public banquets given in these same places at which those present were entertained by artists such as pantomimes' (185). These definitions demonstrate the dialectics between public and private performances as well as the mutual exchange of roles in the respective spaces of the symposion and the theatre: the rooms and gardens of a house and the parts of a theatre building may serve the same function (cf. Pliny, *Epistles* 9.36 = *CAD* 280 IV 102). For a documentation of the phenomenon in the first century AD, Petronius' *Cena Trimalchionis* (*Satyricon* 26.7–78.8) is the classic text (the setting is a Greek city in Campania). For private troupes see *CAD* 281 IV 105–9; Jones (1991) 188. For the recitation of passages from comedy see Teodorsson (1989–96) III 120, while Jones (1991) makes the case for the production of whole plays (193).

The tone and vocabulary used in the discussion of these two opposing 'camps' is strikingly aggressive. It is a reminder that the testimony under examination is not a casual comment by a dispassionate observer of a contemporary cultural event, but a forceful speech by a partisan in support of his cause. The speaker (ἐκεῖνος) is an unnamed sophist of a Stoic persuasion (710B) who is more than eager (οὐδὲν μελλήσας) to argue for his conviction that Plato should be the only dinner theatre acceptable. Upholding such an extreme thesis is one out of many features that mark this intellectual's idiosyncratic temperament. He does not feel very comfortable with his presence at that gathering, as if his virulent comments on the 'effeminacy' of those who cannot appreciate Plato performances were made on purpose to attack some of his fellow-symposiasts (711C–D). It is not difficult to see that Plutarch has not portrayed him in the most attractive of ways. As a speaker he seems to address him in a manner that may be thought of as verging on irony (711B). As an author he chooses Philip of Prusias, a friend of his, to launch a counter-attack and attempt to silence the sophist (711D); while in the introductory remarks of the episode he clearly identifies with those who defended the party from the sophist's 'onslaught' (πράγματ' εἴχομεν ἀμυνόμενοι 711B). Scholarly consensus has it therefore that Plutarch disapproves of whatever the sophist says or does.[97]

So far so good, but this does not tell the whole story. The Stoic is as much an inhabitant of the memory islands of Plutarch the man as the literary creation of Plutarch the writer. It has been noted that this figure combines the features of the disturber and the offended guest, both typical characters of sympotic literature.[98] Certain elements in his characterisation, for instance the apparent lack of humour, the extreme views and strong language, the violation of the rules of good convivial behaviour, may stem from the needs of literary convention more than any personal animosity on the part of the author. His anonymity could very well be

97 As Babut (1969) puts it, 'le sophiste paraît tout à fait déplacé dans la société des amis de Plutarque' (258). Cf. Teodorsson (1989–96) III 111 on 711C–D; Frazier and Sirinelli (1996) 222 n. 176.

98 See Martin (1931) 64–79. Cf. Teodorsson (1989–96) III 101 on 710B and 105 on 710D–E for parallels elsewhere in Plutarch.

part of the same plot, since it encourages the reader to think less of an eccentric individual than of a representative of a general outlook.[99] His philosophical orientation is another case in point. Plutarch, himself a Platonist, is known to have written a number of treatises and often, in his other works, argued against the doctrines and tenets of Stoicism.[100] When he describes the sophist as a wise man, free from passions (σοφόν, ἀπαθής 711B), the unmistakable reference is to the Stoic ideal of the uniquely happy human being, ultimate model of life for every adherent of that school.[101] The veiled irony of the address then would seem in place. But the fact that Philip of Prusias, the sophist's main opponent and Plutarch's friend, is also a Stoic (710B) indicates that an explanation on the basis of an inter-school rivalry would be utterly simplistic. This is not only because in the Roman period there was greater room for convergence between the major philosophical schools.[102] In fact, this symmetrically antithetical portrayal of Philip and the sophist follows a pattern of differentiation between the 'good' and the 'bad' Stoic, a general principle of character-drawing throughout the Plutarchan corpus. This division, emanating as it does from the writer's complex relations with Stoicism and its exponents, cuts across doctrinal disagreements. Any evaluation of the sophist's words and deeds therefore is coloured by his depiction as the foil to his fellow-Stoic and thus playing by the rules of this particular typology.[103]

The influence and function of literary motifs aside, the unqualified negation of an 'unsympathetic' character's reliability as a

99 So I cannot see the absence of a name as specifically a sign of Plutarch's dissociation from the sophist as Teodorsson (1989–96) does (III 101 on 710B).

100 Three extant and six lost works are devoted to the polemics against the Stoics. See Hershbell (1992) 3336–7.

101 As Donini in Inwood and Donini (1999) remarks, 'the wise man is totally free from passions. The ideal of the suppression of passions . . . remained, throughout all antiquity, one of the most famous features of Stoic ethics' (723). See in particular sections IV 'The goal of life' (684–7) by Inwood, VII 'Passions' (699–705) and IX 'Virtue and wisdom' (714–24) by Donini. In an ironic twist Plutarch the character calls the Stoic σοφός, whereas Plutarch the narrator has just used the word σοφιστής.

102 Dillon (2000) 923; Trapp (2007c) 16–18.

103 The classic study on Plutarch's relationship with Stoicism is Babut (1969) who introduces the distinction between the two groups of Stoics that appear as characters in the works of Plutarch (260–7). See also Hershbell (1992), who rightly stresses the inconclusive nature of any thesis on Plutarch's attitude to the Stoa (3350–1).

source is not a legitimate conclusion. It does not follow from an unattractive portraiture that the author denies any truth to each and every word of this character. In the present case the inference is that since Plutarch used a negatively portrayed character as an exponent he must have objected to Plato performances. The argument goes as follows: (a) the sophist favours the productions of Plato; (b) Philip and others strongly disagree; (c) the author takes the side of those refuting the sophist; therefore (d) Philip's objections reflect Plutarch's views, so (e) Plutarch is opposed to the productions of Plato. This line of thought is backed up by these latent assumptions: (1) Philip is the author's mouthpiece; (2) as a Platonist Plutarch could not have felt comfortable with dramatised dialogues. The weakness of this argument is that there is no textual support for the move from (c) to (d) and (e). Nothing suggests that Plutarch *necessarily* belongs to the group of protesters led by Philip (ἡμᾶς, ἡμεῖς 711D). In fact, the reference to the same group by the author in the third person (ἐνίους 711C) indicates quite the opposite. The alleged move rests solely on assumption (1), itself an unwarranted premise violating the principle of economy. As a speaker in the discussion at his own house Plutarch's mouthpiece is obviously himself. There is hardly any hint in his speech (712E–714A) that he is either for or against Plato productions. The question is simply not raised.[104] As for assumption (2), suffice it to say for the present that it is a Stoic, not a Platonist, who opposes the dramatisation for reasons absolutely irrelevant to the ones notoriously put forward in the *Republic*. No one raises any objections against the dramatisation of the dialogues *per se*.[105] In sum, we cannot know with absolute certainty Plutarch's attitude towards the performances of Plato's dialogues. The picture is a

[104] It is true that, after Philip's harsh reply to the sophist (711D), the issue does not surface again in the discussion. This may be taken as another sign of the author's endorsing Philip's views. It may also be thought that had Plutarch been favourable to the performances of the dialogues he would not have presented a friend of his as a stern critic or spoken about them through such an unfavourably depicted character. This interpretation evidently begs the question.

[105] As Blondell (2002) correctly remarks, 'it is not the mode of performance but the setting – over food and wine, Plato as party entertainment – that upsets the company' (24 n. 71).

little more complicated than the story of 'Plutarch and his friends *vs* the arrogant foreigner' may suggest.

To move away from the simplistic model it is imperative to notice how carefully this piece of sympotic literature is constructed. Questions 7 and 8 form a unity highlighted by the reference both at the beginning and end of the section to the subject of the recorded discussion: the types of musical performances (ἀκροαμάτων 710B, 713E). There appear four speakers, two Stoics and two Platonists, each allotted a set speech to promote his views on the right sort of entertainment in the course of a symposion. Philip of Prusias (710C–711A) does not favour a certain type in particular but seems happy to indulge in the existing variety of happenings (cf. 712D), with the exception of the performances of Plato (711D). Diogenianos of Pergamon (711E–712D) rejects Tragedy and Old Comedy, accepts grudgingly and for exceptional reasons only one type of Pantomime, but embraces wholeheartedly the plays of New Comedy.[106] Plutarch disagrees with the performances of mimes and instrumental music but has no objection to singing with the accompaniment of music.

A number of underlying themes permeate the narrative. First, the reader is invited to view the succession of speeches as a contest: each of the speakers engages in the construction of his 'ideal' sympotic entertainment. They are strongly committed to reforming actual practices by means of restricting the number of accepted types. At least two of them are practically partisans of certain performance genres. Second, this contest reflects the atmosphere of a symposion, where most of the competitors are half-serious and their debate therefore is not exactly comparable to any one undertaken in other, more sober social gatherings. At a number of points the relaxing mood of the occasion is stressed (e.g. 711A), while the participants are warned not to let their playful competition inappropriately turn into serious strife.[107] A third theme relates

[106] For Diogenianos and Philip see Puech (1992) 4846 (I) and 4869–70 respectively.

[107] Philip's words summarise neatly the context in which this section of the *Sympotic Questions* may be better read: τὸν δὲ τῶν ζῳδιογλύφων ἀγῶνα βραβεύσομεν αὔριον, ἂν δοκῇ τῷ ξένῳ καὶ Διογενιανῷ, νήφοντες (712D–E). The two symposiasts are singled out because they promote one type of ἀκρόαμα at the expense of all the others and are, therefore, more likely to perceive the discussion in terms of a contest.

to the intertextuality of the narrative. References and allusions to earlier literary works establish a framework in which the sympotic dialogues of Plato and Xenophon are given a prominent place (710C). The dominant literary figure in the speakers' minds is Sokrates. Philip mentions him by name more than once (710C), while Plutarch cites him as an authority to lend support to his own views (713C). The extreme example of such a deferential attitude is Diogenianos. His only reason for not rejecting pantomime in its entirety but accepting a certain type of dance is that this type seems to have been praised by Sokrates (711E).[108]

Seen in this context the anonymous Stoic is found to interact with the rest of the characters in a less straightforward manner. In terms of stagecraft he is given a lively portraiture as his presence is made conspicuous throughout the scene. Despite his persistent attempts to have his views promoted, he has the smallest speaking part: his voice is heard only once in a set speech of a little over ten lines.[109] Twice his views are given in reported speech (710B, 711B), while on two occasions he is prevented from entering the discussion (711A, 712D). His companions try to 'control' him mainly because of his competitive temperament (cf. βουλόμενον αὖθις ἀντιλέγειν 711A) and his extreme points of view. But he is hardly alone in exhibiting these traits of behaviour. All are willing to participate in the contest for the best type of entertainment and ready to reject existing practices as inappropriate. His outbreak at the end of his speech, though almost offensive, is understandable as a reply to some not particularly tactful remarks made by Philip a little earlier.[110] The real point of difference between the sophist and the rest of the symposiasts is that he does not share in the jocular mood of the occasion. He takes things very seriously and

[108] In both cases it is the Sokrates of Xenophon's *Symposium* who is cited as an authority (711E ~ 2.15–16, 713C ~ 2.3).

[109] For the sake of comparison, Diogenianos, the only other character who is not given a second speaking part, has a set speech more than four times longer.

[110] Both the common, rustic men with whom Philip and the rest have to associate (ἡμεῖς δὲ μεμιγμένοι . . . ὅταν οὕτω τύχωμεν, ἰδιώταις καὶ ὑπαγροικοτέροις 710D) and the ridiculed philosopher who leaves the symposion as soon as the music starts (φιλόσοφος δ' ἀνὴρ . . . οὐ καταγέλαστός ἐστι 710E) are thinly disguised caricatures of the Stoic sophist and his likes. On the character of the 'rustic man' (ἄγροικος) in ancient comedy see Konstantakos (2004) and (2005a).

he expects a similar attitude on the part of his interlocutors.[111] All the same, this rigid, far from flexible stance makes him an easy target. The others like to tease him by capitalising on his self-image as a responsible and authoritative speaker.[112] Commentators have perceptively pointed out that the description of the banquet at Chaironeia is full of comic elements.[113] In this comedy the sophist has the 'privilege' of playing the (unwilling) jester of the company.

It is that particular role that brings to the forefront a basic feature in the depiction of the sophist: his special relation with the author and the characters of the Platonic dialogues. It is not difficult to see that Plutarch has to some degree modelled this Stoic on a comic figure from the earlier tradition of sympotic literature, namely Plato's Aristophanes. In a lengthy reference to a number of scenes in the *Symposium* Aristophanes' comic *persona* comes to the fore, as it is stated that his speech is to be likened to a comedy (710C). Having been sufficiently alerted, the reader will not fail to notice that the sophist is prevented from speaking twice as was exactly the case with Aristophanes (*Symp.* 185c, 212c). The parallel becomes explicit by the fact that, on the second occasion he is interrupted, the sophist is about to recite some Aristophanic verses, presenting himself in the role of the self-proclaimed defender of Old Comedy (712D).[114]

111 Philip is exactly hitting the point when he remarks that δέδια μὴ μετὰ σπουδῆς τινος οὐ παιδιᾶς λέγεσθαι πρός σε δόξῃ (711D).

112 See Plutarch's ambiguous eulogy (711B) and Diogenianos' fear expressed in mock-judicial terminology (711E). Significantly, Diogenianos, in his criticism of Old Comedy plays, avoids carefully any mention of the name or the works of Aristophanes (712A), the sophist's favourite comedian.

113 Frazier and Sirinelli (1996) 13.

114 Interestingly, the passages in Plutarch appear in the reverse order from the Platonic passages they recall. The first interruption comes when the sophist is ready to reply to a speech that contained personal hints against him, as is Aristophanes after Sokrates' speech (711A ~ 212c), while the verbal and structural resonances in the construction of the second passage (παυσάμενος ~ παυσαμένου; the interruption occurs at the beginning of a section and leads to a change of speakers) point to the earlier episode of Aristophanes' hiccups (712D ~ 185c). Another point of difference is that, whereas in Plato Aristophanes is forced to stop by largely fortuitous and unpremeditated factors (hiccups, the unexpected arrival of Alkibiades), in the *Sympotic Questions* it is the fellow-symposiasts themselves who intervene, predictably and purposely, to silence the sophist. The chiastic order and the variations in details show how delicately Plutarch incorporates Platonic motifs in his own text.

Aristophanes is not the only Platonic character or the *Symposium* the only dialogue the Stoic sophist invokes. When we first hear of him he argues, with an eye to the present gathering, against those banqueters who resort to musicians for their entertainment because they are unable to engage in discussion with each other (710B). This is precisely the argument applied by Sokrates in the *Protagoras* in order to force the reluctant Abderite to abandon the interpretation of poems and acquiesce in the question-and-answer pattern (347c–d).[115] This identification with Plato's literary hero is the first of a series of Socratic guises. The rest are fashioned for him by his interlocutors. The philosopher who abandons the banquet in a hurry when he sees the musicians ready to play (710E) brings to mind the Platonic motif of the ridiculed intellectual/philosopher, found in a number of dialogues.[116] Philip distorts the sophist's self-image, projecting onto him a parody of the Socratic role. The third guise comes closer to the overall theme of music and its influence. When Plutarch suggests that the sophist's lack of susceptibility to passions guarantees the soundness of his judgement on the best type of entertainment, he calls him ἀκήλητος 'uncharmed' (711B). Philip had earlier brought in the parallel of the Sirens' song to describe how the sophist and his like viewed the musical entertainment at dinners (ὥσπερ [τὰς] Σειρῆνας ἐπιούσας φεύγοντες 710D). The same word and the same image are employed by Sokrates when he urges Phaidros to continue their discussion and avoid falling asleep under the plane-tree, thus lulled by the song of the cicadas that is likened to that of the Sirens

115 Paradoxically Plutarch's sophist defends a position originally intended to defeat the archetypal sophist. It should be noted that the Stoic is referred to as 'sophist' only in the course of the narrative (710B, 711A, 712D). The characters address him as 'wise' (710B), 'friend' (711D) and 'guest' (712E).

116 The placement of the ridiculed philosopher in a symposiac context fits better the description of the philosophers in the *Theaetetus* (173c–175b). There Sokrates says, not without a dose of (self-)mockery, that the leading exponents of philosophical life (ἐν φιλοσοφίᾳ 173c9, 174b1; φιλόσοφον 175e1 ~ φιλόσοφος 710E), by avoiding all the activities of a normal social life, banquets and revels among them (δεῖπνα καὶ σὺν αὐλητρίσι κῶμοι 173d5 ~ αὐλὸν ἐκ συμποσίου φεύγων 710E), become the butt of ridicule by their fellow-citizens (καταγελᾶται 175b5 ~ καταγέλαστος 710E). For the motif of the laughed-at philosopher, in reality a tragicomic portrait of Sokrates, see also *Resp.* 517a–518b (the escaped prisoner who descends back to the cave) and, with an explicit reference to Sokrates' life, *Grg.* 473e–474a, 484c–486d.

(διαλεγομένους καὶ παραπλέοντάς σφας ὥσπερ Σειρῆνας ἀκηλήτους *Phdr.* 259a7–b1). The fact that ἀκήλητος is a rare and poetic word, nowhere else used by Plato and Plutarch,[117] and the allusions to the ethics of music, soon to be taken up in the sophist's speech, leave no doubt that the Sokrates of the *Phaedrus* is one more paradigm informing the character of the anonymous Stoic.

The sophist's Platonic affinities become conspicuous in the most unobjectionable terms in his set speech. He is a staunch supporter of a new type of dinner theatre, the performances of Plato's dialogues. Intrigued by the presence of his opponents he goes so far as to suggest that every other kind of entertainment should be banned from the banquets and uses strong language against them. It is highly suggestive that these views are expressed through a rigid structure of antithetical pairs built on familiar Platonic vocabulary and imagery.[118] The banishing of the other kinds of performance to the public space of theatre (711B) with the exclusive appropriation for Plato productions of the symposion recalls the 'ancient quarrel' between poetry and philosophy and the subsequent banishment of most poetry from the ideal city in the *Republic*. The reference to the 'many' (711B), who have not yet experienced the novelty, may also carry something of the unflattering tone it has when used by Sokrates in the *Protagoras* or the *Gorgias*. Similarly, the combination of gender, political and literary/musical discourse at the climactic finale (711C) of the speech points not only to the programme for the education of the Guardians in the *Republic* but also to the story about the emergence of theatrocracy in the *Laws*. In sum, the sophist revolves around the following pairs: symposion/theatre, private/public, few/many, manly/effeminate, educated/uncultured, gentleman/vulgar.[119]

117 The adjective occurs only once more in the Plutarchan corpus in a quoted line from the *Odyssey* where Kirke addresses Odysseus (*Quom. Adul.* 61B = *Od.* 10. 329). It is also a Homeric *hapax*.

118 Cf. Lakmann (2000) 284–5.

119 On the allusion to *Resp.* 376e–412b see Lakmann (2000) 285, who also takes the repetition of the verb ἐκβάλλω as a reference to Homer's expulsion from Kallipolis (286). In *Lg.* 700a–701c we hear of 'vulgar shouts from the crowd' (ἄμουσοι βοαὶ πλήθους 700c2) and of poets who taught the many how to become lawless in music (τοῖς πολλοῖς ἐνέθεσαν παρανομίαν εἰς τὴν μουσικὴν 700e5–6; cf. 700d3). Similarly in *Lg.* 659a–b we come across the judge of theatrical performances who pronounces a false

This complete identification with Plato on the part of the sophist is also evident in the way his main rival chooses to confront him. Philip himself resorts to motifs from the dialogues, thereby denying the sophist the monopoly of Platonic diction. Already in his first speech he has referred to the musical sympotic activities as 'harmless pleasures' (ἀβλαβεστάτας ἡδονάς 710E), a familiar notion examined in the *Philebus* and elsewhere.[120] In his brief reply (711D) he attempts to defeat the sophist at his own game by appropriating the voice of the Platonic Sokrates. At the very start he calls his fellow-Stoic ὦ τᾶν 'my dear friend', a purely Attic form of address that occurs only once in the dialogues, in the section of Meletos' cross-examination by Sokrates (*Ap.* 25b6). As he fashions himself in the image of a new Sokrates who sustains the unjust invectives of a confused accuser, Philip deprives the sophist of the mantle of authority and puts him on the defensive, associating him with one of Plato's most despised 'villains'. At the end he quotes from Sokrates' introductory remarks to his famous palinode in the *Phaedrus* (ποτίμῳ λόγῳ ἁλμυρὰν ἀκοὴν κατακλύσαι), challenging his rival in one of his guises.[121] In between Philip launches his formidable counter-attack. He reacted against the productions of the dialogues because he could not stand watching Plato as just one among several convivial entertainments. The easy-going occasion of a drinking party is definitely not the place for the performance of philosophical works, given that even Sappho's and Anakreon's songs, standard sympotic ἀκροάματα, deserve a better audience.

verdict succumbing to the power of the masses and his own cowardice (ἐκπληττόμενον ὑπὸ θορύβου τῶν πολλῶν καὶ τῆς αὑτοῦ ἀπαιδευσίας . . . δι' ἀνανδρίαν καὶ δειλίαν a5–7). Moreover, by accusing his opponents of lack of taste and culture (δι' ἀμουσίαν καὶ ἀπειροκαλίαν 711C) the sophist identifies them with the vulgar lover of Kallipolis who cannot control his lustful drive and, therefore, ψόγον ἀμουσίας καὶ ἀπειροκαλίας ὑφέξοντα (*Resp.* 403c1–2; cf. 405b6–c6 where the reference is to the practitioner of rhetoric). In the denouement of his speech the Plutarchan sophist assumes the role of Plato's leading characters in his two great, all-embracing dialogues.

120 See *Phil.* 50e–53e; also 49e, 63a. Plutarch's phrasing echoes more closely *Resp.* 357b7 and *Lg.* 667e5.

121 The passage in the *Phaedrus* runs as follows: ἐπιθυμῶ ποτίμῳ λόγῳ οἷον ἁλμυρὰν ἀκοὴν ἀποκλύσασθαι (243d4–5). In the Platonic context Sokrates' second speech in praise of Eros will wash away the 'salty' encomium of the non-lover. Philip's choice answers to the sophist's (ab)use of gender/erotic discourse (notice the parallel between αἰδούμενος 711D and αἰσχυνόμενος 243d3). This Platonic passage is quoted once more in the *Sympotic Questions* (706D), where Plato is mentioned by name, and alluded to in at least three other places in Plutarch.

Whoever therefore tolerates, let alone supports, this new fashion trivialises Plato in the most insulting manner. By acting out of respect for and a will to preserve the decency of Plato Philip has outwitted the sophist, proving that he himself is actually more faithful to the philosopher than his rival.[122]

The elaborate construction and the abundance of cross-references and intertextual allusions leave little room for any simplistic interpretation of the section or its characters. Plato's presence is prominent throughout and especially in the rivalry between Philip and the sophist.[123] The author presents two diametrically opposite attitudes towards the performances of Plato's dialogues. Their symmetrical incompatibility suggests that they stand for typical reactions, representative of different viewpoints rather than of personal taste. There is no hard evidence that Plutarch clearly favours one stance over the other. For the sophist is more than the anti-social eccentric who needs to be exposed and silenced. After all, it is Plutarch the host who draws him into the discussion and gives him the opportunity to express his opinion without being interrupted (710B).[124] More importantly, the richness of the sophist's characterisation and his association with Plato and his writings suggest that a certain degree of caution is commendable.

[122] This part of Philip's reply is worth quoting in full: ἡμεῖς γάρ ἐσμεν οἱ πρῶτοι τοῦ πράγματος εἰσαγομένου δυσχεράναντες ἐν Ῥώμῃ καὶ καθαψάμενοι τῶν ἀξιούντων Πλάτωνα διαγωγὴν ἐν οἴνῳ ποιεῖσθαι καὶ τῶν Πλάτωνος διαλόγων ἐπὶ τραγήμασι καὶ μύροις ἀκούειν διαπίνοντας· ὅτε καὶ Σαπφοῦς ἂν ᾀδομένης καὶ τῶν Ἀνακρέοντος ἐγώ μοι δοκῶ καταθέσθαι τὸ ποτήριον αἰδούμενος (711D). This passage echoes and balances the sophist's speech through (a) the use of common or similar vocabulary (cf. εἰσάγειν, παρεισηγμένον, τῶν Πλάτωνος διαλόγων 711B) and (b) the exactly reversed treatment of the aspects of Plato productions: Philip, almost obsessively, focuses on the convivial context, a feature artfully suppressed by the sophist with a passing reference (εἰς τὰ συμπόσια 711B), whereas he bypasses with an unimpressive ἀκούειν, sandwiched between sympotic terms, the details of performance, dealt with in detail by his opponent. Interestingly, Plutarch uses the verb 'to listen' for hearing what is clearly a fully dramatised performance.

[123] That two Stoics would argue in full earnest in the name of Plato may seem rather strange to us (especially in the presence of two Platonists), but hardly so to a contemporary reader. Not only were the Stoics as a school in dialogue with or even influenced by some of (early) Platonic ethical tenets (cf. Striker 1994) but also Plato was a highly popular author in the second century AD (de Lacy 1974; Glucker 1991). He was esteemed by divergent groups of readers such as Platonists, professional philosophers, other intellectuals and the general public (albeit possibly for different reasons). The confrontation of the Stoics illustrates precisely that point.

[124] This mirrors ingeniously what Plutarch the author does when recording his character's words in direct speech.

For what it is worth, the anonymous Stoic is chosen to speak as a partisan of Plato. Philip's Socratic *persona* is mainly a countermeasure, derived from the sophist's identification with the Platonic Sokrates. The sophist's somewhat rigid theses and provocative tone qualify but do not cancel his genuine support for everything Platonic. Besides, it is not without significance that his reservations about music in banquets on the authority of Plato, an argument ridiculed and rejected by Philip, are repeated and endorsed with qualifications by Plutarch himself (713D). This argument is to be found at the very beginning and near the end of the section, rounding off the narrative in the manner of *Ringkomposition.*[125]

There is a further point that illustrates how far this engagement with Plato may go. Throughout his narrative the anonymous Stoic attempts consistently to project his own concept of a symposion. The question put by Plutarch is an opposite one: namely, which is the best kind of convivial entertainment. All speakers keep this dimension in mind and answer accordingly. When they reject certain performance genres they do so because they consider them inappropriate for a sympotic context, mainly for practical reasons.[126] All take as their starting points the practices and character of actual gatherings. This is also the main thrust of Philip's critique. Contrariwise, the sophist reverses and radically redefines the notion of a drinking party. Not only does he suppress the sympotic element in his description of the Plato productions; by expelling every other type of performance he actually claims the

[125] Plutarch holds that banqueters who are able to entertain each other with words of philosophy have no need of music. His use of φιλοσοφία echoes the φιλόσοφος ἀνήρ in Philip's caricature of the sophist (710E). Here the author implicitly recognises the sophist's viewpoint. On the other hand, the self-reflective remarks about a symposion full of strife and abuse (λοιδορίαν 713F ~ λοιδορῶν 711D), about to dissolve into a series of contests (713E–F), show that the banquet at Chaironeia may have failed to live up to the ideal envisaged by Plato and accepted by Plutarch and the sophist – the latter's behaviour being largely responsible for any such failure. The final part of Plutarch's words echoes and reconciles themes from the speeches by Philip and the sophist (cf. the story about the Persian King who was thought of as ἀπειρόκαλος and ἀγροῖκος (713E), both terms of abuse used by the Stoics against each other: ὑπαγροικοτέροις 710D, ἀπειροκαλίαν 711C).

[126] Diogenianos banishes tragedy ὡς οὐ πάνυ τι συμποτικόν (711E), the Pyladeian pantomime for being, among other things, πολυπρόσωπον (711E) and the Old Comedy as ἀνάρμοστος ἀνθρώποις πίνουσιν (711F). Similarly, Plutarch (712E) rejects both types of pantomime because ἁρμόζειν δ' οὐδέτερον οἶμαι συμποσίῳ γένος.

occasion of a private gathering as the exclusive domain of a decent and edifying happening. Significantly, he resorts to the vocabulary of *Republic* 10 in order to rewrite the 'quarrel between poetry and philosophy' in new terms: common theatre in public spaces, Plato's 'theatre' in private spaces. For some reason the sophist believes that the introduction of these productions could bring back something lost.

Plutarch has provided the reader with a clue as to what the sophist's and like-minded people's self-image may have been. He introduces him to the readers as the 'long-bearded Stoic sophist'. The adjective βαθυπώγων (710B) is nowhere else used in the whole Plutarchan corpus. Its emphatic position as a constituent of the character's identity means that the reader is expected to respond by locating the sophist's ideological background. For already from Hellenistic times onwards the beard had become one of the 'trademarks' of the public image of the philosopher.[127] The thinker who grew his beard could thereby lay a claim to some intellectual authority and link himself to a centuries-old tradition. The anonymous Stoic is definitely a traditionalist, who wishes to reintroduce the values of the past to an indifferent or, even, hostile present. He defends Aristophanes in a period of Menander's domination (712D) and in music has a longing for the enharmonic, a genus already obsolete for some centuries (711C).[128] The length of his beard may also be seen as a conscious reminder of the portraits of Zenon, the founder of Stoicism, and even read back to Plato.[129] It is this love for tradition that leads him to the wholehearted support for the performances of the dialogues.

But wearing a long beard takes on a new meaning during the centuries of Roman occupation. As a clean-shaven face was the norm for the Romans, the cultivation of a beard became a defining

[127] Zanker (1995) 108–10.

[128] See West (1992a) 160–6; Hagel (2009) 413–29. Plutarch jokingly alludes to the sophist's preferences when addressing him (ποῖον ἂν μάλιστα γένος εἰς πότον ἐναρμόσειεν 711B). I cannot see any anti-Platonic hint in the praise of the enharmonic genus. *Republic* 7.530d–531c does not prove that Plato disliked it (*pace* Teodorsson (1989–96) III 111 on 711C). Plato's professed high esteem of Damon, who held that enharmonic made people brave, suggests rather the opposite. On Damon see West (1992a) 246–9; Wallace (2005).

[129] Cf. Richter (1965) II figs 1084–1105; Zanker (1995) 76–7, 92–7.

element of the Greek identity. An emphatically bearded intellectual could have been perceived as asserting his will to defy the directives of the dominant power.[130] I believe the sophist's personality should rather be seen in this context. His identification with Plato is not the result of an impersonal appreciation of a long-dead philosopher by a gentleman scholar,[131] but derives from the passionate love for one of the pillars of one's own tradition. For him, dramatised Plato as an ἀκρόαμα in a reformed symposion is a welcome development in an attempt to reaffirm an alternative Greek cultural discourse in the context of foreign rule. The denouement of his speech, full of the language of power, shows that he thinks a lot in terms of domination/subordination. In short, through this character Plutarch may have wished to give voice to a view not uncommon among his contemporaries, as may be seen from his own and other works.[132]

[130] This identification was helped by a standard Roman attitude that 'everything that concerned culture and learning was clearly the domain of the conquered Greeks' (Zanker 1995, 199). Or as Henderson (1996) puts it, 'so far as the Roman conquerors of the Greek world are concerned, Greek thinkers, theorists and speakers were a bunch of elderly males with wild locks and shaggy beards, staring eyes and hollow cheeks – not at all like themselves' (334). This was the case throughout Roman times, although the demarcating line between Greek and Roman had to be renegotiated after Hadrian appropriated for himself the 'philosopher's' or the 'Greeks' beard'. A solution was found in growing a longer beard. Cf. Zanker (1995) 198–226. It is worth mentioning that the same cultural division continues in the image of the priests and bishops of the Roman Catholic (clean-shaven) and Greek Orthodox Church (long-bearded).

[131] For the concept of gentleman scholar Zanker (1995) 203–10.

[132] Significantly, the next question in the *Sympotic Questions* (714A–C) constructs another boundary between Greek and a foreign culture: deliberation while drinking is proved to be not a Persian but a Greek custom. The insertion of such a character in a sympotic context may be more appropriate than thought because, as we read in the end of Book 7, wine liberates by taking away τὸ δουλοπρεπές (716B). The following passage from the *Borystheniticus* by Dion of Prusa, a contemporary of Plutarch, provides, in my view, the best commentary on the anonymous Stoic's speech: πάνυ μὲν οὖν ἄν τις ἥσθη τῇ ὄψει φιλόσοφος ἀνήρ, ὅτι ἅπαντες ἦσαν τὸν ἀρχαῖον τρόπον, ὥς φησιν Ὅμηρος τοὺς Ἕλληνας, κομῶντες καὶ τὰ γένεια ἀφεικότες, εἷς δὲ ἐν αὐτοῖς μόνος ἐξυρημένος, καὶ τοῦτον ἐλοιδόρουν τε καὶ ἐμίσουν ἅπαντες, ἐλέγετο δὲ οὐκ ἄλλως τοῦτο ἐπιτηδεύειν, ἀλλὰ κολακεύων Ῥωμαίους καὶ τὴν πρὸς αὐτοὺς φιλίαν ἐπιδεικνύμενος· ὥστε εἶδεν ἄν τις ἐπ' ἐκείνου τὸ αἰσχρὸν τοῦ πράγματος καὶ οὐδαμῇ πρέπον ἀνδράσιν (36.17 Russell). Similarly, another contemporary of theirs, the author of the *On the Sublime*, a work attributed to Longinos, uses a philosopher to voice one of the most powerful cries of protest against the servility of the Greeks towards their Roman rulers: 'οἱ δὲ νῦν ἐοίκαμεν' ἔφη 'παιδομαθεῖς εἶναι δουλείας δικαίας . . . καὶ ἄγευστοι καλλίστου καὶ γονιμωτάτου λόγων νάματος, τὴν ἐλευθερίαν' ἔφη 'λέγω, διόπερ οὐδὲν ὅτι μὴ κόλακες ἐκβαίνομεν μεγαλοφυεῖς' (44.3–4 Russell; cf. Segal 1959;

Athenaios

We have to wait almost a century before we hear again of performances of Plato's dialogues. The second testimony is found in Athenaios' *Deipnosophists*, composed in the period 193–7 AD.[133] The work takes the form of a reported dialogue, in which the author narrates to a certain Timokrates the words and deeds of the diners at the house of the Roman official and bibliophile Larensis, evidently on more than one occasion. In the ninth book a cook astonishes the banqueters with the refined quality of his dishes and his delivery of comic passages in praise of the art of cookery and its practitioners (376c–383f). After one such recitation the host makes the following remark:

ὁ καλὸς ἡμῖν ἑστιάτωρ Λαρήνσιος "καὶ πόσῳ κάλλιον", ἔφη, "τὰ τοιαῦτα ἐκμανθάνειν τοὺς μαγείρους ἢ ἅπερ παρά τινι τῶν πολιτῶν ἡμῶν, ὃς ὑπὸ πλούτου καὶ τρυφῆς τοὺς τοῦ θαυμασιωτάτου Πλάτωνος διαλόγους ἠνάγκαζεν ἐκμανθάνοντας τοὺς μαγείρους φέροντάς τε τὰς λοπάδας ἅμα λέγειν 'εἷς, δύο, τρεῖς· ὁ δὲ δὴ τέταρτος ἡμῖν, ὦ φίλε Τίμαιε, ποῦ τῶν χθὲς μὲν δαιτυμόνων, τὰ νῦν δ' ἑστιατόρων;' ἔπειτ' ἄλλος ἀπεκρίνατο 'ἀσθένειά τις αὐτῷ ξυνέπεσεν, ὦ Σώκρατες.' διεξήρχοντό τε τοῦ διαλόγου τὰ πολλὰ τὸν τρόπον τοῦτον, ὡς ἄχθεσθαι μὲν τοὺς εὐωχουμένους, ὑβρίζεσθαι δὲ τὸν πάνσοφον ἐκεῖνον ἄνθρωπον ὁσημέραι, καὶ διὰ τοῦτο πολλοὺς τῶν καθαρείων ἐξόμνυσθαι τὰς παρ' ἐκείνῳ ἑστιάσεις. οἱ δὲ ἡμέτεροι οὗτοι ἅμα ἴσως ταῦτ' ἐκμανθάνοντες οὐκ ὀλίγην ὑμῖν θυμηδίαν παρέχουσιν." (9. 381f–382b)

Boot 1980). Evidently a common mentality underlies all three passages exemplified in the construction of an anti-Roman resistance voice (apparently shared by another first-century AD figure of the author of the Revelation of John, for that matter; cf. Perry 2007). Because of the founding dogma of 'Greco-Romanism', however, there is a general tendency in scholarship, often cutting across disciplinary boundaries (cf. Shiffman 2008), to gloss over any such references in the works of the Greeks of the so-called Imperial period. Even the undoubtedly anti-Roman tone of the passage in Dion (cf. Russell 1992, 220; Moles 1995, 186; Swain 1996, 215–16) has been suppressed or qualified by some commentators (cf. Braund 1997, 130–1 who surprisingly remarks that the clean-shaven Olbian is hated not because he is a Romaniser but because he is a 'flatterer'!). For a product of the dominant ideology on the subject see, for instance, Goldhill (2001). On Greek identity in the Roman Empire (and beyond) see Swain (1996) 17–131; Alcock (1997); (2002) 36–98; Konstan and Said (2006); Mellor (2008); Barchiesi (2009); Whitmarsh (2009); Spawforth (forthcoming). For Plutarch see Swain (1996) 135–86 and (1997); Lamberton (1997); Duff (1999) 287–309; Preston (2001); Teodorsson (2005). For Dion see Moles (1995) and (2005); Swain (1996) 187–241; Whitmarsh (2001a) 156–66 and (2001b) 285–94.

133 Braund (2000) 13.

Our good host, Larensis, said: 'How much better is it for the cooks to learn these kinds of things instead of the things they learned at the house of a certain fellow-citizen of ours. He was so puffed up by wealth and luxury that he forced his cooks to learn the dialogues of the wonderful Plato and to say as they brought in the dishes: "One, two, three. Where, my dear Timaios, is the fourth of our guests of yesterday and hosts of today?" Then the other replied: "Some illness befell him, Sokrates." And the cooks would recite most of the dialogue in that manner. The result was that the guests were vexed and that all-wise man was insulted every day, and, for this reason, the men of taste boycotted the parties of that fellow. But these cooks of ours, by learning these things, give no little pleasure.' (after Gulick (1927–33) IV)

This passage recalls the episode in the *Sympotic Questions* in a number of points. The Plato productions Larensis speaks of are clearly of the dramatised type as in Plutarch (ἔπειτ' ἄλλος ἀπεκρίνατο). The performances were also part of the after-dinner entertainment (τοὺς εὐωχουμένους) offered at elite gatherings in Rome (τινι τῶν πολιτῶν ἡμῶν).[134] There is also recorded a fierce reaction against these performances on the part of the guests, reminiscent of Philip's and his friends' stance (ἄχθεσθαι, ἐξόμνυσθαι). For these reasons Athenaios' passage has been so far treated as the natural complement to the earlier testimony, filling in any gaps left by Plutarch's narrative. Even when the distance in time is noted, the supposition that in both authors the same type of productions is under discussion is never contested. Consequently, conclusions valid for Larensis' satirical description have been single-handedly transferred to the context of the banquet at Chaironeia. It may not be too much of an exaggeration to claim that were it not for the passage in Athenaios performances of Plato might have had a warmer scholarly reception.[135]

Under closer scrutiny the picture becomes more complex and important differences come to the surface. At one level there is the obvious shift from a polyphonic to a univocal mode of discourse. Plutarch has chosen to present the matter through two characters strongly committed to their opposite (hence complementary) points of view. It is not easy to determine whose side the author

[134] The character of the passage suggests that a well-known figure in the social life of contemporary Rome is targeted. Cf. Braund (2000) 5–6.

[135] Teodorsson (1989–96) III 110 on 711C; Lakmann (2000) 286–9.

takes. In Athenaios there is only one speaker who happens to be the host of the symposion, a central figure throughout the *Deipnosophists*, lavishly praised, and the author's patron.[136] In this case the reader is left with little room for ambiguity on the authority of the utterance. The use of a single speaker means a channelling of the perspective. Larensis is not the ideal, objective recorder of a social event. As is clear from the way he begins and ends his little speech, he indulges for a moment in a display of an air of superiority in an ongoing contest between Roman notables. The applause his cook elicited from the diners reflects on him as the tasteful host who knows how to please his guests, wisely picking the right type of entertainment for the occasion. The contrast with his *nouveau riche* fellow-citizen (ὑπὸ πλούτου καὶ τρυφῆς), who succeeded in alienating himself from his social circle, could not be more vivid. The satirical tone of the passage allows for some comic exaggeration.[137] The depiction of the unnamed host in the role of anti-Larensis should also be added to the picture. In other words, this is very likely a true story mediated by a sole, unsympathetic observer in a piece of sympotic literature.

The really striking feature, though, is how dissimilar the descriptions of these Plato performances in Plutarch and Athenaios are. The Stoic sophist had spoken of carefully designed productions with the full arsenal of professional directing and acting, supported by a sound theoretical background. The dialogues were performed in full and their selection was based on their suitability for staging. The dramatisations Larensis has in mind could not be further removed from this model. The lack of professionalism is conspicuous at all levels. The performers were mere cooks with no particular talent or enthusiasm for their new task (ἠνάγκαζεν). Their training was presumably undertaken by their master himself whose motives were hardly affected by any artistic or philosophical worries. Not the whole works but selections from the dialogues seem to have been dramatised (τοῦ διαλόγου τὰ πολλά). More

136 Larensis is defined by the epitomator as the subject of the whole work (1. 1a) while Athenaios opens the main body of the dialogue with a eulogy of him (1. 2b–3d). See Braund (2000).

137 For instance in the image of the cooks who are forced to learn the *Timaeus* and quote from the dialogue while carrying the dishes or in the description of the guests' reactions.

importantly, the choice of the particular dialogue should come as a surprise if we take for granted the identity of the performances in both authors. The *Timaeus* is not the type of dialogue that would normally be thought of as conforming to the criteria described by the anonymous sophist. But one detail in Larensis' description speaks decisively against any such thesis. It is clearly said that the cooks deliver the words *while bringing in the dishes* (φέροντάς τε τὰς λοπάδας ἅμα λέγειν). This implies the absence of any dividing line between their performing their professional duties and performing Plato. They do not assume the role of the Platonic characters whose lines they have memorised; they rather speak in their own person with borrowed texts. Instead of role-playing the audience watches a (transparent) imitation of role-playing. The self-reflective use of theatrical conventions means that the pieces of drama in the house of Athenaios' wealthy Roman must have been of a very different kind from the ones mentioned in Plutarch.

This discrepancy is explicable because of the dissimilar nature of the respective events. Larensis describes, in effect, a *parody of Plato performance*. Unlike their earlier counterparts, the dramatisations in Athenaios are presented as eccentricities, the product of a single person's vanity and bad taste. Instead of being performed in their own right, Plato's dialogues became simply the means for the display of the particular cooks' competence in mastering the delivery of unusual or difficult texts. Larensis' remark that these eccentricities did violence to and insulted Plato accords well with the satiric spirit of parody.[138] Moreover, this interpretation

[138] The phrase ὑβρίζεσθαι δὲ τὸν πάνσοφον ἐκεῖνον ἄνθρωπον is usually taken as a reference to the unlucky host (Gulick 1927–33 (IV); Lakmann 2000). The latter points to (a) the parallel construction of the clauses (μέν ~ δέ), which requires a mention of the host to balance that of the guests (εὐωχουμένους), and (b) the repetition of the ἐκεῖνος a little later in the same sentence with an obvious reference to the wealthy Roman (Lakmann 2000, 287 n. 41). Now neither of these points is compelling. A corollary of this reading would be that πάνσοφος is here used ironically. But the *only other time* Athenaios uses the word is in connection with Euripides in a straightforward manner (14. 665a). I cannot see why Plato could not be called 'all-wise' by Larensis in his speech. The more so since the reference to Plato by name in the passage (τοῦ θαυμασιωτάτου Πλάτωνος) should be taken at face value, given that the phrase is a standard manner of reference to an author already or about to be quoted (2. 48c: Homer; 3. 78e: Herodotos; 3. 99b: Plato; 6. 268e: Kratinos; 8. 335d, 15. 686f: Chrysippos). Therefore, the phrase is most likely a reference to Plato.

provides a satisfactory answer to the puzzle of the *Timaeus*. It is not easy to see in what sense this dialogue could pass as an ἐλαφρότατος one (p. 199 n. 91).[139] If we abandon the association with the performances in Plutarch, as I think we should, we need an alternative explanation for such a strange choice, to say the least. On the hypothesis of a production with elements of parody, however, the *Timaeus* emerges as an attractive text to dramatise. To begin with, it was the most widely read and known dialogue at the time.[140] Most of the diners would have been familiar with the basics of the plot and the content of the work and, therefore, better prepared to attend an 'alternative' presentation. Another advantage would be the number of suitable themes treated. As the only dialogue about the physical world, it offers sections on the creation of the world out of the first elements and detailed descriptions of the physiology of the body that would turn into a fascinating spectacle in the context of lavishly prepared dishes.[141] The strongest argument, however, in favour of the dramatisation of the *Timaeus* as a piece of dinner theatre is that Plato has chosen to dress up his text with the imagery of the symposion. From the very first words the interlocutors are cast

[139] Lakmann (2000) 288 realises the difficulty and tries to overcome it with an admittedly ingenious suggestion. She points out that the opening words of the dialogue were susceptible to arrangement in more than one rhythmical pattern, a feature noticed already in antiquity (Quint. *Inst. Orat.* 9.4.77–8; cf. Rahn 1975, 339 n. 395). This made the *Timaeus* easy to learn and follow and in this sense a performable text. The weakness of this thesis is that Lakmann is forced to hold, arbitrarily, that only the initial discussion between the interlocutors before Kritias' narration of the Atlantis myth, that is 17a–21a at most, could have been recited by the cooks ('die Vorträge der Köche . . . über die leichteren Eingangskapitel nicht hinausgekommen sind'). Since this blatantly contradicts the evidence (τοῦ διαλόγου τὰ πολλά) the explanation has to be abandoned or revised.

[140] Notice, for example, how often this dialogue is cited or referred to in the works of the Middle Platonists as indicated by Dillon (1977) 428, Index II. According to Niehoff (2007) from the second century AD onwards the *Timaeus* 'helped to construct a textual community, which sought to preserve the original Greek tradition against its appropriation by Christian readers' (162). Significantly, Proklos mentions that the third-century critic Longinos had commented on the style of its opening sentence (Procl. *In Ti.* 1.14.7–20. Cf. Heath 1999, 62).

[141] Particularly liable to a comical treatment would be the part in which Timaios gives an account of the structure and functions of the mortal parts of the soul and the rest of the body (44d–46c, 69a–81e), joined by the passages on the body of the world (31b–34a) and the senses (61c–69a). Especially the denouement of the dialogue, where the creation of the women and the animals of land, air and sea is attributed to different types of men, has a 'surrealistic' potential easily exploitable amidst dishes of stuffed pork or fishes (90e–92c).

into the roles of 'diners' and 'hosts' (δαιτυμόνων . . . ἑστιατόρων 17a2–3), their subsequent discussion, that is the main body of the dialogue, is described as 'feast of speeches' (τὰ τῶν λόγων ξένια 20c1).[142] It takes no more than a literal reading of the text to justify any production of the *Timaeus* in a convivial context. Such a producer could always claim that he simply conforms to the 'stage directions' of the author himself.

There are two points following from the parodic nature of the Plato performance in Athenaios. First, the negative response of the diners may be seen under the correct perspective. The guests are not said to object to the dramatisation of a Platonic dialogue. They expressed their discomfort at the selection of the particular text: unconvinced by the sympotic overtones of the *Timaeus* they could not see why the cooks should start speaking about the creation of the universe instead of their usual extracts from comedy.[143] The καθάρειοι, in particular, must have reacted to what they perceived as a bad joke at the expense of one of the greatest men of the past. Their decision to place an 'embargo' on their visits to that host recalls the fierce opposition of Philip and his friends in Plutarch and stems from the same principle: their belief that Plato is an inappropriate author for convivial entertainment.[144] Second, a parody is by definition secondary to the object on which it exercises itself. The eccentricity in the unnamed Roman's house presupposes proper productions of the dialogues, in full accordance with the theatrical conventions. The joke becomes more intelligible and pointed

[142] For the sympotic vocabulary in the *Timaeus* and the description of Socratic conversation in terms of a word-feast in that and other dialogues see Schoos (1999) 98–102; Slaveva-Griffin (2005); Worman (2008) 184–6 (*Republic* 1).

[143] It is noteworthy that Larensis' cook recites only passages from cooks' speeches, almost without exception (even the lines quoted in 381a cannot be shown with certainty to deviate from the rule).

[144] There are indeed a number of elements common to the two narratives. The anonymous Roman patron pairs with the anonymous sophist. The negative reception of the performances features in both, while Larensis in his description shares Philip's viewpoint. The reference to the καθάρειοι corresponds to the αὐστηροὶ καὶ χαρίεντες mentioned by the Stoic. In view of these parallels the question of intertextuality may be raised. Athenaios was well versed in Plutarch (Berra 2005) and it cannot be excluded that he could have had his predecessor in mind when composing the episode. It is difficult, however, to be sure about the extent of the dependence. For instance, the passage in Athenaios ostensibly aims at praising Larensis' education and good taste. Plato is mentioned incidentally, in stark contrast to the partisanship in the name of Plato in Plutarch.

if some of the guests were acquainted with serious performances of the *Timaeus*, in which the imagery of the symposion would have been alluded to in a less realistic manner. If these mock-performances were held on a daily basis (ὁσημέραι), they might have included more than one dialogue (τοὺς . . . διαλόγους) and perhaps reflected a practice about the presentation of related dialogues in groups.[145] It is reasonable then to conclude that Athenaios provides indirect evidence for performances of Plato's dialogues, of a type similar to but not identical with those already suggested by Plutarch's Stoic sophist almost a hundred years earlier.[146]

The combined testimony of these authors indicates the existence of a tradition of dramatised Plato productions at least throughout the second century AD.[147] This tradition was important enough to be parodied at the dinners of wealthy Romans. The next question naturally refers to the origin and duration of the tradition. The reader needs to ask himself whether these performances were a short-lived fashion, born and dead in Rome in the course of a century, or whether Plutarch and Athenaios describe the contemporary phase of a phenomenon that preceded and outlived both of them. It has to be admitted right from the start that the impression given by the literary record leans heavily towards the first alternative. No other writer before or after provides a similar testimony, something quite difficult to account for if performed Plato was indeed a long-established tradition. The evidence from these two authors themselves also tells the same story: Plutarch speaks of

[145] The arrangements in trilogies and tetralogies would be particularly suitable for such a purpose.

[146] Alternatively, the anonymous Roman may have produced these dramatisations merely out of vanity, in his attempt to advertise his supposed familiarity with the great classics of literature, not unlike Petronius' Trimalchio. On this reading there is no need to postulate any actual Plato performances that were parodied by that Roman. True, but then why not dramatise any one of the short, 'light' dialogues or, alternatively, the *Symposium* for an after-dinner entertainment? The choice of the *Timaeus* indicates a strong theoretical background that only a serious study could provide.

[147] This tradition *might* also be reflected in a difficult passage from Pliny the Younger, if the correction of the editors *Sotadicos* is abandoned in favour of the unanimous reading of the manuscripts *Socraticos*. There the Socratic dialogues are apparently associated with comedies, mimes and lyric poetry: *facio non numquam versiculos severos parum, facio; nam et comoedias audio et specto mimos et lyricos lego et Socraticos intellego; aliquando praeterea rideo iocor ludo* (*Ep.* 5.3.2). The inference that these are references to performed literature has been made by Csapo (1997) 169 n. 23.

a novelty that may not have survived its initial attempts at winning over general approval.[148] De Vries (1984), in fact, believes that the passage from the *Sympotic Questions* provides evidence against the hypothesis of Plato performances before Roman times. He bases his argument on (1) Plutarch's silence – his knowledge of the history of the Academy would make him the one person likely to report any relevant evidence from the classical period had it existed – and (2) his elaborate description of the performances: Plutarch would not have any reason to spend so much time on them if his readers had been acquainted with them even outside the convivial context (144). In view of this overwhelming silence of the sources the natural conclusion is that Plato performances were a marginal artistic trend associated with the intellectual life of the Second Sophistic. It may have originated out of a pedantic desire to contribute to the veneration of Plato or, even worse, an insatiable appetite for inventing new convivial pastimes.[149]

Legitimate though this conclusion may be, it can by no means be considered final. And there is a very simple reason, namely *the inconclusive nature of the evidence*. In the face of so poor a record the interpretation of the available information is so much conditioned by the perspective implicit in the questions asked. Take for example argument (1). It is based on the following facts: (a) Plutarch says that Plato productions had been recently introduced at dinners in Rome and (b) he was also versed in the history of Plato's Academy. But then (c) that the dialogues were never performed by Plato does not necessarily follow from (a) and (b). Nothing compelled Plutarch to mention anything more than he needed in that context, if he ever had any relevant information. If, on the other hand, as is more likely, he was unaware of productions of the dialogues during Plato's lifetime, his ignorance is not an argument for disproving events which purportedly took place almost five centuries before. Besides, there seems to be some

[148] This is an inference from the sophist's last words (καὶ οὐ θαυμάσαιμ' ἂν εἰ τὸ πάμπαν ἐκβαλοῦσιν 711C), if interpreted as a remark with the privilege of hindsight – in other words, a 'prophecy' *post eventum*. Braund (2000) 6 has suggested that Athenaios could very well describe an obsolete practice, as implied by the use of the imperfect tense (ἠνάγκαζεν). This seems to me rather a weak point.

[149] Suggested by Anderson (1997) 2180 and Teodorsson (1989–96) III 109–10 on 711B respectively.

uncertainty as to what the novelty about this type of dinner theatre is. Most commentators take it for granted that it was the dramatised performances themselves. A close reading of the text makes it more probable that the new element was the venue, namely the after-dinner entertainment in symposia at Rome. The choice of παρεισηγμένον may hint at these performances being transported from another location, either outside Rome or outside the convivial milieu or both. This interpretation is lent some credibility by a parallel in Plutarch himself, when he uses the same verb in a similar context to refer to types of entertainment of Greek origin introduced into the symposia of barbarian leaders.[150] The objection to this reading, expressed in argument (2), is that the elaborate description of the performances must be due to the fact that Plutarch's readers were hearing of them for the first time. Hardly a fatal objection, since a number of other reasons may have led to this decision: for example, the need for making clear that the dialogues were performed and not recited, indicating the theoretical and professional background of the novelty, or balancing Philip's speech (p. 211 n. 122). As for Athenaios, the brief life of a wealthy host's experiment tells us nothing about the duration of the phenomenon lying behind the parody. In sum, there is hardly anything in these two authors that decisively disproves the existence of pre- (or post-) Roman Plato productions.

A hypothesis

I would like now to draw attention to a couple of points that may be interpreted as indicating exactly the opposite. The first is the type of texts that yield the evidence. Both the *Sympotic Questions* and the *Deipnosophists* belong to the genre of prose

[150] In his *Life of Crassus* he mentions the joint feasts between the Parthian Orodes and the Armenian Artavazes: ἑστιάσεις τε καὶ πότοι δι' ἀλλήλων ἦσαν αὐτοῖς, καὶ πολλὰ παρεισήγετο τῶν ἀπὸ τῆς Ἑλλάδος ἀκουσμάτων (*Crassus* 33.1–2). In addition to the identity between ἀκούσματα and ἀκροάματα the common theme between the two passages may be noted: Greek types of entertainment introduced in foreign lands. Soon to be mentioned a little later in the *Life* is one of the most celebrated pieces of dinner theatre in literature: Jason of Tralleis sings Agave's part from Euripides' *Bacchae*, and acts using Crassus' severed head in the place of the mask of Pentheus (33.3–7). The overtly theatrical nature of the context offers one more point of contact with the passage from the *Sympotic Questions* (cf. Easterling 1997, 221–2).

sympotic literature.[151] It is well known that Plato's *Symposium* was the founding text and a standard work of reference for all writers of the genre afterwards. Although there is nothing special about mentioning productions of Platonic dialogues in a composition of this type, the construction by both Plutarch and Athenaios of their authorial *personae* as successors/rivals of Plato gives the testimonies another dimension.[152] A sympotic dialogue presents itself as the natural textual environment for providing information on the performance of the dialogues.

A second point would be the theoretical background behind the productions. The distinction between dramatic and narrated dialogues was obviously much earlier than the second century AD. It can be traced back to the late first century BC[153] and may very well belong to the hermeneutic arsenal of the Old Academy, given that it is probably based on Sokrates' division of poetry in *Republic* 2. The application of this taxonomy to the Platonic corpus was a primary concern to the students of the Academy and later to Platonists throughout antiquity. It would be reasonable to assume that the use of this scheme in support of performances of the dialogues must have originated in the circles of Plato's followers.

A third suggestive feature would be the context in which these performances are presented. In both cases the dramatised Platonic dialogues are set in opposition to performances of dramatic literature. In the *Sympotic Questions* the sophist makes it clear that the

[151] For Plutarch see Fuhrmann (1972) xvi–xvii; Teodorsson (1989–96) I 12, who holds that the *Sympotic Questions* is a fusion of two genres, the symposion and the collection of problems. For Athenaios see Anderson (2000), Romeri (2000). Both texts are star examples among those prose works that feature miscellanistic characteristics according to König (2007) 43–7 (Plutarch) and (2008) 90–3 (Athenaios). On the symposion as an institution of the polis see Hobden (2009); Murray (2009).

[152] In the introduction to the *Sympotic Questions* Plutarch locates himself in the tradition of authors of convivial writings that is, naturally, headed by Plato (612D. Cf. Teodorsson 1989–96, I 35–6). Plato's presence is also evident in the choice of the opening question throughout the work. Athenaios also consciously models his own work on Plato (Δραματουργεῖ δὲ τὸν διάλογον ὁ Ἀθήναιος ζήλῳ Πλατωνικῷ 1. 1f): his opening section is a merging of the first lines of the *Phaedo* and the *Symposium* (1. 2a–b), while in the last paragraph of the whole work there seems to be a reference to Plato's *Second Letter* (14. 702b–c). For Athenaios' complex relation to Plato see Trapp (2000b).

[153] This is the most likely date for the composition of the *Anonynous Commentary to Theaetetus* where this division is presupposed. See Bastianini and Sedley (1995) 254–6; Sedley (1997) 112. For arguments in favour of a date around AD 100 see Brittain (2001) 249–54.

new type of drama he favours is incompatible with the current ones that are suitable only for the theatre (711B). Plato's dialogue is set in a contest for the best type of dinner theatre with Tragedy, Old and New Comedy, Mime and Pantomime (711E–713F). In the *Deipnosophists* the tasteless anonymous host offers a parody of the *Timaeus*, whereas Larensis' cook recites passages from comic plays. The practice of these two authors may reflect an established view that Plato's literary productions constituted an alternative to the existing works of theatre in all aspects. There are reasons to believe that this idea was already present and cultivated in Plato's Academy.

In view of these considerations the following hypothesis may be worth pondering: dramatisations of Plato's dialogues were first produced in the Academy during Plato's lifetime on the occasion of dinners at his house. There is nothing inherently surprising in this suggestion given that the symposion was the appropriate place for the composition, performance and transmission of literature long before Plato.[154] The symposia at Plato's house are constantly described in the extant literature as simple and elegant.[155] Such a description leaves enough room for the above hypothesis as it indicates that the alternative and unique character of a Platonic dinner would be the proper place to introduce an exclusively Platonic type of drama. We also know that later Platonists celebrated Sokrates' and Plato's birthday with discussions on issues taken from Plato's dialogues while in Plotinos' school the festivities included a competition between new compositions in prose or verse.[156] A

[154] See Latacz (1990); Bowie (1993a); Whitmarsh (2004) 52–67.

[155] See Plutarch *De San. Praec.* 127A–B: Τιμόθεος εἶπε τῇ προτεραίᾳ δεδειπνηκὼς ἐν Ἀκαδημείᾳ παρὰ Πλάτωνι μουσικὸν καὶ λιτὸν δεῖπνον, ὡς οἱ παρὰ Πλάτωνι δειπνήσαντες καὶ εἰς αὔριον ἡδέως γίγνονται. Cf. also Plut. *QC* 686A–D; Ael. *Var. Hist.* 2.18; Ath. 10. 419c–d. According to Plutarch another feature of Plato's dinners was ἡ τῶν λαληθέντων παρὰ πότον ἀναθεώρησις (*QC* 686B–C). This may refer, among other things, to the type of dinner theatre the guests watched and may hint at a possible discussion after the performance of a given dialogue. Plutarch goes on to mention that Platonists of his time evidently tried to keep the tradition and model their gatherings on what they thought of as the Platonic standard: ὅπου καὶ νῦν τῶν Σωκρατικῶν συμποσίων μετουσία καὶ ἀπόλαυσίς ἐστι τοῖς φιλολόγοις, ὥσπερ αὐτοῖς ἐκείνοις τοῖς τότε δειπνοῦσι (686C).

[156] For the discussions see Plut. *QC* 7. 718C; Procl. *In Remp.* 1. 368A Kroll. For the performance of literature see Porph. *Plot.* 2.40–3, 15.1–6 Brisson. Cf. Brisson (1982) 103–4, Brisson et al. (eds.) (1982–92) II 265–9.

persuasive case has been made that these celebrations may go back to the first generation of Plato's successors or even the Master himself, at least as far as Sokrates' birthday is concerned.[157]

Of course, the greatest argument against this hypothesis is once again the silence of the sources, this time as regards the fourth century BC. By now, however, it may have hopefully become clear that this is not so powerful a reason to deter us from envisioning the possibility. Not only because such silence relates mainly to written sources – this chapter provides non-literary evidence that points in the opposite direction – but also because this silence is less impenetrable than may seem. Perhaps if texts like Speusippos' *Perideipnon*, which narrates the events at the memorial dinner after Plato's funeral, were extant, the picture would have been slightly different. In sum, it would be admittedly imprudent, to say the least, to ignore the lack of any *direct literary* evidence for productions of the dialogues by Plato himself. But is it really plausible for one to argue that the evident potential of the dialogues for performance was not realised until four or five centuries after Plato's death?

The notation

One of the basic features of the Plato productions as described in Plutarch was that the performers changed their voices according to the demands of the text at any given moment (φωνῆς πλάσμα *QC* 8. 711C). They would improvise their own delivery of the lines or follow the directions of their trainer. But the professional actor, singer, orator or any other kind of performer, in addition to his talent for learning, storing and (re)creating vocal modulation, musical phrases and melodies, would normally have access to a code of written symbols that would help him to memorise, for instance, the melodic pattern, or guide him on how to modify the tone, quality or speed of the utterances. That was the function of the systems of musical notation developed and used by the Greeks at different periods, vestiges of which have come down to us usually in association with texts to be sung or recited. In this

157 White (2000) 153–63.

Figure 2. Plato *Protagoras* 356c. *POxy* xiii 1624, early 3rd cent. AD.

context, the possibility that a Plato papyrus from the late Imperial period might contain signs suggestive of a type of recitation opens up an interesting new perspective.

The papyrus under discussion is *POxy* xiii 1624, which in its original form contained the complete text of Plato's *Protagoras*. The extant fragments cover the section 337b3–357b2. On the basis of the style of writing it has been dated to the beginning of the third century AD. An interesting feature is the number of corrections and alternative readings introduced by a second hand, possibly later in the century. It was some of these later insertions found in col. LXIV, fr. 25 ii, lines 2–4 [590–2] that have attracted the attention of one papyrologist and led her to an alternative interpretation (fig. 2). Basing her interpretation on the three dots over μέν in line 2 [590] and the oblique strokes between σμικρότεραι and φαῖεν in line 4 [592], Jourdan-Hemmerdinger has spoken of traces of a musical notation, designed not for the recording of melodies and singing but for providing guidelines for ornamental reading.[158]

158 *POxy* xiii 1624 was first published by Grenfell and Hunt (1919) 199–208 (their numbering of the lines is given in brackets). It has been excellently re-edited by Tulli

Before the discussion of this new interpretation it is fair to say that scholars have not been unaware of these particular signs. They simply rendered them differently, in a rather straightforward manner. The standard explanation is that in both cases we encounter two of the means used by the *corrector* for the excision of words and signs of punctuation. He athetises μέν by putting a dot over each letter and deletes the double dots marking the change of speaker in 356c8 by crossing each of them with a stroke. Given that these were common practices followed by all those who checked the correct copying of a text, there seems to be no need to suspect a different use. The combination of both methods in the immediately preceding line for the deletion of αἵ (LXIV, 1 [589]) shows that hardly any surprises are to be expected here. In short, reading these signs as elements of textual criticism is an economic, reasonable explanation and, very likely, the most natural one.[159]

It does not follow, however, that any alternative theory should be dismissed out of hand as an unnecessary waste of scholarly energy and time. If nothing else, the alleged rationale of the interventions in lines 2 [590] and 4 [592] leaves some room for speculation. It is not very easy to see why μέν should be deleted, since its presence is perfectly accountable on syntactical grounds – it balances the following δέ.[160] Even less clear is the reason that led the *corrector* to cross the double dots. This is not a self-evident decision since he was responsible for most of these dots, presumably as another sign for the change of speakers in replacement of

(1999) with bibliography of previous discussions (310–11); cf. also Tulli (2003). Jourdan-Hemmerdinger presented her views very briefly in a short note at the proceedings of a conference on papyrology (1984) and repeated her claim in a later article (1991, 24).

159 Tulli (1996) has commented excellently on the *corrector*'s work in *POxy* xiii 1624. For his signs in col. LXIV see Grenfell and Hunt (1919) 207–8; Tulli (1999) 329–30. Dots and strokes for excising words are used in the following columns: XVII 22 [176], XXXVII 2 [319], LIX 31 [431], 36 [436], LXI 5 [481], 10 [486],14 [490], LXVI 3 [665] (dots); IX 1 [114], XXIII 4 [272] (strokes). Cf. Tulli (1996) 457–8. Notice, however, that the strokes are placed above the words, they do not cross them. For the work and methods of a *corrector* see Turner (1987) 15–16.

160 Grenfell and Hunt (1919) 207 on 590. Their suggestion that, because of the neighbouring μείζους, the word would be easily omitted or inserted (so also Tulli 1999, 330) is not very satisfactory.

the *paragraphi* of the original.[161] One may think of two possible answers:

(a) He may have taken the phrase from καὶ αἱ φωναί up to φαῖεν ἄν inclusive (356c7–8) as spoken by the same person, possibly Sokrates. Then the retention of the double dots in LXIV 5 [593] is inexplicable, because there is no room for a second speaker in the whole passage 356c7–e3 except for φαῖεν ἄν. The only way to account for these dots would be to attribute 356c7–8 not to Sokrates but Protagoras – hardly an option in view of the demands of the argumentation. In any case, the strongest objection against the removal of the dots after σμικρότεραι is that the incorporation of the verbal phrase into its preceding sentence presupposes an elementary mistake in reading the optative as a form not of φημί but of φαίνομαι.

(b) The dots in LXIV 4 [592] signify a brief reply by Protagoras. This is the only place in the extant fragments where the dots introduce someone other than Sokrates, if, of course, the question of the hypothetical objector in 355d6 (LXI 9 [485]) is interpreted in terms of reported speech as a Socratic utterance. But it is difficult to see why the *corrector* would choose to mark Sokrates' part only, with no regard for the ensuing confusion of the reader.

The argument for the interpretation of these dots and strokes as recitation signs is based on two interrelated premises. The first is their apparent resemblance to elements of a musical notation amply documented in manuscripts of the Byzantine period. This notation is known by the term ekphonetic, because it was used for regulating the recitation (ἐκφώνησις) of the Lessons from the Old and New Testament at services in Greek Orthodox churches. The system was in full use throughout the history of the Byzantine Empire with the evidence starting as early as the eighth and reaching well into the fifteenth century. Five tables of ekphonetic notation have been preserved in manuscripts of the Byzantine period (Sinait. gr. 213, Sinait. gr. 217, Sinait. gr. 8, Lesbos Leimon. 38, Tbilisi Q 908). A comparison of the papyrus signs with one of these lists yields some interesting results. There is a striking similarity between the three dots in LXIV 2 [590] and the ekphonetic sign called *kentēmata* (κεντήματα). The strokes in LXIV 4 [592] could be paralleled

161 Grenfell and Hunt (1919) 200; Tulli (1999) 312. For the use of *paragraphi* see Johnson (1994b).

to the *apesō exō* (ἀπέσω ἔξω), if taken together, or, separately, the lower would correspond to the *apostrophos* (ἀπόστροφος) and the upper one to the *oxeia* (ὀξεῖα). According to Byzantine practice the signs were written at the beginning and at the end of the relevant word or phrase. If then, for the sake of argument, one accepts the identification and postulates a similar principle for the papyrus text, two phrases from Plato's *Protagoras* were furnished with notation for ornamental recitation in the early third century AD.[162]

This line of thought may be challenged by the following counter-arguments. Judged by Byzantine standards the papyrus notation yields unparalleled combinations of signs. The compound sign *apesō exō* always encompasses the word or phrase, never precedes or follows it. The *kentēmeta* are almost always followed by other *kentēmata* and not by an *apostrophos*. The *oxeia* cannot be combined with double dots, a sign that does not appear in the manuscript lists. More important, however, is the objection to the basic premise of the theory. One may wonder whether it is legitimate to explain some signs on a Plato papyrus by resorting to a notation associated with religious texts five centuries later. The chronological distance and the divergence in the context in which the signs operate in each case make it all the more likely that a theory built on the assumption of such a relation is unfounded and any resemblance coincidental or imagined.

The force of these objections notwithstanding, there are still grounds for granting some plausibility in the original premise. Let us start from the gap of five centuries between the papyrus and the earliest attested manuscripts with ekphonetic notation. On the one hand, it may be turned around and used against the first type of objections. A supposed relation in no way means that

[162] For recent surveys of the ekphonetic notation see Engberg (1996) and Engberg (2001) 48–9 (with bibliography); Levy and Troelsgård (2001) 734–5, 749–50; Martani (2003a) 23–6; Porter (2007). Höeg (1935) remains the standard work of reference. Other studies include Wellesz (1961) 246–60; Jourdan (1968–9), Panţiru (1973); Hannick (1979), Revell (1979) and Martani's valuable articles (2002a), (2002b), (2002c), (2003a), (2003b), (2004). Martani (2003a) gives a useful overview of all five tables (35). For a discussion and transcriptions of the tables see Höeg (1935) 17–35 (who was unaware of the list in the Tbilisi manuscript) and, more recently, Martani (2003a) 26–33. A transcription of the most famous of the three, namely Cod. Leimon. 38 from Lesbos, is also reproduced in Wellesz (1961) 251 followed by a list of the relevant signs (252).

the typology and function of the Byzantine notation should be, without any qualifications, read back to late Roman times. On the other hand, although the gap is impressive, the mere distance in time cannot rule out the possibility of an association between written symbols developed in the same area and serving a similar purpose – if this is the case. As evidence for the conservative nature of such semiotic systems it may be pointed out that the number and shape of the Byzantine signs remained virtually unchanged from the eighth to the thirteenth centuries. In principle, some degree of uniformity may be expected of the system, at least in some respects, even before that period. The reason is that the eighth-century manuscripts present us with a fully developed notation. It must therefore have been in use long before its earliest documentation, sufficiently long to account for such a level of standardisation. In fact, scholars date the introduction of the ekphonetic signs to the end of the fourth century.[163]

There is one more element that brings the papyrus signs even closer to their later counterparts. All the evidence, the nomenclature most prominently, points to the prosodic signs of the Hellenistic grammarians as the ultimate origin of the Byzantine ekphonetic notation.[164] This development is not surprising given the musical character of both systems. It may have also been facilitated by the change from a predominantly musical to a predominantly dynamic pronunciation of the Greek language. In any case, a transitional period may be assumed during which a musical notation develops from a grammatical one. The early third century may well belong to such a period.

The musical character of the ancient prosody brings us to the second premise. It is known that teachers and practitioners of rhetoric postulated certain rules regulating the different kinds of proper delivery. In the context of a public performance, be it a deliberative speech, a lecture or a declamation, the skilful handling of features such as the rhythm, intonation and modulation of the delivery

163 Höeg (1935) 38–9; Wellesz (1961) 246–7. Cf. Tardo (1938) 52.

164 Tillyard (1935) 13–14; Tardo (1938) 47–8, 51; Wellesz (1961) 250. Cf. Höeg (1955–7) 410. For a comparative study of the Greek signs with the Hebrew accents see Engberg (1966) and Revell (1979).

contribute significantly to the success of the speaker.[165] Jourdan-Hemmerdinger (1991), on the basis of the testimonies of Dionysios of Halikarnassos and other authors of the Hellenistic and Roman periods, has suggested that a recitative style of delivery, oscillating between plain speech and song, was common practice among public orators, especially in the case of panegyric discourse. She has also argued that palaeographical evidence points to chanted readings as the papyri yield evidence for another system of musical notation, based on dots and their different positions in the line. This system was allegedly used for Christian and pagan texts alike and is said to lie behind Nikanor's taxonomy of eight types of stops (στιγμαί). It was parallel with but unrelated to the ancient alphabetical notation which was still in use during the early stages of the Byzantine system.[166]

The most interesting part of these speculations is that they remind us of the presence of the musical element in the performance of texts other than songs in ancient Greek culture. A chanted type of delivery is associated with παρακαταλογή, the recitation of non-lyric verses with musical accompaniment. This technique, an invention of Archilochos according to tradition, was also employed in theatre, mainly in the parts of plays composed in anapaests or trochaic and iambic tetrameters.[167] As for dramatic poetry, in particular, music infiltrated gradually more portions of the text, so that from the Hellenistic period onwards not only choral odes or monodies but messenger speeches and other spoken parts might be sung. It was a tendency that led to the emergence of a new kind of actors who specialised in singing excerpts from plays.[168] Similarly, Aristeides Kointilianos, possibly an author of

165 Aulus Gellius testifies to the influence that a skilful reading of Plato's *Symposium* could have had on an audience – one composed of students of philosophy at that (*NA* 17.20). For reading in antiquity as 'textual performance' see Gregory Snyder (2000) 1–4.

166 Jourdan-Hemmerdinger (1979). The author attributes musical value to the differentiation between τελεία στιγμή, μέση στιγμή and ὑποστιγμή. All three stops occur in the *POxy* xiii 1624.

167 See *DFA*[2] 156–65; West (1992a) 40 with notes 6, 7 and 8; *CAD* 334–6.

168 Known as τραγῳδοί and κωμῳδοί, two older terms taking on a new meaning. See Hall (2002) 12–24, 30–5. Cf. also West (1992a) 311, 317–18; Webb (2008a) 26–7. For fragments of dramatic texts with musical notation in non-lyric parts, all dating from the Roman period, see *DAGM* figs. 38–40, 42; Pöhlmann (2005); Prauscello (2006). Interestingly, the verse furnished with four alternative melodies in the latter item, a

the third century AD, reports that a special type of delivery, intermediate between plain speech and song, was used for the reading of poetry. A chanted style for oral performance in general, not restricted to poetry-reading, was known to Nikomachos of Gerasa a couple of centuries earlier. Both passages may be traced back to a similar claim found in Aristoxenos on the differences between the continuous-speaking and intervallic-singing voice. In the field of rhetoric Longinos' advice that an orator should shift to a chanted delivery in these moments of his speech which are emotionally charged reflects one of Aristoxenos' precepts in the same section that the emotionally disturbed voice comes closer to singing. Moreover, Dionysios Thrax, the famous Hellenistic grammarian (*c.*170–90 BC), assigns to the various literary genres a special type of reading. There is little doubt that at least in the case of elegiac, lyric and lament poetry an ornamental style is described (the illuminating remarks of the scholiasts indicate that a similar practice was carried on during Roman and Byzantine times).[169]

papyrus from the third century AD (*POxy* liii 3705), has been identified with Menander's *Pk.* 796. It follows that 'this fragment gives evidence of a practice of setting selections of Menandrean dialogue to music' (Huys 1993, 32). In their own edition of musical documents Pöhlmann and West raise the possibility that 'the intention was to illustrate different ways in which an actor might *speak* the verse, the musical notation being used in an attempt to describe speech intonations' (*DAGM* 185). Cf. Hall (2002) 34–5. On the survival of Greek dramatic music down to Roman times see Fleming (1999).

169 Here are the relevant passages: (a) Aristid. Quint. *De Mus.* 1.4: ἡ μὲν οὖν συνεχής [φωνὴ] ἐστιν ᾗ διαλεγόμεθα, μέση δὲ ᾗ τὰς τῶν ποιημάτων ἀναγνώσεις ποιούμεθα, διαστηματικὴ δὲ ἡ κατὰ μέσον τῶν ἁπλῶν φωνῶν ποσὰ ποιουμένη διαστήματα καὶ μονάς, ἥτις καὶ μελῳδικὴ καλεῖται. (b) Nikom. *Harm.* 239. 13–17 Jan: εἰ γάρ τις ἢ διαλεγόμενος ἢ ἀπομνημονεύων τινὸς ἢ ἀναγιγνώσκων γε ἔκδηλα μεταξὺ καθ' ἕκαστον φθόγγον ποιεῖ τὰ μεγέθη . . . οὐκέτι λέγειν ὁ τοιοῦτος οὐδὲ ἀναγιγνώσκειν ἀλλὰ μελεάζειν λέγεται. (c) Aristox. *Harm.* 1.9.26–32 da Rios: ἀλλὰ γὰρ ἵστασθαί τε δοκεῖ [τὴν φωνὴν] καὶ πάντες τὸν τοῦτον φαινόμενον ποιεῖν οὐκέτι λέγειν φασὶν ἀλλὰ ᾄδειν. διόπερ ἐν τῷ διαλέγεσθαι φεύγομεν τὸ ἱστάναι τὴν φωνήν, ἂν μὴ διὰ πάθος ποτὲ εἰς τοιαύτην κίνησιν ἀναγκασθῶμεν ἐλθεῖν. In this section (1.8.14–10.10) Aristoxenos discusses the two types of vocal movements and concludes that ἡ μὲν συνεχὴς λογική τις ἐστιν ἡ δὲ διαστηματικὴ μελῳδική (1.9.10). (d) Longin. *Rh.* 312.14–16 Spengel: οἰκτιζόμενον δὲ δεῖ μεταξὺ λόγου τε καὶ ᾠδῆς τὸν ἦχον ποιήσασθαι. (e) Dion. Thr. *Gramm.* 6.5–11 Uhlig: Ἀναγνωστέον δὲ καθ' ὑπόκρισιν, κατὰ προσῳδίαν, κατὰ διαστολήν. ἐκ μὲν γὰρ τῆς ὑποκρίσεως τὴν ἀρετήν, ἐκ δὲ τῆς προσῳδίας τὴν τέχνην, ἐκ δὲ τῆς διαστολῆς τὸν περιεχόμενον νοῦν ὁρῶμεν. ἵνα τὴν μὲν τραγῳδίαν ἡρωϊκῶς ἀναγνῶμεν, τὴν δὲ κωμῳδίαν βιωτικῶς, τὰ δὲ ἐλεγεῖα λιγυρῶς, τὸ δὲ ἔπος εὐτόνως, τὴν δὲ λυρικὴν ποίησιν ἐμμελῶς, τοὺς δὲ οἴκτους ὑφειμένως καὶ γοερῶς (for the scholiasts' interpretations of the passage see *Scholia in Dion. Thr.* 16.11–21.29,

It is reasonable to ask whether this practice was ever associated with some kind of notation to facilitate the task of the reader. So far there is evidence for two types of ancient musical notation, two series of letters of the alphabet for vocal and instrumental music respectively.[170] But there is no necessary reason why a separate system of symbols should exclusively be used for recitation purposes. It makes perfectly good sense that the same signs would serve more than one function. A case in point is the double dot or dicolon (:). In addition to its use in scholia and commentaries to mark the end of lemmata and individual notes, it is employed to mark the change of speaker in both theatrical and Platonic texts. Not infrequently, however, it is found in places where no such change takes place. It is interpreted there as a pause symbol signalling a strong stop.[171] Both uses may even be present in the same document. For instance, in the slightly earlier *POxy* xlvii 3326 (second century AD) the dots in cols i 17, 21, ii 13 and iii 12 distinguish Sokrates' and Glaukon's lines (*paragraphi* are also employed), whereas those in cols ii 2, 9, 23 and iii 4 divide Sokrates' long questions into smaller sections. The latter use seems to be a peculiarity of Plato papyri from that period (Turner 1987, pl. 19), but is not so common in other literary texts with the exception of drama. The explanation offered is that this feature is one more *aide-lire* prompted by the complexity of the Platonic sentence.[172] It is reasonable to ascribe to the sign a 'musical' character in accordance with the demands of a recited text. That the relevant dots

172.1–174.13, 305.24–308.27, 473.33–477.15, 568.43–570.3 Hilgard). For the relation between the passages (a), (b) and (c) and further references see Barker (1989) 404 n. 25. Cf. Barker (1989) 133 nn. 39 and 40.

170 See West (1992a) 254–73; Landels (1999) 206–17; Johnson (2000b); Sandin (2007) 214–21, esp 214 n. 17; Hagel (2009) 1–102. For the origins of the notation from Greek local scripts of the fifth century BC see West (1992a) 36–42. For ancient Greek music in general West (1992a) is the definitive study, supplemented by Mathiesen (1999), Barker (2007) and Hagel (2009). *DAGM* is the standard edition of all extant documents. Cf. also Comotti (1989); Anderson (1994); Landels (1999); Bundrick (2005); Levin (2009); Rocconi (2009). For the influence of ancient Greek musical theory on the Byzantine chant manuals see Troelsgard (1988).

171 See Turner (1987) 8–9. For the use of dicolon in the *POxy* xiii 1624 see Tulli (1996) 462. In a third-century BC papyrus fragment with musical notes the dicolon signals 'an antiphonal exchange between two musicians' (Rawles 2006, 9).

172 So Haslam (1980) 38. Johnson (1994b) suggests a similar role for the *paragraphus*, namely that it was introduced in prose texts 'prmarily to assist with reading aloud' (68).

in *POxy* xlvii 3326 appear in pairs (ii 2–ii 9 and ii 23–iii 4), thus 'isolating' certain phrases, may be not unrelated to the manner of delivery of these phrases.[173]

A similar 'ekphonetic' interpretation has been suggested for another sign, namely the oblique stroke. Another papyrus from the late second century AD, with fragments from Menander's *Epitrepontes*, namely *POxy* l 3533, documents the use of the stroke to mark the end of clauses (ll. 2, 6, 8) (Turner 1987, pl. 86). The position of the strokes on the line followed by a space indicates that these were already present in the exemplar. It has been plausibly suggested that the latter was an actor's edition of the text or of selected excerpts from plays.[174] In this case the oblique stroke may have served a function similar to that of the Byzantine *oxeia*, being typologically the same sign. An even greater affinity with *oxeia* is evident in the strokes on the text of the *Iliad* 2.147–62 in two wooden tablets of the third century AD (Schubart 1921, 23 fig. 4).[175] It is remarkable how similar the employment of the strokes in these tablets looks to that found in another tablet recording Psalms 28 and 29, dated earlier than the eighth and, possibly, the seventh century AD (Pintaudi 1982, pl. III). In all these cases the strokes are evidently not grammatical but 'ekphonetic' signs.

Two conclusions may be drawn from these considerations. First, the prosodic signs were used as markers for a more or less musical reading of the texts. Employed in a dramatic text these signs may indicate either reading aloud or dramatisation. In any case the element of performance, in a public or private context, is evidently presupposed by the mere use of such a notation. Second, similar symbols were applied in the recitation of pagan and Christian

[173] On this hypothesis it would be attractive to see the dicolon as the ancestor of the Byzantine ekphonetic sign with the suggestive name of *hypokrisis* (ὑπόκρισις) (⁝). The shape and function might point in the same direction: the number and position of the hooks correspond to those of the dots (an earlier version of the ancient sign with three dots is documented from the third century BC according to Turner 1987, 9); while both signs indicate pause (Wellesz 1961, 253).

[174] Turner (1987) 144. The author properly distinguishes between the recitative and the other possible meanings of the sign when he remarks that he is 'inclined to think its purpose is not a punctuation or part division, but as *a divider to aid reading aloud or dramatic delivery*' (italics mine).

[175] Schubart (1921) 24–6; Pack (1967) 52 no. 637.

texts.[176] This resemblance is only natural in the context of the cultural continuum: the Byzantine ekphonetic notation originated from the Hellenistic prosodic signs while the recitation of liturgical texts in Orthodox churches may go back to those modes of delivery taught and practised throughout antiquity.[177] Furthermore, in the transitional period of the first Christian centuries it is normal to find old and new forms used side by side. The striking example in the case of music is *POxy* XV 1786, a strip of papyrus of the late third century AD, that has on its *verso* a hymn to the Holy Trinity with the music in the alphabetical notation (*DAGM* fr. 59). It is the latest of the extant documents in ancient Greek notation and the earliest piece of Christian hymnody.[178] The text recalls the opening lines from the *prooemium* of the hymn to the Sun by Mesomedes, a composer active at the times of Hadrian and Pius (Mesomedes 2.2.1–6 Heitsch). Since this *prooemium*, a standard request to the whole of nature for silence before the arrival of the divinity, was in all probability a traditional composition, the Oxyrhynchos hymn appropriately illustrates the manner in which the religious poetry and music of Byzantium evolved from that of Greek antiquity.[179]

[176] An association neatly brought out by Turner (1987) 144.

[177] For the origins of the ekphonetic system see Höeg (1935) 137–53. The author points to the presence of an ἀναγνώστης in the philosophical and rhetorical schools, in some respect a predecessor of the namesake church official (151–2; cf. Turner 1977, 84–6; on chanted reading of the Old Testament in Byzantine churches see Engberg 1987). He also remarks that 'la valeur musicale de l'accentuation grecque a été un fait décisif pour la création de cette déclamation artistique [sc. l'ekphonèse byzantine]' (153).

[178] Musicology provides evidence that one of the standard principles of composition in Byzantine music, namely that the accented syllable of a word carries the highest note, was used by composers between the second century BC and the second century AD (Cosgrove and Meyer 2006). Intriguingly, the late third century AD is the most likely date for the *corrector*'s interventions. See Tulli (1996) 457.

[179] The importance of the Oxyrhynchos hymn cannot be overestimated (*pace* MacKinnon 2000, 773). The most recent discussion is to be found in *DAGM* 190–4. For earlier contributions see Grenfell and Hunt (1922) 21–5; Abert (1921–2) and (1926); Pighi (1941); Wellesz (1945) and (1961) 152–6; Heitsch (1963) 159–60; West (1992b) 47–54 and (1992a) 283 no. 51, 324–6. Wellesz is almost alone in denying that the recorded music is part of the Greek tradition but derives it instead from Syro-Palestinian and Jewish sources (1945, 44–5; cf. 1961, 156). West proves decisively that this position is mistaken and shows that textually and musically 'the hymn stands squarely in the Greek tradition' (1992b, 54. Cf. 1992a, 325; *DAGM* 192). Wellesz's line of argument follows from his theory of the 'Oriental', Semitic origins and character of Byzantine music and the corresponding remoteness of the latter from Greek culture (see e.g. Wellesz 1961, 32–45, 70–1, 146–52). This view had been, for quite a long period, an article of faith for many a Western interpreter of Byzantine music (cf. Höeg 1955–7), along with

It is time to return to *POxy* xiii 1624. Let us, for a moment, assume that the signs added by the *corrector* are indeed of an 'ekphonetic' type. The next question is what were his motives for doing so, or, to put it differently, on what type of occasion would a Platonic text with such a notation be required. The issue is particularly interesting given that the *Protagoras* had not been a very popular text among the philosophers.[180] One possibility would be to refer to the gatherings of Platonists to commemorate the Master. The celebration of Plato's birthday provided the occasion for the reading/recitation of the dialogues and discussion on selected topics (pp. 225–6). An attractive speculation has it that, in view of the quasi-religious status Plato's works enjoyed in Neoplatonism, there could have been an ongoing reciprocity as regards the treatment of their sacred texts between the Neoplatonic schools and the Church.[181] In this case an analogy in usage would encourage a convergence in notation. Another option may be that such papyri were used by the performers of dramatised dialogues. As with the actors' editions of plays, annotated Plato papyri of this kind would provide the guidelines for the proper delivery of the dialogues either in full or in the manner of selected passages. From

(a) an almost complete identity between Byzantine and Western chant (Tillyard 1935, 13; Wellesz 1961, 22) and (b) the discontinuity between Byzantine and post-Byzantine practice owing to the detrimental [sic] influence of 'Oriental', i.e. Arabic and Turkish elements, such as the establishment of chromaticism in the tonal system (Wellesz 1961, 22, 128). These premises, deriving mainly from an inability or unwillingness to appreciate the significance of living tradition, both oral and written, are in need of revision: for instance, Makris (2005) has proved the existence of chromatic scales in late Byzantium. An excellent survey of the cultural politics behind the Western reading of the Greek practice is given by Lingas (2003). His article in the *Oxford Handbook* series is the best starting point for an updated introduction to Byzantine music with a comprehensive survey of the secondary literature (Lingas 2008). For an alternative to the Western method of transcription of Byzantine notation the reader is referred to the seminal studies of Karas (1955) and (1982); Troelsgard (2011). Cf. also Stathis (1979); Zannos (1991); Arvanitis (1997); Troelsgard (1997), (1999). On the change and continuity in Greek musical tradition see Dragoumis (1966); Beaton (1980); Baud-Bovy (1991); Wolfram (2008); Kallimopoulou (2009) 1–46. For Mesomedes see Bowie (1993b) 85–90; West (1992a) 280 no. 18, 304–6; *DAGM* 92–115. Interestingly, Synesios (AD 370–413), who sang Mesomedes' compositions (West 1992a, 273), offers an early Byzantine version of the same motif in his third hymn (Synesios III 72–85 Christ–Paranikas). See Pighi (1941) 214 n. 1; West (1992b), esp. 49–50 for more parallels.

180 See Tulli (1996) 457 n. 1 and (1999) 313.

181 A similar hypothesis is hinted at by Jourdan-Hemmerdinger (1991) 24.

this point of view the *Protagoras* would be a perfect text because of its particularly theatrical character.[182]

In sum, the evidence from a Plato papyrus, not least the work of the *corrector*, raises the question of whether some signs were to be interpreted as bearing a musical function. This cannot be answered with certainty owing to the inconclusive nature of the evidence. In principle, however, it is not implausible that some of Plato's texts were furnished with some musical notation in the early third century AD. The notation was useful to those who would recite Plato on public or private ceremonial occasions and participate in dramatised performances of the dialogues at symposia and elsewhere.

The mosaic

In the preceding section Menander was mentioned twice in relation to a couple of documents containing lines from his plays with musical notation. In the present section his name features prominently as the building in which the next piece of evidence was found was named after him. The House of Menander is a late Roman villa excavated in the early 1960s at Chorafa, Mytilene. The floors were decorated with mosaics. A panel of Orpheus the charmer of animals occupied the central room (S), while the *triclinium* (T) and the north side of the peristyle (P) featured illustrations related to theatre, for the most part scenes from Menander's comedies, including a portrait bust of the poet (hence the naming of the house). Panels with masks and a long illustration of fishermen and fishes in the west side of the peristyle complete the picture. Two alternative dates have been suggested for the mosaics, the late third (around 300) or the late fourth century AD, in or near the reign of Julian (AD 361–3). The ownership of the villa is equally disputed. It may have been the residence of a wealthy individual with real

182 See Capra (2001) 37–95; Charalabopoulos (2001). For the performance aspect of the dialogue see also Schofield (1992) 132. Another possibility would have been that extracts from Plato were recited by schoolchildren in their competitions organised by the cities as a kind of exam. See p. 264 n. 17.

or pretended literary interests or, less plausibly, the property of the local association of the Artists of Dionysos.[183]

The Mytilene mosaics provide the richest illustration of the world of theatre from Roman times. From this point of view the decoration of the *triclinium* proves of particular importance. Ten mosaics have been deployed in a T-shaped arrangement: four are placed in a row that covers the whole width of the room from wall to wall, while the other six, divided in two series of three, occupy the central space of the room. All ten have been allotted separate square panels and share the same orientation facing north. The single row of four seems to play a programmatic role. The outer panels illustrate the portrait busts of Menander and Thaleia, the patron-Muse of his art, holding the mask of an old man. Next to Menander there is a three-actor scene from Act II of his *Plokion*. This panel serves as the bridge between the two groups since the six mosaics of the centre equally illustrate scenes from Menander's comedies. In all these instances, three actors are depicted while the title of the play, the number of the act and the names of the *dramatis personae* are all inscribed.[184]

This wealth of theatrical imagery makes it all the more surprising therefore to find, among the scenes from Menandrean plays, a representation of Sokrates with two of his associates (fig. 3). The paradox is even more striking since the Sokrates panel is located in such a position that its uniqueness could by no means be missed by the viewer. It is the only mosaic of the dining-room completely unrelated to comedy. Furthermore, it is emphatically placed in the upper zone, next to Thaleia, standing in the same relation to the

183 The standard study is Charitonidis et al. (1970), while the most recent discussion is found in Csapo (2010) 140–67. See also Charitonidis (1962); Kahil (1969); Tsirivakos (1975); Berczelly (1988); Stefanou (1996); Csapo (1997); Handley (1997); Ellinghaus (1998/9). Berczelly (1988) has argued for the late fourth-century date instead of the earlier one suggested by Charitonidis et al. (1970) 12, 90, 96. The later date has been accepted by Green (1994) 164; Green and Handley (1995) 78; *MINC*^{3} 75, 469 6 DM 2; Dunbabin (1999) 217 n. 26. For the ownership of the house see Charitonidis et al. (1970) 105; Green (1994) 165; Dunbabin (1999) 217 (the latter two opting for a single owner). On the importance of illustrations related to the classical past see Uytterhoeven (2009).

184 For the mosaics of the *triclinium* see Charitonidis et al. (1970) 26–52; *MINC*^{3} 86–95; Csapo (1997); Handley (2002) 171–3; Konstantakos (2005b) 194–8. Cf. Charitonidis et al. 1970, 26 fig. 4; pl. 9, 1. For illustrations of the mosaics see Charitonidis et al. (1970) pls 2–8 (colour), 15–22; Csapo (2010) 141, fig. 5.1.

Figure 3. Scene from Plato's *Phaedo*: Simmias, Sokrates, Kebes. Mosaic (T3) from the House of Menander.

Muse as the scene from *Plokion* does with respect to the poet. The symmetrical juxtaposition and the unexpected illustration of a different subject, in lieu of the otherwise expected comic scene, indicate that the paradox was intentional or, at least, evidently felt as such. A mosaic with a Socratic theme appears under any consideration as a bit of a mystery in a decoration dedicated to the celebration of Menander and his art.[185]

The first step towards shedding some light on this mystery is a close look at the panel. Sokrates stands in the middle wearing a long white mantle over a white cloak. Depicted in a frontal position he turns his head three-quarters to the left. He raises his right hand in the familiar gesticulation of speech, or teaching, with his first two fingers upright, while with his left hand he supports his mantle and holds a book-roll. He is flanked on his right by Simmias and on his left by Kebes. They both share the same outfit, attributes,

[185] For this mosaic and illustrations see Charitonidis et al. (1970) 33–6 with pl. 3, 2 (colour), pl. 17, 1; Berczelly (1988) 119–22 with pl. 3A; Csapo (1997) 168–9; Lapatin (2006) 152 n. 11.

gesticulation and posture with Sokrates – except that Simmias' raised hand points to his right. The only real differentiation relates to the design of the heads and faces. Each of the heads is turned in a different direction, although the students direct their look in some sense towards the centre. All three figures wear long hair and beards but the artist has used *tesserae* of a different colour for each one of them, yellow-brown for Simmias, grey-blue for Sokrates, predominantly black for Kebes. More significantly, the students have a youthful and a somehow 'naturalistic' complexion, while Sokrates stands in marked contrast with his yellow face and strange, cat-like eyes. This diversification counter-balances the otherwise uniform representation of the figures.[186]

Now the identical gesticulation and their facial confrontation suggest that Sokrates and Kebes are involved in an argument while Simmias remains rather disengaged. The representation of this kind of action may be an indication that a literary text is alluded to in the picture. Despite the context, a comedy by Menander seems a highly unlikely candidate. The lack of any testimony for New Comedy plays featuring Sokrates and his Theban associates and the absence of the iconographical conventions of the other *triclinium* mosaics tell strongly against this idea. Conversely, the particular combination of interlocutors makes it more likely that the mosaic offers an illustration of Plato's *Phaedo*, the only known text that brings together all three characters.[187] Therefore, the paradox of a Socratic theme in the midst of comic scenes takes on an additional dimension, that of the characters of a Platonic dialogue 'intruding' in a world dominated by the protagonists of New Comedy.

The next step is to explore the reasons that may have led the owner of the villa to include the Sokrates panel in the decoration. According to a hypothesis put forward by the editors of the mosaics, the answer lies in the 'philosophical' qualities of Menander's plays. In view of his later use as a source of proverbial, maxim-like wisdom, Menander may have easily been associated with the philosophers. His art as a playwright may be seen to bear

[186] Charitonidis et al. (1970) 33–4 and 81.

[187] So Charitonidis et al. (1970) 34b, 35b followed by all later scholars. Alexis is known to have written a comedy called *Phaedo* or *Phaidrias* but the title is probably corrupt. See *PCG* II 161–2.

affinities with the dialectical character of Sokrates' teachings. It has been suggested therefore that a Sokrates panel, along with comedy scenes, was originally part of an illustrated edition of Menander. It was specifically to be found in the section devoted to the poet's life together with the originals of the panels of the top zone, whereas comedy scenes, such as those in the centre of the room, were used to illustrate the text of their respective plays. These book-illustrations eventually became the models for reproductions in frescoes and mosaics. The mosaicist in Mytilene copied the pictures of such an edition. The supposition of a common origin for all the panels of the *triclinium* and, especially, of a separate group for the decoration of the introductory chapter of the poet's life, accounts for the positioning of the Socratic scene between the portraits of Menander and Thaleia.[188]

This hypothesis has the obvious merit of providing a unified explanation for the iconographical programme of the banquet-room. At the same time it does not obliterate the significance of distinguishing between the two zones of panels but instead accommodates this arrangement accordingly. The well-attested existence of illustrated editions of playwrights, such as Euripides and Terence, also gives a certain air of plausibility to this theory.[189] On the other hand, the presence of a scene from the *Plokion* in this upper zone is left unexplained – a point conceded by the editors themselves.[190] The weakness of the hypothesis, however, lies in the unconvincing reason given for the incorporation of a Socratic theme, let alone this particular Platonic dialogue, into a theatrical context. There is some difference in the application of the method of question-and-answer by comic characters and philosophically minded interlocutors. But even if the point had been to underline the poet's credentials as a thinker by alluding to his affinities with the philosopher *par excellence*, a depiction of Plato's *Phaedo* does not seem the obvious choice. A more generic image, a portrait of Philosophy for example, might be more in

[188] Charitonidis et al. (1970) 36b with n. 7, 103b. Cf. Billig (1977) 42 n. 76. Acording to Bassett (2008) the depiction of Menander in the company of philosophers and intellectuals 'emphasizes his membership in a specifically literary and philosophical canon at the expense of his theatrical output' (218).

[189] Weitzmann (1947) 44, 73, 80 fig. B.

[190] Charitonidis et al. 1970, 36b.

place next to Thaleia rather than the invocation of a particular text. It may be concluded then that, regardless of its soundness as a reconstruction of the history of the comedy scenes, the theory of the illustrated Menander edition does little to explain why an illustration of the *Phaedo* should be there in the first place.

A second hypothesis focuses precisely on this question. Moving away from the idea of an original association of the Socratic scene with the rest of the panels, Berczelly (1988) studies the odd-mosaic-out on its own terms. Capitalising on an editor's passing remark, he draws attention to the striking resemblance between the iconographical type of the *Phaedo* scene with representations from early Christian art. Sokrates with Simmias and Kebes is strongly reminiscent of Christ flanked by two apostles, usually Peter and Paul.[191] In some cases, Christ raises his hand in the gesture of speech, while He and the Apostles hold papyrus-rolls. The affinities with a relief group from a roughly contemporary 'passion sarchophagus' in the cemetery of S. Sebastiano in Rome (AD 350–75) put the interpretation of the Mytilene mosaic in a different, subtler perspective. The theory goes that the patron of the villa commissioned the production of a Socratic mosaic in conscious imitation of the style of Christian iconography because he wanted to declare his personal affiliations with the pagan intelligentsia. For it is suggested that throughout the fourth century, after the Peace of the Church, there took place an appropriation of Christian literary and artistic motifs by the pagans in order to defeat their opponents at their own game (in fact, a reversal of the norm during the preceding three centuries). The exemplary figure of Sokrates plays a prominent role in this movement as a legitimate alternative to that of Christ. The scene from the *Phaedo*, a dialogue describing the last day of Sokrates, reminds the pagan viewer that he could also commemorate his own executed Master, much like his Christian neighbour.[192]

191 This triadic pattern, especially associated with the motif of Christ as the dispenser of the Law (*traditio legis*), is later developed in the Byzantine iconography of the Transfiguration (Μεταμόρφωσις, Christ with Moses and Elias) and the Supplication (Δέησις, Christ with His Mother and John the Baptist).

192 Berczelly (1988) 121–2. For the sarcophagus from the cemetery of S. Sebastiano see Deichmann (1967) 119–20 no. 189. For representations of Christ flanked by his

This is an attractive thesis overall. The dialectic between pagans and Christians was a major phase in the cultural history of the people experiencing the transition from the Late Roman to the early Byzantine Empire. Because of a shared background of mixed ethnic traditions, interaction and 'infiltration' between the two camps was inevitable. Therefore the importance of interpreting literary and artistic products from that period under a dual perspective, whenever applicable, cannot be stressed enough. The theory of repaganisation of Christian motifs for the purposes of anti-Christian propaganda points to an important development in fourth-century art, reaching its culmination under the reign of Julian the Apostate (AD 361–3). A classic example of this process is the famous mosaic in Apameia in Syria, dated to precisely these years (Charalabopoulos 2007, 123 fig. 7.1). There Sokrates, the only person whose name is inscribed, sits in the middle of a seated group among six other intellectuals, in an iconographical type strongly suggestive of representations of Christ with six of His disciples, itself modelled on an earlier classical motif (Hanfmann 1951, fig. 6). The unnamed figures have been variously identified with the remaining six of the Seven Sages, Sokrates' associates, or philosophers. An association with the reform programme of the pagan emperor who stayed in Antioch in 362 and 363 persuasively suggests itself.[193]

On the other hand, the limitations of the above theory cannot be ignored. Sokrates was by no means the exclusive property of militant pagan intellectuals. Already from the second century he had secured a prominent place in the Christian consciousness as an exemplary figure of martyrdom and a bearer of the Divine Logos. While recording ambivalent responses as well, the literary sources testify to the popularity of the notion of Sokrates as, in some

disciples see the references in Hanfmann (1951) 230 n. 70 (with fig. 6) and Berczelly (1988) 121 nn. 21 and 22. The following images of Christ with Peter and Paul bear particular resemblances with the Sokrates panel: (a) church mosaic, second half of fifth century (Charitonidis et al. 1970, 35a with pl. 3); (b) catacomb painting, *c.* AD 320–50 (Ferrua 1990, 120–1 fig. 105; (c) catacomb mosaic, *c.* AD 366–84 (Mathews 1993, 122 fig. 92); (d) relief from an ivory book cover, sixth century AD (Mathews 1993, 139–40 fig. 108); (e) relief from a silver casket *c.* AD 400 – although the identification of the Apostles here is uncertain (Mathews 1993, 86 fig. 57).

193 Charalabopoulos (2007) 106–10. On the transitional nature of late antiquity and its contested boundaries with Byzantium see Ando (2008); James (2008); Whittow (2009).

sense, a forerunner of Christ.[194] In the field of artistic representation the development of the iconography of Christ as the teacher of the true philosophy made the analogy with Sokrates conspicuous, while signalling the continuity of the imagery of the intellectual from antiquity to Byzantium.[195] It follows that the intricacies of religious politics may not be the only or even the most appropriate explanation for the commissioning of the *Phaedo* panel in Mytilene. The assumed parallel between Sokrates and Christ does not *necessarily* imply a statement of partisan adherence to the former over the latter.[196] Some of the other mosaics of the villa tell a similar story. Theatrical iconography cannot be identified *ex hypothesi* with anti-Christian ideology.[197] Similarly, the Orpheus from the reception-hall and the fishes and fishermen from the peristyle may perfectly well be read from a Christian perspective. As the coexistence of mythical and biblical stories in the paintings from a fourth-century Roman catacomb shows, the use of motifs from the pagan past is not always a matter of religious affiliations. Without

[194] For the reception of Sokrates in the first centuries of Christianity see Malingrey (1975); Döring (1979) 143–61; Stegemann (1999) (Sokrates and Paul); Frede (2006); Edwards (2007b); Taylor (2007). The testimonia from Greek and Latin Church fathers is conveniently collected in *SSR* I 312–41. For the Apostle Andrew of the apocryphal *Acts of Andrew* (*c.*200) cast in the role of a Christianised Sokrates see MacDonald (1994) 211–12, 249–75. For Gregory Nazianzenos' self-portrait as a latter-day Sokrates see Vinson (1993).

[195] Zanker (1995) 289–97. The author rightly remarks that '[t]he Christian priest and the monk are the true successors of the ancient philosopher, and it is no coincidence that they early assumed both the beard and the cloak' (335). For Christianity as revealed and true philosophy see Hadot (2002) 237–52; Rhee (2005) 50–71; Löhr (2010). Wasserman (2008) proves that in his treatment of sin St Paul appropriates the Platonic discourse on the death of the soul. For what it is worth, in a relief on an ivory pyxis showing an enthroned Christ among the Apostles with Peter and Paul next to Him, Paul's head evidently recalls that of Sokrates (Zanker 1995, 304–5 fig. 165).

[196] Lyman (2002) insightfully remarks that '[i]n late antiquity Christian "orthodoxy" as a rhetorical presentation of transcendent identity could become a dominant form of "Hellenism" as a universal system because it occupied many of the same cognitive and authoritative spaces' (219). The gradual osmosis between Hellenic and Christian identity (cf. Schott 2008) and the cultural continuity between the Late Roman and the Byzantine world problematise the legitimacy of the absolute antithesis between 'pagan' and 'Christian': Ruprecht (2008), for one, considers this 'a historically falsifying contrast' and reads late antiquity as 'Neo-Hellenic, not necessarily anti-Hellenic at all' (81). The student of Plato, in particular, should remind himself of Ramelli's (2009) caveat: 'Christian Platonism is no less legitimate, "authentic", or "Platonic" than pagan Platonism' (252).

[197] See, for example, Easterling and Miles (1999) 103–6 for the constructive relationship of the Greek Fathers with tragedy. Cf. Bergjan (2005).

any supporting evidence an association of the *triclinium* mosaics with the reactionary programme of Julian remains plausible but doubtful.[198]

Whether part of the mechanisms of politico-religious propaganda or not, the Sokrates mosaic at Mytilene must have appealed in its own special way to the viewers. It is singled out for inclusion in a decorative pattern in honour of Menandrean comedy. Most probably it is a later addition to an already fixed iconographic programme. There is no difficulty in supposing that the Sokrates mosaic replaced the comic scene that would normally take its place next to Thaleia. For these representations are not inventions of the late Roman–early Byzantine mosaicist but belong to an established tradition of illustrations of Menander's plays as proved by a comparison of the *Synaristosai* and the *Theophoroumene* from Mytilene with the late Hellenistic Dioskourides mosaics from Pompeii. The originals may have been either book-illustrations from editions of Menander or, more likely, in view of the limited variety in the depiction of individual plays, a group of wall-paintings commemorating successful comedies. In either case, these illustrations were intrinsically associated with the action on stage as depicting the title or a memorable scene from the performance that would help the viewer identify the play. Either inherited from this iconographical tradition or reflecting contemporary practices, the theatrical background of the Mytilene mosaics is their indisputable feature. The iconography of the *triclinium* therefore may be considered a celebration of Theatre in the person of Menander.[199]

[198] As Stefanou (1996) rightly remarks, 'in einer solchen Zeit des Übergangs zwischen Heidentum und Christentum sind Mosaikfußböden "traditionell-paganer" Thematik selbst in einem "christlichen" Haus nicht völlig undenkbar' (224). On the catacomb see Ferrua (1990) 130–9. The paintings are to be dated between AD 320 and 350 (158). The explanation favoured by the editor for the presence of so many pagan paintings in this catacomb is that the mythological scenes reflected the beliefs of pagan members of families who were buried among their Christian relatives (159). It cannot be ruled out, however, that scenes like Alkestis' return from the Underworld or Herakles' choice of Virtue over Vice would by the fourth century have been familiarised to a Christian audience as images of the Resurrection and the virtuous life respectively (an option discussed but rejected by Ferrua 1990, 159).

[199] See *MINC*[3] 85–6; Handley (2002) 171–3. Charitonidis et al. (1970) 103–4 argue for illustrations in manuscripts as sources for the iconographical tradition, whereas the alternative theory of wall-paintings as originals, dated around 300–280 BC, is supported by Csapo (1997) 170–6 (cf. *MINC*[3] 85; Handley 1997, 191). Csapo also postulates the

It is in the light of such a theatrical context that the *Phaedo* panel may be interpreted. The artist has been particularly careful to present the incorporation of this non-comic scene in the smoothest possible way, while at the same time underlining its unique character by means of a delicate combination of similarities and differences between the philosophers and the rest of the mosaics of the room. To begin with, the illustration of Plato's dialogue shares the size, shape and iconographical conventions of the theatrical scenes. There is a plain background, made similarly of white *tesserae* while the characteristic yellow strip on brown layer is also present. The philosophers, however, stand on an additional blue strip, a feature to be found not in the *triclinium* but in two of the peristyle scenes, the *Kybernetai* and the *Leukadia*. The Platonic characters have their names inscribed like their comic counterparts. What is not there, though, is the inscription giving the title and the respective part of the dialogue to which the scene belongs.[200] It may be noted that in the peristyle scenes the inscriptions with the names of the *dramatis personae* are missing, while the *Leukadia* scene also lacks the act inscription.[201]

At this point a direct comparison between the neighbouring illustrations of the *Plokion* and the *Phaedo* may prove instructive, particularly since their juxtaposition in the middle of the upper zone covering the space between the portrait busts invites the

use of 'notebooks of models' by painters and mosaicists for the transmission of these scenes *pace* Bruneau (1984). For the Mytilene mosaics as evidence for contemporary theatrical production of Menander see *MINC*² ix; Handley (1969) 90; Green and Handley (1995) 79. Csapo (2010) makes a powerful case for undermining such a connection (143–56). On the other hand, a more nuanced view, leaving some space for fourth-century performances, may be found in *MINC*³ 75. Cf. Jones (1993) 42–3. For the reception of Menander in Roman times see Fantham (1984), who concludes that the poet was mainly known through textbooks not stage productions (309), while Jones (1993) believes that Menander continued to be staged throughout antiquity (48). On the independence of Menander's iconographic tradition from both performance practices and textual tradition see Nervegna (2010).

200 Stefanou (1996) interprets this as an attempt to decontextualise Sokrates from the Platonic dialogues and to turn him into an iconic figure for Philosophy in general (225). A more practical explanation may also suggest itself: the names of Sokrates, Simmias and Kebes make any inscription with the title of the dialogue superfluous, while the traditional division in acts or parts was evidently not applicable to a Platonic dialogue.

201 There is no sufficient reason to suspect that the two groups of comedy mosaics do not belong to the same period.

viewer to do so. In iconographical terms, both scenes comply with the three-figure rule. The arrangement is identical: the two outer figures look towards the central one, who, in turn, speaks with the figure to his left. All six characters also gesticulate in a similar manner, namely raising their right hand to their left (except Simmias) in the gesture of speech (except Laches). In other words, here the artist follows the principle of 'twin pairs', one of the two types of arrangement of the Menander mosaics in Mytilene, according to which the paired panels share a common configuration. In the other type, that of 'balanced pairs', the panels stand to each other in a mirror-like complementary symmetry.[202]

The real differences seem to relate to the presence or absence of the theatrical element. The *Plokion* panel makes its stage character perfectly clear. The depicted figures are three actors, as is evident from their masks and costumes and the scene illustrates a certain moment of the play.[203] Contrariwise, the *Phaedo* panel lacks any ostensible signs of a theatrical nature. The philosophers do not seem to wear a stage costume, as the uniformity of their attire shows. The scale of the colours applied, hardly anything more than white and blue, contrasts with the bright yellow of Charinos in the *Messenia* or the feast of colours one comes across in the *Theophoroumene* and *Synaristosai* mosaics. Additionally, the faces of the philosophers do not recall any of the known types of New Comedy masks. More significantly, the Sokrates mosaic does not seem to recall any particular scene from the dialogue – as would, for instance, a depiction of Sokrates drinking the hemlock. It looks more like an allusion to the dialogue, not an illustration of a certain moment in the plot. For all these reasons the figures of the three philosophers are not actors but representations of Platonic characters instead. Consequently, the *Phaedo* mosaic bears no relationship to the world of theatre.[204]

202 This taxonomical principle was introduced by Csapo (1997) 177. He divides the *triclinium* mosaics into the following pairs: *Plokion* – *Samia*, *Epitrepontes* – *Theophoroumene* (both 'twin'), *Encheiridion* – *Messenia* ('balanced'). It is not clear which is the pair of the *Synaristosai* (177–9).

203 Cf. Charitonidis et al. (1970) 32–3.

204 See Charitonidis et al. (1970) 34, 81. Cf. also *MINC*^{3} 299 YM 2 (1568) A 3; Berczelly (1988) 119.

All the same there is enough room for some second thoughts. As regards the costume, the white tunic of the philosophers is worn by certain male actors as well, while some details, such as sleeves, are shared by both groups.[205] The narrow range of colours is not a decisive point by itself since the *Leukadia* is slightly more colourful. From an alternative perspective, the philosopher's outfit could be seen as a plain type of the male actor's costume. The relation between masked and unmasked characters is more complicated still. Although the 'naturalistic' faces of Simmias and Kebes seem unproblematic, Sokrates' strange face gives enough reasons for pause. By using yellow *tesserae* the artist associates Sokrates with Laches, Smikrines and the rest of the Old Men of the *triclinium* mosaics with their yellow masks. By designing an unconventional complexion, unrelated to the actual types of masks, he dissociates Sokrates from Menander's characters. In fact, the bald head and snub nose may be an attempt to reproduce the notorious silenic features of the Socratic iconography.[206] In this case, the traditional image of Sokrates the Wise Silenos resurfaces and his portrait becomes once again the *locus classicus* where the human face and the silenic mask converge and fuse with each other (pp. 162–5). In this reading, the position of the *Phaedo* mosaic between the *Plokion* and the Thaleia panel may not be without significance as Sokrates' mask-like face may be compared to the masked face of the actor on his right and the mask of the Old Man held by Thaleia on his left.

Another iconographical feature may lead us to an alternative theory as to the nature of the present illustration. The way the mosaicist has designed the eyes leaves the viewer with the impression of something extraordinary about Sokrates' look. Now there is a passage in the *Phaedo* that may possibly come to mind. Simmias has just finished his speech and Phaidon, the narrator of the dialogue, immediately says:

205 'Ces personnages [sc. the philosophers] portent, *comme les acteurs*, la tunique blanche, longue . . . les manches à damier du sous-vêtement sont, elles, *identiques à celles des acteurs*' (Charitonidis et al. 1970, 81, my italics). Cf. Daux's (1963) remark that Sokrates and his associates are dressed up as comedians (823), a view accepted by Richter (1965) I 118.

206 So Charitonidis et al. (1970) 34b.

διαβλέψας οὖν ὁ Σωκράτης, ὥσπερ τὰ πολλὰ εἰώθει, καὶ μειδιάσας, 'δίκαια μέντοι', ἔφη, 'λέγει ὁ Σιμμίας... δοκεῖ μέντοι μοι χρῆναι πρὸ τῆς ἀποκρίσεως ἔτι πρότερον Κέβητος ἀκοῦσαι τί αὖ ὅδε ἐγκαλεῖ τῷ λόγῳ... ἀλλ' ἄγε,' ἦ δ' ὅς, 'ὦ Κέβης, λέγε, τί ἦν τὸ σὲ αὖ θρᾶττον [ἀπιστίαν παρέχει].' 'λέγω δή,' ἦ δ' ὃς ὁ Κέβης. (86d5–e6)

Socrates looked at us keenly, as was his habit, smiled and said: 'What Simmias says is quite fair... However, I think that before we answer him, we should hear Cebes' objection... Come then, Cebes. What is troubling you?' 'I tell you', said Cebes'. (after Cooper 1997, 75)

The text makes it perfectly clear that here is a reference to Sokrates' customary idiosyncratic stare.[207] The action described in this passage may seem somehow familiar. Sokrates has just heard Simmias, who remains silent, and turns to Kebes and asks for his contribution to the discussion. Kebes readily accepts the invitation and launches into his own speech. Some resemblance with the action depicted in the mosaic at Mytilene may not be coincidental. Simmias' disengagement and his raising his hand in the opposite direction from that of his companions may be the mosaicist's way of denoting that Simmias has just stopped talking. Even more pertinent is the context of the above extract. In their respective speeches, Sokrates' associates from Thebes raise their formidable objections to his latest proof for the immortality of the soul. These will pose the greatest challenge for Sokrates' arguments and lead him to the introduction of the theory of recollection. So powerful were these objections that they caused despair to all those present in Sokrates' cell (88c). Moreover, Plato takes an unusual step and exceptionally reintroduces the initial narrative setting so that the emotional reactions of Phaidon's audience may be heard as well. By these means the importance of the section for the structure of the dialogue is properly emphasised. In other words, the moment at which Simmias and Kebes intervene and challenge Sokrates is a turning point for the action of the dialogue. The parallel with the convention for the Menander scenes is striking indeed.

[207] Rowe (1993) 206 on 86d5. On the dangerous associations of Sokrates' gaze see Borthwick (2001).

There is also a last point that may lend some support to the present hypothesis. It has been suggested that the design of the illustrations and even the productions of plays may have reflected reading preoccupations. The characters are arranged on the mosaic (or the stage) in the order of speaking with the first speaker in the relevant passage on the left-hand side, in the manner of scene-headings.[208] Significantly, this principle is applicable to the Platonic scene: the arrangement Simmias – Sokrates – Kebes corresponds precisely to their order of speaking in *Phd.* 85c–88c. It is possible, then, that the *Phaedo* mosaic, like its theatrical counterparts, illustrates a particular scene from a dramatic work, namely *Phd.* 86d–e.[209]

This complex interplay between the Menandrean and the Platonic images attests to the rich semantics of the 'programmatic' zone of the *triclinium* mosaics. The *Phaedo* panel has been fully incorporated into a group of theatre-related illustrations by means of a mechanism of simultaneous assumption and undermining of the theatrical identity. Sokrates and his associates are presented as sharing the same world with, but breathing a different air from, Moschion or Demeas. There is little doubt that, though a later addition, the philosophers' mosaic is given a prominent place and its presence may have even influenced the character of the composition. For no compelling reason has been given so far for the choice of the *Plokion* as the play to accompany Menander's portrait.[210] The answer becomes evident when the *Plokion* mosaic is viewed in connection with the one on its left. Out of all the Mytilene scenes that particular comedy was the only one featuring a role whose name could be found among the cast of Plato's works. The name of the old man flanked by his son and wife is Laches, and so is the Athenian general in the eponymous Platonic dialogue. It

[208] So Handley (1997), who claims that 'the Mytilene *Samia* works perfectly in this way – Cook, Demeas, Chrysis – and possibly that was the way the play was staged' (197). Cf. Handley (2002) 171–3.

[209] One wonders whether the peculiar design of Sokrates' mouth (note the position of a black *tessera* on the viewer's left) was an attempt at a visual representation, admittedly a rudimentary one, of the μειδιάσας from Plato's text.

[210] Charitonidis et al. (1970) 103b admit that their theory of an illustrated edition of the poet's *vita* leaves the *Plokion* mosaic unaccounted for, while Berczelly (1988) does not raise the question.

seems reasonable to suppose that this play would be considered more than appropriate to pair with the *Phaedo* scene. To remind the viewer that Menander and Plato had created characters bearing the same names is to underline one more parallel between the two authors, thereby justifying the agenda behind the structure of the four-panel zone.

There is one remaining point to be commented on, namely the selection of the *Phaedo* to stand for Plato amidst the plays of Menander. The mosaicist or his patron(s) may have had more than one reason for this particular choice. It may be that the immortality of the soul and its fate in the afterlife complemented the vivid scenes from Menander, so exemplifying the familiar contrast in a sympotic context between life and death. The educated banqueters would appreciate the interplay and engage themselves in thoughtful discussion over these issues.[211] Another reason could have been the continuous fame of this dialogue throughout antiquity and early Byzantium. The *Phaedo* had established its position as one of the standard Platonic texts among the philosophers, while its subject matter, a narrative of the last day of Sokrates, guaranted its appeal among the general public as well.[212] Furthermore, the combination of two key themes in Plato, Sokrates' life and the Theory of Forms, make the *Phaedo* a pivotal text. In the Mytilene panel Plato is evoked by a sufficiently 'Platonic' dialogue with which every viewer would be familiar. In any case, the *Phaedo* seems to have held a special place in the circles of Platonisers. One may envisage its being presented in those Neoplatonic celebrations in honour of Sokrates and Plato that offered the context for a reading of the dialogues. A recently argued thesis has it that these feasts reflected similar rites in the Old Academy and that the *Phaedo* was precisely the founding text for the establishment of Sokrates as the patron-hero of the new philosophical community of the Academy. An illustration from the text that commemorates the martyrdom of Sokrates bears evident religious overtones, especially in the

211 Ellinghaus (1998–9) 268–9.

212 For a brief sketch of the reception of the dialogue and the philosophical commentaries see Westerink (1976) 7–20; Dörrie and Baltes (1993) 28–39, 185–93; Barnes (1993) 136–8.

context of an intended parallel with Christ. The structural and thematic parallels with tragedy demonstrate the dramatic elements in the composition of the dialogue. A work that may be considered equally a 'philosophical tragedy' or a 'passion play' fits comfortably in a group of panels associated with theatre.[213]

Finally, the *Phaedo* is credited with an additional 'prerogative' that few other dialogues share. It had its own history in the visual arts. Illustrations of the dialogue had been in circulation long before the Mytilene panels were commisioned. Loukianos attests to the existence of paintings depicting Sokrates on his deathbed surrounded by his disciples already in the second century AD.[214] The manner of the reference suggests that this image was not a novelty but descended from an earlier tradition. This is confirmed by the illustration on an Etruscan gem dated around 300 BC (Albizzati 1937, pl. I.2). There a bearded old man wearing a *himation* and seated on a *diphros* offers another standing man with similar features a cock. Three more figures may be seen in the background. In all probability the gem provides an illustration of the very last scene of the *Phaedo*. The two men in the forefront are Sokrates and Kriton. Sokrates gives his friend the cock he mentions in his last words as an offering to Asklepios (a clear allusion to *Phd.* 118a). The young men behind Kriton could be two of the philosopher's disciples while the man behind Sokrates has been interpreted as the prison official who prepared the hemlock. The image may be safely attributed to an earlier Greek original, possibly a painting or

[213] As White (2000) remarks, in writing the *Phaedo* Plato 'imitated Sophocles and the tragedians in dramatizing a hero's final day' (153) while 'the point of remembering and venerating Socrates, after all, is to live like Socrates, and that is a thoroughly ecumenical religion' (168). For the analogy between the Oidipous of the *Oedipus at Colonus* and the Sokrates of the *Phaedo* see 151–2 (cf. also 169 n. 8). For the *Phaedo*'s affinities with tragedy see p. 67 with n. 99. On the religious and sacramental tone of the dialogue see Bacon (1990) 149–51 and Morgan (1990) 55–79.

[214] In his invective *On the death of Peregrinus* Loukianos gives an openly inimical account of the life of a person whom the author believed to have been a charlatan presenting himself as a 'holy man'. Having described, purportedly as an eyewitness, how Peregrinos died by throwing himself into the fire, Loukianos records his invitation to the Cynic followers of the deceased to stop mourning in silence around the burning corpse and abandon the place: ἢ περιμένετε ἔστ᾽ ἂν γραφεύς τις ἐπελθὼν ἀπεικάσῃ ὑμᾶς οἵους τοὺς ἐν τῷ δεσμωτηρίῳ ἑταίρους τῷ Σωκράτει παραγράφουσιν; (37). Although Plato is not mentioned by name, there can be no doubt that the painters were inspired by the finale of the *Phaedo*. This was apparently the only text dealing with the last moments of Sokrates in prison and received very early a canonical status.

a relief of the late fourth century BC.[215] It follows that illustrations of the Platonic dialogues, in this case the *Phaedo*, were a familiar artistic presence at least a few decades after Plato's death.

The possibility that the iconography of Sokrates' death originated in the milieu of the Academy at the instigation of its founder cannot be ruled out. In fact, some references by Aristotle in his *Topics* to a seated Sokrates have been plausibly interpreted as indirect evidence for the existence in his lecture-room of a picture of Sokrates in the prison. Since the text of the *Topics* along with the rest of the logical works may be traced back to Aristotle's lectures in the Academy, it is reasonable to suppose that the painting in question was to be found in the peristyle of the public gymnasium or Plato's own premises nearby. This artefact may well have been the one that set off the whole series of similar representations.[216] When the Mytilene mosaicist, then, chose to illustrate the *Phaedo* out of the Platonic dialogues he presented his audience with a familar image drawing on a centuries-old tradition. Moving away from the standard depiction of Sokrates' last moments he shifts from the finale to another section of the dialogue. At the same time he appropriates for his own version the vocabulary of the religious iconography of his era. By reshaping the traditional typology in

[215] Hanfmann (1951) 229 n. 51, who opts for the relief. On the Etruscan gem see Albizzati (1937) 1–7. The author associates the gem with the commemoration of Sokrates established in Italy by Plato and continued by Archytas and other Pythagoreans and implies a connection of the use of gems as seals and the circulation of copies of the *Phaedo* (6–7).

[216] The existence of a painting of Sokrates in prison has been conjectured by Jackson (1920) 194–5, on the basis of *Top.* 160^{b}26–8: οἷον ἐάν τις λάβῃ τὸν καθήμενον γράφειν, Σωκράτη δὲ καθῆσθαι· συμβαίνει γὰρ ἐκ τούτων Σωκράτη γράφειν. The author also points to Aristotle's frequent references to Sokrates the μουσικός, a clear allusion to the *Phaedo*. The *Topics* must have been composed in the 350s (Düring 1966, 49). The image on the Etruscan gem supports Jackson's hypothesis as Sokrates is indeed depicted seated. It is tempting to see in it a copy of the painting in the Academy. On the other hand, the text of the *Topics* offers another alternative. Sokrates may have been not only seated but writing as well. Such an image could very well be taken as a standard illustration of the *Phaedo*, since only in this dialogue is Sokrates presented as an author, a composer of a hymn to Apollo and a versification of some Aesop's fables (60d, 61b). Furthermore, on the basis of *APr.* 43^{a}35–6 (φαμὲν γάρ ποτε τὸ λευκὸν ἐκεῖνο Σωκράτη εἶναι καὶ τὸ προσιὸν Καλλίαν), in relation to similar references to Sokrates and Kallias in *Metaph.* 6. 1033^{b}24, 1034^{a}6–7, Jackson (1920) 195–6 postulates the presence of a second painting, this time an illustration of *Prt.* 335c. As the *Prior Analytics* was a work of Aristotle's Academic period (cf. Düring 1966, 50) the picture could also belong to Plato's school – of course, similar paintings might decorate the Lyceum as well.

this way the artist smoothly incorporates his composition into the principles of the *triclinium* decoration (three-figure scenes from dramas) while retaining the emotional and symbolic appeal of older representations.

In sum, the presence of the *Phaedo* mosaic among scenes from Menander's comedies in Mytilene suggests that even as late as the second half of the fourth century AD the association between Plato's dialogues and the world of theatre was a living tradition. That the Sokrates panel shares the basic iconographical conventions with, but also stands apart from, the comic scenes demonstrates the essential affinities and the points of differentiation between these two kinds of dramatic literature. More significantly, the decoration of the *triclinium*, apart from being a statement of identification with Greek culture, may have been inspired by the types of literature performed in that very room as part of sympotic entertainment.[217] Whether still staged in public theatres or not (pp. 246–7 n. 199), the comedies of Menander could have been produced, in the form of complete plays or selected passages, in that Mytilene villa. There is absolutely no reason to rule out the possibility that the *Phaedo* mosaic reflected similar productions of Plato's dialogues.[218] In this case, the mosaic provides the visual equivalent of the literary testimonies of Plutarch and Athenaios, while attesting to the longevity of the tradition of Plato performances in the context of dinner theatre.[219]

[217] Dunbabin (1999) 217.

[218] Barnes (1993), who does not seem aware of the Mytilene mosaic, remarks that '[n]o doubt the *Phaedo* was among the works which rich Romans trained their slaves – or their chefs – to memorize and to recite to their guests at dinner parties' (136). Dunbabin (1999) thinks also of 'recitations from Plato' (217). Both refer to the passages from Plutarch and Athenaios. But these authors, as already shown (pp. 197–226), clearly state that the dialogues were dramatised not recited.

[219] Alternatively, if the House of Menander belonged to the local guild of the Artists of Dionysos the *triclinium* mosaics could have represented scenes from the company's repertoire. It should be noted, however, that there is no evidence for a theatrical company in Mytilene.

5

FINALE

The Mytilene mosaic is an appropriate point at which to conclude this travel in time as it brings us back to the Silenic Sokrates, the hero commemorated in the dialogues and in his statue in the Academy. The evidence examined so far represents a variety of archaeological and literary material that spans a considerable amount of time. The 'fragments' of the last chapter in combination with the testimonies of literary theorists (Demetrios, the Anonymous of *POxy* xlv 3219) and other authors indicate that there was throughout antiquity a tradition of interpreting the Platonic dialogue as a piece of dramatic performance literature. It may be argued that this reading constituted a basic feature of the Platonic interpretation from the fourth century BC onwards. The recognition of this dimension may have some interesting implications for the history of the reception of the dialogues. It would be interesting, for instance, to see how different types of readers had responded to the close relationship between Plato and the playwrights.

More than in the study of reception, the image of 'Plato the metatheatrical dramatist' is particularly helpful for a reconstruction of the function of the dialogues in a fourth-century BC context. By founding his own school Plato may have intended to establish himself as an alternative voice of authority in the polis. By constructing a new hero, the philosopher, he offered a model for emulation by anyone willing to attempt it. By creating his own type of theatre, he claimed for himself the role of the educator of his community traditionally attributed to Homer and the tragedians. The presentation of a dialogue in the Academy may be seen as the (Platonic) equivalent of the staging of a play in the theatre. The continuous interplay with and transformation of the theatrical language supports this view. Plato's contemporaries would not have failed to see in him a 'renegade' dramatist who attempted to encompass and supplant the received beliefs of his community with a way and vision of life (and death) he called philosophy.

A reading of Plato's dialogues as performance texts may also pave the way for their interpretation in the context of performance literature in fourth-century Athens. If they were composed for an oral presentation (recitation and dramatisation) in front of an audience on certain occasions, it follows that for a full appreciation of their meaning one may not leave out elements usually associated with the experiences of 'theatre-goers', as, for instance, the emotional response, and not with the responses of a reflective solitary reader. It may be the case that Plato's way of writing about and doing philosophy engaged many more aspects of the human psyche than the rational faculty.

These brief remarks refer to only a few points that further research based on a reading of Plato in his original context may elaborate. The aim of the present study has been much narrower, namely to present the evidence from the dialogues themselves and from the later tradition that attests to the metatheatrical character of Plato's texts. That Plato is mainly known as a great philosopher is nothing to be surprised about: he certainly was one. The point is that for him to be a writer of philosophy meant primarily to be the composer of the 'truest tragedy'. Let it be said in conclusion that to see Plato as a fellow-dramatist and successor of Euripides may not be so far from the truth after all.

APPENDIX

AN ACADEMY INSCRIPTION

The archaeologists' labour of about seven decades in the grounds of the ancient gymnasium of the Academy has yielded a number of important findings reflecting the history of the area in different periods.[1] One of them is of special interest as it has been associated with Plato's legacy. I refer to an inscribed marble fragment unearthed by P. Aristophron in the excavations of 1933–4. It was found in the vicinity of a building known as the 'Square Peristyle' or 'Peripatos' in the northern part of the precinct and bears traces of four proper names. The reading of these names and the date of the fragment have so far been a matter of dispute. The inscription, which should be dated to the second century BC, reads as follows:[2]

[.].[- -]

Χαρ[μίδης?]

Ἀρισ[τ – -]

Μενεκρ[ ]

Κρίτων?[- – -]

π[- – - – - -]

[1] The most comprehensive account available is Billot (1989). The articles by Stavropoullos (1962) and Travlos (1971) 42–51 remain the basic works of reference. See also Dillon (1983) and (2003) 1–16. For a complete list of the reports of the findings see Glucker (1978) 237 n. 32. Cf. Jones (1999) 231 n. 51. For a recent report and some findings that may lead to a partial revision of Travlos's plan see Lynkouri-Tolia (1988). Topographical plans of the Academy may be found in Travlos (1971) 50 fig. 62 and 318 fig. 417.

[2] I owe this transcription to Yiannis Tzifopoulos. The most recent discussion of the inscription is Brumbaugh (1992) 172 (cf. *SEG* XLII 1992 no. 144) who reads it ΧΑΡ... | ΑΡΙΣ... | ΜΕΝΕΚ?... | ΚΡΙΤΩΝ. The inscription was first published by Karo (1934) 140. He had read it as Χαρμ[ίδες?], Ἀρίσ[τον], Ἀξί[οχος], Κρίτων (sic) and suggested a date in the fifth century BC. His reading and date were reproduced in *SEG* XIII (1956) no. 28 and followed by Tod (1957) 135. Stavropoullos (1962) 343 produced a drawing, on the basis of which a revised reading and a Hellenistic date (2nd c. BC) are suggested in *SEG* XXI (1965) no 638, followed by Billot (1989) 724.

We lack virtually all the necessary information for a proper understanding of this fragment. We do not know whether it was found *in situ* or anything about the size of the original inscription, i.e. how many more names, if any at all, were included in the list. Similarly, the nature of the inscription remains a mystery since the type of structure that supported it is unknown. Nothing short of a personal inspection of the fragment can yield reasonable results. In the present circumstances any explanation of the rationale behind the dedication of this inscription belongs firmly to the world of speculation.

Apart from the inscription itself the only other useful piece of evidence is the area in which it was found. The 'Peripatos' is a roughly square building with sides of about 40m and walls made of large and well-cut blocks of limestone. These are preserved to some considerable height and are evidently the product of high-quality craftsmanship. A series of columns must have run on all four sides, as their conglomerate foundations indicate. The edifice may have been constructed in the second half of the fourth century BC. Its date and size make its identification with the *palaestra* in the Academy, mentioned by Hypereides (5.6.26 Worthington), an attractive hypothesis.[3] The impression of a public wrestling-ground is reinforced by the discovery around it of about seventy inscriptions, dating from the fourth century BC up to Roman times. Many of them belong to honorific decrees, a large number of which were commissioned during the rule of Demetrios of Phaleron.[4] It seems likely then that the 'Peripatos' was built on the site of the original gymnasium and that its facilities were open to the public.

The nature of the evidence evidently allows a wide range of possible explanations. One that suggests itself is the inscribed names found in gymnasia throughout the Greek world in the Hellenistic and Roman periods. Our fragment may just belong to those ephebic lists or graffiti reflecting the life of the youngsters in the

[3] Cf. Whitehead (2000) 443–6.
[4] Cf. Stavropoullos (1962) 342; Travlos (1971) 43; Billot (1989) 724–5.

place of their training. The Attic flavour of the names lends some support to this latter view.[5]

A different type of answer is reached from another direction. A fragmentary marble stele from Piraeus dated around 100 BC preserves a catalogue of literary works from the fifth down to the second century BC.[6] The list has been composed on a simple principle: the author's name in the genitive is followed by the title of one or more of his works in the nominative. The majority of the listed writers are playwrights, mainly tragedians. The names of at least two comedians are also restored while in the midst of these works of theatre a Socratic dialogue is surprisingly mentioned.[7] It has been suggested that this is a catalogue of books related to the library of a gymnasium, allegedly the Ptolemaion in Athens.[8] Similarly, the fragmentary inscription from the Academy discussed above could be interpreted as part of such a list. A genitive case for the names cannot be ruled out and the stone seems common in both cases. A library in the Academy at that period is also a possibility. For the sake of the discussion, the fragment can be restored so that the names correspond to comic poets from the fifth to the second century BC. The reading would then be something on the following lines:

ΧΑΡ[ΙΚΛΕΙΔΟΥ ?]

ΑΡΙΣ[ΤΟΦΑΝΟΥΣ ?]

ΜΕΝΕΚΡ[ΑΤΟΥΣ ?]

ΚΡΙΤΩΝ[ΟΣ] [9]

5 Guarducci (1967–74) II 388–410 (ephebic lists) and III 365–70 (graffiti). On the possible names that would originally have appeared on the first three lines of the inscription see *LPGN* II 51–63, 473–7 and 305–6 respectively.

6 *IG* ii^2 2363. Cf. *SEG* XXXVII (1987) no. 130. For an edition and commentary see Burzachechi (1963) 93–6.

7 Tragic poets: Nikomachos (as author of the play of l. 2), Sophokles (l. 19), Euripides (restored l. 38), Achaios (l. 15), Asklepiades (l. 16), Silenos (l. 17). Comic poets: Krates (l. 30), Diphilos (l. 33) and possibly Menander (as author of the plays of ll. 5–7). The Socratic dialogue is Eukleides' *Aeschines* (l. 10). Demosthenes and Hellanikos are the only other prose writers mentioned.

8 For libraries as a feature of the Hellenistic gymnasium all over the Greek world see Marrou (1956) 187–9; Delorme (1960) 331–2. Burzachechi (1963) provides a collection of the relevant epigraphical evidence.

9 Charikleides was active in the third, Menekrates in the fifth and Kriton in the second century (*PCG* IV 70–1, 346–8 and VII 1–2 respectively). Aristophanes may be replaced

These are attractive hypotheses, yet necessarily of limited interpretative value. It is not so easy to see how our fragment would fit into the usual formulaic pattern of the graffiti or library catalogues. There is no sign, for example, of short phrases arranged in the form of a continuous text. Unless evidence turns up to the contrary, we have to presume a succession of names in the vertical axis, in the manner of the citizens' lists of various purposes. Catalogues with the names of citizens killed in action, of members of phratries, religious associations or families fall into this category. A hypothesis that interprets the Academy inscription in this way, though not unlikely in itself, somehow fails to account satisfactorily for the presence of these particular names. The logic of their selection and order of arrangement remains unexplained. In other words, there is no way to tell whether our fragment refers, for instance, to books, playwrights or relatives.

On the other hand, the fact that the inscription was found in the Academy makes it tempting to postulate a 'Platonic connection'.[10] In fact the association with Plato has been a standard point of reference throughout the history of the interpretation of the fragment. The first editor thought that the list comprises 'Platonic names', while his reading was later published under the heading 'names of pupils of Sokrates'.[11] This would presuppose an inscription with names of persons who are related to each other. Often these are grouped together as participants in some common activity (e.g. dedication of a certain offering) or, less likely, as 'students' and the inscription would stand for a 'matriculation' document in the

by any one of those comedians whose name fits the first four letters of the fragment, say Aristagoras, Aristomenes or Aristophon (for all the candidates see *PCG* II 558–74 and IV 1–11). Alternatively if the names are in the nominative we would have had a list of comic playwrights, one unrelated to victories in dramatic festivals (but the typical phraseology is missing).

10 It may not be overlooked, however, that throughout antiquity the Academy was first and foremost a public gymnasium, a focal urban space with particular religious and cultural overtones. Cf. Billot (1989) 703. The only other finding possibly associated with Plato's Academy is the foundations of a house excavated at the north-western end of the gymnasium, presumably outside its grounds. Stavropoullos (1963) confidently identifies it with the building of the school at some point during the Hellenistic period (esp. 17–19).

11 'Resten der vier Platonikernamen' (Karo 1934, 140) and 'Nomina discipulorum Socratis' (*SEG* XIII 1956, 28) respectively.

manner of the ephebic lists.[12] Following the complete revision of the third line Stavropoullos (1962) offered a new explanation for the names, namely 'titles of Platonic dialogues'.[13] This signals a shift from a list of persons to one of literary works, in the manner of the catalogue of books from the library at the Ptolemaion. In this case we might be dealing with a list of Plato's dialogues deposited in the library of the gymnasium of the Academy. Unfortunately this explanation could not account for the second name, as there is no work of Plato beginning with *Aris-*. Owing to this discrepancy and the postulation of a Hellenistic date it was felt that the idea of a 'Socratic/Platonic connection' had to be abandoned. The names did not refer either to a group of Sokrates' friends or to a catalogue of Plato's books.[14]

In a later article, however, Brumbaugh (1992) renounces his earlier doubts and argues that the fragment is related to Plato's Academy and that the names on it come from his dialogues. He restores the second name as ΑΡΙΣ[ΤΕΙΔΗΣ, the son of Lysimachos and grandson of Aristeides the Just, who appears in the cast

[12] Cf. *SEG* XLIV (1994) no. 1149 II, XXXVII (1987) no. 725, XXXII (1982) no. 426C (*IG* vii 3224). In this respect, the content of a graffito cut on the steps of the north-east side of the Tower of the Winds (Plaka, Athens) deserves to be mentioned. The inscription reads as follows: φίλοι | Πλάτων | [Σ]ω[κράτ]ης (*SEG* XXXVII 1987, no. 204). The identification of the second name looks pretty much certain since the two letters after ω may possibly be read as Κ and Ρ. No date has been given but the place and the shape of the letters point to the Roman period. Although the names might belong to young ephebes, one is tempted to think more of the renowned philosophers of the past. Oikonomides (1987), the first editor, who conveniently offers a drawing of the graffito, believes that the names reflect 'a student's enthusiastic appraisal of the well-known friendship between Plato and his teacher Sokrates' (33). If this interpretation is sound, it follows that at least in Roman times it was possible for members of the Socratic circle to be listed together in the manner of the φίλοι-inscriptions. This graffito may shed a different light on a piece of evidence from the *Suda* lexicon. In the entry on *Academy* we read: λέγεται δὲ Ἀκαδημία ἡ τῶν φίλων διατριβή (I 775 Adler). Glucker (1978) 162 and Dorandi (1988) 578 correct φίλων to φιλοσόφων, plausibly explaining the error as a misreading of a scribal abbreviation. I would like to suggest that the unanimous manuscript reading probably preserves a tradition reflected in the graffito, according to which the Academy was the community, the school of the friends, namely Plato and Sokrates (for the meaning of the word διατριβή see Glucker 1978, 162–5).

[13] 'ὀνόματα πλατωνικῶν διαλόγων' (Stavropoullos (1962) 343). This is the excavator's only claim in relation to the inscription. He does not commit himself either to the date or the reading of the last letter of the third name (*pace* Brumbaugh 1992, 171).

[14] This was the verdict of Brumbaugh and Wells (1968) 161. They were building on the entry in *SEG* XXI (1965) no. 638, where the fragment, described merely as a list of names ('catalogus nominum'), was thought to be unrelated to Sokrates ('lapidem hunc nihil cum discipulis Socratis philosophi commune habere').

of Plato's *Laches*. He then goes on to suggest that the fragment has preserved 'a list of names of schoolboys from Platonic dialogues, one each for the set V 2 – VI 1 in Thrasyllus' tetralogical order' (171–2). Kriton's presence in the list is considered justified because at the end of the *Euthydemus* he evidently agrees to become a student again alongside Sokrates.[15] He summarises the correspondence between Thrasyllos' arrangement, the dialogues and the names of the Academy fragment in the following table (172):

Tetralogy	Dialogue	Cast	Inscription
V 2	*Charmides*	Charmides	ΧΑΡ...
V 3	*Laches*	Aristides	ΑΡΙΣ...
V 4	*Lysis*	Menexenus	ΜΕΝΕΚ?...
VI 1	*Euthydemus*	Kriton	ΚΡΙΤΩΝ

If one were to follow the same provisional line of argument, the question of the purpose of such an inscription comes to the fore. The selection of one character from each dialogue indicates that this is different from the catalogues found in the papyri and manuscripts, which record the cast of a single play or dialogue. Therefore the Academy list may have served a special purpose. One wonders whether this list could be associated with the practice of some of the dialogues being performed by members of Plato's school. That all of the characters are either of school age or in need of education suggests that a pedagogical motif may be at work here. It could be interpreted as a statement on the relevance of the dialogues and the teaching methods of the Academy for the proper education of the youngsters (a more than appropriate theme in the context of a public gymnasium).[16] It is not inconceivable that the students of the Academy performed the dialogues as part of their

[15] For some possible textual support see *Euthd.* 272d, 307c.

[16] An ephebic inscription informs us that in the archonship of Demetrios (123/2 BC) the youth of Athens attended lectures by philosophers in the Academy as part of their curriculum (*IG* ii² 1006, 19–20). That the ephebes frequented the gymnasium for their physical training in the early second century is shown by another inscription dated around 184–171 BC (*Agora Invent.* I 4512, 3–4). Cf. Billot (1989) 726; Reinmuth (1961) 15–7.

training.[17] If the Hellenistic date is accepted, there is, moreover, reason to believe that the anti-doctrinal orientation of the school in the second century BC, favoured a reception of the dialogues tuned with a particular emphasis on issues of characterisation and the polyphony of the dialogue form.[18] Last but definitely not least, the testimony of Demetrios, a literary critic of the second or early first century BC, has to be brought into the picture. His remark that an actor could very well deliver the opening lines of the *Euthydemus* may not be irrelevant to events that might have led to the creation of the Academy inscription.

This hypothesis is the only one that conforms so fully to the principle of economy since it offers a binding reason for the presence of these particular names in precisely that order. The introduction of Thrasyllos' taxonomy provides the explanatory pattern that accounts for the original form and position of *all* four names. Nothing is left out as the list of names takes the form of a group with internal consistency and unity. The suggestion that the names correspond to young boys from Platonic casts seemed to have paved the way for an answer to the riddle.

Brumbaugh's theory is an attractive piece of reasoning. That is why it needs to be tested against a close reading of the inscription itself, as it appears in a set of photographs taken and published here with the permission of the Third Ephorate of Classical Antiquities (fig. 4a–b).[19] The dimensions of the fragment (M 3120) are as follows: height 0.0058m, width 0,0055m and depth 0,0021m. The

[17] We know that the Hellenistic cities organised competitions of performances (songs, recitations) of poetry and prose among schoolchildren as a kind of exam. See Marrou (1956) 166.

[18] From the time of Arkesilaos (*c.* 268 BC) until almost its final years in the early first century BC the Academy adopted a sceptical stance. For the reception of Sokrates and Plato in the Hellenistic Academy see Annas (1994). A collection of the evidence concerning the scholarchs in the period 265–110 BC is found in Mette (1984) and (1985); cf. also Dorandi (1992) 3778–88. A chronological survey of the Academy from Plato's death onwards with a list of scholarchs is given by Dorandi (1999) 31–5, 48–9, 53–4. For separate periods see Dillon (2003) on the Old Academy; Thorsrud (2010) and Lévy (2010) on the New Academy; Glucker (1978), Brittain (2001) and Sedley (forthcoming) on the last years of Plato's school. The basic epistemological tenets of Karneades, the most influential scholarch of the second century, are surveyed in Schofield (1999) 334–50 and Thorsrud (2010) 70–8.

[19] I wish to thank E. Lynkouri-Tolia for the permission. I am also much indebted to J. Reynolds for her invaluable help in reading the photographs.

(a)

(b)

Figure 4(a–b) Fragment of a marble inscription from the Academy.

left side is the only one preserved and it is clear that the original must have been larger both in height and in breadth, but we do not know how much. There is not much to be said about its function, but the formal cutting of the letters and the material used (marble) suggest that the inscription was erected for some semi-official purpose. There are visible traces of another name in a fifth line: the upper part of the second letter may be Γ, Ε or Π.[20] Only one out of the four names survives in full (ΚΡΙΤΩΝ).[21] Its open-bottomed *omega* may point to a Hellenistic date,[22] although a date as early as the fourth century BC cannot be excluded. In the case of the first name the letters Χ and Α are clearly visible followed by a possible but doubtful Ρ. There are also no doubts about the first four letters of the second name (ΑΡΙΣ), possibly followed by a doubtful Τ. So far, then, the evidence is compatible with Brumbaugh's theory. But the crux lies in the final, badly preserved, letter of the third name.[23] The photograph suggests that Ρ is the more plausible reading[24] but I do not feel that we can be absolutely confident that the issue is settled, at least not before an autopsy of the inscription itself.[25] All in all, the case for the Platonic names does not rest on solid

[20] If it is a list of Platonic names, then a Π would be appropriate as suggestive of Hippokrates, Sokrates' young associate. Nails (2002) opts for an Ε (93).

[21] Owing to the fragmentary state of the inscription the possibility of another name for the last line must always remain open. On the other hand, the only other attested name in Attica that fits the bill is Κριτωνιανός, dated to a much later period, possibly Byzantine (*LGPN* II 274).

[22] Tracy would have tentatively dated the fragment to *c.*229–150 BC (personal correspondence). It was the discovery that this letter was an omega and not an omicron as the first editor would have it that led to the suggestion of a Hellenistic date. See Glucker (1978) 239 n. 40. At any rate the presence of an omicron does not by itself guarantee a fifth-century date since there is evidence for confusion of Ω and Ο in the late classical and Hellenistic period, especially in inscriptions of a more private character (see Threatte 1980, 50–1, 224–7). For what it is worth, the writing of the fragment seems to resemble that of the cutter of *IG* ii^2 913 (Tracy 1990, 72 fig. 6).

[23] Stavropoullos' drawing was instrumental in the reconstruction of the third line. The newly revealed name was completely different from the original suggestion. To have transcribed ΑΞΙ . . . for ΜΕΝΕΚ . . . , as Karo had done, is a rather striking case of misreading, though epigraphically less absurd than might at first seem.

[24] So *SEG* XXI (1965) no. 638. In his catalogue of Athenian personal names Trail (2003) reads the name of Menekrates (209a, no. 643670). According to Tzifopoulos (personal correspondence) the letter is almost certainly a *rhō* ('80%, perhaps even more').

[25] For the reading ΜΕΝΕΞΕΝΟΣ either Σ or Ξ would do. There appear only two instances of ΚΣ for Ξ, both in texts of Roman period (Threatte 1980, 555). The cluster ΚΞ for Ξ, though rare, was not unknown (Threatte 1980, 555). But a cross-like shape for Ξ is attested only in Doric alphabets outside Attica (Guarducci 1967 table I).

ground. Therefore the hypothesis that this inscription is somehow related to a more performance-oriented study, although attractive in itself, must be dropped – at least until an examination of the marble fragment based on autopsy calls for a reconsideration.[26]

[26] This section has greatly benefited from the invaluable comments by Joyce Reynolds, Yiannis Tzifopoulos and Stephen Tracy. Any 'residual' mistakes still present are, needless to say, my responsibility.

REFERENCES

The bibliography contains only works cited in the main text and footnotes. Edited volumes are given a separate entry only when the volume as a whole has been mentioned or where more than one essay from the volume is listed in the bibliography. I have tried to refer to the most recent editions in all cases. Editions of ancient texts are cited here only when they contain material, other than the original text, which has been discussed.

Abert, H. (1921–2) 'Ein neu entdeckter früchristlicher Hymnus mit antiken Musiknoten', *ZMW* **4**: 524–9.

(1926) 'Das älteste Denkmal der christlichen Kirchenmusik', *Die Antike* **2**: 282–90.

Acheson, K. (2008) 'Science as gesture: rethinking the nature of communicative silences', *Communication Theory* **18**: 535–55.

Achtemeier, P. J. (1990) '*Omne verbum sonat*: the New Testament and the oral environment of late Western antiquity', *JBL* **109**: 3–27.

Adomenas, M. (2001) 'Self-reference, textuality, and the status of the political project in Plato's *Laws*', *OSAPh* **21**: 29–59.

Ahbel-Rappe, S. and R. Kamtekar (eds.) (2006) *A Companion to Socrates*. Malden, Mass. and Oxford.

Albizzati, C. (1937) 'Due intagli d'arte italica', in *Scritti in Onore di Bartolomeo Nogara*. Vatican: 1–10.

Alcock, S. E. (1997) 'Greece: a landscape of resistance?', in *Dialogues in Roman Imperialism: Power, Discourse and Discrepant Experience in the Roman Empire*. ed. D. J. Mattingly. Ann Arbor: 103–15.

(2002) *Archaeologies of the Greek Past: Landscapes, Monuments, and Memories*. Cambridge.

Alker, H. R., Jr (1988) 'The dialectical logic of Thucydides' Melian dialogue', *APSR* **82**: 805–20.

Allan, D. J. (1980) 'Ἀναγιγνώσκω and some cognate words', *CQ* **30**: 244–51.

Allen, R. E. (1991) *The Dialogues of Plato Volume II: The Symposium*. New Haven and London.

Alline, H. (1915) *Histoire du texte de Platon*. Paris.

Aloni, A. (2009) 'Elegy: forms, functions and communication', in Budelmann (ed.): 168–88.

Alrivie, J. J. (1971) 'Les prologues du "Théétète" et du "Parménide"', *RMM* **76**: 6–23.

Alter, J. (1990) *A Sociosemiotic Theory of Theatre*. Philadelphia.
Altman, W. H. F. (2010a) '*Laches* before *Charmides*: fictive chronology and Platonic pedagogy', *Plato* **10** <http://gramata.univ-paris1.fr/Plato/article95.html>.
(2010b) 'The reading order of Plato's dialogues', *Phoenix* **64**: 18–51.
Álvarez Salas, O. (2007) 'I frammenti filosofici di Epicarmo: una rivisitazione critica', *SIFC* **5**: 23–72.
Anagnostopoulos G. (2009) 'Aristotle's works and the development of his thought', in *A Companion to Aristotle*, ed. G. Anagnostopoulos. Oxford: 14–27.
Anderson, D. E. (1993) *The Masks of Dionysos: A Commentary on Plato's 'Symposium'*. Albany.
Anderson, G. (1997) 'Athenaeus: the sophistic environment', *ANRW* II **34**.3: 2173–85.
(2000) 'The banquet of belles-lettres: Athenaeus and the comic symposium', in Braund and Wilkins (eds.): 316–26, 572–3.
Anderson, J. M. (1993) 'Myth, tragedy and dialogue: the language of philosophy', in Georgopoulos (ed.): 187–216.
Anderson, W. D. (1994) *Music and Musicians in Ancient Greece*. Ithaca and London.
Ando, C. (2008) 'Decline, fall, and transformation', *JLA* **1**: 31–60.
Andronicos, M. (1984) *Vergina: The Royal Tombs*. Athens.
Annas, J. (1982) 'Plato's myths of judgement', *Phronesis* **27**: 119–43.
(1994) 'Plato the skeptic', in Vander Waerdt (ed.): 309–40.
Annas, J. and C. J. Rowe (eds.) (2002) *New Perspectives on Plato, Modern and Ancient*. Cambridge, Mass. and London.
Anton, J. P. (1962–3) 'Some Dionysian references in the Platonic dialogues', *CJ* **58**: 49–55.
(1964) 'Plato's philosophical use of myth', *GOTR* **9**: 161–80.
Arieti, J. A. (1991) *Interpreting Plato: The Dialogues as Drama*. Savage, Md.
(1993) 'Plato's philosophical *Antiope*: the *Gorgias*', in Press (ed.): 197–214.
Armstrong, C. B. (1953) 'Plato's Academy', *PLPLS* **7**: 89–106.
Arvanitis, I. (1997) 'A way to the transcription of Old Byzantine chant by means of written and oral tradition', in Troelsgard (ed.): 123–41.
Atherton, C. (ed.) (1997) *Form and Content in Didactic Poetry*. Bari.
Avlonitis, S. (1999) 'Aristophanes βωμολόχος: Platon, Symposion 185C-189B', *RhM* **142**: 15–23.
(2008) 'Πρὸς τὴ φιλοσοφικὴ ποιητικὴ καὶ παραίνεση τοῦ πλατωνικοῦ *Συμποσίου*', *Ἑλληνικά* **58**: 27–45.
Babut, D. (1969) *Plutarque et la Stoïcisme*. Paris.
Bacon, H. H. (1959) 'Socrates crowned', *VQR* **35**: 415–30.
(1990) 'The poetry of *Phaedo*', in *Cabinet of the Muses: Essays on Classical and Comparative Literature in Honor of Thomas G. Rosenmeyer*, ed. M. Griffith and D. Mastronarde. Atlanta: 147–62.

Bailey, D. M. (1974) 'A caricature of Socrates', *AJA* **78**: 427.
Bailey, D. T. J. (2008) 'Excavating Dissoi Logoi 4', *OSAPh* 249–64.
Bakker, E. J. (ed.) (2010) *A Companion to Ancient Greek Language*. Oxford.
Bakola, E. (2010) *Cratinus and the Art of Comedy*. Oxford.
Balaudé, J.–F. (1999) 'Livre VIII 1–23, 51–91', in Goulet-Cazé (ed.): 921–60, 980–1019.
Balogh, J. (1927) 'Voces paginarum', *Philologus* **82**: 84–109, 202–40.
Baltes, M. (1993) 'Plato's School, the Academy', *Hermathena* **155**: 7–28. reprinted in *ΔΙΑΝΟΗΜΑΤΑ: Kleine Schriften zu Platon und zu Platonismus*. ed. A. Hüffmeier, M.-L. Lakmann and M. Vorwerk. Stuttgart and Leipzig, 1999: 249–73.
(1997) 'Is the Idea of the Good in the *Republic* beyond being?', in Joyal (ed.): 3–23.
Baltussen, H. (2002) 'Philology or philosophy? Simplicius on the use of quotations', in Worthington and Foley (eds.): 173–89.
Barchiesi, A. (2009) 'Roman perspectives on the Greeks', in Boys-Stones et al. (eds.): 98–113.
Barker, A. (1989) *Greek Musical Writings Vol. II: Harmonic and Acoustic Theory*. Cambridge.
(2007) *The Science of Harmonics in Classical Greece*. Cambridge and New York.
Barnes, J. (1982) *The Presocratic Philosophers*. London and New York.
(1991) 'The Hellenistic Platos', *Apeiron* **24**: 115–28.
(1993) 'Imperial Plato', *Apeiron* **26**: 129–51.
Barnes, J. and J. Griffin (eds.) (1997) *Philosophia Togata II: Plato and Aristotle at Rome*. Oxford.
Barney, R. (2006) 'The sophistic movement', in Gill and Pellegrin (eds.): 77–97.
Barney, R., T. Brennan and C. Brittain (eds.) (forthcoming) *Plato and the Divided Self*. Cambridge.
Bartol, K. (2000) 'Ion of Chios and the king (Ion, 27, 1–3 W. = 2, 1–3 G.-P.)', *Mnemosyne* **53**: 185–92.
Bassett, S. E. (2008) 'The late antique image of Menander', *GRBS* **48**: 201–25.
Bastianini, G. and D. N. Sedley (1995) 'Commentarium in Platonis "Theaetetum"', in *CPF* **III**: 227–562.
Battezzato, L. (2009) 'Techniques of reading and textual layout in ancient Greek texts', *CCJ* **55**: 1–23.
Baud-Bovy, S. (1991) 'Les modes dans la musique byzantine et le chant populaire et dans la musique grecque antique', in Meyer (ed.): 67–75.
Baumgarten, R. (2009) 'Dangerous tears? Platonic provocations and Aristotelian answers', in *Tears in the Graeco-Roman World*, ed. T. Fögen. Berlin and New York: 85–104.
Beard, M. and J. Henderson (2001) *Classical Art from Greece to Rome*. Oxford.
Beaton R. (1980) 'Modes and roads: factors of change and continuity in Greek musical tradition', *ABSA* **75**: 1–11.

Beck, M. C. (2006) *Tragedy and the Philosophical Life* (3 vols). Lewiston, Queenston and Lampeter.
Becker, A. and P. Scholz (eds.) (2004) *Dissoi Logoi. Zweierlei Ansichten: Ein sophistischer Traktat*. Munich.
Belfiore, E. (1980) '*Elenchus, epode*, and magic: Socrates as Silenus', *Phoenix* **34**: 128–37.
(2004) 'Wine and *catharsis* of the emotions in Plato's *Laws*', *CQ* **36**: 421–37.
(2011) 'Poets at the Symposium', in Destrée and Herrmann (eds.): 155–74.
Benardete, S. (1989) *Socrates' Second Sailing: On Plato's Republic*. Chicago and London.
(2000) *Plato's "Laws": The Discovery of Being*. Chicago and London.
Benitez, E. (2007) 'Philosophy, myth and Plato's two-worlds view', *EL* **12**: 225–42.
Benson, H. H. (ed.) (2006) *A Companion to Plato*. Oxford.
Bérard, C. and C. Bron (1989) 'Satyric revels', in *A City of Images: Iconography and Society in Ancient Greece*, ed. C. Bérard et al., translated by D. Lyons. Princeton: 131–50.
Berczelly, L. (1988) 'The date and significance of the Menander mosaics at Mytilene', *BICS* **35**: 119–26.
Beresford, A. (2008) 'Nobody's perfect: a new text and interpretation of Simonides *PMG* 542', *CPh* **103**: 237–56.
Bergjan, S.-P. (2005) '"Das hier ist kein Theater und ihr sitzt nicht da, um Schauspieler zu betrachten und zu klatschen" – Theaterpolemik und Theatermetaphern bei Johannes Chrysostomos', *ZAC* **8**: 567–92.
Berra, A. (2005) 'Le Plutarque d' Athénée: masque, modèle et tradition', *Pallas*: **67**: 139–52.
Bers, V. (2010) '*Kunstprosa*: philosophy, history, oratory', in Bakker (ed.): 455–67.
Bertrand, J.-M. (1999) *De l'écriture à l'oralité: lectures des Lois de Platon*. Paris.
Bett, R. (ed.) (2010) *The Cambridge Companion to Ancient Scepticism*. Cambridge.
Beversluis, J. (2000) *Cross-examining Socrates: A Defense of Interlocutors in Plato's Early Dialogues*. Cambridge.
(2006) 'A defence of dogmatism in the interpretation of Plato', *OSAPh* **31**: 85–111.
Bieber, M. (1917) 'Die Herkunft des tragischen Kostüms', *JDAI* **32**: 15–104.
Billig, E. (1977) *Spätantike Architekturdarstellungen 1*. Stockholm.
Billot, M.-F. (1989) 'Académie – topographie et archéologie', in *DPhA*: 693–789.
Blackenhagen von, P. H. (1992) 'Stage and actors in Plato's *Symposium*', *GRBS* **33**: 51–68.
Blank, D. (1993) 'The arousal of emotion in Plato's dialogues', *CQ* **43**: 428–39.
Blome, P. (1999) 'Bildliche Darstellungen von Sokrates', in Pestalozzi (ed.): 98–111.

Blondell, R. (2002) *The Play of Character in Plato's Dialogues*. Cambridge.

Blumenthal, A. von (1939) *Ion von Chios: Die Reste seine Werke*. Stuttgart and Berlin.

Blundell, M. W. (1989) *Helping Friends and Harming Enemies: A Study in Sophocles and Greek Ethics*. Cambridge.

(1992) 'Character and meaning in Plato's *Hippias Minor*', in Klagge and Smith (eds.): 131–72.

Bobonich, C. (1996) 'Reading the *Laws*', in Gill and McCabe (eds.): 249–81.

(2002) *Plato's Utopia Recast: His Later Ethics and Politics*. Oxford.

(ed.) (2010) *Plato's Laws: A Critical Guide*.

Boegehold, A. L. (1999) *When a Gesture was Expected: A Selection of Examples from Archaic and Classical Greek Literature*. Princeton.

Bonazzi, M and F. Trabattoni (eds.) (2003) *Platone e la tradizione platonica*. Milan.

Bonazzi, M., L.-A. Dorion, T. Hatano, N. Notomi and M. van Ackeren (2009) '"Socratic" dialogues', *Plato* **9** <http://gramata.univ-paris1.fr/Plato/article88.html>.

Bonelli, G. (1991) *Socrate Sileno: dinamica erotica e figurazione scenica nel Convito di Platone*. Turin.

Bons, J. A. E. (1993) 'Ἀμφιβολία: Isocrates and written compostion', *Mnemosyne* **46**: 160–71.

Bonzon, S. (1988) 'Sur la "mise en récit" du dialogue chez Platon', in *La narration: quand le récit devient communication*, ed. S. Bonzon et al. Geneva: 205–16.

Boot, P. (1980) 'The place of Longinus' *De Sublimitate* c. 44', *Mnemomsyne* **33**: 299–306.

Borthwick, E. K. (2001) 'Socrates, Socratics and the word *βλεπεδαιμων*', *CQ* **51**: 297–301.

Bos, A. P. (1989) *Cosmic and Meta-Cosmic Theology in Aristotle's Lost Dialogues*. Leiden.

Bosch-Veciana, A. (2007) 'Socrates as a "figure" of the philosopher in the *Gorgias*', in Bosch-Veciana and Monserat-Molas (eds.): 93–136.

Bosch-Veciana, A. and J. Monserrat-Molas (eds.) (2007) *Philosophy and Dialogue: Studies in Plato's Dialogues, vol. 1*. Barcelona.

Bostock, D. (1988) *Plato's Theaetetus*. Oxford.

Bowe, G. S. (2007) 'In defense of Clitophon', *CPh* **102**: 245–64.

Bowie, E. L. (1993a) 'Greek table-talk before Plato', *Rhetorica* **11**: 355–71.

(1993b) 'Greek poetry in the Antonine age', in *Antonine Literature*, ed. D. A. Russell. Oxford: 53–90.

Boyarin, D. (2008) 'Dialectic and divination in the Talmud', in Goldhill (ed.): 217–41.

Boys-Stones, G. (2004) 'Phaedo of Elis and Plato on the soul', *Phronesis* **49**: 1–23.

(2007) 'Physiognomy and ancient psychological theory', in *Seeing the Face, Seeing the Soul: Polemon's Physiognomy from Classical Antiquity to Medieval Islam*, ed. Simon Swain. Oxford: 19–124.

Boys-Stones, G., B. Graziosi and P. Vasunia (eds.) (2009) *The Oxford Handbook of Hellenic Studies*. Oxford.

Boys-Stones, G. R. and J. H. Haubold (eds.) (2010) *Plato and Hesiod*. Oxford.

Brancacci, A. (1997) 'Filosofia e paideia in Antistene', in Giannantoni and Narcy (eds.): 255–77.

(2003) 'Zwei verlorene Schriften des Antisthenes', *RhM* **146**: 259–78.

(2005) 'The double *daimōn* in Euclides the Socratic', in *Socrates' Divine Sign: Religion, Practice, and Value in Socratic Philosophy*, ed. P. Destrée and N. D. Smith. Suppl. *Apeiron* Vol. 38 no 2. Edmonton.

Brancacci, A., D. El Murr and P. Taormina (eds.) (2010) *Aglaïa Autour de Platon. Mélanges offerts à Monique Dixsaut*. Paris.

Brandwood, L. (1976) *A Word Index to Plato*. Leeds.

Braund, D. (1997) 'Greeks and barbarians: the Black Sea region and Hellenism under the early Empire', in *The Early Roman Empire in the East*, ed. S. E. Alcock. Oxford: 121–36.

(2000) 'Learning, luxury and empire: Athenaeus' Roman patron', in Braund and Wilkins (eds.): 3–22, 539.

Braund, D. and J. Wilkins (eds.) (2000) *Athenaeus and his World: Reading Greek Culture in the Roman Empire*. Exeter.

Brillante, C. (1996) 'La realtà del sogno da Omero a Platone', *QUCC* **53**.2: 7–26.

Brisson, L. (1982) 'Notices sur les noms propres', in Brisson et al. (eds.): 49–142.

(1992) 'Diogène Laërce, "Vies et doctrines des philosophes illustres", Livre III: Structure et contenu', *ANRW* **36**.5: 3619–3760.

(1998) *Plato the Myth Maker*, trans. G. Naddaf. Chicago and London.

(1999) 'Livre III: Platon', in Goulet-Cazé (ed.): 370–464.

(2007) 'The role of myth in Plato and its prolongations in antiquity', *EL* **12**: 141–58.

Brisson, L. and J.-F. Pradeau (2006) *Platon Les Lois* (2 vols). Paris.

Brisson, L. et al. (eds.) (1982–92) *Porphyre La Vie de Plotin*, vols I (1982), II (1992). Paris.

Brittain, C. (2001) *Philo of Larissa: The Last of Academic Sceptics*. Oxford.

(2008) 'Plato and Platonism', in Fine (ed.): 526–52.

Brock, R. (1990) 'Plato and comedy', in *Owls to Athens: Essays on Classical Subjects for Sir Kenneth Dover*, ed. E. Craik. Oxford: 39–49.

Brogan, W. A. (1991) 'Is Platonic drama the death of tragedy?', *ISPh* **23**: 75–82.

Brown, A. L. (1996) 'Chaeremon (1)', *OCD*^{3}: **315a**.

Brumbaugh, R. S. (1991) 'Simon and Socrates', *Anc Phil* **11**: 151–2.

(1992) 'An Academy inscription', *AncPhil* **12**: 171–2.

Brumbaugh, R. S. and R. Wells (1968) *The Plato Manuscripts: A New Index*. New Haven and London.

Bruneau, P. (1984) 'Les mosaîstes antiques avaient-ils des cahiers des modèles?', *RA*: 241–72.
Budelmann, F. (ed.) (2009) *Greek Lyric*. Cambridge.
Bundrick, S. D. (2005) *Music and Image in Classical Athens*. Cambridge.
Burkert, W. (1972) *Lore and Science in Ancient Pythagoreanism*, trans. E. L. Minar, Jr. Cambridge, Mass.
Burnyeat, M. F. (1990) *The Theaetetus of Plato*. Indianapolis and Cambridge.
(1997) 'Postscript on silent reading', *CQ* **47**: 74–6.
Burzachechi, M. (1963) 'Ricerche epigrafiche sulle antiche biblioteche del mondo greco', *RAL* **18**: 75–96.
Byrd, M. (2007) 'The summoner approach: a new method of Plato interpretation', *JHPh* **45**: 365–81.
Calame, C. (1986) 'Facing otherness: the tragic mask in ancient Greece', *HR* **26**: 125–42.
Cameron, A. (1978) *Plato's Affair with Tragedy*. Cincinnati.
Cameron, Av. (1998) 'Education and literary culture', in *CAH XIII: The Late Empire A.D. 337–425*: 665–707.
Camp, J. M. (1986) *The Athenian Agora: Excavations in the Heart of Classical Athens*. London.
Campbell, D. A. (1982) *Greek Lyric Poetry*. 2nd edn. Bristol.
Capra, A. (1998) 'Il *Menesseno* di Platone e la commedia antica', *Acme* **51**: 183–92.
(2001) *Ἀγὼν λόγων: Il 'Protagora' di Platone tra eristica e commedia*. Milan.
(2003) 'Dialoghi narrati e dialoghi drammatici in Platone', in Bonazzi and Trabattoni (eds.): 3–30.
(2005) 'Protagoras' Achilles: Homeric allusion as a satirical weapon (Pl. *Prt.* 340A)', *CPh* **100**: 274–7.
(2010) 'Plato's Hesiod and the will of Zeus: philosophical rhapsody in the *Timaeus* and the *Critias*', in Boys-Stones and Haubold (eds.): 200–18.
Carey, C. (2009) 'Iambos', in Budelmann (ed.): 149–67.
Carlini, A. (2003) 'Alcune considerazioni sulla tradizione testuale degli scritti pseudoplatonici', in Döring et al. (eds.): 25–36.
Carlini, A. and F. Montanari (1989) 'Aristoteles 21T: *De Poetis*', in *CPF* **I***: 306–7.
Casertano, G. (ed.) (2000) *La struttura del dialogo platonico*. Naples.
(ed.) (2002) *Il 'Teeteto' di Platone: struttura e problematiche*. Naples.
(2004) 'La struttura del dialogo (o di quando la filosofia si fa teatro)', in *Il Protagora di Platone: struttura e problematiche*, ed. G. Casertano. Naples: 729–66.
(ed.) (2007) *Empedocle tra poesia, medicina, filosofia e politica*. Naples.
Cassio, A. C. (1985) 'Two studies on Epicharmus and his influence', *HSCPh* **89**: 37–51.
Cavallo, G. (2007) *Leggere a Bisanzio*. Milan.

Cerri, G. (2002) 'Dalla dialettica all'epos: Platone, *Republica X, Timeo, Crizia*', in Casertano (ed.): 7–34.
Chadwick, H. (1998) 'Orthodoxy and heresy', in *CAH XIII: The Late Empire A.D. 337–425*: 561–600.
(2001) *The Church in Ancient Society: From Galilee to Gregory the Great*. Oxford.
Chance, T. H. (1992) *Plato's Euthydemus: Analysis of What Is and Is Not Philosophy*. Berkeley, Los Angeles and Oxford.
Chaniotis, A. (1997) 'Theatricality beyond the theater: staging public life in the Hellenistic world', *Pallas* **47**: 219–59.
Charalabopoulos, N. (2000) 'Plato's use of theatrical vocabulary', in *Theatre: Ancient and Modern*, ed. L. Hardwick et al. Milton Keynes: 198–214.
(2001) 'The metatheatrical reader of Plato's *Protagoras*', in *Homer, Tragedy and Beyond: Essays in Honour of P. E. Easterling*, ed. F. Budelmann and P. Michelakis. London: 149–78.
(2007) 'Two images of Sokrates in the art of the Greek east', in Trapp (ed.): 105–22.
Charitonidis, S. I. (1962) 'Ἡ ἀνασκαφὴ Μυτιλήνης', *PAAH*: 134–41.
Charitonidis, S., L. Kahil and R. Ginouvès (1970) *Les mosaïques de la Maison du Ménandre à Mytilène*. Bern.
Chatzidakis, M. (1977) *Εἰκόνες τῆς Πάτμου: Ζητήματα Βυζαντινῆς καὶ Μεταβυζαντινῆς Ζωγραφικῆς*. Athens.
Cherniss, H. (1945) *The Riddle of the Early Academy*. Berkeley.
Chiron, P. (ed.) (1993) *Démétrios: Du style*. Paris.
Choremi-Spetsieri, A. (2009) *Acropolis*. Athens.
Chourmouziadis, N. G. (1974) *Σατυρικά*. Athens.
Christ, W. and M. Paranikas (1871) *Anthologia Graeca Carminum Christianorum*. Leipzig.
Chroust, A.-H. (1965) 'The organization of the corpus Platonicum in antiquity', *Hermes* **93**: 34–46.
Clark, W. P. (1931) 'Ancient reading', *CJ* **26**: 698–700.
Clay, D. (1979) 'Socrates' prayer to Pan', in *Arktouros: Hellenic Studies Presented to Bernard M. W. Knox on the Occasion of his 65th Birthday*. ed. G. W. Bowersock, W. Burkert and C. J. Putnam. Berlin and New York: 345–53.
(1983) 'The tragic and comic poet of the *Symposium*', in *Essays in Ancient Greek Philosophy*, ed. J. P. Anton and A. Preus. Albany, NY: 186–202.
(1992) 'Plato's first words', *YClS* **29**: 113–29.
(1994) 'The origins of the Socratic dialogue', in Vander Waerdt (ed.): 23–47.
(2000) *Platonic Questions: Dialogues with the Silent Philosopher*. University Park, Pa.
(2004) 'Philodemus on the plain speaking of the other philosophers', in *Philodemus and the New Testament World*, ed. J. T. Fitzgerald, D. Obbink and G. S. Holland. Leiden and Boston: 55–71.

Clayton, E. W. (2008) 'The death of Socrates and the *Life of Aesop*', *AncPhil* **28**: 311–28.

Cohn, D. (2001) 'Does Socrates speak for Plato? Reflections on an open question', *NLH* **32**: 485–500.

Collard, C. (1970) 'On the tragedian Chaeremon', *JHS* **90**: 22–34.

Colligne, A. (1989) 'The case of Satyrs', in *Images of Authority: Papers Presented to Joyce Reynolds on the Occasion of Her Seventieth Birthday*, ed. H. M. Mackenzie and C. Roueché. Cambridge: 82–103.

Collins, D. (2004) *Master of the Game: Competition and Performance in Greek Poetry*. Cambridge, Mass. and London.

Comotti, G. (1989) *Music in Greek and Roman Culture*, trans, R. V. Munson. Baltimore and London.

Compton, T. M. (2006) *Victim of the Muses: Poet as Scapegoat, Warrior and Hero in Greco-Roman and Indo-European Myth and History*. Cambridge, Mass. and London.

Conley, T. M. (1985) 'Dating the so-called *Dissoi Logoi*: a cautionary note', *AncPhil* **5**: 59–65.

Cooper, C. (ed.) (2007) *Politics of Orality*. Leiden and Boston.

Cooper, J. M. (ed.) (1997) *Plato: Complete Works*. Indianapolis and Cambridge.

(2007) 'Socrates and philosophy as a way of life', in D. Scott (ed.): 20–43.

Cope, E. M. and J. E. Sandys (1877) *The Rhetoric of Aristotle with a Commentary* (3 vols). Cambridge.

Corlett, J. A. (2005) *Interpreting Plato's Dialogues*. Las Vegas.

Corrigan, K. and E. Glazov-Corrigan (2004) *Plato's Dialectic at Play: Structure, Argument and Myth in the Symposium*. University Park, Pa.

Cosgrove, C. H. and M. C. Meyer (2006) 'Melody and word accent relationships in ancient Greek musical documents: the Pitch Height Rule', *JHS* **126**: 66–81.

Cossutta, F. (2003) 'Dialogic characteristics of philosophical discourse: the case of Plato's dialogues', *Ph&Rh* **36**: 48–76.

Coulloud-Streit, M. (2005) *Fünf platonischen Mythen im Verhältnis zu ihren Textfelden*. Fribourg.

Coulson, W. D. E., O. Palagia, T. L. Shear, Jr, H. A. Shapiro, and F. J. Frost (eds.) (1994) *The Archaeology of Athens and Attica under the Democracy*. Oxford.

Courtonne, Y. (ed.) (1961) *Saint Basile: Lettres Vol. II*. Paris.

Coventry, L. (1990) 'The role of the interlocutor in Plato's dialogues: theory and practice', in *Characterization and Individuality in Greek Literature*, ed. C. B. P. Pelling. Oxford: 174–96.

Crick, N. and J. Poulakos (2008) 'Go tell Alcibiades: tragedy, comedy, and rhetoric in Plato's *Symposium*', *QJS* **94**: 1–22.

Crotty, K. (2009) *The Philosopher's Song: The Poets' Influence on Plato*. Lanham.

Csapo, E. (1997) 'Mise en scène théâtrale, scène de théâtre artisanale: les mosaïques de Ménandre à Mytilène, leur contexte social et leur tradition iconographique', *Pallas* **47**: 165–82.

(2010) *Actors and Icons of the Ancient Theatre*. Oxford.

Csapo, E. and M. C. Miller (eds.) (2007) *The Origins of Theatre in Ancient Greece and Beyond: From Ritual to Drama*. Cambridge.

Cunningham, I. C. (ed.) (1971) *Herodas Mimiambi*. Oxford.

(ed.) (2002a) *Herodas Mimes*. Cambridge, Mass.

(ed.) (2002b) *Sophron and Other Mime Fragments*. Cambridge, Mass.

D'Ancona, C. (2002) Review of Reis (1999), *Mnemosyne* **55**: 613–26.

Daux, G. (1963) 'Chronique des fouilles et découvertes archéologiques en Grèce en 1962', *BCH* **87**: 689–878.

Davies, D. (2008) 'Review of Livy (2006)', *JAAC* **66**: 89–91.

Davies, M. (2004) 'Aristotle *fr. 44* Rose: Midas and Silenus', *Mnemosyne* **57**: 682–97.

Davies, T. C. (ed.) (2008) *The Cambridge Companion to Performance Studies*. Cambridge.

Decleva Caizzi, F. (2006) 'Minor Socratics', in Gill and Pellegrin (eds.): 119–35.

Deferrari, R. J. (ed.) (1928) *Saint Basil: The Letters Vol. II*. London and New York.

Deichmann, F. W. (ed.) (1967) *Repertorium der christlich-antiken Sarkophage Band I: Rom und Ostia*. Wiesbaden.

Delattre Biencourt, J. (2010) (ed.) *Théon de Smyrne Lire Platon. Le recours au savoir scientifique: arithmétique, musique, astronomie*. Toulouse.

Delcogliano, M. (2010) *Basil of Caesarea's anti-Eunomian Theory of Names: Christian Theology and Late-Antique Philosophy in the Fourth Century Trinitarian Controversy*. Leiden and Boston.

Delorme, J. (1960) *Gymnasion: études sur les monuments consacrés à l'éducation en Grèce*. Paris.

Denyer, N. C. (ed.) (2001) *Plato 'Alcibiades'*. Cambridge.

Depew, D. (2007) 'From hymn to tragedy: Aristotle's genealogy of poetic kinds', in Csapo and Miller (eds.): 126–49.

Depew, M. and D. Obbink (eds.) (2000) *Matrices of Genre: Authors, Canons, and Society*. Cambridge, Mass. and London.

Desideri, P. (1978) *Dione di Prusa: un intellettuale greco nell' impero romano*. Messina and Florence.

Desjardins, R. (1988) 'Why dialogues? Plato's serious play', in Griswold (ed.): 110–25.

Destrée, P. and F.-G. Herrmann (eds.) (2011) *Plato and the Poets*. Leiden.

Detienne, M. (ed.) (1988) *Les savoirs de l'écriture en Grèce ancienne*. Lille.

De Vita, M. C. (2004) '*Protagora* 314c3–316a5: "door opening scene" (314c–e2): al di là della soglia (314e3–316a5)', *Vichiana* **6**: 41–58.

Dickey, E. (1996) *Greek Forms of Address: From Herodotus to Lucian*. Oxford.

Dihle, A. (2007) 'Zur datierung der Schrift des Demetrios *Über den Stil*', *RhM* **150**: 298–313.

Dillon, J. M. (1977) *The Middle Platonists: A Study of Platonism 80 B.C. to A.D. 220*. London.

(1983) 'What happened to Plato's garden?', *Hermathena* **134**: 51–9.

(2000) 'Philosophy', in *CAH XI²: The High Empire, A.D. 70–192*: 922–42.

(2003) *The Heirs of Plato: A Study of the Old Academy 347–274* BC. Oxford.

Dillon, S. (2006) *Ancient Greek Portrait Sculpture: Contexts, Subjects, and Styles*. Cambridge.

Dobrov, G. W. (2001) *Figures of Play: Greek Drama and Metafictional Poetics*. Oxford.

(2007) 'Comedy and the satyr-chorus', *CW* **100**: 251–65.

Dodds, E. R. (ed.) (1959) *Plato 'Gorgias'*. Oxford.

Dorandi, T. (1988) 'Four testimonia on the Academy', *CQ* **38**: 576–8.

(1991) *Filodemo, Storia dei filosofi [.] Platone e l'Academia*. Naples.

(1992) 'Il quarto libro delle "Vite" di Diogene Laerzio: l'Academia da Speusippo a Clitomacho', *ANRW* II **36**.5: 3761–92.

(1999) 'Organization and structure of the phiosophical schools', in *CHHP*: 55–62.

(2009) *Laertiana: Capitoli sulla tradizione manoscritta e sulla storia del testo delle Vite dei filosofi di Diogene Laerzio*. Berlin and New York.

Döring, K. (1979) *Exemplum Socratis: Studien zur Sokratesnachwirkung in der kynisch-stoischen Popularphilosophie der frühen Kaiserzeit und im frühen Christentum*. Wiesbaden.

(1989) 'Gab es eine dialektische Schule?', *Phronesis* **34**: 293–310.

(2011) 'The students of Socrates', in D. R. Morrison (ed.): 24–47.

Döring, K., M. Erler and S. Schorn (eds.) (2003) *Pseudoplatonica*. Stuttgart.

Dorion, L.-A. (2006) 'Xenophon's Socrates', in Ahbel-Rappe and Kamtekar (eds.): 93–109.

(2008) 'Héraklès entre Prodicos et Xénophon', *Philosophie Antique* **8**: 85–114.

(2011) 'The rise and fall oft he Socratic problem', in D. R. Morrison (ed.): 1–23.

Dörrie, H. (1987) *Der Platonismus in der Antike Band 1: Die geschichtlichen Wurzeln des Platonismus*. Stuttgart.

(1990) *Der Platonismus in der Antike*, ed. and rev. M. Baltes and F. Mann, *Band 2: Der hellenistische Rahmen des kaiserzeitlichen Platonismus*. Stuttgart.

Dörrie, H. and M. Baltes (1993) *Der Platonismus in der Antike Band 3: Der Platonismus im 2. und 3. Jahrhundert nach Christus*. Stuttgart.

Dougherty, C. (2009) 'Just visiting: the mobile world of classical Athens', in Boys-Stones et al. (eds.): 391–400.

Dover, K. J. (1965) 'The date of Plato's *Symposium*', *Phronesis* **10**: 2–20.

(1966) 'Aristophanes' speech in Plato's *Symposium*', *JHS* **86**: 41–50.

(1968) 'Portrait-masks in Aristophanes', in *Komoidotragemata: Studia Aristophanea Viri Aristophanei W. J. W. Koster in honorem*. Amsterdam: 16–28.

reprinted in K. J. Dover, *The Greeks and their Legacy: Collected Papers Vol. I.* London 1987: 267–78.
(ed.) (1980) *Plato Symposium.* Cambridge.
(1986) 'Ion of Chios: his place in the history of Greek literature', in *Chios: A Conference at the Homereion in Chios 1984*, ed. J. Boardman and C. E. Vaphopoulou-Richardson. Oxford: 27–37. Reprinted in K. J. Dover, *The Greeks and their Legacy, Collected Papers Volume II: Prose Literature, History, Society, Transmission, Influence.* Oxford, 1988: 1–12.
Downey, G. and A. F. Norman (eds.) (1971) *Themistii Orationes Vol. II.* Leipzig.
Dragoumis, M. (1966) 'The survival of Byzantine chant in the monophonic music of the modern Greek Church', *SEC* **1**: 9–36.
Drodzek, A. (2005) 'Euclides of Megara: God = phronesis = the good', *AAHung* **45**: 27–34.
Duff, T. (1999) *Plutarch's Lives: Exploring Virtue and Vice.* Oxford.
Dunbabin, K. M. D. (1999) *Mosaics of the Greek and Roman World.* Cambridge.
Duncan, A. (2006) *Performance and Identity in the Classical World.* Cambridge.
Dunn M. R. (1976) 'Iamblichus, Thrasyllus, and the reading order of the Platonic dialogues', in *The Significance of Neoplatonism*, ed. R. B. Harris. New York: 59–80.
Dunshirn, A. (2008) 'In welcher Reihenfolge die Dialoge Platons lessen?', *Gymnasium* **115**: 103–22.
Düring, I. (1957) *Aristotle in the Ancient Biographical Tradition.* Göteborg.
(1966) *Aristoteles: Darstellung und Interpretation seines Denkens.* Heidelberg.
Duvoisin, J. A. (1996) 'The rhetoric of authenticity in Plato's *Hippias Major*', *Arethusa* **29**: 363–88.
Earle, B. (2003) 'Plato, Aristotle, and the imitation of reason', *Ph&Lit* **27**: 382–401.
Easterling, P. E. (1993) 'The end of an era? Tragedy in the fourth century', in Sommerstein et al. (eds): 559–69.
(ed.) (1997) *The Cambridge Companion to Greek Tragedy.* Cambridge.
(2009) 'Sophocles and the wisdom of Silenus: a reading of *Oedipus at Colonus* 1211–1248', in Karamalengou and Makrygianni (eds.): 161–70.
Easterling, P. E. and E. Hall (eds.) (2002) *Greek and Roman Actors: Aspects of an Ancient Profession.* Cambridge.
Easterling, P. E. and B. M. W. Knox (eds.) (1985) *The Cambridge History of Classical Litterature, Vol. I: Greek Literature.* Cambridge.
Easterling, P. E. and R. Miles (1999) 'Dramatic identities: tragedy in late antiquity', in *Constructing Identities in Late Antiquity*, ed. R. Miles. London and New York: 95–111.
Ebert, T. (2002) 'Platon als philosophischer Dramaturg: Bemerkungen zu Personal und Szenerie der *Politeia*', in *Interpretation und Argument: Festschrift für Gerhard Steel*, ed. H. Linneweber-Lammerskitten and

G. Mohr. Würzburg: 59–74; reprinted in T. Ebert, *Gesammelte Aufsätze, Band II: Zur Philosophie und ihrer Geschichte*. Paderborn 2004: 93–111.

(2003) 'The role of the frame dialogue in Plato's *Protagoras*', in Havlíćek and Karfík (eds.): 9–20.

Edelstein, L. (1945) 'The role of Eryximachus in Plato's *Symposium*', *TAPhA* **76**: 85–103.

Edmunds, L. and R. W. Wallace (eds.) (1997) *Poet, Public and Performance in Ancient Greece*. Baltimore and London.

Edwards, M. (2007a) 'Alcidamas', in Worthington (ed.): 47–57.

(2007b) 'Socrates and the early Church', in Trapp (ed.): 127–41.

Eidinow, E. and C. Taylor (2010) 'Lead-letter days: writing, communication and crisis in the ancient Greek world', *CQ* **60**: 30–62.

Eisner, R. (1982) 'Socrates as hero', *Ph & Lit* **6**: 106–18.

Elam, K. (1980) *The Semiotics of Theatre and Drama*. London and New York.

Elias, J. (1984) *Plato's Defense of Poetry*. New York.

Ellinghaus, C. (1998–9) 'Das Trikliniumsmosaik im Haus des Menander in Mytilene/Lesbos: Menander und Sokrates laden zum Symposion ein', *Boreas* **21/22**: 261–9.

Else, G. F. (1957) *Aristotle's Poetics: The Argument*. Cambridge, Mass.

(1965) *The Origin and Early Form of Greek Tragedy*. Cambridge, Mass.

Emlyn-Jones, C. (2004) 'The dramatic poet and his audience: Agathon and Socrates in Plato's "Symposium"', *Hermes*: **132**: 389–405.

(2008) 'Poets on Socrates' stage: Plato's reception of dramatic art', in Hardick and Stray (eds.): 38–49.

Engberg, S. G. (1966) 'Greek ekphonetic neumes and Masoretic accents', *SEC* **1**: 37–49.

(1987) 'The Greek Old Testament lectionary as a liturgical book', *CIMA* **54**: 39–48.

(1996) 'Greek ekphonetic notation: the classical and the pre-classical systems', in *Palaeobyzantine Notations II*, ed. G. Wolfram and C. Troelsgard. Hernen: 33–55.

(2001) 'Ekphonetic notation', in *NGDM* **8**: 47–51.

England, E. B. (1921) *The Laws of Plato*. London.

Erbse, H. (1961) 'Überlieferungsgeschichte der griechischen klassischen und hellenistischen Literatur', in *Geschichte der Textüberlieferung der antiken und mittelalterlichen Literatur*, vol. I, ed. H. Hunger et al. Zurich: 207–83.

Erler, M. (1998) 'Idealità e storia. La cornice dialogica del *Timeo* e del *Crizia* e la *Poetica* di Aristotele', *Elenchos* **19**: 5–28.

(2003) 'To hear the right thing and to miss the point', in Michelini (ed.): 153–73.

Erler, M. and L. Brisson (eds.) (2007) *Gorgias – Menon: Selected Papers from the Seventh Symposium Platonicum*. Sankt Augustin.

Fantham, E. (1982) *Seneca's 'Troades'*. Princeton.

(1984) 'Roman experience of Menander in the late Republic and early Empire', *TAPhA* **114**: 299–309.

Faraone, C. A. (2008) *The Stanzaic Architecture of Early Greek Elegy*. Oxford.

Fedwick, P. J. (ed.) (1981) *Basil of Caesarea: Christian, Humanist, Ascetic: A Sixteen-Hundredth Anniversary Symposium* (2 vols). Toronto.

Fendt, G. and F. Rozema (1998) *Platonic Errors: Plato, a Kind of Poet*. Westport and London.

Ferber, R. (2003) 'L'Idea del Bene è o non è transcendente? Ancora su ἐπέκεινα τῆς οὐσίας', in Bonazzi and Trabattoni (eds.): 127–49.

Ferrari, G. R. F. (2003) *City and Soul in Plato's Republic*. Sankt Augustin.

(2007a) 'The three-part soul', in Ferrari (ed.): 165–201.

(2007b) 'Editor's introduction', in Ferrari (ed.): xv–xxvi.

(ed.) (2007c) *The Cambridge Companion to Plato's Republic*. Cambridge.

(2008) 'Socratic irony as pretence', *OSAPh* **34**: 1–33.

Ferrua, A. (1990) *The Unknown Catacomb: A Unique Discovery of Early Christian Art*, trans. I. Inglis. Florence.

Findlay, J. N. (1978) 'The myths of Plato', *Dionysius* **2**: 19–34.

Fine, G. (ed.) (2008) *The Oxford Handbook of Plato*. Oxford.

Fischer-Lichte, E. (1992) *The Semiotics of Theatre*, trans. J. Gaines and D. L. Jones. Bloomingtoon and Indianapolis.

Fitzgerald, T., D. D. Obbink and G. Holland (eds.) (2004) *Philodemus and the New Testament World*. Leiden and Boston.

Fleming, T. J. (1999) 'The survival of Greek dramatic music from the fifth century to the Roman period', in *La colometria antica dei testi poetici greci*, ed. B. Gentili and F. Perusino. Pisa and Roma: 17–29.

Floyd, E. D. (1992) 'Why Parmenides wrote in verse', *AncPhil* **12**: 251–65.

Foley, H. P. (2008) 'Generic boundaries in fifth-century Athens', in Revermann and Wilson (eds.): 15–36.

Ford, A. (2003) 'From letters to literature: reading the "song culture" of classical Greece', in Yunis (ed.): 15–37.

(2008) 'The beginnings of dialogue: Socratic discourses and fourth-century prose', in Goldhill (ed.): 29–44.

(2009) 'Performance, text, and the history of criticism', in Boys-Stones et al. (eds.): 628–36.

(2010) 'Σωκρατικοὶ λόγοι in Aristotle and fourth-century theories of genre', *CPh* **105**: 221–35.

Fornara, C. W. and D. C. Yates (2007) '*FGrHist* 328 (Philochorus) F 181', *GRBS* **47**: 31–37.

Forti, S. (2006) 'The biopolitics of soul: racism, nazism and Plato', *Political Theory* **34**: 9–32.

Fox, M. (2009) 'Heraclides of Pontus and the philosophical dialogue', in *Heraclides of Pontus: Discussion*, ed. W. W. Fortenbaugh, and E. E. Pender. New Brunswick: 41–67.

Frazier, F. and J. Sirinelli (eds.) (1996) *Plutarque: œuvres Morales Tome IX. 3 Propos de table Livres VII–IX*. Paris.
Frede, D. (1996) 'The hedonist's conversion: the role of Socrates in the *Philebus*', in Gill and McCabe (eds.): 213–48.
Frede, M. (1992) 'Plato's arguments and the dialogue form', in Klagge and Smith (eds.): 201–19.
(2006) 'The early Christian reception of Socrates', in *Remembering Socrates: Philosophical Essays*, ed. L. Judson and V. Karasmanis. Oxford: 188–202.
Frère, J. (2010) 'La mort et le statut des morts d'Eschyle à Platon', in Brancacci et al. (eds.): 275–88.
Freydberg, B. (2000) 'Retracing Homer and Aristophanes in the Platonic texts', in *Retracing the Platonic Text*, ed. J. Russon and J. Sallis. Evanston: 99–112.
(2007) 'Homeric μέθοδος in Plato's Socratic dialogues', in G. A. Scott (ed.): 111–29.
Fronterotta, F. (2010) 'Plato's *Republic* in the recent debate', *JHP* **48**: 125–51.
Fuhrmann, F. (ed.) (1972) *Plutarque: œuvres Morales Tome IX. 1 Propos de table Livres I–III*. Paris.
Fussi, A. (2000–1) 'The myth of the last judgement in the *Gorgias*', *RMeta* **54**: 529–52.
Gabrici, E. (1903) Review of Sogliano (1902), *RFIC* **31**: 369–71.
Gagarin, M. (1999) 'The orality in Greek oratory', in Mackay (ed.): 163–80.
Gain, B. (1985) *L' Église de Cappadoce au IVe siècle d'après le correspondance de Basile de Césarée*. Rome.
Gaiser, K. (1959) *Protreptik und Paränese bei Platon: Untersuchungen zur Form des platonischen Dialogs*. Stuttgart.
(1973) 'Die Platon-Referate des Alkimos bei Diogenes Laertios (III 9–17)', in *Zetesis: Festschrift für E. de Strycker*. Antwerp and Utrecht: 61–79.
(1980) 'Plato's enigmatic lecture "*On the Good*"', *Phronesis* **25**: 5–37.
(1982) 'Philochoros über zwei statuen in Athen', in *Praestant Interna: Festschrift für U. Hausmann*, ed. B. von Freytag gen. Löringhoff, D. Mannsperger and F. Prayon. Tübingen: 91–100.
(1989) 'Das Gold der Weisheit: zum Gebet des Philosophen am Scluß des *Phaidros*', *RM* **132**: 105–40.
Gallop, D. (1971) 'Dreaming and waking in Plato', in *Essays in Ancient Greek Philosophy*, ed. J. P. Anton and G. L. Kustas. Albany, NY: 187–201.
(2001) 'Emotions in the *Phaedo*', in *Plato's Phaedo*, ed. A. Havlíček and F. Karfík. Prague: 275–86.
(2003) 'The rhetoric of philosophy: Socrates' swan-song', in Michelini (ed.): 313–32.
Gangloff, A. (2006) *Dion Chrysostome et les mythes: Hellénisme, communication et philosophie politique*. Grenoble.
Gaspari, C. and A. Veneri (1986) 'Dionysos', in *LIMC* **III1**: 414–514.
Gavrilov, A. K. (1997) 'Techniques of reading in classical antiquity', *CQ* **47**: 56–73.

Geiger, J. (2007) 'Socrates and his companions in art', in Trapp (ed.): 89–103.

Geffcken, J. (1934) *Griechische Literatur II: Von Demokritos bis Aristoteles*. Heidelberg.

Gemelli Marciano, M. L. (2008) 'Images and experience: at the roots of Parmenides' *Aletheia*', *AncPhil* **28**: 21–48.

Gentili, B. (1988) *Poetry and its Public in Ancient Greece: From Homer to the Fifth Century*, trans. A. T. Cole. Baltimore and London.

Georgopoulos, N. (ed.) (1993) *Tragedy and Philosophy*. Basingstoke.

Gera, D. L. (1993) *Xenophon's Cyropaedia: Style, Genre, and Literary Technique*. Oxford.

(2000) 'Two thought experiments in the *Dissoi Logoi*', *AJPh* **121**: 21–45.

(2007) 'Xenophon's Socrateses', in Trapp (ed.): 33–50.

Gerson, L. P. (2005) 'What is Platonism?', *Journal of the History of Philosophy* **43**: 253–76.

Ghira, D. (2004) 'Soph. *OC* 1556–1779 e Plat. *Phaed.* 113d–118a', *Maia* **56**: 511–24.

Ghiron-Bistagne, P. (1991) 'Le drame satyrique dans les concours dramatiques', *Dioniso* **61**: 101–19.

Giannantoni, G. (2001) 'L' *Alcibiade* d'Éschine et la littérature socratique sur Alcibiades', in Romeyer Dherbey and Gourinat (eds.): 289–307.

(2005) *Dialogo socratico e nascita della dialettica nella filosofia di Platone*. Naples.

Giannantoni, G. and M. Narcy (eds.) (1997) *Lezioni Socratiche*. Rome.

Gifford, M. (2001) 'Dramatic dialectic in *Republic* Book 1', *OSAPh* **20**: 35–106.

Gigante, M. (1953) 'Epicarmo, Pseudo-Epicarmo e Platone', *PP* 8: 161–75.

Gigon, O. (ed.) (1987) *Aristotelis Opera Vol III: Librorum Depertitorum Fragmenta*. 2nd edn. Berlin and New York.

Gilead, A. (1994) *The Platonic Odyssey: A Philosophical-Literary Inquiry into the Phaedo*. Amsterdam.

Gill, C. (1996) *Personality in Greek Epic, Tragedy, and Philosophy: The Self in Dialogue*. Oxford.

(2006) 'The Platonic dialogue', in Gill and Pellegrin (eds.): 136–50.

(2007) 'Form and outcome of arguments in Plato's *Gorgias*', in Erler and Brisson (eds.): 62–5.

Gill, C. and M. M. McCabe (eds.) (1996) *Form and Argument in Late Plato*. Oxford.

Gill, M. L. and P. Pellegrin (eds.) (2006) *A Companion to Ancient Philosophy*. Oxford.

Gilliard, F. D. (1993) 'More silent reading in antiquity: *non omne verbum sonabat*', *JBL* **112**: 689–96.

Gioia, F. (2004) 'La forma dialógica y su nueva función el les *Leyes* de Platón', in Santa Cruz et al. (eds.): 131–45.

Giuliani, L. (1997) 'Das älteste Sokrates-Bildnis: ein physiognomisches Porträt wider die Physiognomiker' in *Bildnisse: Die europäische Tradition der Portraitkunst*, ed. W. Schlink. Freiburg: 11–55.

Giuliano, F. B. (2000a) 'Filosofia in letteratura: il dialogo platonico e la sua interpretazione', *A&R* **45**: 1–43.

(2000b) 'Filosofia *versus* poesia: Platone davanti a un antica disputa', in *Letteratura e riflessione sulla letteratura nella cultura classica*, ed. G. Arrighetti and M. Tulli. Pisa: 377–400.

(2005) *Platone e la poesia: teoria della composizione e prassi della ricezione*. Sankt Augustin.

Glucker, J. (1978) *Antiochus and the Late Academy*. Göttingen.

(1991) 'Images of Plato in late antiquity', in *Physics, Cosmology and Astronomy, 1300–1700: Tension and Accommodation*, ed. S. Unguru. Dordrecht, Boston and London: 3–18.

Goldberg, L. (1983) *A Commentary on Plato's Protagoras*. New York.

Goldhill, S. (ed.) (2001) *Being Greek under Rome: Cultural Identity, the Second Sophistic and the Development of Empire*. Cambridge.

(2004) *Love, Sex & Tragedy: How the Ancient World Shapes Our Lives*. London.

(ed.) (2008) *The End of Dialogue in Antiquity*. Cambridge.

Goldhill, S. and R. Osborne (eds.) (1999) *Performance Culture and Athenian Democracy*. Cambridge.

Goldhill, S. and S. von Reden (1999) 'Plato and the performance of dialogue', in Goldhill and Osborne (eds.): 257–89.

Gomme, A. W. (1958) 'The structure of Plato's *Crito*', *G&R* **5**: 45–51.

Gonzalez, F. J. (ed.) (1995) *The Third Way: New Directions in Platonic Studies*. Lanham.

(2000) 'The Eleatic Stranger: his master's voice?', in Press (ed.). 161–81.

Göransson, T. (1995) *Albinus, Alcinous, Arius Didymus*. Göteborg.

Gordon, J. (1999) *Turning Toward Philosophy: Literary Device and Dramatic Structure in Plato's Dialogues*. University Park, Pa.

Gottschalk, H. B. (2000) 'Demetrius of Phalerum: a politician among philosophers and a philosopher among politicians', in *Demetrius of Phalerum: Text, Translation and Discussion*, ed. W. W. Fortenbaugh and E. Schütrumpf. New Brunswick and London: 367–80.

Goulet, R. (1989) 'Alcimos', in *DPhA* **I**: 110–1.

(1997) 'Trois cordonniers philosophes', in Joyal (ed.): 119–25.

Goulet-Cazé, M.-O. (ed.) (1999) *Diogène Laërce: Vies et doctrines des philosophes illustres*. Paris.

Gow, A. S. F. and D. L. Page (eds.) (1965) *The Greek Anthology: Hellenistic Epigrams* (2 vols). Cambridge.

Graham, D. W. (1992) 'Socrates and Plato', *Phronesis* **37**: 141–65.

Granger, H. (2007) 'Poetry and prose: Xenophanes of Colophon', *TAPhA* **137**: 403–33.

(2008) 'The proem of Parmenides' poem', *AncPhil* **28**: 1–20.
(2010) 'Parmenides of Elea: rationalist or dogmatist?', *AncPhil* **30**: 15–38.
Gray, V. (2006) 'The linguistic philosophies of Prodicus in Xenophon's "Choice of Heracles"', *CQ* **56**: 426–35.
Grazzini, B. J. (2007) 'Of physic maieutics and dialogical bondage in Plato's *Theaetetus*', in G. A. Scott (ed.): 130–51.
Green, J. R. (1994) *Theatre in Ancient Greek Society*. London.
(1999) 'Tragedy and the spectacle of the mind: messenger speeches, actors, narratives, and audience imagination in fourth-century BCE vase-painting', in B. Bergmann and C. Kondoleon (eds.) *The Art of Ancient Spectacle*. New Haven and London: 37–63.
Green, J. R. and E. W. Handley (1995) *Images of the Greek Theatre*. London.
Greenberg, N. A. (1965) 'Socrates' choice in the *Crito*', *HSCPh* **70**: 45–82.
Greenwood, E. (2008) 'Fictions of dialogue in Thucydides', in Goldhill (ed.): 15–28.
Gregory. J. (1999–2000) 'Comic elements in Euripides', *ICS* 24–5: 59–74.
Gregory Snyder, H. (2000) *Teachers and Texts in the Ancient World: Philosophers, Jews and Christians*. London and New York.
Grenfell, B. P. and A. S. Hunt (1898) *The Oxyrhynchus Papyri I*. London.
(1919) *The Oxyrhynchus Papyri XIII*, London.
(1922) *The Oxyrhynchi Papyri XV*, London.
Griffith, M. (2002) 'Slaves of Dionysos: satyrs, audience, and the end of the *Oresteia*', *CAnt* **21**: 195–258.
(2008) 'Greek middlebrow drama (something to do with Aphrodite?)', in Revermann and Wilson (eds.): 59–87.
Griswold, C. L., Jr (ed.) (1988) *Platonic Writings: Platonic Readings*. New York and London.
(1999) '*E pluribus unum*? On the Platonic "corpus"', *AncPhil* **19**: 361–97.
(2000) '*E pluribus unum*? On the Platonic "corpus": the discussion continued', *AncPhil* **20**: 195–201.
(2008) 'Reading and writing Plato', *Ph&Lit* **32**: 205–16.
Groningen, B. A. van (1963) '"Ἔκδοσις', *Mnemosyne* **16**: 1–17.
(1971) 'Empédocle, poète', *Mnemosyne* **24**: 169–88.
Guarducci, M. (1967–74) *Epigrafia greca*, vols I (1967), II (1969), III (1974). Rome.
Gulick, C. B. (1927–33) *Athenaeus: The Deipnosophists*, vols I (1927); IV (1930); V (1933). London and New York.
Hadot, P. (1974) 'La figure de Socrate', *Eranos-Jb* **43**: 51–90.
(1979) 'Les divisions des parties de la philosophie dans l'Antiquité', *MH* **36**: 201–23.
(2002) *What is Ancient Philosophy?*, trans. M. Chase. Cambridge, Mass. and London.

Hagel, S. (2009) *Ancient Greek Music: A New Technical History*. Cambridge.
Hagel, S and C. Harrauer (eds.) (2005) *Ancient Greek Music in Performance*. Vienna.
Hagen, C. (1994) *Simplicius: On Aristotle's Physics 7*. London.
Hall, E. (2002) 'The singing actor in antiquity', in Easterling and Hall (eds.): 3–38.
(2006) *The Theatrical Cast of Athens: Interactions between Ancient Greek Drama and Society*. Oxford.
Halliwell, S. (1984) 'Plato and Aristotle on the denial of tragedy', *PCPhS* **30**: 50–8.
(1986) *Aristotle's Poetics*. London.
(1993) 'The function and aesthetics of the Greek tragic mask', in *Intertextualität in der griechisch-römischen Komödie*, ed. N. W. Slater and B. Zimmerman. Stuttgart: 195–211.
(1996) 'Plato's repudiation of the tragic', in Silk (ed.): 332–49; rev. version in Halliwell (2002): 98–117.
(1997) 'The *Republic*'s two critiques of poetry (Book II 376c–III 398b, X 595a–608b)', in *Platon: Politeia*, ed. O. Höffe. Berlin: 313–31.
(2000) 'The subjection of muthos to logos: Plato's citations of the poets', *CQ* **50**: 94–112.
(2002) *The Aesthetics of Mimesis: Ancient Texts and Modern Problems*. Princeton.
(2008) *Greek Laughter: A Study of Cultural Psychology from Homer to Early Christianity*. Cambridge.
(2011) 'Antidotes and incantations: is there a cure for poetry in Plato's *Republic*?', in Destrée and Hermann (eds.): 241–66.
Hamilton, R. (1991) 'Comic acts', *CQ* **41**: 346–55.
Handley, E. W. (1969) 'Notes on the *Theophoroumene* of Menander', *BICS* **16**: 8–101.
(1997) 'Some thoughts on New Comedy and its public', *Pallas* **47**: 185–200.
(2002) 'Acting, action and words in New Comedy', in Easterling and Hall (eds.): 165–88.
Hanfmann, G. M. A. (1951) 'Socrates and Christ', *HSPh* **60**: 205–33.
Hannick, C. (1979) 'Les lectionnaires grecs avec notations ekphonétiques', *SEC* **4**: 76–80.
Hardwick, L. and C. Stray (eds.) (2008) *A Companion to Classical Receptions*. Oxford.
Harris, D. (1992) 'Bronze statues on the Athenian Acropolis: the evidence for a Lycurgan inventory', *AJA* **96**: 637–52.
Harris, W. V. (1989) *Ancient Literacy*. Cambridge, Mass. and London.
Harrison, G. W. M. (ed.) (2005) *Satyr Drama: Tragedy at Play*. Swansea.
Harrison, J. C. (1978) 'Plato's prologue: *Theaetetus* 142a–143c', *TSP* **27**: 103–23.
Hart, R. and V. Tejera (eds.) (1997) *Plato's Dialogues: The Dialogical Approach*. Lewiston.

Haslam, M. W. (1972) 'Plato, Sophron, and the dramatic dialogue', *BICS* **19**: 17–38.
(1975) 'The authenticity of Euripides *Phoenissae* 1–2 and Sophocles *Electra* 1', *GRBS* **16**: 149–74.
(1977) '3219. Treatise on Plato?', in *The Oxyrhynchus Papyri XLV*, ed. A. K. Bowman et al. London: 29–39.
(1980) '3326. PLATO *Republic* 8. 545C–546A', in *The Oxyrhynchus Papyri XLVII*, ed. R. A. Coles and M. W. Haslam. London: 37–41.
Hathaway, R. (1969) 'Sceptical maxims about the "publication" of Plato's dialogues', in *The Progress of Plato's Progress*, ed. R. Freis Berkeley, 28–42.
Havelock, E. A. (1963) *Preface to Plato*. Cambridge, Mass. and London.
(1966) 'Pre-literacy and pre-socratics', *BICS* **13**: 44–67.
(1982) *The Literate Revolution in Greece and its Cultural Consequences*. Princeton.
(1986) *The Muse Learns to Write: Reflections on Orality and Literacy from Antiquity to the Present*. New Haven and London.
Havlíček, A. and F. Karfík (eds.) (2003) *Plato's 'Protagoras': Proceedings of the Third Symposium Platonicum Pragense*. Prague.
Heath, J. (2005) *The Talking Greeks: Speech, Animals, and the Other in Homer, Aeschylus, and Plato*. Cambridge.
Heath, M. (1999) 'Longinus, *On Sublimity*', *PCPhS* **45**: 43–74.
Hedreen, G. M. (1992) *Silens in Attic Black-figure Vase-painting: Myth and Performance*. Ann Arbor.
(2007) 'Myths of ritual in Athenian vase-paintings of silens', in Csapo and Miller (eds.): 150–95.
Heitsch, E. (1963) *Die griechischen Dichterfragmente der römischen Kaiserzeit Vol. I*, 2nd edn. Göttingen.
(2002) *Dialoge Platons vor 399 v. Chr.?* Göttingen.
(2003) 'Hat Sokrates Dialoge Platons noch lesen können?', *Gymnasium* **110**: 109–19.
Henderson, J. (1996) 'Seeing through Socrates: portrait of the philosopher in sculpture', *Art History* **19**: 327–52.
Herington, C. J. (1985) *Poetry into Drama: Early Tragedy and the Greek Poetic Tradition*. Berkeley, Los Angeles and London.
Hershbell, J. P. (1983) 'The oral-poetic religion of Xenophanes', in Robb (ed.): 125–31.
(1992) 'Plutarch and Stoicism', in *ANRW* II **36**.5: 3336–52.
(1995) 'Reflections on orality and literacy of Plato's dialogues', in Gonzalez (ed.): 25–39.
Hildebrand, S. M. (2007) *The Trinitarian Theology of Basil of Caesarea: A Synthesis of Greek Thought and Biblical Truth*. Washington.
Hine, H. M. (ed.) (2000) *Seneca 'Medea'*. Warminster.
Hirzel, R. (1895) *Der Dialog: Ein literarhistorischer Versuch* (2 vols). Leipzig.

Hobbs, A. (2000) *Plato and the Hero: Courage, Manliness and the Impersonal Good*. Cambridge.
Hobden, F. (2009) 'The politics of the *sumposion*', in Boys-Stones et al. (eds.): 271–80.
Hobein, H. (1927) 'Simon (6)', *RE* **III.1**: 163–73.
Hock, R. F. (1976) 'Simon the shoemaker as the ideal Cynic', *GRBS* **17**: 41–54.
Höeg, C. (1935) *La notation ekphonétique*. Copenhagen.
(1955–7) 'Les rapports de la musique chrétienne et de la musique de l'antiquité classique', *Byzantion* 25–7: 383–412.
Hoepfner, W. (1976) *Das Pompeion und seine Nachfolgerbauten. Kerameikos: Ergebnisse der Ausgrabungen*, vol. X. Berlin.
Hoerber, R. G. (1957) 'Thrasylus' Platonic canon and the double titles', *Phronesis* **2**: 10–20.
Hoffmann, P. (2006) 'What was commentary in late antiquity? The example of the Neoplatonic commentators', in Gill and Pellegrin (eds.): 597–622.
Holowchak, M. (2007) 'Sleeping with mother, men, gods, and beasts: virtuous rule and vicious dreams in *Republic* IX', *Plato* **7** <http://gramata.univ-paris1.fr/Plato/article73.html>.
Hopkins, P. (2007) '"To say what is most necessary": expositional and philosophical practice in Thucydides and Plato', in G. A. Scott (ed.): 15–40.
Hordern, J. H. (2004) *Sophron's Mimes: Text, Translation and Commentary*. Oxford.
Hornblower, S. (1987) *Thucydides*. London.
(1991–6) *A Commentary on Thucydides*, vols I (1991), II (1996). Oxford.
Howland, J. (1993) *The Republic: The Odyssey of Philosophy*. New York.
(1998) *The Paradox of Political Philosophy: Socrates' Philosophical Trial*. Lanham and Oxford.
(2005–6) 'The mythology of philosophy: Plato's *Republic* and the odyssey of the soul', *Interpretation* **33**: 219–41.
(2008) 'Plato's *Apology* as tragedy', *Review of Politics* **70**: 519–46.
Hudson-Williams, H. Ll. (1949) 'Isocrates and Recitations', *CQ* **43**: 65–9.
Hunter, R. L. (2003) 'Reflecting on writing and culture: Theocritus and the style of cultural change', in Yunis (ed.): 213–34.
(2004) *Plato's 'Symposium'*. Oxford.
Huß, B. (1999) *Xenophons Symposion: Ein Kommentar*. Stuttgart and Leipzig.
Huys, M. (1993) 'P.Oxy. LIII 3705: a line from Menander's "Periceiromene" with musical notation', *ZPE* **99**: 30–2.
Hyland, D. A. (1968) 'Why Plato wrote dialogues', *Ph & Rh* **1**: 38–50.
(1990) 'Plato's three waves and the question of utopia', *Interpretation* **18**: 91–109.
(1993) 'Philosophy and tragedy in the Platonic dialogues', in Georgopoulos (ed.): 123–38.
(2008) *Plato and the Question of Beauty*. Bloomington and Indianapolis.

Imbert, C. (1993) 'Le dialogue platonicien en quête de son identité', *Rhetorica* **11**: 375–94.
Immerwahr, H. R. (1964) 'Book rolls on Attic vases', in *Classical, Mediaeval and Renaissance Studies in Honor of B. L. Ullmann*, ed. C. Henderson, Jr. Rome: 17–48.
(1973) 'More book rolls on Attic vases', *AK* **16**: 143–7.
(2007) 'Nonsense inscriptions and literacy', *Kadmos* **45**: 136–72.
(2008) 'Aspects of literacy in the Athenian Ceramicus', *Kadmos* **46**: 153–98.
Innes, D. C. (ed.) (1995) *Demetrius: On Style*. Cambridge, Mass.
Inwood, B. (2002) 'Comments on Taylor', in Annas and Rowe (eds.): 85–92.
Inwood, B. and P. Donini (1999) 'Stoic ethics', in *CHHP*: 675–738.
Irwin, T. H. (1988) 'Socrates and the tragic hero', in *Language and the Tragic Hero: Essays on Greek Tragedy in Honor of Gordon M. Kirkwood*, ed. P. Pucci. Atlanta: 55–83.
(2008) 'The Platonic corpus', in Fine (ed.): 63–87.
Isnardi Parente M. (1986) 'L'Accademia antica: interpretazioni recenti di metodo', *RFIC* **114**: 350–78.
Jackson, H. (1920) 'Aristotle lecture-room and lectures', *JPhil* **35**: 191–200.
Jacobson, H. (1983) *The Exagoge of Ezekiel*. Cambridge.
Jäkel, S. (1992) 'Platonic dialogue as a specific genre between tragedy and comedy: tragic and comic elements in the early dialogues of Plato', *SIFC* **10**: 1001–13.
James, E. (2008) 'The rise and function of the concept "late antiquity"', *JLA* **1**: 20–30.
James, L. (ed.) (2010) *A Companion to Byzantium*. Oxford.
Jeffreys, E. (2008) 'Rhetoric', in Jeffreys et al. (eds.): 827–37.
Jeffreys, E., J. Haldon and R. Cormack (eds.) (2008) *The Oxford Handbook of Byzantine Studies*. Oxford.
Jennings, V. and A. Katsaros (eds.) (2007) *The World of Ion of Chios*. Leiden.
Jirsa, J. (2009) 'Authenticity of the *Alcibiades I*: some reflections', *Listy filologické* **132**: 225–44.
Johne, R. (1991) 'Zur Entstehung einer "Buchkultur" in der zweiten Hälfte des 5. Jahrhunderts v.u.z.', *Philologus* **135**: 45–54.
Johnson, W. A. (1994a) 'Oral performance and the compostion of Herodotus' *Histories*', *GRBS* **35**: 229–54.
(1994b) 'The function of the paragraphus in Greek literary prose texts', *ZPE* **100**: 65–8.
(1998) 'Dramatic frame and philosophical idea in Plato', *AJPh* **119**: 577–98.
(2000a) 'Toward a sociology of reading in classical antiquity', *AJPh* **121**: 593–627.
(2000b) 'Musical evenings in the early Empire: new evidence from a Greek papyrus with musical notation', *JHS* **120**: 57–85.
(2010) *Readers and Reading Culture in the High Roman Empire: A Study of Elite Communities*. Oxford.

Johnson, W. A. and H. N. Parker (eds.) (2009) *Ancient Literacies: The Culture of Reading in Greece and Rome*. Oxford.

Jones, C. P. (1966) 'Towards a chronology of Plutarch's works', *JRS* **56**: 61–74.

(1978) *The Roman World of Dio Chrysostom*. Cambridge, Mass. and London.

(1991) 'Dinner theater', in *Dining in a Classical Context*. ed. W. J. Slater. Ann Arbor: 185–98.

(1993) 'Greek drama in the Roman empire', in Scodel (ed.): 39–52.

Jones, N. F. (1999) *The Associations of Classical Athens: The Response to Democracy*. New York and Oxford.

Jouët-Pastré, E. (2006) *Le jeu et le sérieux dans les 'Lois' de Platon*. Sankt Augustin.

Jourdan, D. (1968–9) 'La notation ekphonétique archaïque (*Vaticanus gr.* 2144)', *AEHE* **107**: 557–60.

Jourdan-Hemmerdinger, D. (1979) 'Nouveaux fragments musicaux sur papyrus (une notation antique par points)', *SEC* **4**: 81–111.

(1984) 'Le *POxy*1624 de Platon et les notations musicales dites "ekphonétiques"', in *Atti del XVII Congresso Internazionale di Papirologia*. Naples: 82.

(1991) 'Fonction du chant dans les discours et lectures publics', in Meyer (ed.): 15–42.

Joyal, M. (ed.) (1997) *Studies in Plato and the Platonic Tradition: Essays Presented to John Whittaker*. Aldershot.

(2000) *The Platonic Theages*. Stuttgart.

Jülicher, A. (1903) 'Diodoros 57', *RE* V.1 Stuttgart.

Kaelin, E. F. (1993) 'The role of philosophy in the development of tragic drama', in Georgopoulos (ed.): 86–103.

Kahil L. (1969) 'Remarques sur l'iconographie des pièces de Ménandre', in *Ménandre: Entretiens XVI*, ed. E. G. Turner. Paris: 231–51.

Kahn, C. H. (1981) 'Did Plato write Socratic dialogues?', *CQ* **31**: 305–20.

(1983) 'Philosophy and the written word: some thoughts on Heraclitus and the early Greek uses of prose', in Robb (ed.): 110–24.

(1990) 'Plato as a Socratic', *RPhLang* 12. *Hommage à Henri Joly*. Grenoble: 287–301; reprinted in *SIFC* 10 (1992): 580–95.

(1994) 'Aeschines on Socratic eros', in Vander Waerdt (ed.): 87–106.

(1996) *Plato and the Socratic Dialogue: The Philosophical Use of a Literary Form*. Cambridge.

(2000) 'Response to Griswold', *AncPhil* **20**: 189–93.

(2002) 'On Platonic chronology', in Annas and Rowe (eds.): 93–127.

(2003) 'Writing philosophy: prose and poetry from Thales to Plato', in Yunis (ed.): 139–61.

(2010) 'L' importance philosophique dans le forme du dialogue', in Brancacci et al. (eds.): 69–81.

Kalligas P. G. (1994) 'Ἡ περιοχὴ τοῦ ἱεροῦ καὶ τοῦ θεάτρου τοῦ Διονύσου στὴν Ἀθήνα', in Coulson et al. (eds.): 25–30.

Kallimopoulou, E. (2009) *Paradosiaká: Music, Meaning, and Identity in Modern Greece*. Aldershot.
Kannicht, R. (1980) '"Der alte Streit zwischen Philosophie und Dichtung": zwei Vorlesungen über Grundzüge der griechischen Literaturauffassung', *AU* **23**: 6–36.
Karamalengou E. and Eugenia Makrygianni (eds.) (2009) *Ἀντιφίλησις: Studies on Classical, Byzantine and Modern Greek Literature and Culture in Honour of John-Theophanes A. Papademetriou*. Stuttgart.
Karas, S. I. (1955) *Ἡ Ὀρθὴ Ἑρμηνεία καὶ Μεταγραφὴ τῶν Βυζαντινῶν Μουσικῶν Χειρογράφων*. Athens.
(1982) *Μέθοδος τῆς Ἑλληνικῆς Μουσικῆς* (2 vols). Athens.
Kargas, A. (1998) *The Truest Tragedy: A Study of Plato's Laws*. London.
Karo, G. (1934) 'Archäologische Funde vom Juli 1933 bis Juli 1934: Griechenland und Dodekanes', *AA* **49**: 123–96.
Kelly, D. (1996) 'Oral Xenophon', in Worthington (ed.): 149–63.
Kerkhof, R. (2001) *Dorische Posse, Epicharm und attische Komödie*. Munich and Leipzig.
Kim, L. (2008) 'Dio of Prusa, *Or.* 61, *Chryseis*, or reading Homeric silence', *CQ* **58**: 601–21.
Kivy, P. (2006) *The Performance of Reading: An Essay in the Philosophy of Literature*. Malden, Mass.
Klagge, J. C and N. D. Smith (eds.) (1992) *Methods of Interpreting Plato and his Dialogues*. *OSAPh* Suppl. Oxford.
Klauck, H.-J. (2007) 'Nature, art, and thought: Dio Chrysostom and the *Theologia Tripertita*', *JR* **87**: 333–54.
Klein, J. (1965) *A Commentary on Plato's 'Meno'*. Chapel Hill.
Klonoski, R. J. (1993) 'The preservation of Homeric tradition: heroic reperformance in the *Republic* and the *Odyssey*', *Clio* **22**: 251–71.
Knab, R. (2006) *Platons Siebter Brief*. Hildesheim, Zurich and New York.
Knox, B. M. W. (1968) 'Silent reading in antiquity', *GRBS* **9**: 421–35.
(1979) 'Euripidean comedy', in *Word and Action: Essays on the Ancient Theater*, ed. B. M. W. Knox. Baltimore: 250–74.
(1985a) 'Books and readers in the Greek world: from the beginings to Alexandria', in Easterling and Knox (eds.): 1–16.
(1985b) 'Minor tragedians', in Easterling and Knox (eds.): 339–45.
Kofman, S. (1998) *Socrates: Fictions of a Philosopher*, trans. C. Porter. London.
König, J. (2007) 'Fragmentation and coherence in Plutarch's *Sympotic Questions*', in König and Whitmarsh (eds.): 43–68.
(2008) 'Sympotic dialogue from the first to the fifth centuries CE', in Goldhill (ed.): 85–113.
König, J. and T. Whitmarsh (eds.) (2007) *Ordering Knowledge in the Roman Empire*. Cambridge.
Konstan, D. and S. Said (eds.) (2006) *Greeks on Greekness: Viewing the Greek Past under the Roman Empire*. Cambridge.

Konstantakos, I. M. (2004) 'Antiphanes *Ἄγροικος*-plays: an examination of the ancient evidence and fragments', *RCCM* **46**: 9–40.

(2005a) 'Aspects of the figure of the ἄγροικος in ancient comedy', *RhM* **148**: 1–26.

(2005b) 'The drinking theatre: staged symposia in Greek comedy', *Mnemosyne* **58**: 183–217.

Korres, M. (1980) 'A *AD* **35** [1988] B1: 8–21.

Korres, S. G. (1955) 'Ἡ ἐπὶ τὸν Πλάτωνα ἐπίδρασις τοῦ Εὐριπίδου', *Platon* **7**: 6–12.

Korshak, Y. (1987) *Frontal Faces in Attic Vase Painting of the Archaic Period*. Chicago.

Kosman, L. A. (1992) 'Silence and imitation in the Platonic dialogues', in Klagge and Smith (eds.): 73–92.

Kowalzig, B. (2008) 'Nothing to do with Demeter? Something to do with Sicily! Theatre and society in the early fifth-century West', in Revermann and Wilson (eds.): 128–57.

Kramer, S. (1987/8) 'Socrates' dream: *Crito* 44a–b', *CJ* **83**: 193–7.

Kraut, R. (ed.) (1997) *Plato's Republic: Critical Essays*. Lanham, Md.

Kremer, M. (ed.) (2004) *Plato's Cleitophon: On Socrates and the Modern Mind*. Lanham and Oxford.

Krentz, A. A. (1983) 'Dramatic form and philosophical content in Plato's dialogues', *Ph & Lit* **7**: 32–47.

Kuch, H. (2003) 'Λόγος und μῦθος in platonischen Jenseitsvorstellungen', *Mnemosyne* **56**: 641–51.

Kuhn, H. (1941–2) 'The true tragedy: on the relationship between Greek tragedy and Plato', I (1941) *HSCPh* **32**: 1–40 and II (1942) *HSCPh* 33: 37–88.

Kullmann, W. (1986) 'Euripides' Verhältnis zur Philosophie', in *Literatur und Philosophie in der Antike*, ed. H. Koskenniemi, S. Jäkel and V. Pyykko. Turku: 35–49.

Kullmann, W. and M. Reichel (eds.) (1990) *Der Übergang von der Mündlichkeit zur Literatur bei den Griechen*. Tübingen.

Kurke, L. (2006) 'Plato, Aesop, and the beginnings of mimetic prose', *Representations* **94**: 6–52.

Kustas, G. L. (1981) 'Saint Basil and the rhetorical tradition', in Fedwick (ed.) I: 221–79.

Kutash, E. (2007) 'What did Plato read ?', *Plato* **7** <http://gramata.univ-paris1.fr/Plato/article74.html>.

Laborderie, J. (1978) *Le dialogue platonicien de la maturité*. Paris.

Lacy, P. de (1974) 'Plato and the intellectual life of the second century A.D.', in *Approaches to the Second Sophistic*, ed. G. W. Bowersock. University Park, Pa.: 4–10.

Laird, A. (1999) *Powers of Expression, Expressions of Power: Speech Presentation and Latin Literature*. Oxford.

Lakmann, M.-L. (2000) 'Dramatische Aufführungen der Werke Platons', in *Skenika: Beiträge zum antiken Theater und seiner Rezeption. Festschrift zum 65. Geburtstag von Horst-Dieter Blume*, ed. S. Gödde and T. Heinze. Darmstadt: 277–89.

Laks, A. (2004) '"Qu'importe qui parle": sur l'anonymat platonicien et ses antécédents', in *Identités d'auteur dans l'Antiquité et la tradition européenne*, ed. C. Calame and R. Chartier. Grenoble: 99–117.

(2005) *Médiation e coercition: pour une lecture de 'Lois' de Platon*. Lille.

(2010) 'Plato's "truest tragedy": *Laws* Book 7. 817a–d', in Bobonich (ed.): 217–31.

Lamberton, R. (1997) 'Plutarch and the Romanizations of Athens', in *The Romanization of Athens*, ed. M. C. Hoff and S. I. Rotroff. Oxford: 151–60.

Lamprellis, D. N. (1995) *Ἐπιθυμία καὶ Τραγωδία: Ἡ Ὕστατη Πλατωνικὴ Ἀνθρωπολογία*. Athens and Ioannina.

Landels, J. G. (1999) *Music in Ancient Greece and Rome*. London and New York.

Lane, M. (2006) 'The evolution of *eironeia* in classical Greek texts: why Socratic *eironeia* is not Socratic irony', *OSAPh* **31**: 49–83.

(2011) 'Reconsidering Socratic irony', in D. R. Morrison (ed.): 237–59.

Lang, M. L. (1978) *Socrates in the Agora*. Princeton.

Lapatin, K. (2006) 'Picturing Socrates', in Ahbel-Rappe and Kamtekar (eds.): 110–55.

Latacz J. (1990) 'Die Funktion des Symposions für die entstehende griechische Literatur', in *Der Übergang von der Mündlichkeit zur Literatur bei den Griechen*, ed. W. Kullmann and M. Reichel. Tubingen: 227–64.

Laurenti, R. (2003) 'Aristote de Stagire: les "dialogues"', in *DPhA Suppl.*: 379–471.

Lavery, J. (2007) 'Plato's *Protagoras* and the frontier of genre research: a reconnaisance report from the field', *PT* **28**: 191–246.

Lech, M. L. (2008) 'A possible date of the revival of Aeschylus' *The Seven against Thebes*', *CQ* **58**: 661–4.

Lee, M.-K. (2008) 'The *Theaetetus*', in Fine (ed.): 411–36.

Lemaire, A. (2008) 'The spread of alphabetic scripts (*c.* 1700–500 BCE)', *Diogenes* **55**: 45–58.

Lesher, J., D. Nails and F. Sheffield (eds.) (2006) *Plato's 'Symposium': Issues in Interpretation and Reception*. Cambridge, Mass. and London.

Lesky, A. (1983) *Greek Tragic Poetry*, trans. M. Dillon. New Haven and London.

Leurini, A. (2000) *Ionis Chii Testimonia et Fragmenta*. 2nd edn. Amsterdam.

Levin, F. R. (2009) *Greek Reflections on the Nature of Music*. Cambridge.

Levin, S. B. (2001) *The Ancient Quarrel between Philosophy and Poetry Revisited: Plato and the Greek Literary Tradition*. Oxford.

Lévy, C. (2010) 'The sceptical Academy: decline and afterlife', in Bett (ed.): 81–104.

Levy, K. and C. Troelsgard (2001) 'Byzantine chant', in *NGDM* **4**: 734–56.

Liatsi, M. (2008) *Die semiotische Erkenntnistheorie Platons im Siebten Brief: eine Einführung in den sogenannten philosophischen Excurs*. Munich.

Lingas, A. (2003) 'Performance practice and the politics of transcribing Byzantine chant', *AMB* **6**: 56–76.

(2008) 'Music', in Jeffreys et al. (eds.): 915–35.

Lisi, F. L. (ed.) (2001) *Plato's Laws and its Historical Significance*. Sankt Augustin.

(2004) 'Arte, legge e dialogo nelle *Leggi* di Platone', *SIFC* n.s. **2**: 42–61.

Li Volsi, R. (2001) 'Sulla cronologia dei dialoghi platonici', *GM* **23**: 217–56.

Lloyd, G. E. R. (1979) *Magic, Reason and Experience*. Cambridge.

Lobel, E. (1929) 'A crux in the *Poetics*', *CQ* **23**: 76–9.

Löhr, W. (2010) 'Christianity as philosophy: problems and perspectives of an ancient intellectual project', *VChr* **64**: 160–88.

Long, A. (2008) 'Plato's dialogues and a common rationale for dialogue form', in Goldhill (ed.): 45–59.

Long, A. A. (1985a) 'Philosophical poets and Heraclitus', in Easterling and Knox (eds.): 245–53.

(1985b) 'Sceptics, Cynics and other post-Aristotelian philosophers', in Easterling and Knox (eds.): 636–41.

Loraux, N. (1995) *The Experiences of Tiresias: The Feminine and the Greek Man*, translated by P. Wissing. Princeton.

Lorenz, H. (2008) 'Plato on the soul', in Fine (ed.): 243–66.

Louis, P. (1945) *Les métaphores de Platon*. Rennes.

Lowe, N. J. (2007) 'Old Comedy and Aristophanes', *G&R* **54**: 21–62.

Lowenstam, S. (1986) 'Aristophanes' hiccups', *GRBS* **27**: 43–56.

Luraghi, N. (2010) 'The local scripts from nature to culture', *ClAnt* **29**: 68–91.

Lucas, D. W. (ed.) (1968) *Aristotle Poetics*. Oxford.

Lukinovich A. (1990) 'The play of reflections between literary form and the sympotic theme in the *Deipnosophistae* of Athenaeus', in O. Murray (ed.): 263–71.

Luljak, D. A. (1994) 'Plato's two comic Apologies of Socrates: comedy and laughter in the *Symposium* and the *Phaedo*'. Diss. State University of New York.

Lyman, R. (2002) 'Hellenism and heresy', *JECS* **11**: 209–22.

Lynch, J. P. (1972) *Aristotle's School: A Study of a Greek Educational Institution*. Berkeley, Los Angeles and London.

Lynkouri-Tolia, E. (1988) *AD* 43 [1993] B1- Χρονικά: 36–9.

MacCabe, M. M. (2000) *Plato and his Predecessors: The Dramatisation of Reason*. Cambridge.

(2006) 'Form and the Platonic dialogue', in Benson (ed.): 39–54.

(2008) 'Plato's ways of writing', in Fine (ed.): 88–113.

MacDonald, D. R. (1994) *Christianizing Homer: The Odyssey, Plato and The Acts of Andrew*. New York and Oxford.

MacDonald, J. M. S. (1931) 'Character Portrayal in Epicharmus, Sophron and Plato'. Diss. Columbia University.
Mackay, E. A. (ed.) (1999) *The Oral Tradition and its Influence in the Greek and Roman World*. Leiden.
(2001) 'The frontal face and "you": narrative disjunction in early Greek poetry and painting', *AClass* **44**: 5–34.
MacKinnon J. W. (2000) 'Music', in *The Early Christian World Vol. II*, ed. P. F. Esler. London and New York: 773–90.
MacLean, D. R. (2007) 'The Socratic corpus: Socrates and the physiognomy', in Trapp (ed.): 65–85.
MacMinn, J. B. (1990) 'Plato's mantic myths in the service of Socrates' maieutic art', *Kernos* **3**: 219–34.
Mader, M. (1977) *Das Problem des Lachens und der Komödie bei Platon*. Stuttgart.
Mainz, V. (2007) 'Bringing the hemlock up: Jacques-Louis David's Socrates and the invention of history', in Trapp (ed.): 249–75.
Makris, E. (2005) 'The chromatic scales of the Deuteros modes in theory and practice', *PMM* **14**: 1–10.
Malingrey, A.-M. (1975) 'Le personnage de Socrate chez quelques auteurs chrétiens du IVe siècle', in *Forma Futuri: Studi in Onore del Cardinale Michele Pellegrino*. Turin: 159–78.
Mann, W.-R. (1996) 'The life of Aristippus', *AGPh* **78**: 97–119.
(2006) 'Plato in Tübingen', *OSAPh* **31**: 349–400.
Mansfeld, J. (1994) *Prolegomena: Questions to be Settled Before the Study of an Author, or a Text*. Leiden, New York and Cologne.
Mara, G. M. (2008) *The Civic Conversations of Thucydides and Plato: Classical Political Philosophy and the Limits of Democracy*. Albany.
Marini, N. (2007) *Demetrio: Lo Stile*. Roma.
Marinis, M. de (1993) *The Semiotics of Performance*, trans. A. O'Healy. Bloomington and Indianapolis.
Markovich, M. (ed.) (1999) *Diogenis Laertii Vitae Philosophorum*, vol. I. Stutgart and Leipzig.
Marrou, H. I. (1956) *A History of Education in Antiquity*, trans. G. Lamb. London.
Mársico, C. T. (2005) 'Antístenes y la prehistoria de la noción de campo semántico', *Nova Tellus* **23**: 69–99.
Martani, S. (2002a) 'Ekphonetische Notation: Die Probleme der Entzifferung', in *Theorie und Geschichte der Monodie*, ed. M. Pischlöger. Plenven: 62–8.
(2002b) 'L'ekphonesis delle Sacre Scritture: alcune osservazioni sulla notazione dell'evangeliario Mutin. a.W.2.6. (gr. 73)', in *Gedenkenschrift für Walter Pass*, ed. M. Czernin. Tutzing: 245–60.
(2002c) 'L'evangeliaire de Iaşi et le système ekphonétique dans les manuscrits en majuscule', *AMB* **4**: 20–5.
(2003a) 'The theory and practice of ekphonetic notation: the manuscript *Sinait. Gr. 213*', *PMM* **12**: 15–42.

(2003b) Die griechischen datierten Evangelien Handschriften mit ekphonetischer Notation. Quellen und palaeographische Anmerkungen', in *The Past in the Present*, vol. 2, ed. L. Dobszay. Budapest: 23–44.

(2004) 'Heilige Schrift und Ekphonesis: wie der Text die Musik formt', *Studia Musicologica* 45: 149–63.

Martin, J. (1931) *Symposion: Die Geschichte einer literarischen Form*. Paderborn.

Martin, R. P. (1993) 'The Seven Sages as performers of wisdom', in *Cultural Poetics in Archaic Greece: Cult, Performance, Politics*, ed. C. Dougherty and L. Kurke. Cambridge: 108–28.

Mason, H. A. (1979–80) 'Plato's comic masterpiece?', *CamQ* **9**: 114–42.

Mastronarde, D. J. (2010) *The Art of Euripides: Dramatic Technique and Social Context*. Cambridge.

Mathews, T. F. (1993) *The Clash of Gods: A Reinterpretation of Early Christian Art*. Princeton.

Mathiesen, T. J. (1999) *Apollo's Lyre: Greek Music and Music Theory in Antiquity and the Middle Ages*. Lincoln, Neb. and London.

Mathieu, M.-A. (1988) 'Théâtralité des dialogues de Platon', *CGITA* **1**: 75–9.

Matthews, G. B. (2006) 'Socratic ignorance', in Benson (ed.): 103–18.

Medda, E., M. S. Mirto and M. P. Patoni (eds.) (2006) *ΚΩΜΩΙΔΟΤΡΑΓΩΙΔΙΑ: Intersezioni del tragico e del comico nel teatro del V secolo a.C.* Pisa.

Meinwald, C. (2011) 'Reason v. literature in Plato's *Republic*: does the dialogue rule itself out?', *Anc Phil* **31**: 25–45.

Mejer, J. (1978) *Diogenes Laertius and his Hellenistic Background*. Wiesbaden.

(1992) 'Diogenes Laertius and Greek philosophy', in *ANRW* II 36.**5**: 3556–602.

Mellor, R. (2008) '*Graecia capta*: the confrontation between Greek and Roman identity', in Zacharia (ed.): 79–125.

Méndez, E.-A. and A. Angeli (eds.) (1992) *Filodemo: testimonianze su Socrate*. Naples.

Mette, H. J. (1984) 'Zwei Akademiker heute: Krantor und Arkesilaos', *Lustrum* **26**: 7–94.

(1985) 'Weitere Akademiker heute: von Lakydes bis zu Kleitomachos', *Lustrum* **27**: 39–148.

Meyer, C. (ed.) (1991) *Aspects de la musique liturgique au Moyen Age: actes des colloques de Royaumont de 1986, 1987 et 1988*. Paris.

Michelini, A. N. (2000) 'Socrates plays the buffoon: cautionary protreptic in *Euthydemus*', *AJPh* **121**: 509–35.

(ed.) (2003a) *Plato as Author: The Rhetoric of Philosophy*. Leiden and Boston.

(2003b) 'Plato's Socratic mask', in Michelini (ed.): 45–65.

Milani, L. A. (1903) 'Dionysoplaton. Nota alla monografia di questo titolo del Sogliano', *RFIC* **31**: 220–2.

Miller, D. L. (1978) 'Rhythms of Silenos in a poetics of Christ: images of the Great Teacher', *Eranos-Jb* **47**: 67–121.

Miller, F. D., Jr (2006) 'The Platonic soul', in Benson (ed.): 278–93.
Miller, M. H., Jr (1995) 'The choice between the dialogues and the "unwritten teachings": a Scylla and Charybdis for the interpreter?', in Gonzalez (ed.): 225–43.
(2008) 'The pleasures of the comic and of Socratic inquiry: aporetic reflections on *Philebus* 48A–50B', *Arethusa* **41**: 263–89.
Minar, E. L. (ed.) (1961) *Table Talks Books VII–VIII* in *Plutarch's Moralia Vol. IX (697C–771E)*, ed. E. L. Minar. Cambridge, Mass.
Mitchel, F. W. (1970) *Lycurgean Athens 338–322. Lectures in Memory of Luise Taft Sample*. Cincinnati.
Moes, M. (2000) *Plato's Dialogue Form and the Care of the Soul*. New York.
Moles, J. (1995) 'Dio Chrysostom, Greece, and Rome', in *Ethics and Rhetoric: Classical Essays for Donald Russell on his Seventy-Fifth Birthday*, ed. D. Innes, H. Hine and C. Pelling. Oxford: 177–92.
(2005) 'The thirteenth oration of Dio Chrysostom: complexity and simplicity, rhetoric and moralism, literature and life', *JHS* **125**: 112–38.
(2006) 'Jesus and Dionysus in *the Acts of the Apostles* and early Christianity', *Hermathena* **180**: 65–104.
Momigliano, A. (1993) *The Development of Greek Biography*. 2nd edn. Cambridge, Mass. and London.
Monoson, S. S. (2000) *Plato's Democratic Entanglements: Athenian Politics and the Practice of Philosophy*. Princeton.
Montiglio, S. (2000) *Silence in the Land of Logos*. Princeton.
Moors, K. F. (1982) *Platonic Myth: An Introductory Study*. Washington, DC.
Morgan, K. A. (2003a) 'The tyranny of the audience in Plato and Isocrates', in *Popular Tyranny: Sovereignty and its Discontents in Ancient Greece*, ed. K. A. Morgan. Austin, Tex.: 181–213.
(2003b) 'Plato's dream: philosophy and fiction in the *Theaetetus*', in *The Ancient Novel and Beyond*, ed. S. Panayotakis, M. Zimmerman and W. Keulen. Leiden and Boston: 101–13.
Morgan, M. L. (1990) *Platonic Piety: Philosophy and Ritual in Fourth-Century Athens*. New Haven and London.
Morgan, T. J. (1999) 'Literate education in classical Athens', *CQ* **49**: 46–61.
Morrison, D. R. (2006) 'Socrates', in Gill and Pellegrin (eds.): 101–18.
(ed.) (2011) *The Cambridge Companion to Socrates*. Cambridge.
Morrison, J. V. (2000) 'Historical lessons in the Melian episode', *TAPhS* **130**: 119–48.
(2007) 'Thucydides' *history* live: reception and politics', in Cooper (ed.): 217–33.
Morrow, G. W. (1960) *Plato's Cretan City: A Historical Intepretation of the Laws*. Princeton.
Most, G. W. (2000) 'Generating genres: the idea of the tragic', in Depew and Obbink (eds.):15–35.

(2011) 'What ancient quarrel between poetry and philosophy?', in Destrée and Herrmann (eds.): 1–20.
Moulinier, L. (1967) 'Dans quel sens et dans quelle mesure les dialogues de Platon sont-ils les pièces de théâtre?', *Dioniso* **41**: 186–93.
Mourelatos, A. P. D. (1987) 'Quality, structure, and emergence in later pre-Socratic philosophy', *BACAP* **II**: 127–94.
Mouze, L. (1998) 'La dernière tragédie de Platon', *RPhA* **16**: 79–101.
(2005) *Le législateur et le poète: une interprétation de* Lois *de Platon*. Villeneuve d'Ascq.
Muir, J. V. (ed.) (2001) *Alcidamas: The Works and Fragments*. London.
Müller, C. W. (1975) *Die Kurzdialoge der Appendix Platonica*. Munich.
Mullet, M. (2010) 'No drama, no poetry, no fiction, no readership, no literature', in James (ed.): 227–38.
Mulroy, D. (2007) 'The subtle artistry of the *Minos* and the *Hipparchus*', *TAPhA* **137**: 115–31.
Murray, O. (ed.) (1990) *Sympotica: A Symposium on the Symposion*. Oxford.
(2009) 'The culture of the *symposion*', in Raaflaub and van Wees (eds.): 508–23.
Murray, P. (ed.) (1996) *Plato on Poetry*. Cambridge.
(1999) 'What is a *muthos* for Plato?', in *From Myth to Reason? Studies in the Development of Greek Thought*, ed. R. Buxton. Oxford: 251–62.
(2003) 'Plato and Greek theatre', in *Attitudes to Theatre from Plato to Milton*, ed. E. Theodorakopoulos. Bari: 1–19.
Naddaf, G. (2000) 'Literacy and poetic performance in Plato's *Laws*', *AncPhil* **20**: 339–50.
(2007) 'The role of the poet in Plato's ideal cities of Callipolis and Magnesia', *Kriterion* **116**: 329–49.
Naddaff, R. A. (2002) *Exiling the Poets: The Production of Censorship in Plato's 'Republic'*. Chicago and London.
Nagy, G. (1989) 'Early Greek views on poetry and poets', in *The Cambridge History of Literary Criticism Vol I: Classical Criticism*, ed. G. A. Kennedy. Cambridge: 1–77.
(1996) *Poetry as Performance: Homer and Beyond*. Cambridge.
(2009) 'Performance and text in ancient Greece', in Boys-Stones et al. (eds.): 417–31.
Nails, D. (1995) *Agora, Academy, and the Conduct of Philosophy*. Dordrecht, Boston and London.
(2002) *The People of Plato: A Prosopography of Plato and Other Socratics*. Indianapolis and Cambridge.
(2006) 'Tragedy off-stage', in Lesher at al. (eds.): 179–207.
Narcy, M. (1989) 'Alexamenos de Téos', in *DPhA*: **117**.
(1997) 'La religion de Socrate dans les *Mémoires* de Xenophon', in Giannantoni and Narcy (eds.): 97–120.
Narcy, M. and A. Tordesillas (eds.) (2008) *Xénophon et Socrate*. Paris.

Natorp, P. (1894) 'Alexamenos', *RE* **I**.1: 1375.
Navia, L. E. (2001) *Antisthenes of Athens: Setting the World Aright.* Westport and London.
Nehamas, A. (2007) 'Beauty of body, nobility of soul: the pursuit of love in Plato's *Symposium*', in Scott, D. (ed.): 97–135.
Nervegna, S. (2010) 'Menander's *Theophoroumene* between Greece and Rome', *AJPh* **131**: 23–68.
Nesselrath, H.-G. (ed.) (2003) *Dion von Prusa, menschliche Gemeinschaft und göttliche Ordnung: die Borysthenes-Rede.* Darmstadt.
(2009) *Dion von Prusa: der Philosoph und sein Bild.* Tübingen.
Neumann, H. (1966) 'On the comedy of Plato's Aristophanes', *AJPh* **87**: 420–6.
Nichols, M. P. (2004) 'Socrates' contest with the poets in Plato's *Symposium*', *Political Theory* **32**: 186–206.
Nieddu, G. F. (1984) 'Testo, scrittura, libro nella Grecia arcaica e classica: note e osservazioni sulla prosa sientifico-flosofica', *S&C* **8**: 213–61.
Niehoff, M. R. (2007) 'Did the *Timaeus* create a textual community?', *GRBS* **47**: 161–91.
Nightingale, A. W. (1992) 'Plato's *Gorgias* and Euripides' *Antiope*: a study in generic transformation', *ClAnt* **11**: 121–41.
(1993) 'Writing/reading a sacred text: a literary interpretation of Plato's *Laws*', *CPh* **88**: 279–300.
(1995) *Genres in Dialogue: Plato and the Construct of Philosophy.* Cambridge.
Nünlist, R. (2009) *The Ancient Critic at Work: Terms and Concepts of Literary Criticism in Greek Scholia.* Cambridge.
Nussbaum, M. C. (2001) *The Fragility of Goodness: Luck and Ethics in Greek Tragedy and Philosophy.* 2nd edn. Cambridge.
(2003) 'Philosophy as literature', in Sedley (ed.): 211–41.
Nüsser, O. (ed.) (1991) *Albins Prolog und die Dialogtheorie des Platonismus.* Stuttgart.
O'Connor, D. K. (2007) 'Rewriting the poets in Plato's characters', in Ferrari (ed.): 55–89.
(2011) 'Xenophon and the enviable life of Socrates', in Morrison (ed.): 48–74.
Oikonomides, Al. N. (1987) '"Resting sites" (Λέσχαι) in ancient Athens and Attica', *AncW* **16**: 29–34.
Olivieri, A. (1930) *Frammenti della commedia greca e del mimo nella Sicilia e nella Magna Grecia.* Naples.
Olson, S. D. (1999) 'Kleon's eyebrows (Cratin. Fr. 228 K–A) and late 5th-century comic portrait-masks', *CQ* **49**: 320–1.
O'Mahoney, P. (2011) 'On the "hiccupping episode" in Plato's *Symposium*', *CW* **104**: 143–59.
Opsomer, J. (1998) *In Search of Truth: Academic Tendencies in Middle Platonism.* Brussels.
Osborne, C. (1997) 'Was verse the default form for presocratic philosophy?', in Atherton (ed.): 23–35.

(2006) 'Socrates in the Platonic dialogues', *Philosophical Investigations* **29**: 1–21.

Osipovich, D. (2006) 'What is a theatrical performance?', *JAAC* **64**: 461–70.

Ostwald, M. and J. P. Lynch (1994) 'The growth of schools and the advance of knowledge' in *CAH VI: The Fourth Century*. 2nd edn. 592–635.

O'Sullivan, L. (2001) 'Philochorus, Pollux, and the *nomophulakes* of Demetrius of Phalerum', *JHS* **121**: 51–62.

(2008) 'Athens, intellectuals, and Demetrius of Phalerum's *Socrates*', *TAPhA* **138**: 393–410.

O'Sullivan, N. (1996) 'Written and spoken in the First Sophistic', in Worthington (ed.): 115–27.

(2008) 'The authenticity of [Alcidamas'] *Odysseus*: two new linguistic considerations', *CQ* **58**: 638–47.

Pack, R. A. (1967) *The Greek and Latin Literary Texts from Greco-Roman Egypt*. 2nd edn. Ann Arbor.

Palpacelli, L. (2009) *L''Eutidemo' di Platone: una commedia straordinariamente seria*. Milan.

Palumbo, L. (2000) 'Struttura narrativa e tempo nel *Teeteto*', in Casertano (ed.): 225–37.

(2008) *Μίμησις: rappresentazione, teatro e mondo nei dialoghi di Platone e nella 'Poetica' di Aristotele*. Naples.

Panno, G. (2007) *Dionisiaco e alterità nelle* Leggi *di Platone: ordine del corpo e automovimento dell'anima nella città-tragedia*. Milan.

Panţiru, G. (1973) 'Une nouvelle interprétation de la notation ecphonétique d' un manuscrit à Iaşi, Roumanie', *SEC* **3**: 124–38.

Papalexandrou, A. (2010) 'The memory culture of Byzantium', in James (ed.): 108–22.

Paris, N. T. (2002) 'The ekphonesis in the Orthodox Divine Liturgy', *AMB* **4**: 46–51.

Partenie, C. (ed.) (2009) *Plato's Myths*. Cambridge.

Patterson, R. (1982) 'The Platonic art of comedy and tragedy', *Ph&Lit* **6**: 76–93.

Patzer, A. (1999) 'Der Xenophontische Sokrates als Dialektiker', in Pestalozzi (ed.): 50–76.

Pavis, P. (1982) *Languages of the Stage: Essays in the Semiology of Theatre*. New York.

Payne, T. (1983) 'The *Crito* as a mythological mime', *Interpretation* **11**: 1–23.

Pelling, C. (2007) 'Ion's *Epidemiai* and Plutarch's Ion', in Jennings and Katsaros (eds.): 75–109.

Pender, E. E. (2007) 'Poetic allusions in Plato's *Timaeus* and *Phaedrus*', *GFA* **10**: 51–87.

Penella, R. J. (2000) *The Private Orations of Themistius*. Berkeley, Los Angeles and London.

Penner, T. (2002) 'The historical Socrates and Plato's early dialogues: some philosophical questions', in Annas and Rowe (eds.): 189–212.

(2007) 'The death of the so-called "Socratic elenchus"', in Erler and Brisson (eds.): 3–19.

Pepin, J. (1992) 'Philólogos / Philósophos', in Brisson et al. (eds.): 477–501.

Perry, P. S. (2007) 'Critiquing the excess of empire: a synkrisis of John of Patmos and Dio of Prusa', *JSNT* **29**: 473–96.

Pestalozzi, K. (ed.) (1999) *Der fragende Sokrates*. Stuttgart and Leipzig.

Petraki, Z. (2011) *The Poetics of Philosophical Language: Plato, Poets, and Presocratics in the 'Republic'*. Berlin and New York.

Petre, Z. (2009) 'Revenants et sauveurs. Le *Ménexène* de Platon et le théâtre attique', in *Memory, Humanity, and Meaning*, ed. M. Neamtu and B. Tataru-Cazaban. Bucharest: 149–62.

Pfeiffer, R. (1968) *History of Classical Scholarship: From the Beginnings to the End of the Hellenistic Age*. Oxford.

Philip, J. A. (1970) 'The Platonic corpus', *Phoenix* **24**: 296–308.

Pickard, C. (1953) 'La mosaîque de Socrate à Apamée-sur-l'Oronte', *RA* **41**: 100–2.

Pighi, G. B. (1941) 'Ricerche sulla notazione ritmica greca: l'inno cristiano del POxy 1786', *Aegyptus* **21**: 189–220.

Pintaudi, R. (1982) 'Una tavoletta lignea della biblioteca Vaticana: Vat. Gr. 2657 (LXX Ps 28; 29,1–7)', *ZPE* **48**: 97–104.

Pittakis, K. S. (1839) 'Ἀρ. 325', *AEph*: 282–3.

Planinc, Z. (2003) *Plato through Homer: Poetry and Philosophy in the Cosmological Dialogues*. Columbia and London.

(2004) 'Ascending with Socrates: Plato's use of Homeric imagery in the *Symposium*', *Interpretation* **31**: 325–50.

Poe, J. P. (1999) 'Entrances, exits and the structure of Aristophanic comedy', *Hermes* **127**: 189–207.

Pöhlmann, E. (2005) 'Dramatische Texte in den Fragmenten antiker Musik', in Hagel and Harrauer (eds.): 131–46.

Polansky, R. (1992) *Philosophy and Knowledge: A Commentary on Plato's 'Theaetetus'*. Lewisburg.

Porter, W. J. (2007) 'The use of ekphonetic notation in Vienna New Testament manuscripts', in *Akten des 23. Internationalen Papyrologenkongress*, ed. B. Palme. Vienna: 581–5.

Postlewait, T. and T. C. Davis (2003) 'Theatricality: an introduction', in *Theatricality*, ed. T. C. Davies and T. Postlewait. Cambridge: 1–39.

Pownall, F. (2007) 'From orality to literacy: the moral education of the elite in fourth-century Athens', in Cooper (ed.): 235–49.

Pradeau, J.-F. (2005) 'Enchanting the souls: on Plato's conception of law and "preambles"', *BACAP* **21**: 125–37.

(2009) *Platon, l'imitation de la philosophie*. Paris.

Pratt, N. T. (1983) *Seneca's Drama*. Chapel Hill and London.

Prauscello, L. (2006) *Singing Alexandria: Music between Practice and Textual Transmission*. Leiden.
Press, G. A. (ed.) (1993) *Plato's Dialogues: New Studies and Interpretations*. Lanham.
(1997) 'The dialogical mode in modern Plato studies', in Hart and Tejera (eds.): 1–28.
(ed.) (2000) *Who Speaks for Plato? Studies in Platonic Anonymity*. Lanham.
(2007) *Plato: A Guide for the Perplexed*. London and New York.
Preston, R. (2001) 'Roman questions, Greek answers: Plutarch and the construction of identity', in Goldhill (ed.): 86–119.
Price, J. J. (2001) *Thucydides and Internal War*. Cambridge.
Prince, S. (2006) 'Socrates, Antisthenes, and the Cynics', in Ahbel-Rappe and Kamtekar (eds.): 75–92.
Prior, W. J. (1997) 'Why did Plato write Socratic dialogues?', in *Wisdom, Ignorance and Virtue: New Essays in Socratic Studies*, ed. M. L. McPherran. Edmonton: 109–23.
(2006) 'The Socratic problem', in Benson (ed.): 25–35.
Puchner, M. (2010) *The Drama of Ideas: Platonic Provocations in Theater and Philosophy*. Oxford.
Puchner, W. (2002) 'Acting in the Byzantine theatre: evidence and problems', in Easterling and Hall (eds.): 304–24.
Puech, B. (1992) 'Prosopographie des amis de Plutarque', *ANRW* II **33.6**: 4831–93.
Raaflaub, K. and H. van Wees (eds.) (2009) *A Companion to Archaic Greece*. Oxford.
Rahn, H. (1975) *Marcus Fabius Quintilianus: Ausbildung des Redners, Band II: Bücher VII–XII*. Darmstadt.
Ramage, E (1961) 'An early trace of Socratic dialogue', *AJPh* **82**: 418–24.
Ramelli, I. L. E. (2009) 'Origen, patristic philosophy, and Christian Platonism: re-thinking the Christianisation of Hellenism', *VC* **63**: 217–63.
Rankin, H. D. (1967) 'Laughter, humour and related topics in Plato', *C&M* **28**: 186–213.
(1986) *Antisthenes Sokratikos*. Amsterdam.
(1993) 'Socrates, Plato and fiction', *Scholia* **2**: 31–44.
Rau, P. (1967) *Paratragodia: Untersuchung einer komischen Form des Aristophanes*. Munich.
Rawles, R. (2006) 'Musical notes on the new anonymous lyric poem from Köln', *ZPE* **157**: 8–13.
Reeve, C. D. C. (2006) 'A study in violets: Alcibiades in the *Symposium*', in Lesher et al. (eds.): 124–46.
Reich, H. (1902) *Der Mimus: ein literarentwicklungsgeschichtlicher Versuch*. Berlin.
Reinmuth, O. W. (1961) 'Ephebic texts from Athens', *Hesperia* **30**: 8–22.

Reis, B. (1999) *Der Platoniker Albinos und sein sogenannter Prologos*. Wiesbaden.
Reitz, C. (2003) 'Mündlichkeit und Schriftlichkeit in Platons *Theätet*', *Hermes* **131**: 397–406.
Revell, E. J. (1979) 'Hebrew accents and Greek ekphonetic neumes', *SEC* **4**: 140–70.
Revermann, M. (2006a) 'The competence of theatre audiences in fifth- and fourth-century Athens', *JHS* **126**: 99–124.
(2006b) *Comic Business: Theatricality, Dramatic Techinque, and Performance Contexts in Aristophanic Comedy*. Oxford.
Revermann, M. and P. Wilson (eds.) (2008) *Performance, Iconography, Reception: Studies in Honour of Oliver Taplin*. Oxford.
Rhee, H. (2005) *Early Christian Literature: Christ and Culture and the Second and Third Centuries*. London and New York.
Rhys Roberts, W. (ed.) (1902) *Demetrius: On Style*. Cambridge.
(1984) 'Rhetoric', in *The Complete Works of Aristotle: The Revised Oxford Translation*, vol. 2, ed. J. Barnes. Princeton: 2152–269.
Richter, G. M. A. (1965) *The Portraits of the Greeks* (3 vols). London.
(1984) *The Portraits of the Greeks*, 2nd edn, abbreviated and revised by R. R. R. Smith. Ithaca.
Riginos, A. Swift (1976) *Platonica: The Anecdotes Concerning the Life and Writings of Plato*. Leiden.
Rivera, O. (2007) 'The comedy of patricide (or: a passing sense of manliness): Socrates' overcoming of andreia', *Epoche* **11**: 353–69.
Robb, K. (1983a) 'Preliterate ages and the linguistic art of Heraclitus', in Robb (ed.): 153–206.
(ed.) (1983b) *Language and Thought in Early Greek Philosophy*. La Salle.
(1994) *Literacy and Paideia in Ancient Greece*. New York and Oxford.
Robertson, D. (2009) 'Plato on conversation and experience', *Philosophy* **84**: 355–69.
Robinson, S. (2004) 'The contest of wisdom between Socrates and Agathon in Plato's *Symposium*', *AncPhil* **24**: 81–100.
Robinson, T. M. (1979) *Contrasting Arguments: An Edition of Dissoi Logoi*. New York.
(2003) 'Protagoras, the *Protagoras*, and the *Dissoi Logoi*', in Havlíček and Karfík (eds.): 233–45.
Rocconi, E. (2009) 'Music', in Boys-Stones et al. (eds.): 569–78.
Rokem, F. (2008) 'The philosophers and the two playwrights: Socrates, Agathon, and Aristophanes in Plato's *Symposium*', *TS* **49**: 239–52.
Rolley, C. (1999) *La sculpture grecque*, vol. 2: *La période classique*. Paris.
Romani, S. (2006) 'Il volto in movimento (per una lettura del πρόσωπον in Platone)', *SIFC* **99**: 141–59.
Romeri, L. (2000) 'The λογόδειπνον: Athenaeus between banquet and anti-banquet', in Bowersock et al. (eds.): 256–71, 563–7.

Romeyer Dherbey, G. (2001) 'Le deux discours de la guerre d'Antisthène', in Romeyer Dherbey and Gourinat (eds.): 333–50.
Romeyer Dherbey, R. and J. B. Gourinat (eds.) (2001) *Socrate et les Socratiques*. Paris.
Romilly, J. de (1984) 'D'Euripide à Platon: l'exemple des Phéniciennes', *EClás* **26**: 259–65.
Roochnik, D. L. (1988) 'The tragic philosopher: a critique of Martha Nussbaum', *AncPhil* **8**: 285–95.
(1990) *The Tragedy of Reason: Toward a Platonic Concept of Logos*. New York and London.
(2003) *Beautiful City: The Dialectical Character of Plato's Republic*. Ithaca.
Rood, T. (1998) *Thucydides: Narrative and Explanation*. Oxford.
Rorty, A. O. (2008) 'The dramatic sources of philosophy', *Ph & Lit*: **32**: 11–30.
Rose, V. (1886) *Aristotelis qui Ferebantur Libroram Fragmenta*. Leipzig.
Rosen, R. M. (1999) 'Comedy and confusion in Callias' *Letter Tragedy*', *CPh* **94**: 147–67.
Rosen, S. (1968) *Plato's Symposium*. New Haven and London.
(2005) *Plato's Republic: A Study*. New Haven and London.
Rosenbecker, K. A. and J. L. Adamitis (eds.) (1999) *Representations of Philosophy in the Classical World*. Ancient Philosophy Special Issue. Pittsburgh.
Rosenbloom, D. (2004) '*Ponêroi* vs *Chrêstoi*: the ostracism of Hyperbolos and the struggle of hegemony in Athens after the death of Perikles', *TAPhA* **134**: 55–105 (Part I), 323–58 (Part II).
Rosenmeyer, T. G. (1993) 'Seneca's *Oedipus* and the performance: the Manto scene', in Scodel (ed.): 235–44.
Rösler, W. (2002) 'The *Histories* and writing', in *Brill's Companion to Herodotus*, ed. E. J. Bakker, I. J. F. De Jong and H. van Wees: 79–94.
(2009) 'Books and literacy', trans. F. Spiegel, in Boys-Stones et al. (eds.): 432–41.
Ross, W. D. (1955) *Aristotelis Fragmenta Selecta*. Oxford.
Rossetti, L. (1980) 'Ricerche sui "dialoghi Socratici" di Fedone e di Euclide', *Hermes* **108**: 183–200.
(1993) 'Where philosophy and literature merge in the Platonic dialogues', *Argumentation* **6**: 433–43.
(2005) '"*Logoi Sokratikoi*": le contexte littéraire dans laquelle Platon a écrit', in *La philosophie de Platon*, vol. 2, ed. M. Fattal. Paris: 51–80.
(2007) 'A context for Plato's dialogues', in Bosch-Veciana and Monserrat-Molas (eds.): 15–31.
Rostagni, A. (1926–7) 'Il dialogo Aristotelico Περὶ Ποιητῶν', *RFIC* **4** (1926): 433–70 and 5 (1927): 145–73.
Rotondaro, S. (1998) *Il sogno di Platone*. Naples.
Rotstein, A. (2010) *The Idea of Iambos*. Oxford.
Rousseau, P. (1994) *Basil of Caesarea*. Berkeley, Los Angeles and Oxford.

(2008) 'Human nature and its material setting in Basil of Caesarea's sermons on the creation', *HeyJ* **49**: 222–39.

Rowe, C. J. (1991) 'The speech of Eryximachus in Plato's *Symposium*', in *Traditions of Platonism: Essays in Honour of John Dillon*, ed. J. J. Cleary. Aldershot: 53–64.

(ed.) (1993) *Plato Phaedo*. Cambridge.

(ed.) (1998) *Plato Symposium*. Warminster.

(2002) 'Comments on Penner', in Annas and Rowe (eds.): 213–25.

(2003a) 'Plato', in Sedley (ed.): 98–124.

(2003b) 'What might we learn from the *Clitophon* about the nature of the Academy?', in Döring et al. (eds.): 213–24.

(2006a) 'The literary and philosophic style of the *Republic*', in Santas (ed.): 7–24.

(2006b) 'The *Symposium* as a Socratic dialogue', in Lesher et al. (eds.): 9–22.

(2006c) 'Socrates in Plato's dialogues', in Ahbel-Rappe and Kamtekar (eds.): 159–70.

(2007a) *Plato and the Art of Philosophical Writing*. Cambridge.

(2007b) 'The moral psychology of the *Gorgias*', in Erler and Brisson (eds.): 90–101.

Ruijgh, C. J. (2001) 'Le *Spectacle des Lettres*, comédie de Callias, (Athénée X 453c–455b)', *Mnemosyne* **54**: 257–335.

Ruprecht, L. A., Jr (2008) 'Greek exercises: the modern Olympics as Hellenic appropriation and reinvention', *Thesis Eleven* **93**: 72–87.

Russell, D. A. (ed.) (1992) *Dio Chrysostom: Orations VII, XII, XXXVI*. Cambridge.

Russo, J. (1997) 'Prose genres for the performance of traditional wisdom in ancient Greece: proverb, maxim, apophthegm', in Edmunds and Wallace (eds.): 49–64.

Rusten, J. (1982) 'Dicaearchus and the *Tales from Euripides*', *GRBS* **23**: 357–67.

Rutherford, R. B. (1995) *The Art of Plato*. London.

Ryle, G. (1966) *Plato's Progress*. Cambridge.

Ryssel, V. (1893) 'Der pseudosokratische Dialog über die Seele', *RhM* **48**: 175–95.

Sales-Coderch, J. (2007) 'Between artlessness and ability: an interpretation of *Hippias Minor*', in Bosch-Veciana and Monserrat-Molas (eds.): 59–76.

Sallis, J. (2004) 'The flow of φύσις and the beginning of philosophy: on Plato's *Theaetetus*', in *BACAP* XX, ed. J. J. Cleary and G. M. Gurtler: 177–93.

Sandin, P. (2007) 'Aeschylus, *Supplices* 86–95, 843–910, and the early transmission of antistrophic lyrical texts', *Philologus* **151**: 207–29.

Sansone, D. (1996a) 'Plato and Euripides', *ICS* **21**: 35–67.

(1996b) 'Socrates' "tragic" definition of color (Pl. *Meno* 76D–E)', *CPh* **91**: 339–45.

(2004) 'Heracles at the Y', *JHS* **124**: 125–42.

Santa Cruz, M. I., G. B. Marcos and S. G. Di Camillo (eds.) (2004) *Diálogo con los griegos: Estudios sobre Platón, Aristóteles y Plotino*. Buenos Aires.
Santas, G. (ed.) (2006) *The Blackwell Guide to Plato's Republic*. Oxford.
(2010) *Understanding Plato's Republic*. Oxford.
Saunders, T. J. and L. Brisson (2000) *Bibliography on Plato's Laws*. Sankt Augustin.
Sauvé-Meyer, S. (2011) 'Legislation as a tragedy (on *Laws* VII, 817b–d)', in Destrée and Herrmann (eds.): 387–402.
Saxonhouse, A. (2009) 'The Socratic narrative: a democratic reading of Plato's dialogues', *Political Theory* **37**: 728–53.
Sayre, K. M. (1995) *Plato's Literary Garden: How to Read a Platonic Dialogue*. Notre Dame and London.
Schauer, M. and S. Merkler (1992) 'Äsop und Sokrates', in *Der Äsop-Roman: Motivgeschichte und Erzählstruktur*, ed. N. Holzberg. Tubingen: 85–96.
Schefold, K. (1959) 'Sokratische Wolkenverehrer', *AK* **2**: 21–6.
(1997) *Die Bildnisse der antiken Dichter, Redner und Denker*. 2nd edn. Basel.
(1992) 'Prose usages of ἀκούειν "to read"', *CQ* **42**: 129–41.
Schironi, F. (2005) 'Plato at Alexandria: Aristophanes, Aristarchus, and the "philological tradition" of a philosopher', *CQ* **55**: 423–34.
Schofield, M. (1992) 'Socrates and Protagoras', in *Socratic Questions: New Essays on the Philosophy of Socrates and its Significance*, ed. B. S. Gower and M. C. Stokes. London and New York: 122–36.
(1999) 'Academic epistemology', in *CHHP*: 323–51.
(2006) *Plato: Political Philosophy*. Oxford.
(2008) 'Plato in his time and place', in Fine (ed.): 36–62.
Schoos, D. J. (1999) 'Timaeus' banquet', in Rosenbecker and Adamitis (eds.): 97–107.
Schöpsdau, K. (1994) *Platon IX 2: Nomoi (Gesetze). Buch I–III*. Göttingen.
(2003) *Platon IX 2: Nomoi (Gesetze). Buch V–VII*. Göttingen.
Schott, J. M. (2008) '"Living like a Christian, but playing the Greek": accounts of apostasy and conversion in Porphyry and Eusebius', *JLA* **1**: 258–77.
Schubart, W. (1921) *Das Buch bei den Griechen und Römern*. 2nd edn. Berlin and Leipzig.
Scodel, R. (ed.) (1993) *Theater and Society in the Classical World*. Ann Arbor.
Scolnicov, S. and L. Brisson (eds.) (2003) *Plato's Laws: From Theory into Practice. Selected Papers from the Sixth Symposium Platonicum*. Sankt Augustin.
Scott, D. (ed.) (2007) *Maieusis: Essays in Ancient Philosophy in Honour of Myles Burnyeat*. Oxford.
(2008) 'The *Republic*', in Fine (ed.): 360–82.
Scott, G. A. (ed.) (2007) *Philosophy in Dialogue: Plato's Many Devices*. Evanston.
Scott, L. (2005) *Historical Commentary on Herodotus Book 6*. Leiden and Boston.

Seaford, R. (ed.) (1984) *Euripides: Cyclops*. Oxford.
Sedley, D. N. (1977) 'Diodorus Cronus and Hellenistic philosophy', *PCPhS* **23**: 74–120.
(1997) 'Plato's *auctoritas* and the rebirth of the commentary tradition', in Barnes and Griffin (eds.): 110–29.
(2002) 'A Socratic interpretation of Plato's *Theaetetus*', in *BACAP* 18, ed. J. J. Cleary and G. M. Gurtler: 277–313.
(2003a) *Plato's Cratylus*. Cambridge.
(ed.) (2003b) *The Cambridge Companion to Greek and Roman Philosophy*. Cambridge.
(2004) *The Midwife of Platonism: Text and Subtext in Plato's Theaetetus*. Oxford.
(2007) 'Philosophy, the forms and the art of ruling', in Ferrari (ed.): 256–83.
(2009) 'A Thrasyllan interpretation of *Theaetetus*', *The Oxyrhynchus Papyri* **73**: 65–71.
(2010) 'Hesiod's *Theogony* and Plato's *Timaeus*', in Boys-Stones and Haubold (eds.): 246–58.
(ed.) (2012) *The Philosophy of Antiochus*. Cambridge.
Seery, J. E. (1988) 'Politics as ironic community: on the themes of descent and return in Plato's *Republic*', *Political Theory* **16**: 229–56.
Segal, C. (1959) '῞Υψος and the problem of cultural decline in the *De Sublimitate*', *HSCPh* **64**: 121–46.
(1978) '"The myth was saved": reflections on Homer and the mythology of Plato's *Republic*', *Hermes* **106**: 315–36.
Segoloni, L. M. (1994) *Socrate a Bancchetto: Il Simposio di Platone e i Banchettanti d'Aristophane*. Rome.
Seidensticker, B. (1999) 'Philologisch-literarische Einleitung', in *Das griechische Satyrspiel*, ed. R. Krumeich, N. Pechstein and B. Seidensticker. Darmstadt: 1–40.
Sellars, J. (2003) 'Simon the shoemaker and the problem of Socrates', *CPh* **98**: 207–16.
Sheffield, F. C. C. (2001) 'Alcibiades' speech: a satyric drama', *G&R* **48**: 193–209.
(2006) *Plato's 'Symposium': The Ethics of Desire*. Oxford.
Shelley, C. (2003) 'Plato on the psychology of humour', *Humor* **14**: 351–67.
Sheppard, A. (2008) 'Rhetoric, drama, and truth in Plato's *Symposium*', *IJPT* **2**: 28–40.
Shiffman, M. (2008) 'Plutarch among the postcolonialists', *PPS* **37**: 223–30.
Sider, D. (1980a) 'Plato's *Symposium* as Dionysian festival', *QUCC* **33**: 41–56.
(1980b) 'Did Plato write dialogues before the death of Socrates?', *Apeiron* **14**: 15–9.
(1997) *The Epigrams of Philodemos: Introduction, Text, and Commentary*. Oxford.

Sifakis, G. M. (1997–8) 'Agonismata in Thucydides and Aristotle', *BICS* **42**: 21–7.

Silk, M. S. (1993) 'Aristophanic paratragedy', in Sommerstein et al. (eds.): 477–504.

(ed.) (1996) *Tragedy and the Tragic: Greek Theatre and Beyond*. Oxford.

(2000) *Aristophanes and the Definition of Comedy*. Oxford.

Silverman, A. (2007) 'Ascent and descent: the philosopher's regret', in *Freedom, Reason, and the Polis: Essays in Ancient Greek Political Philosophy*, ed. D. Keyt and F. D. Miller Jr: 40–69.

Simon, E. (1986) 'Silenoi', in *LIMC* VIII **1** Suppl.: 1108–33.

(1989) 'Satyrspielbilder aus der Zeit des Aischylos', in *Satyrspiel*, ed. B. Seidensticker. Darmstadt: 362–403.

Slater, N. W. (2002) 'Dancing the alphabet: performative literacy on the Attic stage', in Worthington and Foley (eds.). Leiden: 117–29.

(2005) 'Nothing to do with satyrs? *Alcestis* and the concept of prosatyric drama', in Harrison (ed.): 83–101.

Slater, W. J. (1986) *Aristophanis Byzantii Fragmenta*. Berlin and New York.

Slaveva-Griffin, S. (2005) '"A feast of speeches": form and content in Plato's *Timaeus*', *Hermes* **133**: 312–27.

Slings, S. R. (ed.) (1999) *Plato: Clitophon*. Cambridge.

Sluiter, I. (2000) 'The dialectics of genre: some aspects of secondary literature and genre in antiquity', in Depew and Obbink (eds.): 183–204.

Smith, J. A. (2003) 'Clearing up some confusion in Callias' *Alphabet Tragedy*: how to read Sophocles *Oedipus Tyrannus* 332–33 et al.', *CPh* **98**: 313–29.

Smith, N. D. (2004) 'Did Plato write the *Alcibiades* I?', *Apeiron* **37**: 93–108.

Smyth, H. W. (1956) *Greek Grammar*. 2nd edn. Cambridge, Mass.

Soares, L. (2004) 'El rol del poeta legislador y su antecedente en la figura del poeta guardian en *República*', in Santa Cruz et al. (eds.): 159–80.

Sogliano, A. (1902) *Dionysoplaton. Contributo alla iconografia platonica*. Naples.

Solmsen, F. (1981) 'The Academic and Alexandrian editions of Plato's works', *ICS* **6**: 102–111.

Solomos, A. (1964) *Ὁ Ἅγιος Βάκχος: Ἄγνωστα Χρόνια Θεάτρου*. Athens.

Sommerstein, A., S. Halliwell, J. Henderson and B. Zimmerman (eds.) (1993) *Tragedy, Comedy and the Polis*. Bari.

Souilhé, J. (ed.) (1930) *Platon œuvres complètes XIII. 2: Dialogues suspects*. Paris.

Spawforth, A. J. S. (forthcoming) *Greece and the Augustan Cultural Revolution*. Cambridge.

Speliotis, E. (2007) 'Image, myth, and dialectic in Plato', *EL* **12**: 211–23.

Spetsieri-Choremi, A. (1994) 'Ἡ ὁδὸς τῶν Τριπόδων καὶ τὰ χορηγικὰ μνημεῖα στὴν ἀρχαία Ἀθήνα', in Coulson et al. (eds.): 31–42.

Speyer, A. (2001) 'The earliest bust of Socrates? New observations to Philochoros in *PHerc*. 1021 Col.2', *CErc* **31**: 81–95.

Stampolidis, N. (1982–4) 'Τό σύμπλεγμα ἀρ. 257 τοῦ Ε.Μ. καί οἱ πλατωνικοί Σιληνοί (μια ἀκόμα προσέγγιση στήν προσωπογραφία τοῦ Σωκράτη)', *Archaiognosia* **3**: 123–59.
Stathis, G. Th. (1979) 'An analysis of the Sticheron *Τὸν ἥλιον κρύψαντα* by Germanos, Bishop of New Patras [The old "synoptic" and the new "analytical" method of Byzantine notation]', *SEC* **4**: 177–227.
Stavropoullos, P. (1962) 'Ἀκαδημία Πλάτωνος', in *Μεγάλη Ἑλληνική Ἐγκυκλοπαιδεία*, ed. P. Thrandakis, Suppl. 22. Athens: 340–4.
(1963) 'Ἀνασκαφαὶ ἀρχαίας Ἀκαδημίας', *PAAH* [**1966**]: 5–28.
Steel, S. (2003) 'Katabasis in Plato's *Symposium*', *Interpretation* **31**: 59–83.
Stefanou, D. (1996) 'Die Menander-Mosaiken von Mytilene: ein paganes Glaubensbekenntnis? Bemerkungen zur Deutung der Trikliniumsmosaiken im "Haus des Menander" in Mytilene/Lesbos durch L. Berczelly', *Boreas* **19**: 221–7.
Stegemann, E. W. (1999) 'Paulus und Sokrates', in Pestalozzi (ed.): 115–31.
Stella, L. A. (1933) 'Influssi di poesia e d'arte ellenica nell'opera di Platone: Platone ed il teatro greco II. Platone e la tragedia', *Historia* **7**: 75–123.
Stern, P. (2008) *Knowledge and Politics in Plato's Theaetetus*. Cambridge.
Stern-Gillet, S. (2008) 'Poets and other makers: Agathon's speech in context', *Dionysius* **26**: 9–28.
Stewart, D. J. (2007) 'The structure of the *Fihrist*: Ibn al-Nadīm as historian of Islamic legal and theological schools', *IJMES* **39**: 369–87.
(2009) 'Ibn al-Nadīm's Ismāʿīlī contacts', *JRAS* **19**: 21–40.
Stokes, M. R. (1986) *Plato's Socratic Conversations: Drama and Dialectic in Three Dialogues*. London.
Storey, I. C. (2005) 'But comedy has satyrs too', in Harrison (ed.): 201–18.
Striker, G. (1994) 'Plato's Socrates and the Stoics', in Vander Waerdt (ed.): 241–51.
Susanetti, D. (2002) 'Il cigno antitragico: l'esperienza di teatro dall'*Alcesti* euripideo al *Fedone* platonico', in *Antichi e nuovi dialoghi di sapienti e di eroi*, ed. L. M. Napolitano Valditara. Trieste: 53–76.
Sutton, D. F. (1980) *The Greek Satyr Play*. Meisenham am Glan.
(1986a) 'Named choreuts in satyr plays', *AJPh* **106**: 107–10.
(1986b) *Seneca on the Stage*. Leiden.
Svenbro, J. (1987) 'The voice of letters in ancient Greece: on silent reading and the representation of speech', *C&H* **2**: 31–47.
(1999) 'Archaic and classical Greece: the invention of silent reading', in *A History of Reading in the West*, trans. L. G. Cochrane, ed. G. Cavallo and R. Chartier. Oxford: 37–63.
Swain, S. (1996) *Hellenism and Empire: Language, Classicism, and Power in the Greek World,* AD *50–250*. Oxford.
(1997) 'Plutarch, Plato, Athens, and Rome', in Barnes and Griffin (eds.): 165–87.

(ed.) (2000) *Dio Chrysostom: Politics, Letters, and Philosophy*. Oxford.

Sykoutris, I. (ed.) (1934) *Πλάτωνος Συμπόσιον*. Athens.

(ed.) (1937) *Ἀριστοτέλους Περὶ Ποιητικῆς*. Athens.

Szlezák, T. A. (1999) *Reading Plato*. London.

Tanner, S. (2010) *In Praise of Plato's Poetic Imagination*. Lanham.

Taplin, O. (1977) 'Did Greek dramatists write stage directions?', *PCPhS* **23**: 121–34.

(1986) 'Fifth-century tragedy and comedy: a *synkrisis*', *JHS* **106**: 163–74.

(1996) 'Comedy and the tragic', in Silk (ed.): 188–202.

(1999) 'Spreading the word through performance', in Goldhill and Osborne (eds.): 34–57.

(2007) *Pots and Plays: Interactions Between Tragedy and Greek Vase-Painting of the Furth Century B.C.* Los Angeles.

Tardo, P. L. (1938) *L'antica melurgia bizantina*. Grottaferrata.

Tarrant, D. (1946) 'Colloquialisms, semi-proverbs, and word-play in Plato', *CQ* **40**: 109–17.

(1958) 'More colloquialisms, semi-proverbs, and word-play in Plato', *CQ* **8**: 158–60.

Tarrant, H. A. S. (1993) *Thrasyllan Platonism*. Ithaca and London.

(1996) 'Orality and Plato's narrative dialogues', in Worthington (ed.): 129–47.

(1999) 'Dialogue and orality in a post-Platonic age', in Mackay (ed.): 181–97.

(2000) *Plato's First Interpreters*. London.

(2008) 'The dramatic background of the arguments with Callicles, Euripides' *Antiope*, and an Athenian anti-intellectual argument', *Antichthon* **42**: 20–39.

Taylor, C. C. W. (2002) 'The origins of our present paradigms', in Annas and Rowe (eds.): 73–84.

(2007) 'Socrates and the Severans', in *Severan Culture*, ed. S. Swain, S. Harrison and J. Elsner. Cambridge: 496–507. Reprinted in *Pleasure, Mind, and Soul: Selected Papers in Ancient Philosophy*. Oxford 2008: 327–39.

Tecuşan, M. (1990) '*Logos sympotikos*: patterns of the irrational in philosophical drinking: Plato outside the *Symposium*', in Murray (ed.): 238–60.

Tejera, V. (1999) *Plato's Dialogues One by One: A Dialogical Interpretation*. 2nd edn. Lanham.

Teodorsson, S.-T. (1989–96) *A Commentary on Plutarch's Table Talks*, vols I (1989), II (1990), III (1996). Göteborg.

(2005) 'Plutarch, amalgamator of Greece and Rome', in *Historical and Biographical Values in Plutarch's Works: Studies Devoted to Professor Philip Stadter by the International Plutarch Society*, ed A. Pérez Jiménez and F. Titchener. Málaga and Utah: 433–9.

Tessitore, A. (1994) 'Courage and comedy in Plato's *Laches*', *The Journal of Politics* **56**: 115–33.

Thesleff, H. (1967) *Studies in the Styles of Plato*. Helsinki. Reprinted in Thesleff (2009): 1–142.

(1982) *Studies in Platonic Chronology*. Helsinki. Reprinted in Thesleff (2009): 147–382.

(1990) 'Presocratic publicity', in *Greek and Latin Studies in Memory of Cajus Fabricius*, ed. S.-T. Teodorsson. Göteborg: 110–21.

(2002) 'Plato and his public', in *Noctes Atticae: Studies Presented to Jørgen Mejer*, ed. B. Amden et al. Copenhagen: 289–301. Reprinted in Thesleff (2009): 541–50.

(2007) 'The *Gorgias* re-written – why?', in Erler and Brisson (eds.): 78–82.

(2009) *Platonic Patterns: A Collection of Studies by Holger Thesleff*. Las Vegas, Zurich and Athens.

Thomas, R. T. (1989) *Oral Tradition and Written Record in Classical Athens*. Cambridge.

(1992) *Literacy and Orality in Ancient Greece*. Cambridge.

(1993) 'Performance and written publication in Herodotus and the sophistic generation', in *Vermittlung und Tradierung von Wissen in der griechischen Kultur*, ed. W. Kullmann and J. Althoff. Tübingen: 225–44.

(2000) *Herodotus in Context: Ethnography, Science and the Art of Persuasion*. Cambridge.

(2003) 'Prose performance texts: *epideixis* and written publication in the late fifth and early fourth centuries', in Yunis (ed.): 162–88.

Thompson, D. B. (1960) 'The house of Simon the shoemaker', *Archeology* **13**: 234–40.

Thompson, H. A. (1954) 'Excavations in the Athenian Agora: 1953', *Hesperia* **23**: 31–67.

Thorsrud, H. (2010) 'Arcesilaus and Carneades', in Bett (ed.): 58–80.

Threatte, L. (1980) *The Grammar of Attic Inscriptions*, vol. 1: *Phonology*. Berlin and New York.

Tigerstedt, E. N. (1974) *The Decline and Fall of the Neoplatonic Interpretation of Plato*. Helsinki.

Tigner, S. S. (1970) 'Plato's philosophical uses of the dream metaphor', *AJPh* **101**: 204–12.

Tillyard, H. J. W. (1935) *Handbook of the Middle Byzantine Musical Notation*. Copenhagen.

Tod, M. N. (1957) 'Sidelights on Greek philosophers', *JHS* **77**: 132–41.

Torrance, N. and D. R. Olson (eds.) (2009) *The Cambridge Handbook of Literacy*. Cambridge.

Trabattoni, F. (2003) 'Il dialogo come "portavoce" dell'opinione di Platone: il caso del *Parmenide*', in Bonazzi and Trabattoni (eds.): 151–78.

Tracy, S. (1990) *Attic Letter-Cutters of 229 to 86 B.C.* Berkeley and Los Angeles.

Trail, J. S. (2003) *Persons of Ancient Athens*, vol. 12. Toronto.

Trapp, M. B. (1997) *Maximus of Tyre: The Philosophical Orations*. Oxford.

(2000a) 'Plato in Dio', in Swain (ed.): 213–39.

(2000b) 'Plato in the *Deipnosophistae*', in Braund and Wilkins (eds.): 353–63, 577–8.
(2007a) 'Introduction: questions of Socrates', in Trapp (ed.): xv–xxviii.
(2007b) 'Beyond Plato and Xenophon: some other ancient Socrateses', in Trapp (ed.): 51–63.
(2007c) *Philosophy in the Roman Empire: Ethics, Politics and Society*. Aldershot.
(ed.) (2007d) *Socrates from Antiquity to the Enlightenment*. Aldershot.
Travlos, J. (1971) *Pictorial Dictionary of Ancient Athens*. Princeton.
Trivigno, F. V. (2009a) 'Paratragedy in Plato's *Gorgias*', *OSAPh* **36**: 73–105.
(2009b) 'The rhetoric of parody in Plato's *Menexenus*', *Ph&Rh* **42**: 29–58.
Troelsgard, C. (1988) 'Ancient musical theory in Byzantine environments', *CIMA* **56**: 228–38.
(ed.) (1997) *Byzantine Chant: Tradition and Reform*. Athens.
(1999) 'Musical notation and oral transmission of Byzantine chant', *C&M* **50**: 249–57.
(2011) *Byzantine Neumes: A New Introduction to the Middle Byzantine Musical Notation*. Copenhagen.
Tsirivakos, E. (1975) 'Ἀρχαιότητες καὶ Μνημεῖα Νήσων Αἰγαίου', *AD* **30** B2 [1983]: 314.
Tsitsiridis, S. (1998) *Platons Menexenos: Einleitung, Text und Kommentar*. Stuttgart and Leipzig.
Tsouna, V. (2007) *The Ethics of Philodemus*. Oxford.
Tulli, M. (1996) 'Sul testo del "Protagora" nella tradizione antica: il corrector di POxy 1624', in *ΟΔΟΙ ΔΙΖΗΣΙΟΣ Le Vie della Ricerca: Studi in onore di F. Adorno*, ed. M. S. Funghi. Florence: 457–65.
(1977) *The Typology of the Early Codex*. University Park, Pa.
(1987) *Greek Manuscripts of the Ancient World*, 2nd edn, revised and enlarged by P. J. Parsons. London.
(1999) 'Plato 62: *Protagoras* 337b3–357b2 POxy 1624', in *CPF* **I** ***: 310–34.
(2003) 'Prodico e *POxy 1624*: due note sul testo del *Protagora* di Platone', in *Studi di filologia e tradizione greca in memoria di Aristide Colonna*, ed. F. Benedetti and S. Grandolini. Naples: 807–11.
(2007) 'Il *Gorgia* e la lira di Anfione', in Erler and Brisson (eds.): 72–7.
Tuozzo, T. M. (2011) *Plato's 'Charmides': Positive Elenchus in a 'Socratic' Dialogue*. Cambridge.
Ubersfeld, A. (1999) *Reading Theatre*, trans. F. Collins. Toronto.
Usener, S. (1994) *Isokrates, Platon und ihr Publikum. Hörer und Leser von Literatur im 4. Jahrhundert v. Chr.* Tübingen.
Usher, M. D. (2002) 'Satyr play in Plato's *Symposium*', *AJPh* **123**: 205–28.

Uytterhoeven, I. (2009) 'Know your Classics! Manifestations of "classical culture" in Late Antique elite houses', in *Faces of Hellenism: Studies in the History of the Eastern Mediterranean (4th century B.C.–5th century A.D.)*, ed. P. Van Nuffelen. Leuven: 321–42.
Vanderspoel, J. (1995) *Themistius and the Imperial Court: Oratory, Civic Duty, and Paideia from Constantius to Theodosius*. Ann Arbor.
Vander Waerdt, P. A. (ed.) (1994) *The Socratic Movement*. Ithaca and London.
Vasiliou, I. (1998) 'Conditional irony in the Socratic dialogues', *CQ* **49**: 456–72.
(2002) 'Socrates' reverse irony', *CQ* **52**: 220–30.
Vegetti, M. (1988) 'Dans l'ombre de Thoth: dynamiques de l'écriture chez Platon', in Detienne (ed.): 387–419.
(2006) 'La letteratura socratica e la competizione fra generi letterari', in *L'autore e l'opera. Attribuzioni, appropriazioni, apocrifi nella Grecia antica*, ed. F. Roscalla. Pisa: 119–31.
Velardi, R. (2000) 'Scrittura e tradizione dei dialoghi in Platone', in Casertano (ed.): 108–39.
Vicaire, P. (1960) *Platon: Critique littéraire*. Paris.
Vinson, M. (1993) 'Gregory Nazianzen's Homily 36: a Socratic response to Christian persecution', *C&M* **44**: 255–66.
Vlastos, G. (1991) *Socrates: Ironist and Moral Philosopher*. Cambridge.
Voelke, P. (2001) *Un théâtre de la marge: aspects figuratifs et configurationnels du drame satyrique dans l'Athènes classique*. Bari.
Vogt, S. (ed.) (1999) *Aristoteles Physiognomonica*. Darmstadt.
Voutiras, E. (1994) 'Sokrates in der Akademie: Die früheste bezeugte Philosophenstatue', *MDAI(A)* **109**: 133–61.
Vries, G. J. de (1984) 'Platonic dialogues performed?', *Mnemosyne* 37: 143–5.
(1985) 'Laughter in Plato's writings', *Mnemosyne* **38**: 378–81.
Wagner, C. (1981) 'Geloion bei Sophokles und Platon (zu Soph. Aias 132f.)', *GB* **10**: 77–81.
Wallace, R. W. (1995) 'Speech, song and text, public and private: evolutions in communications media and fora in fourth-century Athens', in *Die athenische Demokratie im 4. Jahrhundert v. Chr.: Vollendung oder Verfall einer Verfassungsform?*, ed. W. Eder. Stuttgart: 199–218.
(2005) 'Performing Damon's *harmoniai*', in Hagel and Harrauer (eds.): 147–58.
Walters, H. B. (1925) 'A portrait-statuette of Socrates', *JHS* **45**: 255–61.
Wardy, R. (1990) *The Chain of Change: A Study of Aristotle's 'Physics' VII*. Cambridge.
(2002) 'The unity of opposites in Plato's *Symposium*', *OSAPh* **23**: 1–61.
Warren, J. (2007) 'Diogenes Laërtius, biographer of philosophy', in *Ordering Knowledge in the Roman Empire*, ed. J. König and T. Whitmarsh. Cambridge: 133–49.
Wasserman, E. (2008) 'Paul among the philsosophers: the case of sin in Romans 6–8', *JSNT* **30**: 387–415.

Watson, J. (ed.) (2001) *Speaking Volumes: Orality and Literacy in the Greek and Roman World*. Leiden.

Watts, E. (2007) 'Creating the Academy: historical discourse and the shape of community in the Old Academy', *JHS* **127**: 106–22.

Waugh, J. (1995) 'Neither published nor perished: the dialogues as speech, not text', in Gonzalez (ed.): 61–77.

Webb, R. (2008a) *Demons and Dancers: Performance in Late Antiquity*. Cambridge, Mass. and London.

(2008b) 'Basil of Caesarea and Greek tragedy', in Hardwick and Stray (eds.): 62–71.

Webster, T. B. L. (1956) *Greek Theatre Production*. London.

Weiss, R. (2006) 'The strategic use of myth in the *Protagoras* and *Meno*', *Interpretation* **33**: 133–52.

(2007) 'Wise guys and smart alecks in *Republic* 1 and 2', in Ferrari (ed.): 90–115.

Weitzmann, K. (1947) *Illustrations in Roll and Codex: A Study of the Origin and Method of Text Illustration*. Princeton.

Wellesz, E. J. (1945) 'The earliest example of Christian hymnody', *CQ* **39**: 34–45.

(1961) *A History of Byzantine Music and Hymnography*. 2nd edn. Oxford.

Welsh, D. (1979) 'Knights 230–3 and Cleon's eyebrows', *CQ* **29**: 214–15.

West, M. L. (1985) 'Ion of Chios', *BICS* **32**: 71–8.

(1992a) *Ancient Greek Music*. Oxford.

(1992b) 'Analecta Musica', *ZPE* **92**: 1–58.

Westerink, L. G. (ed.) (1976) *The Greek Commentaries on Plato's 'Phaedo'*, vol. I. Amsterdam, Oxford and New York.

Westerink, L. G. and J. Trouillard, A. Ph. Segonds (eds.) (1990) *Prolégomènes à la philosophie de Platon*. Paris.

Westermann, H. (2002) *Die Intention des Dichters und die Zwecke der Interpreten. Zu Theorie und Praxis der Dichterauslegung in den platonischen Dialogen*. Berlin and New York.

White, F. C. (2004) 'Virtue in Plato's *Symposium*', *CQ* **54**: 366–78.

(2008) 'Beauty of soul and speech in Plato's *Symposium*', *CQ* **58**: 69–81.

White, S. A. (2000) 'Socrates at Colonus: a hero for the Academy', in *Reason and Religion in Socratic Philosophy*, ed. N. D. Smith and P. B. Woodruff. Oxford: 151–75.

Whitehead, D. (2000) *Hypereides: The Forensic Speeches*. Oxford.

Whitmarsh, T. (2001a) *Greek Literature and the Roman Empire: The Politics of Imitation*. Oxford.

(2001b) '"Greece is the world": exile and identity in the Second Sophistic', in Goldhill (ed.): 269–305.

(2004) *Ancient Greek Literature*. Cambridge and Malden, Mass.

(2009) 'Greece and Rome', in Boys-Stones et al. (eds.): 114–28.

Whittaker, J. (1989) 'The value of indirect tradition in the establishment of Greek philosophic texts or the art of misquotation', in *Editing Greek and Latin Texts*, ed. J. N. Grant. New York: 63–95.
Whittow, M. (2009) 'Early medieval Byzantium and the end of the ancient world', *JACh* **9**: 134–53.
Wilamowitz-Moellendorf, U. von (1879) 'Phaidon von Elis', *Hermes* **14**: 187–93.
(1920) *Platon* (2 vols). 2nd edn. Berlin.
Wiles, D. (2008), The poetics of the mask in Old Comedy', in Revermann and Wilson (eds.): 374–92.
Willi, A. (2008) 'Cows, houses, hooks: the Greco-Semitic letter-names as a chapter in the history of the alphabet', *CQ* **58**: 401–23.
Wilson, A. M. (1977) 'The individualized chorus in Old Comedy', *CQ* **27**: 278–83.
Wilson, J.-P. (2009) 'Literacy', in Raaflaub and van Wees (eds.): 542–63.
Wilson, P. J. (1999) 'The *aulos* in Athens', in Goldhill and Osborne (eds.): 58–95.
Wolfram, G. (ed.) (2008) *Tradition and Innovation in Late- and Postbyzantine Liturgical Chant*. Leuven.
Wolfsdorf, D. (2004a) 'Interpreting Plato's early dialogues', *OSAPh* **27**: 15–40.
(2004b) 'Socrates' avowals of knowledge', *Phronesis* **49**: 75–142.
(2008a) 'Hesiod, Prodicus, and the Socratics on work and pleasure', *OSAPh* **35**: 1–18.
(2008b) *Trials of Reason: Plato and the Crafting of Philosophy*. Oxford.
(2009) 'Empedocles and his ancient readers on desire and pleasure', *OSAPh* **36**: 1–71.
Woodard, R. G. (2010) '*Phoinikēia Grammata*: an alphabet for the Greek language', in Bakker (ed.): 25–46.
Woodruff, P. (ed.) (1982) *Plato's 'Hippias Major'*. Oxford.
Worman, N. (2008) *Abusive Mouths in Classical Athens*. Cambridge.
Worthington, I. (1996a) 'Greek oratory and the oral/literate division', in Worthington (ed.): 165–77.
(ed.) (1996b) *Voice into Text: Orality and Literacy in Ancient Greece*. Leiden, New York and Cologne.
(ed.) (2007) *A Companion to Greek Rhetoric*. Oxford.
Worthington, I. and J. M. Foley (eds.) (2002) *Epea and Grammata: Oral and Written Communication in Ancient Greece*. Leiden, Boston and Cologne.
Wright, M. R. (1997) 'Philosopher poets: Parmenides and Empedocles', in Atherton (ed.): 1–22.
Wycherley, R. E. (1962) 'Peripatos: the Athenian philosophical scene', *G & R* 9: 2–21.
Xanthakis-Karamanos G. (1980) *Studies in Fourth-Century Tragedy*. Athens.
Yaginuma, S. (1995) 'Did Thucydides write for readers or hearers?', in *The Passionate Intellect: Essays on the Transformation of Classical Tradition*, ed. L. Ayres. New Brunswick: 131–42.

Yamagata, N. (2005) 'Plato, memory, and performance', *Oral Tradition* **20**: 111–29.

Yunis, H. (ed.) (2003) *Written Texts and the Rise of Literate Culture in Ancient Greece*. Cambridge.

(2007a) 'Plato's rhetoric', in Worthington (ed.): 75–89.

(2007b) 'The Protreptic rhetoric of the *Republic*', in Ferrari (ed.): 1–26.

Zacharia, K. (1995) 'The marriage of tragedy and comedy in Euripides' *Ion*', in *Laughter Down the Centuries II*, ed. S. Jäkel and A. Timonen. Turku: 45–63.

(ed.) (2008) *Hellenisms: Culture, Identity, and Ethnicity from Antiquity to Modernity*. Aldershot.

Zanker, P. (1995) *The Mask of Socrates: The Image of the Intellectual in Antiquity*, trans. A. Shapiro. Berkeley, Los Angeles and Oxford.

Zannos, I. (1991) 'Ornamentation, improvisation and composition in the oral tradition of Greek Orthodox church music at Constantinople', in Meyer (ed.): 125–47.

Zaslavsky, R. (1981) *Platonic Myth and Platonic Writing*. Washington, DC.

Zeller, E. (1868) *Socrates and the Socratic Schools*, trans. O. J. Reichel. London.

Zuckert, C. H. (2009) *Plato's Philosophers: The Coherence of the Dialogues*. Chicago.

Zwierlein, O. (1966) *Die Rezitationsdramen Senecas*. Meisenham am Glan.

GENERAL INDEX

INDEX LOCORUM

Made in the USA
Las Vegas, NV
02 February 2025

17419141R00197